Economics

Related titles in the series

Accounting
Advertising
Auditing
Book-keeping
Business and the European Community
Business Environment, The
Business French
Business German
Business Italian
Business Law
Business Spanish
Business Studies
Commerce
Cost and Management Accounting
Economics
Elements of Banking
Financial Management
Management Theory and Practice
Marketing
Organizations and Management
Statistics for Business

Economics

Fifteenth edition

Geoffrey Whitehead, BSc(Econ)

**MADE SIMPLE
BOOKS**

Made Simple
an imprint of Butterworth-Heinemann
Linacre House, Jordan Hill, Oxford OX2 8DP
A division of Reed Educational and Professional Publishing Ltd

Ⓡ A member of the Reed Elsevier plc group

OXFORD   BOSTON   JOHANNESBURG
MELBOURNE   NEW DELHI   SINGAPORE

First published 1970
Thirteenth edition 1986
Reprinted 1988, 1989, 1996
Fourteenth edition 1992
Reprinted 1994
Fifteenth edition 1996

British Library Cataloguing in Publication Data
Whitehead, Geoffrey
  Economics – 15th ed.
  1. Economics
  I. Title
  330

ISBN 0 7506 2678 X

Composition by Genesis Typesetting, Laser Quay, Rochester, Kent
Printed and bound in Great Britain

Contents

Preface

This book covers all the basic aspects of the economic organisation of free-enterprise societies, with special reference to Great Britain's position in the European Union. It explains clearly and simply the production, distribution and exchange of goods and services, both within a country and internationally. The activities of plants, firms and industries are examined, so are the influences on them of great institutions; banks, insurance companies, trade unions and local and central government bodies. The part played by governments in controlling abuses, promoting social progress and managing prosperity is fully described. The historical development of Economics is incidentally recounted.

Although principally designed for self-study, the book is of equal value to schools, colleges and universities. Teachers and lecturers will find that it adequately covers the syllabuses of various examining bodies for GCE 'A' Level Economics, the BTEC National Diploma and Certificate Courses and the BTEC Higher National Conversion Course. It also covers relevant material for the professional examinations for Accounting, Company Secretaryship, Management Accounting, etc., the Intermediate Examination for the Chartered Institute of Transport and first year Degree Courses at University level. It is particularly suitable for students reading Economics as a liberal study accompanying main courses in other disciplines. It is a sound background reference book for more elementary studies at GCSE level.

In preparing this book I have received much helpful assistance from a number of public bodies, firms and individuals. I wish to express my thanks to the following: the Controller of HM Stationery Office for permission to reproduce and adapt sundry tables from official publications, particularly the National Income Accounts and the Balance of Payments Accounts; the Clyde Port Authority for permission to reproduce its map on the Maritime Industrial Development Area; the Bank of England for permission to reproduce statistics from its Quarterly Magazine; Barclays Bank Review for permission to reproduce a chart on the advances made by bankers, and the Cooperative Union Ltd, for help with recent statistical data and permission to reproduce its photograph of the original Toad Lane, Rochdale, Cooperative shop.

The statistics in this revised edition present the most recently available statistics, which relate to the year ending December 1993.

Finally, may I thank the editorial and production staff at Butterworth-Heinemann for their unfailing courtesy and meticulous attention to detail.

GEOFFREY WHITEHEAD

Section 1: Introduction

1   Some basic ideas

1.1
What is economics?

Economics was defined by the late Alfred Marshall, one of the great Victorian economists, as 'the study of mankind in the everyday business of life'. There are other definitions which are discussed later in this book, but Marshall's definition draws attention to that unique feature of human society: that unlike other animals, man provides for his everyday needs by means of a complex pattern of production, distribution and exchange. This everyday business of providing the means of livelihood is called by the general term 'economy'. Economics is the study of economies, and in particular of modern economies such as those of Western Europe and the USA. In passing we take note of primitive economies, but it is the advanced economies that interest us most. How do we produce all the things that we need? How do we distribute the products among the various groups in the society? What institutions have we developed to promote economic activity, and how does each institution play its part in the intricate relationships of everyday life?

1.2
'Wants' and 'utilities'

The study of economics begins with understanding human 'wants'. By 'want' the economist means the endless succession of material 'wants' which are displayed by all living things. Everyone needs air, food and water to support life. If we live in some climates we need clothing and shelter from the weather. Everyone needs a home to call his own: some territory which is his, by right.

Even when we have these basic 'wants', other more advanced 'wants' present themselves. We want comfortable homes, entertainment, education, and transport. As the things we need increase in variety and become more and more sophisticated, the economy becomes more intricate too, until thousands of people are cooperating in different countries to produce the raw materials, designs, and specialised machinery which are necessary for a single thing we 'want' – such as an aeroplane or a motor vehicle.

The student of economics has to learn many new words in the course of his studies. There is nothing complicated about these new words; but once they have been learnt and understood they make conversation between economists easier, because everyone then knows exactly what the other person is talking about. Outsiders often dismiss this specialised vocabulary as jargon, but this is a mistake. The words 'table' and 'chair' describe particular household objects: they are the jargon of the dining-room.

The first piece of economic jargon we need to learn is the word **utility**. In ordinary language this means something that has usefulness, and to some extent this is still its meaning in economics; but the particular form that this usefulness takes is to satisfy our 'wants'. Thirst is a 'want', and water has 'utility' because it satisfies this want. A glass of water does not always have the same utility; its satisfying power depends upon the extent of our want. Consider a thirsty child in a school playground: for her a glass of water has utility. To the airman whose plane has crashed in the desert, the same glass of water would have greater utility, for his need is greater. To an Indian peasant in a monsoon flood, water has no utility at all.

When we reduce economics to its basic elements it is the study of how mankind produces utilities to satisfy wants. In satisfying the wants we consume the utilities, so that they cease to exist and we must start producing them again. A large part of the everyday business of life involves the repetitive production of well-tried utilities to satisfy well-known wants. Inventors and designers, however, constantly produce new forms of satisfaction – a blue rose, or a 'whiter' detergent, or a new motive power – so that mankind progresses to higher levels of satisfaction.

1.3
The production of utilities

Satisfaction can be achieved in two ways: by the enjoyment of goods or the enjoyment of services. **Goods** are tangible items which either satisfy the basic requirements of human life or make that life fuller and richer. Common examples are foods, clothing, housing, furniture, books, television sets and motor cars. The actual point of satisfaction occurs when we consume the food, or beverage, wear the clothing, make use of the furniture, and so on, so that the name **consumer goods** is usually applied to these tangible utilities. There is another class of goods, dealt with more fully on page 28, called **producer goods**. These are goods which do not yield personal satisfaction to consumers but are part of the capital assets of production. A drilling machine, or an assembly line in a factory, are examples of producer goods.

Services are intangible 'utilities', which satisfy our needs by personal attention. The dentist who extracts a painful tooth; the surgeon who sets a broken leg; the television personality who brightens an otherwise dull evening; or the hairdresser who prepares us for a social occasion are examples of people offering **personal service**. As with goods, there is a class of services which is not directly personal in this way, but forms part of the productive organisation. Such services are **commercial services**; trade, banking, transport, insurance and communications are the chief examples.

The whole purpose of production, which makes use of producer goods and commercial services in the course of its activities, is to create utilities by providing an endless flow of consumer goods and personal services. In order to achieve this production of utilities the resources available to mankind must be mobilised. These resources are called the **factors of production**.

1.4
The factors of production

There are three factors of production which together enable advanced economies to create the goods and services needed by mankind. These three sets of resources are given the names land, labour and capital.

Land is a term used by the early economists to describe resources provided by the bounty of nature. It includes not only agricultural land but also the mineral resources of the earth, the gases of the atmosphere, the products of the fields, forests and oceans, and even the extra-terrestrial resources which man may one day begin to haul in from space.

Labour includes all the human resources of the earth, the physical and mental abilities of the peoples of the world. It embraces a wide variety of skills in specialised trades and occupations, and abilities of organisation and management that are crucial in the productive processes. We shall see later that a dispute exists between economists as to whether this last type of skill is so different from occupational skills as to deserve being classed as a separate factor. For the moment we will not try to separate off organisational skills in this way.

Capital resources are the 'producer goods' to which we have already referred. They are a store of physical assets owned by businessmen and others which enable the production of consumer goods and services to be carried on more effectively. Capital assets of this sort have to be constructed from natural resources by human skill and energy, so that whatever stock of these assets is available must have been accumulated in an earlier period.

At this point we should mention a difficulty which is dealt with more fully later – money capital. Most people when asked what capital is would think of capital in money terms. When we wish to set up in business we must first find some capital (money capital). We either start to scrimp and save, like the early capitalists, or we turn to the banks who have lots of capital to lend us because they have the savings of countless people tucked away in their vaults. What does this money represent? The answer is that it represents control over other resources, the ability to buy the use of land, labour and producer goods (capital) to start our enterprise. If we use the capital to dig a mine, or build a factory, or buy a heavy goods vehicle we are said to 'fix' the money capital. We turn the *liquid assets* (assets in money form), into *fixed assets* (assets in the form of producer goods).

Money capital is therefore rather different from the term 'capital' as used by economists, but it can be turned into economic capital by using it to create capital assets (producer goods). Creating producer goods takes time. The ordinary working people during the industrial revolution complained bitterly that they never seemed to get any share in the wealth they were creating. It was all 'jam tomorrow – never jam today'. Workers complained about 'pie in the sky'. They never actually became consumers – but their grandchildren did!

1.5 The organisation of production

If the factors of production are to be combined to create utilities which will satisfy man's wants, someone must take the initiative. Even in the most primitive tribes there is some leader who displays above-average ability in hunting, fishing or food-gathering. In more civilised groups other skills become important. Master craftsmen discover, develop and hand down the secrets of spinning, weaving, pottery-making and the smith's arts. Enterprising merchants travel the mountain and forest trails, or cross trackless deserts and seas to bring the precious products of the world to market. In more advanced nations the complexity of production calls forth classes of men who are skilled in making the necessary arrangements. They may possess special technical ability, like the great engineers of the Industrial Revolution. They may possess, or know how to collect, financial resources which will enable production to be organised. They may even be unscrupulous, quick to take advantage of the weakness or indecision of others. Whatever their particular ability, the economic effect is the same. Production is achieved by the enterprising activity of such individuals who combine the factors of production in the best possible way to achieve outputs of goods and services. These organisers of production are called **entrepreneurs**.

1.6 Consumption and production

When production has been achieved, the goods and services produced are used to satisfy the wants of mankind. In consuming the utilities created we destroy the fruits of our earlier labours. The fuel mined is burnt; the cloth woven is worn; the crops harvested are eaten, and the shelter built is enjoyed. Consumption destroys production, and we return to our former condition. We must begin again an endless cycle of production and

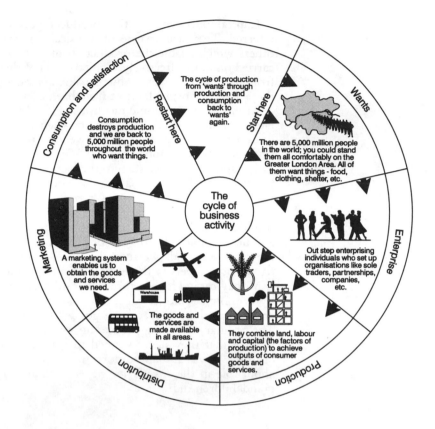

Figure 1.1 The cycle of production

consumption. This cycle of production is shown in Figure 1.1. Study it now.

1.7
Scarcity and choice

No matter how much we produce, we shall never be able to satisfy men's wants, for these develop and extend with every advance of technology. Appetite grows with feeding, and every growth of output which raises man to a new level serves but to reveal a more extensive horizon. In his book, *Nature and Significance of Economic Science*, Lord Robbins defined economics as: 'The science which studies human behaviour as a relationship between "ends" and scarce "means" which have alternative uses.' Man's insatiable 'wants' are Robbins's 'ends' which exist to be satisfied. The resources of the earth are the scarce 'means' which are available to satisfy these ends. Economics becomes a study of how men behave when there are insufficient 'means' to satisfy the 'ends' they have in mind.

If the utilities that can be created are limited compared with the insatiable appetites of men, then we must exercise some sort of choice as to what shall be produced and in what quantities. Just how we exercise this kind of choice depends upon the type of society in which we live. In the so-called 'free-enterprise' societies choice is exercised by a wide range of individuals and groups. Millions of housewives exercise choice when they do their shopping. Motorists buy, or do not buy, from countless garages which they pass on the way to work. Councils and other elected bodies choose equipment and buildings according to their sense of priorities. This apparent freedom of choice is marred a little by influences which are at work to persuade us to exercise choices in a way different from our own natural inclinations. Informative, or persuasive, advertising may influence our demand for goods. In the free-enterprise countries the choices of millions of people take effect through the **market**. The existence of markets is a characteristic feature of such economies, and the major commodity markets and financial markets lie at the root of the prosperity of such nations.

1.8
Cost and opportunity cost

Everyone who is familiar with a money system understands the ordinary meaning of 'cost', as the amount of money that has to be given up in order to obtain a particular commodity or service. In economics we have a term 'opportunity cost', or 'alternative cost', which expresses the cost of a commodity not in money but in terms of the alternative forgone. If we exercise choice we must have alternatives from which to choose. The housewife who decides to give a party on an anniversary or birthday will tend to reduce expenditure on ordinary meals so that she can accumulate reserves for the party. The true cost of the party is the reduced enjoyment at other meals. The student who chooses to cut a lecture in order to escort a young lady to the theatre is sacrificing one opportunity for another. The true cost of the theatre visit is the lecture he has missed.

When we take one opportunity, or follow a particular policy, we shall never know what would have happened if we had taken the other alternative opportunity, or policy. The student who cut the lecture might have had his interests in the subject triggered off into a lifetime pursuit. On the other hand, the theatre visit might end in a more permanent attachment to the young lady, so that he marries and lives happily ever after. Similarly, a decision by a local authority to have only comprehensive schools in its area will divert resources of building accommodation and teaching staff towards this type of education. We shall never know whether these resources would have given greater satisfaction if used in other ways.

1.9
'Free' economies, 'controlled' economies and 'mixed' economies

Economic activity is pursued in a climate which to some extent reflects the political framework of society. In all nations it developed originally in a framework of free enterprise where little interference was made in the activities of those engaging in economic activity. This framework of the free enterprise was described by men like Adam Smith (see page 13), and perhaps today is best represented by the American economy. Outright free enterprise does lead, regrettably, to some abuses. In particular it leads to gross inequalities of incomes, and to various types of monopoly practices. Political solutions to the injustices of outright 'free' enterprise have given us Communist (controlled) economies like the Northern Korean and Chinese economies. Military solutions have given us dictatorships of one sort or another around the world – some durable and some more temporary. In many other countries but notably in the United Kingdom, a 'mixed' economy, featuring certain centrally controlled industries and a rich pattern of other 'free enterprise' industries, has been evolved.

In fact all countries must be, to some extent, mixed economies. It is impossible for bureaucratic supervision of every aspect of production to be achieved even by the most authoritarian governments, while the monopolistic exploitation of the mass of any people in a truly 'free-enterprise' system is totally unacceptable in the increasingly egalitarian atmosphere of the modern world.

This book is largely concerned with the free-enterprise economies and mixed economies of the western world, but readers should relate their readings to the broader world scene.

**1.9.1
The Interpretation
Act, 1978**

Throughout this book terms such as 'entrepreneur' are used without any sexist connotation: the person showing enterprise may be of either sex. It is extremely difficult to eliminate all use of the word 'his' (for example) in such a textbook, without affecting the ease with which ideas may be conveyed. The Interpretation Act, 1978, reenacting the Interpretation Act, 1939, states quite clearly that in any text coming before the courts 'the male includes the female gender' – or as one legal wag put it, 'ever since time immemorial male has embraced female'. Economists have no sexist bias, and find Laura Ashley as interesting as F. W. Woolworth. While every attempt has been made to eliminate phrases which appear to discuss the business world as a male-dominated world, occasionally it has not been possible without stilting the text. Apologies are tendered for any such lapses.

**1.10
Summary of
Chapter 1**

1 Economics is the study of the ways in which man provides for his every-day needs of food, clothing, shelter, etc.
2 'Utilities' are goods and services that have the power to satisfy the 'wants' of mankind.
3 Production of utilities is achieved by making use of the factors of production, land, labour and capital.
4 The initiative in production is taken by businessmen called 'entrepreneurs', who combine land, labour and capital to create goods and services.
5 Consumption destroys production; 'wants' devour 'utilities'.
6 Since the resources available to mankind are limited, we must exercise choice. In choosing, the true cost of one opportunity chosen is the 'next-best' alternative opportunity we did not choose.

Exercises Set 1

1 Draw up a list of 'wants' likely to be experienced by: (*a*) a shipwrecked mariner on a desert island; (*b*) a citizen of an advanced nation.
2 Distinguish between 'consumer goods' and 'producer goods'.
3 What are 'utilities'?
4 What is an entrepreneur?
5 Explain 'the endless cycle of production and consumption'.
6 What do you understand by 'opportunity cost'? Suggest true costs for the following: (*a*) a high level of armament production; (*b*) a bottle of wine at a dinner party; (*c*) a refill of notepaper in a student's ring binder; (*d*) a field of wheat.
7 Aristotle's phrase 'man is a political animal' has been amended by some economists to read 'man is an economic animal'. In what way is man an economic animal – and how does politics enter the picture?

Section 2: Production

2 Basic ideas on production

2.1
What does an economist understand by 'production'?

We have already seen that production is the creation of 'utilities' to satisfy 'wants'. It follows that the creation of both goods and services is 'production' to an economist. Economists do not draw any distinction between the farmer, the factory worker, the lorry driver, the doctor, or the actor as far as production is concerned. All these workers are specialising in the creation of some commodity or service which is required by their fellow men. The farmer is not more productive than the doctor; he is only providing a different sort of utility. Physical labour is not more worthy of reward than mental labour, for all producers are engaged in a common endeavour to satisfy man's wants. If we make the mistake of belittling the 'service' trades because they are unproductive, and divert their workers into other occupations, we shall decrease satisfaction. In fact, it is precisely these occupations which are insusceptible to mechanisation which are expanding fastest in the advanced nations. Whereas fewer and fewer agricultural workers can grow more and more food by a thoughtful use of machinery and fertilisers, it is much more difficult to mechanise personal services. We are unlikely ever to see mass production in the dentist's chair or the operating theatre. Higher levels of satisfaction in health services must therefore be achieved by training more dentists and doctors. In rather a different way the services devoted to distribution and exchange, such as transport, wholesaling, and retailing, must expand as specialisation in large factories or farms produces greater and greater surpluses to be shared out among the population. An increased number of people engaged in the provision of services is therefore inevitable and advantageous.

It follows that workers in service trades are equally entitled to a reward for their activities, for they are just as much part of production as the factory worker or the farm labourer. A manufactured commodity has not been fully 'produced' in the economic sense until it reaches the consumer. It is therefore quite wrong to claim that the actual grower or producer is entitled to the full fruits of his labour, and mean by that the entire price paid by the consumer for the commodity. The middleman who brought it to market and the retailer who handled it are also entitled to a reward. Unless they receive a reward for their efforts they will not handle the goods, and the grower will be unable to realise any reward for his work, while the factory worker will soon be laid off because stocks are rising.

Production to an economist, therefore, is the creation of utilities to satisfy wants; whether that means the creation of a 'good' itself in agriculture or industry; its transport form the point of production to the point of consumption (geographical distribution); its transport through time from the moment of production to the moment of consumption, in stock-piles, cold stores, warehouses, or granaries (distribution through time); or the provision of 'personal services' directly enjoyed by individuals or groups, such as health, education, and entertainment services.

For convenience production is divided into three categories.

Table 2.1 Types of production

(a) The production of goods		(b) The production of services	
1. Primary production	2. Secondary production	3. Tertiary production	
(The production of goods made available by Nature. Man's inheritance of natural wealth)	(The production of sophisticated products which are derived from the natural primary products)	(The production of services)	
		Commercial services	Personal services
Coal miner	Engineer	Wholesaler	Doctor
Gold miner	Electronic engineer	Retailer	Dentist
Tin miner	Builder	Banker	Nurse
Lead miner	Decorator	Insurance agent	Teacher
Oil driller	Cabinet maker	Stockbroker	Lecturer
Lumberjack	Carpenter	Importer	Policeman
Farmer	Plastics engineer	Exporter	Detective
Fisherman	Refinery technologist	Transport driver	Entertainer
Shepherd	Stillman	Merchant-navy	Vocalist
Pearl diver	Potter	captain	TV personality
Herdsman	Tailor	Ship's crew	Clergyman
Fur trapper	Steelworker	Communications	Undertaker
etc.	Shipbuilder	engineer	Editor
	Aeronautical engineer		Author
			Psychologist

2.2 The three classes of production

We all specialise in some sort of work, producing some useful commodity or service, but to study production we must try to sort out the different classes of producers. The three main types of production are known as **primary production, secondary production** and **tertiary production**. Table 2.1 names some of the specialists who work in the three types of production.

Consolidate your understanding of these three types by attempting to think of ten more occupations in each of the four groups shown.

2.3 Direct production and indirect production

2.3.1 Direct production

If a person works directly to satisfy his own wants he is said to engage in **direct production**. Thus a castaway on a desert island would be forced to find his own food, build his own shelter, and make such garments as he could from the leaves of trees or the skins of animals. He must be a jack-of-all-trades: a hunter, farmer, builder, tailor and so on. He would never have the time to do half the things he would like to do, and he would never develop the skill that comes from repetition. Similarly, tribes of primitive peoples, even though they cooperate together in a primitive communal existence, rarely satisfy all their wants, and are easily exterminated by natural disasters. The Bushmen of the Kalahari go naked expect for a leather strap hanging from the shoulders and tied around the waist. They build only the most primitive shelters, for they are constantly on the move following game. Those who are too feeble to keep up are left, in a protective thorn shelter with all the water that can be spared, until thirst or the hyenas or leopards put an end to them. Clearly direct production is an inefficient type of organisation.

**2.3.2
Indirect production**

Indirect production is production by specialisation. People choose an occupation that appeals to them, usually because they have a natural talent or interest in it. They either have already, or hope to achieve, an advantage over their fellow men in that particular field of activity. The advanced nations offer an incredible variety of employment to their citizens. Not only are there many specialist trades, but within each trade there are many separate occupations. A popular television programme, in which a panel of personalities had to guess the occupations of viewers who challenged the panel, ran for ten years before it was retired at last – without having run out of trades.

If production is **indirect** it means that the producer is not attempting to satisfy his own wants directly, except to a very limited extent. A tailor no doubt makes himself a suit occasionally, and an oil-refinery engineer probably buys cheap petrol from the company pump. The bulk of the products of both trades will go to other people – to the general public. In return, the tailor and the refinery engineer will obtain a balanced share of the world's goods through the exchanges arranged by wholesalers and retailers, using money as a medium of exchange.

**2.4
Specialisation and
the division of
labour**

Indirect production takes place when entrepreneurs combine the factors available to them to secure the required goods and services. People are employed in their specialist occupations, to take the fullest advantage of their natural talents or acquired abilities. Adam Smith, the first great economist, drew attention to this specialisation as the chief source of the Wealth of Nations. The reader should know more of this great economist. Let us make a small diversion to consider his contribution to economics.

**2.4.1
Adam Smith – the
optimist who started
the 'dismal science'**

Adam Smith was born in 1723, the son of the Comptroller of Customs at Kirkcaldy in Fife. He went to Oxford, but was dissatisfied with his course because it had nothing much to do with the things that interested him. His great treatise on *The Nature and Causes of the Wealth of Nations* was published in 1776. It was the result of 20 years' study of the industrial developments taking place around him in Britain, which was just passing through the stage known to history as the Industrial Revolution.

Adam Smith started the central economic tradition, which holds that economics attempts to understand and explain the world in which we live, but not unduly to change it. His emphasis on the natural competitive forces in the market as the thing that regulated the economy led to the idea that there were inevitable forces at work which human beings were unable to control, and should leave strictly alone.

His central doctrine was that a system of natural liberty, where free men were able to follow their inclinations, would lead to the best results for both the individual and society itself. Man's natural inclination is to increase his well-being by producing wealth. If each man is thrown on his own resources he will labour for his own enrichment, and will incidentally enrich all society. Adam Smith's book, appearing at the same time as the American colonies declared their independence, prophesied that their system of free enterprise would make them the greatest nation in the world.

The weaknesses of Smith's doctrine lay in its disregard of the distribution of wealth. He was talking about total wealth, or **aggregate wealth**. He had little hope that the distribution of wealth between manufacturers, merchants, and landlords, on the one hand, and the mass of working people, on the other, would ever be such as to benefit the ordinary people. He said, 'We have many Acts of Parliament aimed against combining to raise wages; but none against combining to lower them.' This led Smith and other economists to conclude that although wages could not fall below the point where they would keep the workers alive, they were unlikely to rise much above that point. For this reason economics was referred to as 'The Dismal Science'. It was for later economists such as John Stuart Mill to point to the distribution of wealth as a matter of fundamental importance in society.

Smith died in 1790, a man of international reputation whose central doctrine has passed into history as the doctrine of *laisser faire*: (let things work themselves out). Leave men to please themselves, and they will do the best for themselves, and everyone else too. It remains a doctrine which has much to recommend it. Many politicians today believe the pendulum has swung too far away from free enterprise in recent years. They have developed 'supply-side economics' to reverse this trend. Despite this, the general belief in the twentieth century has been that economic affairs cannot be left entirely to free enterprise but require positive policies if prosperity and economic welfare are to be achieved.

2.4.2
Specialisation – the key to the wealth of nations

In the first chapter of his book Smith described the specialisation of labour used in a local pin factory with which he was familiar. He wrote:

> *A man not educated to this business could scarcely perhaps with his utmost industry make one pin a day, and certainly could not make twenty ... But in the way this trade is carried on it is divided into a number of branches, of which the greater part are likewise peculiar trades. One man draws out the wire, another straights it, a third cuts it, a fourth point it, a fifth grinds it at the top (for receiving of the head). To make the head requires two or three distinct operations. To put it on is a peculiar business, to whiten the pins is another. It is even a trade by itself to put them into the paper, and the important business of making a pin is divided in this way into eighteen different processes, which in some manufactories are all performed by distinct hands.*
>
> *I have seen a small manufactory of this kind where ten men only were employed, and where some of them consequently performed two or three distinct operations. But although they were very poor, and therefore but indifferently accommodated with the necessary machinery they could, when they exerted themselves, make among them twelve pounds of pins a day. There are in a pound upwards of 4000 pins of a middling size. Each person, therefore, could make one-tenth of 48 000 pins in a day. But if they had wrought separately, without having been educated to this peculiar business, they certainly could not have each made twenty, and possible not even one.*

2.4.3
The advantages of specialisation

Adam Smith went on to examine the advantages of specialisation. He found the main advantages to be as follows:

(a) *People are free to choose the work they like.* When a person is free to choose his employment he generally chooses a trade which interests him and in which he was some natural talent. He therefore works more effectively and more willingly, so that output rises and the nation becomes more prosperous.

(b) *The specialist uses the same set of tools all day.* A 'Robinson Crusoe', alone on his desert island, has many tasks to perform every day. He may dig his field for a short while, and then put his spade away while he makes fish hooks for an hour or two before going down to the beach. This is both wasteful of time and an inefficient use of equipment. The specialist uses the same set of tools all day. They are constantly at work, so that they contribute more intensively to production, and there is no waste of time clearing away between different activities. The intensive use of capital equipment is very desirable, because it is then worn out before it is made obsolete by new techniques of production.

(c) *Constant use of the same tools and materials leads to a close study of both, resulting in improved equipment and better methods of work.* A man who specialises in a particular trade soon discovers methods of production that are an improvement on previous methods. These 'tricks of the trade' are often jealously guarded secrets. Even in mass-production systems, where layout and procedure have been carefully planned, improvements are still possible. Many firms offer cash prizes to employees who suggest improvements which save time or materials.

(d) *Specialised production is associated with mechanisation, and machines can be speeded up.* Wherever specialisation enables work to be subdivided into processes, it becomes possible to mechanise the activity. This enables the power of the machine to replace the muscle power of the worker. The activity may be carried on at high speed; machines do not tire like workers, nor do they grow bored with the repetition of actions for which they have been designed or programmed.

(e) *Repetition brings increased skill.* Of course this is over a more limited field. Readers who have marvelled at the intricate windings of an electric motor or the complex circuits of a television set are strongly recommended to visit a factory where such things are made. They are usually assembled by workers who have become so accustomed to the work that they can talk quite freely to their neighbours about everyday affairs and still produce faultless assemblies. Admittedly they are only putting in one or two components each, but over this narrow field they have acquired enormous skills.

(f) *Computerisation and robotics.* Today we have moved beyond mere mechanisation to the computerisation of industrial production and the use of robots – machines which are human-like in their ability to perform a sequence of activities automatically, and to make decisions about problems that arise. Such machines call for very precise engineering, and continuous flow production if they are to be utilised fully, with the result that a flood of output is produced which must be cleared from the production lines and transported to depots around the country, and the world.

2.4.4
The nature of specialisation

The increased output achieved by specialisation is the result of the **division of labour**. The process has proceeded historically along the following lines:

(a) *Specialisation within the family or tribal group.* We have seen that direct production generally results in poverty. Man quickly finds that working together gives better results. The best hunters go hunting, the best anglers fish, the best potter makes pots for the entire village, and so on. The fruits of their labours are then shared among the whole family or tribe.

(b) *Specialisation into trades.* Here the natural divisions of production are performed by specialists: bakers, butchers, engineers, doctors and so on. The medieval guilds were combinations of such skilled tradesmen, designed to keep trade secrets within the guild, admission to which could be achieved only by properly trained apprentices. The persistence of trades into modern advanced societies has produced the great craft unions like the printers, engineers and electricians. The organisation of doctors, dentists, accountants and similar groups is an extension of specialisation, into higher levels of professional and administrative life. Originally organisations were small and centred in towns all over the country; now they have grown to national importance.

(c) *Specialisation into sub-trades.* The further division of work into particular aspects of a particular trade increased skill by concentrating the attention of tradesmen on those jobs that for some reason (usually profit) interested them most. In the early days of the cotton industry a division soon sprang up between spinning and weaving, between dyeing and fabric-printing, etc. Skill increased, but for each entrepreneur it was over a more limited field. This spreading of specialised activities through a region led to the localisation of production, which is dealt with more fully on page 71.

(d) *Specialisation into processes.* Here the division of labour reaches its greatest concentration. The manufacturing process is broken down into a series of separate activities, each of which is performed by a separate operative. This operative becomes highly skilled over a very limited field, and mass production results.

The term **mass production** is used to describe any system which aims at producing, with the fewest workers, the greatest output of goods. In nearly every industry today techniques have been developed which allow manufacturing processes to be carried on continuously, often day and night. The work flows through the factory in an endless stream, and workers at various stages perform individual operations with specially designed machinery.

Henry Ford in America developed the motor-car industry from a system whereby one man built a car completely to a system where hundreds of men, each performing one operation repeatedly, produce a continuous flow of cars. At one time a car was rolling off the production lines every ten seconds. Henry Ford's definition of mass production reads: 'It is the focusing upon a manufacturing project of the principles of power, accuracy, economy, system, continuity, speed, and repetition.'

Two other factors have been found to affect greatly the volume of production. They are **simplification** and **standardisation**. Together with **specialisation** they are the source of wealth in our affluent society. These three methods, simplification, standardisation and specialisation, are sometimes called **the three Ss**.

Simplification is the process of making a manufactured article as simple and functional as possible. Many modern plastic household articles, such as bowls and buckets, display this quality of simplicity. There are no decorative embellishments of any sort. The design is such that once the plastic has been pressed into shape that article will fall out of the press instantly. The surface of the mould is polished to a mirror finish by the toolmaker, and this perfect finish is reproduced on the plastic article, which is consequently shiny and attractive to the customer.

Standardisation is the process of making things in standard parts, which can be used in many similar articles. For instance, a printed circuit in one manufacturer's radio set is very like the printed circuit in another make of set. Where standard parts can be used in many appliances the factory making these parts has very long production runs indeed. These long runs means that the unit cost per component is reduced, because the expensive design costs are shared out among millions of units of output.

Automation and computerisation in industry. These modern developments carry specialisation to its highest levels. When a design has been reduced to its simplest, most standardised form automation becomes possible. The whole process is not only mechanised but also automated so that human operatives are not required. Computerisation adds a further refinement, enabling, for example, decisions to be made about dynamic changes in the operation of plant. These developments open up very great possibilities for the future satisfaction of wants, and it is these prospects that have led economists such as Prof. Galbraith to assert that man is approaching a final solution to the problems of the production of wealth.

(e) *International specialisation of labour.* Modern technology has developed specialisation so fully that a further geographical change becomes possible. Instead of regional specialisation, national specialisation becomes a distinct possibility. Italian styles of shoes are sold all over the world, American machine tools are universally recognised, Japanese cameras, Scotch whisky, and Swiss watches are demanded everywhere.

We therefore see that technically the division of labour has moved through the following stages:

(i) The use of individual skills and talents.
(ii) The development of specialised trades.
(iii) The subdivision of these trades into specialised aspects.
(iv) The further subdivision of these aspects into processes.
(v) The mechanisation and automation of processes.
(vi) The computerised control of automatic processes.

These changes have resulted in a growth of large-scale industries which have developed territorially in the following way:

(i) From the family to the village or tribal unit.
(ii) From the countryside to the medieval borough or town.
(iii) From the town to the geographical region.
(iv) From the regional to the national level, with particular nations supplying a major part of the world's requirements.

The advantages offered by a fuller development of specialisation are not achieved without some adverse effects. We must now consider the disadvantages of specialisation.

2.5
The disadvantages of specialisation

Despite the obvious advantages of simplification, standardisation and specialisation, there are certain disadvantages to offset the gains achieved. The net effect is still a higher level of satisfaction of human 'wants', but it is not as high as at first seemed possible. The chief disadvantages are:

1 The growth of tertiary production.
2 The monotonous nature of many highly specialised employments.

3 The decline of craftsmanship.
4 Structural, regional and general unemployment.
5 Industrial unrest and social discontent.

2.5.1
The growth of tertiary production

Specialisation concentrates production in large factories, most of whose output is surplus to the requirements of the employees in each factory. This means that the commercial activities of distribution and marketing are greatly increased. Wholesalers specialise in warehousing stocks at appropriate points until they are required by consumers. This clears the production lines, which would otherwise be choked by the volume of goods produced. Retailers buy from wholesalers and display goods where consumers can inspect and purchase them. Clearly some of the gains achieved by mass production must be dissipated in these activities.

2.5.2
The monotonous nature of many highly specialised employments

The work involved in a particular process can soon become an automatic activity which the operator performs without difficulty. Some people prefer this type of employment, which carries little responsibility and finishes as soon as the factory siren blows. Others find it irksome in the extreme. Often such employees feel trapped in a manufacturing system from which there is no escape. This is particularly true in areas where one or two large enterprises dominate the local employment scene and few alternative occupations exists for those who dislike work as operatives.

2.5.3
The decline of craftsmanship

Mass production greatly reduces the skills required of ordinary workers. They become highly skilled at particular processes but know little of the entire range of activities in their craft. Of course, a few super-craftsmen on the design staff still play an influential part in the whole enterprise, but the mass of employees are unable to take part in any truly creative activity. This leads them to regard work as of little importance, for their true personalities can be developed only in leisure hours. Thus production suffers and the total effectiveness of enterprises is reduced.

2.5.4
Structural, regional and general unemployment

Structural unemployment is unemployment caused by changes in the world demand for a particular product. The whole structure of an industry changes as world demand falls. Even if world demand grows, but is supplied from a different source, serious unemployment can occur in the formerly prosperous supplier's industry. In 1870–1900 the UK shipbuilding industry built ships for the whole world, and her merchant navy carried about 80 per cent of world trade. Today she builds ships for only a few nations and carries only 11 per cent of world trade. The consequent structural changes in the British shipbuilding industry are a cause for concern to men, management and governments. The risk of being laid off is understandably unsettling to a labour force, and causes unrest and hardship.

Regional unemployment arises when an area of a country has too high a proportion of its work force tied to a particular industry. Technology is not static, but dynamic. Advances in technology make previously prosperous industries obsolete: victims of declining world demand. For instance, synthetic fibres such as nylon and Acrilan have made serious inroads into the markets for natural fibres such as silk, cotton and wool, and earlier synthetic fibres such as rayon. In rather a different way a region may suffer setbacks because its previously advantageous position is eroded away for some reason. Perhaps it is the exhaustion of natural supplies of raw material, or economic changes may reduce the demand for its products. For example, the change to oil, gas and electric central heating affected the coalmining industry very seriously, while cheap clothing imports from the Far East have reduced the UK clothing industry. Where a region is over-specialised, a serious depression in one major industry leads to a general decline in associated industries in the area; migration of skilled workers and a general decline in prosperity follows.

General unemployment in the advanced nations arises from insufficient demand in their economies for the products they themselves can make. That the effects are made worse by fierce competition from the newly industrialised countries seems undeniable, since there is little point in managing the economy to increase demand if it only results in a flood of imports. This is a very difficult problem and is discussed more fully in later chapters.

2.5.5
Industrial unrest and social discontent

If high degrees of specialisation are introduced, mechanisation and automation must replace existing labour forces. It is generally recognised that such trends are inevitable and benefit the whole community by raising the volume of production. The displaced workers must be retrained to new employment, and these new jobs will inevitably be in tertiary production rather than in primary or secondary production. Even with the fullest cooperation between management and unions, it is often difficult to resolve these problems – particularly as, by its very nature, specialist production is easy to disrupt. If work flows continuously through a factory any operative who downs tools interrupts the production line, 'One out – all out' is the cry, and it is easily achieved.

The trend towards increased computerisation is even affecting employment in the tertiary services, particularly the commerical services, where large numbers of low-paid clerical workers are likely to be replaced. The shift to tertiary services therefore needs to be made into the labour-intensive personal services, like education, health services and entertainments. There must also be some increase in leisure, rather than enforced idleness – with earlier retirement and longer vacations assisting the sharing of work. If this is seen as an improvement in the standard of living, extra leisure being regarded as a desirable satisfaction to be achieved, it can be regarded as economic sense.

Industrial unrest tends to be local, but social unrest can be country-wide. If advanced societies are to prosper everyone must share in the prosperity, for disruption is easily arranged. Some reasonable distribution of wealth has to be achieved which, without disrupting incentives to hard work, keeps society stable.

2.6
Limitations to the division of labour

Although the division of labour will usually result in lower costs per unit of output, there are limitations to its effective use. These limitations are:

(a) *The extent of the market.* There is little point in mass production of goods which are not in mass demand. Therefore refined division-of-labour techniques are inappropriate in industries serving a small market only. Artificial limbs are unlikely to be mass produced, for the number of disabled persons is fortunately small. Similarly, a shop in a country district, sparsely inhabited, is unlikely to employ specialist bacon cutters, ham slicers, etc. The sole assistant will perform such activities to the best of his/her ability at times when customers are not present waiting to be served.

(b) *Technical impossibility.* Sometimes it is impossible to subdivide a technical process beyond a certain point. When each process has been reduced to a minimum activity further division of labour is impossible, and increased output will have to be achieved by duplication of the existing processes. Parallel units of production in an industry indicate that no further economies could be achieved by the subdivision of labour.

(c) *An inadequate monetary system.* If the money system is inadequate in some way, perhaps because of general distrust of the currency or fear of depreciation, the production of large outputs becomes more risky. Entrepreneurs will play safe and content themselves with lower levels of production than in more favourable circumstances.

2.7 Production and welfare

Many economists have defined economics in terms of welfare. In Britain the Welfare State was established in the years following the Second World War, and although it has its critics, it also has many staunch supporters. If the aim of an economy is to create utilities to satisfy wants, and if social unrest develops in societies where manifest inequalities exist, then it seems inevitable that some attempt at a Welfare State must be made in most societies. The alternative appears to be repression of some sort.

At this point economics merges with politics. It is inappropriate in *Economics Made Simple* to go further than this. Applied economics, usually regarded as a field of study that can be approached only when basic principles have been examined, inevitably merges into politics, and instead of merely observing man in the everyday business of life attempts to suggest acceptable policies which will maximise human welfare.

2.8 The pattern of production in an advanced economy

An advanced economy has all three types of production taking place, primary, secondary and tertiary production of goods and services. Collecting data on this enormous range of activities is not simple. It involves problems of definition – how shall we classify the production of each type of factory, for example; of collection – how shall we deal with manufacturers who refuse to send in their figures; and of statistical presentation.

The data are presented as part of the United Kingdom National Accounts in the CSO Blue Book, published each year about August, giving the figures to the end of the previous year. The 1994 book gives the figures to 1993, which are shown in Table 2.2. The figures for 1983 are shown alongside the 1993 figures, to show the change over the ten-year period, and we can see that the figures increased in every case except one – the figure for mining, quarrying, oil and gas. The decline in this field was almost entirely due to the collapse of the mining industry and the closure of pits. However, this comparision of the two years does not give a true picture, because of inflation over the ten-year period, and the consequent fall in the value of money. If we apply a correction to the 1993 figures to show them at 1983 prices, we have a very different set of figures. In the first place we see that the growth in all the figures was not as dramatic as at first appears, and the fall in the mining output was even worse. We say that 'in real terms' agricultural output, for example, rose from £5429 million to £8084 million, and not to £10 373 million as at first appeared.

Table 2.2 Production in the United Kingdom in 1993

Industry	1983 figures (£ millions)	1993 figures (£ millions)	1993 figures at 1983 prices (£ millions)
Agriculture, hunting, forestry & fishing	5 429	10 373	8 084
Mining, quarrying, oil and gas	20 234	12 147	9 466
Manufacturing	64 738	118 294	92 189
Electricity, gas and water supply	8 682	13 994	10 905
Construction	15 929	29 221	22 773
Wholesale & retail trade, repairs, hotels etc	33 491	78 348	61 058
Transport, storage and communication	19 727	46 263	36 053
Financial intermediation, real estate, rent and business activities	49 645	133 956	104 395
Public administration, defence and social security	18 599	38 199	29 769
Education, health and social work	22 997	57 457	44 778
Other services including sewage and refuse disposal	13 752	31 292	24 387
	273 223	569 544	443 857

2.9 Summary of Chapter 2

1 To an economist all workers are producers, whether they are engaged in producing goods or services.
2 Production can be divided into primary production (natural resources), secondary production (manufactures), and tertiary production (commercial services and personal services).
3 Direct production is the production of goods for one's own immediate personal use.
4 Indirect production is production by specialists, who perform either in particular trades or in processes arranged along mass-production lines.
5 The division of labour secures high levels of productivity and achieves a high national income. This national income must be shared fairly if industrial and social unrest is to be avoided.

Exercises Set 2

1 Discuss whether (*a*) the conductor of a symphony orchestra, and (*b*) a dental mechanic, are productive workers.
2 How might the following be made to increase their productivity: (*a*) a garage foreman in the repair section, (*b*) a bus conductor; (*c*) a tailor; (*d*) a schoolteacher; (*e*) a politician?
3 What similarities, and what differences, as far as production is concerned are there between: (*a*) a peasant fishing from a balsa raft in the Peruvian Current: (*b*) an owner-operator fishing from a modern trawler outside the Icelandic limit?
4 Consider the advantages and disadvantages of specialisation in the motor-vehicle-servicing industry from the points of view of: (*a*) a large motor-vehicle manufacturer considering to whom he should give his sole agency for servicing in Transitshire; (*b*) a householder about to go on holiday who wants his car to be serviced cheaply and reliably; (*c*) Ivor Waywivem, a motor-vehicle mechanic.

5 'To an economist all occupations are productive.' Explain.

6 'We factory workers made the goods – we are entitled to the full rewards from them.' Explain why they can't have the full rewards from the sale of these goods.

7 Eskimos practised polyandry (one wife having many husbands) because of the killing-off in infancy of girl children. Why do you think the Eskimos killed off children in this way?

8 What do you understand by the division of labour?

9 List the advantages of specialisation and illustrate them by considering some industry you know about.

10 'Mass production is the focusing upon a manufacturing project of the principles of power, accuracy, economy, system, continuity, speed and repetition' (H. Ford). Explain these principles as applied to the motor-vehicle industry.

11 'In primitive societies man is preoccupied with satisfying his basic wants; in advanced societies he is still preoccupied with production, but now services are his main interest.' Discuss.

3 The factors of production

3.1
Introduction

We have already seen that enterprising individuals organise production by employing what are called **factors** (land, labour and capital) in such proportions as seem the most appropriate to them. In making business decisions the aim is generally to achieve the greatest output of utilities from the minimum input of factors. This will usually result in the greatest profit to the enterprise, but if not some conflict may develop between the greatest output of utilities and the greatest profit to the owners. The true aim in this case is probably profit maximisation. Generally speaking, economists expect entrepreneurs who are behaving rationally to maximise profits; but some entrepreneurs may have reasons for deliberately not doing so. For instance, the prospect of labour unrest may lead them to use more labour and less capital (e.g. machinery) so that, instead of maximising profits, they maximise satisfactions. There are some satisfactions which are not monetary, and the employment of our fellow men in useful and rewarding labour may be one of them.

3.2
The factors of production – land

By 'land' the economist means those resources made available by the bounty of Nature. At present these resources are found only on earth, because although man has reached the moon he has not yet started to exploit extra-terrestrial sources of minerals. Land therefore consists of the following:

(*a*)   The agricultural areas of the earth's surface.
(*b*)   The natural grasslands, woodlands and jungles.
(*c*)   The deserts and ice deserts.
(*d*)   The oceans and seas.
(*e*)   The chemicals of the earth's crust and of the atmosphere.

The last are of three types: the elements formed before the earth was born in the atomic furnance of some great Sun; the compounds resulting from the interaction of elements, for example, sodium chloride and carbon dioxide: and other compounds which are the accumulation of animal and vegetable material resulting from life on earth. Sometimes these compounds are very complex, or are mixtures of many chemicals – for example, crude oil. Sometimes they are simple, like the chalk which forms the white cliffs of Dover.

3.2.1
Land as a free gift of nature

Since land has either existed in its present form from time immemorial or is provided annually by the bounty of Nature, it is often regarded as a free gift which all citizens should be entitled to share. In some countries, even today, reasonable quantities of land may be taken by anyone. In Tanzania, for example, nationals may build a house anywhere they like without permission, provided the holding taken is a reasonable one for a family. In the US in the nineteenth century land was similarly available to settlers, so that the workman of today became the independent landed proprietor of tomorrow. In Australia the word 'squatter' came to mean 'independent landowner': he acquired his rights to a farm or ranch by occupying and working the land. In that great Australian song 'Waltzing Matilda' it is the squatter who is the property owner and is harassing the swagman, or tramp, for stealing his sheep. In Britain the ownership of natural resources has developed from an original seizure of the land during the Norman invasion of AD 1066 through the granting of leases and freeholds to a situation where many people own land, but all land is owned. There are no free gifts of Nature except atmospheric ones. For instance, anyone who gets planning permission could set up a factory to obtain oxygen by liquefying air, but even he would need some land on which to build his plant.

3.2.2
Land as a
geographical site

Like the entrepreneur referred to above, every enterprise requires a geographical location. The location of industry is an interesting topic and is dealt with on page 66. Geographical location is also of importance to individuals who must have some territory they can call their own. Where peoples are dispossessed of their land they become refugees seeking a geographical location by the kind permission of other nations.

3.2.3
Land – mobile factor
or immobile factor?

The mobility of factors is important, since it is often necessary to move them if they are to be combined with other factors. Alaskan oil is of little use in Alaska, and Burmese teak is not appreciated as greatly there as in the fashionable homes of Western Europe. But some resources are immobile. We cannot move Niagara Falls to a more desirable location, but must utilise its electrical potential *in situ*. We cannot move a building site we wish to dispose of to a more desirable location, where it will fetch a higher price. An important aspect of mobility of land is the short period taken by crops to grow. This increases the mobility of land, in that it can be turned over to other uses very quickly. For instance, once a field is sown with wheat it is 'immobilised' until harvest time: but after the wheat has been harvested the land can be used for growing a different crop or for rearing cattle or sheep. If it is converted to industrial or domestic uses by being built on its mobility declines considerably, for it cannot now be turned over to different uses until the buildings have served their useful purpose, which may not be for 100 years.

3.2.4
Land – limited in
supply or
inexhaustible?

The early economists were much impressed by the limited supply of land, and our inability to increase it. This may have been because they were British, and in Britain, unlike some other countries, land has been wholly owned since 1066. Today some economists are preoccupied with the possibility that we may soon exhaust the resources of the earth's crust. It is commonly believed that oil resources are only sufficient to last about twenty-five years at the present rate of consumption. World supplies of many minerals are scarce, and the destruction of many slow-growing jungle hardwoods as the pace of rain-forest clearing accelerates is likely to lead to severe shortages of timber for some trades such as furniture-making. It appears that while most natural resources are still in abundant supply, we may soon exhaust supplies of one or two products. We are also in danger of over-hunting some creatures, and population pressures are seriously reducing wild life in Africa and South and Central America.

Even though the actual territory of the earth is limited, it can be used much more intensively than at present, as those who live in Hong Kong or Singapore have proved. Reclamation of land also takes place on quite an extensive scale, as in Holland, and irrigation can restore deserts to fertility. A particularly large discovery of underground water reserves in Libya during the 1970s was estimated to be sufficient to fill the River Nile for 200 years. This should enable huge areas of desert to be irrigated, so perhaps the early economists were pessimistic in their statement that the supply of land could not be increased.

3.2.5
Land – subject to the law of diminishing returns

The early economists held that land was a factor which suffered particularly from the law of diminishing returns. This early doctrine held that, given a certain quantity of the factor land, with which the entrepreneur combined increasing quantities of labour or capital, sooner or later the addition of further quantities of these other factors would result in diminishing returns, that is less output per unit of other factors applied.

An example of this is given in Table 3.1. Successive increments of capital (in the form of artificial fertiliser) are being added to an acre of land by a smallholder growing potatoes. Untreated, the land yields 5 tonnes per acre. When successive increments of fertiliser are added output rises. The first sack yields an increase of 1 tonne per acre, the second sack yields an extra 2 tonnes per acre, and the third sack an extra 2½ tonnes per acre. The fourth sack only yields an increase of 1 tonne, so that diminishing returns have already set in, while the fifth sack produces no better results at all, tonnage actually decreasing. At this point the fertiliser has become too concentrated. Maximum output is achieved at four sacks of fertiliser, but by this time both the marginal output (i.e. the extra output achieved from each sack) and the average extra output have begun to decline.

Diminishing returns must inevitably follow the addition of successive increments of capital to land.

The early economists were wrong in thinking that the law of diminishing returns applied particularly to land. Industry appeared to them to be able always to achieve increasing returns, because in general industry in their day was on a fairly small scale. Today we know that diminishing returns can set in when firms become too large. Difficulties over communication between the board of directors and the ordinary work-people may result in production losses which are greater than the gains achieved by a more perfect division of labour.

The law of diminishing returns can be seen in operation in real life almost everywhere. The following will illustrate this point, but the reader is urged to find local examples drawn from his own experience.

Table 3.1 Diminishing returns from land

Area of land (in acres)	Weight of fertiliser used (in 50 kg sacks)	Output of potatoes (in tonnes)	Increase in output over untreated land	Marginal output (i.e. output achieved by each extra sack used)
1	–	5	–	–
1	1	6	1	1
1	2	8	3	2
1	3	10.5	5.5	2.5
1	4	11.5	6.5	1
1	5	9	4	–2.5

Example 1. A firm moves into a new town to set up a clothing factory. At first it employs only fully qualified machinists. As it expands production, the supply of suitably trained machinists is exhausted and it has to recruit inexperienced staff and train them. Expenses incurred in the training period, wastage, etc., reduce over-all profitability. Later still, when it has trained the suitable labour it has to accept for training less and less satisfactory labour. Training periods have to be lengthened and larger wastage (due to spoilt work) accepted as inevitable. Finally, it may have to adopt a home-sewing scheme for out-workers, because the pool of workers available to travel daily to the factory is exhausted. This will involve extra expense in delivery and collection of the product.

Example 2. A country attempts to increase agricultural output. At first it utilises all the best land; but as the programme develops, more and more unsatisfactory land has to be cultivated. Diminishing returns at each successive stage of expansion are inevitable.

3.3
The factors of production – labour

'Labour' to an economist is the supply of human resources, both physical and mental, which is available to engage in the production of goods and services. The supply of labour depends on two things: (*a*) the total labour force available, i.e. the population less any sections of the population who do not work; and (*b*) the number of hours per week the population is prepared to work.

3.3.1
The working population

The working population of the United Kingdom is about 26 million. The 'groups who do not work', referred to above, consist of:

(i)   *Young people.* The number of young people available for work varies with the education available. If education is largely a matter of parental instruction and the handing down of techniques from father to son, as in many peasant communities, children will participate in production from an early age. If education is a matter of specialist tuition by professional educators the labour supply will be correspondingly reduced as pupils and students are withheld from the labour force during their schooling.

(ii) *Married women.* Where it is traditional for married women to cease work when they have young children to care for, the labour force is correspondingly reduced. In Britain since the end of World War II the employment of married women has been the greatest single change in the labour force. Despite recent legislation calling for equal opportunities for women it remains true that for many married women the family is more important than the career. Decisions to take up career opportunities are deferred while the children's welfare requires it. Instead employment is deliberately taken in fields where good incomes can be earned without irksome responsibilities. It is impossible to generalise, of course, and many gifted women carry both home and family responsibilities with an equanimity which inspires the admiration of all who know them.

(iii) *Retired persons.* The age of retirement affects the supply of labour. If, for example, retirement at the age of 60 is normal, so that perfectly healthy and energetic men and women retire compulsorily at that age, the supply of labour is reduced. Many people of retirement age today are quite capable of continuing in productive employment.

**3.3.2
The hours worked
per year**

If the working week is reduced the supply of labour falls, unless the resultant improvement in health enables more efficient labour to take place in the shorter working week. For instance, in early industrial Britain men, women and children commonly worked a 12–14-hour day. It is probable that the Ten Hour Act, introduced in 1847 to reduce the working day, improved the effectiveness of the work done in the ten hours to offset the shorter day. This is probably not true of present-day conditions, where, for example, reducing the 40-hour week to 35 hours almost certainly lowers the supply of labour. Productivity may still rise if the reduction of hours is secured by the workers in return for an agreement to use new machinery, etc., but the factor capital has produced the increase. Holiday periods operate in a similar way to reduce the supply of labour. An extreme example is the case of the Californian shipyard which is currently giving its workers 91 days' holiday a year. In the US generally a 30-hour week is quite common. Some workers prefer extra income to shorter working hours, so that 'moonlighting' (doing one job by day and another in the evening) is quite common. 'Moonlighting' therefore increases the supply of labour available to entrepreneurs.

**3.3.3
The quality of labour**

More important perhaps than the actual supply of labour is the quality of the labour. Is it skilled, semi-skilled or unskilled? Is it willing? Is it adaptable? Skilled labour is labour which has either mastered a particular craft, like toolmaking or printing, or has been professionally trained, like doctors, dentists, lawyers and accountants. Semi-skilled labour is in some ways a misnomer, since the operatives who are described as semi-skilled have in fact reached very high degrees of skill over a very limited range of activities. A spot-welder in a motor-vehicle assembly plant and a stator winder in a vacuum-cleaner factory are examples. Such labour can be very quickly trained, in from four to six weeks at the most. Similarly, one manufacturer of word-processing machines considers that an operator can be fully trained in two days. Unskilled labour, as its name implies, requires little specialised training. What training there is can be acquired on the job itself. Even so this labour becomes more efficient as it grows used to the work. When the canals were dug in Britain, and later when railways were laid, the entrepreneurs found it took a full year to turn a strong, healthy ploughboy into a navvy. Not only did he need to learn the economy of effort which would enable him to work long hours without tiring but his whole physique had to change. To build the muscles that were necessary for the work, and to acquire the strength of character to withstand the rough life was not the work of a single day.

Generally speaking, skilled labour tends to be more *specific* than semi-skilled or unskilled labour. The idea of 'specificity' is an important one in economics. If a factor of production is specific it can be used in only one particular task: for instance, a dentist must be employed in dentistry if his true talents are to be used. If we take a dentist and turn him into the fields to cut sugar cane we shall be wasting his talents. Of course it may do the dentist a world of good to find out what a hard life the cane-worker leads, but this is no substitute for the efficient use of his services in caring for his patients' teeth. A spot-welder in a motor-car factory is a less specific form of labour. He will probably be equally useful servicing cars in a garage, or drilling assemblies in an electronics factory.

Factors affecting the efficiency of labour include:

(*a*) The general education and background knowledge of the labour force. If it has been born into the television era of an advanced society it will be knowledgeable, adaptable and sophisticated. If it has only recently left a peasant community it will be unsophisticated, superstitious, nervous and slow to adapt itself.

(b) The general health of the labour force. This may be improved by diet, and by adequate welfare services of all sorts. A developing nation's progress may be slow because a fully effective labour force depends on raising the standard of living. This is a slow process and depends on an efficient labour force. We therefore have a vicious circle, which spirals slowly upwards, but at an increasing pace as the years go by.

(c) The incentives offered to labour. Where there are few incentives labour will be less efficient. Where the incentives are great labour will apply itself more assiduously.

(d) The availability of other factors of high quality. This is the commonest method of increasing the efficiency of labour. If it is backed by good quality land, labour itself will be more efficient. If it is backed by well chosen tools and adequate power supplies, even a poor labour force will be highly productive. One explanation of the great wealth of the US, despite the short working week and long holidays of its citizens, is that during his or her working hours every worker is supported by an array of power tools appropriate to his or her activities.

3.4
The factors of production – capital

The word 'capital' is used in many different ways today, but all its meanings refer to some stock of physical assets which have been created in the past and are available for present use. Thus **social capital**, such as schools, roads, and municipal swimming baths, has been created over the years by contributions in the form of rates and taxes. As a factor of production, capital means the stock of **producer goods** which are available to entrepreneurs for use in production.

Producer goods are defined as goods which are not made to satisfy wants directly but are made to increase the eventual output of consumption goods by raising productivity in the fields, forests and factories of the earth. Thus a motor-driven saw raises the volume of timber cut by workers in the forestry and timber trades, resulting in an increased flow of timber products at cheaper prices into our homes. A refinery fractionating column turns the experimental work of the research chemist into a productive reality, yielding up a flow of hydrocarbon products into the petrol tanks and oil sumps of our cars and the service bays of garages.

(a) Types of producer goods

The commonest types of factor capital are:

(a) Constructional works of every sort: factories, offices, mines, power stations, dams, piers, docks and harbour improvements, aerodromes, roads, railways, canals, hospitals, schools, etc.

(b) Plant, machinery, tools and equipment of every sort.

(c) Stocks of raw materials and partly finished goods. Some economists hold that stocks of finished consumer goods which are being transported (either geographically or in time) are 'capital' too. This idea ties in with our definition of 'production' as a process that continues until the final consumer actually receives the goods; but for practical purposes it is probably better to leave this class of finished goods out of our calculations of the factor capital.

(b) Specific capital

Capital assets tend to be more specific than either land or labour. Many types of plant are purpose-built, and are of little use if the demand for the product they make changes. Many tools are designed to do particular jobs: a hammer is less specific than a press tool for making plastic tea-plates. The extent to which his capital assets are specific may vitally affect the decisions made by an entrepreneur. For example, a tailor faced with a reduced demand for suits may use his sewing machines to make overalls or skirts – for sewing machines are non-specific. A cement manufacturer faced with reduced demand must either stock-pile or shut down, for a cement works can only make cement.

(c) Capital, income and wealth

These words are clearly connected but what is the actual relationship? Viewed from the point of view of a modern sophisticated economy with a money system we can say:

(a) Income is reckoned in money terms. It is the sum of money which a person acquires in any accounting period (usually a year) which he/she is free to spend as desired. Much of our incomes we spend in purchasing a balanced 'basket' of goods and services to meet our personal needs or the needs of our dependents. Any unspent income is money wealth, and if we buy long-term assets (durable consumer goods of various sorts and landed property) these are also part of our wealth. One other aspect of income is that we are all liable for 'income tax', a share of our income demanded by central government for social purposes.

(b) If we decide to make some of our 'money wealth' available for the use of others who need to be able to command resources for productive purposes this is 'money capital'. We can invest directly in such enterprises, but more likely we simply save our money in banks and other financial institutions and they make it available to 'capitalists' who require capital to develop businesses. As they do so the money capital (often called liquid capital) is said to be fixed – it is turned into fixed assets, (often called 'fixed capital').

(d) The accumulation of capital

In order to create capital assets of the types listed above it is necessary for work to be performed without any immediate gain or reward in the form of consumer goods. In primitive societies the workers making stone axes must be kept alive by the other members of the tribe who hunt or collect food. These hunters and food gatherers must eat less today so that capital assets can be produced which will increase productivity in the future. In other words, we must postpone current consumption to provide future improvements in living standards. Economists put it in the form of an equation:

Consumption postponed = Savings = Capital available for investment

The early stages in any country's accumulation of capital are very bitter years. Promises of jam tomorrow do not compensate the poor eating dry bread today. Were the early capitalists of Great Britain, whom Dickens called 'The Iron Gentlemen', justified in paying such low wages to accumulate the capital for their industries? At least they practised self-denial themselves too. Similarly, Henry Ford, the American industrialist, asked by his son for some money, reputedly gave the boy a penny. The boy indignantly flung it into a bush in the garden. Ford insisted on finding it, and read the boy a lecture on the value, and unique properties, of copper. Was Stalin right to let five million Russians die of starvation while he built up heavy industry. The almost universal denigration today of the 'man of steel' testifies to the bitterness of the process. 'You dared not go out,' said one witness 'for fear people would eat you.' Stalin may have built up heavy industry, but this might have been achieved equally well in other ways.

(e) Skills as capital

Hidden behind the actual producer goods themselves there is another kind of capital, the accumulated skill and knowledge of the people. This can be established only over lengthy periods of time, although the process is speeded up by modern education. Great Britain took a great many years to discover the basic industrial processes which brought her to greatness. From about 1700 until 1850 these skills and processes were slowly mastered. Other nations, like France, Germany and the US, made more rapid progress because they benefited from lessons already learned in Britain. They sprang to industrial power in fifty years (1860–1910). The Japanese made even more rapid strides. In each case there is the further point that when you come in later you start from a better base. Germany rose to power in the electrical age rather than the steam age, and Japan has made its progress in the electronic era. Leapfrogging in this way, the late developers not only challenge but surpass others who, having invested capital in earlier technologies, are slow to destroy what they have so painfully accumulated. The process of accumulating capital is perhaps less bitter for those who begin today than in the early days of industrialism.

Once a nation has advanced through the initial period of the accumulation of capital it is much easier for it to accumulate capital, because it already has a skilled and sophisticated labour force. The best example of this was the rapid recovery of Germany after World War II. Despite the appalling devastation of the country's resources and the punitive reparations demanded, Western Germany rose like a phoenix from the ashes. This was not entirely due to her own efforts. Enlightened behaviour by the Allies contributed a great deal, but the hard work and skill of the West Germans themselves were chiefly responsible for restoring a shattered economy to a leading position in Europe in the space of a dozen years. It has been calculated that the total capital assets of even an advanced nation represent less than two years of national income. The rebuilding of Germany in such a short time appears to support this calculation.

3.4.1
Net capital formation and savings

The following ideas about capital formation are important:

(a) *Capital formation is possible only if consumption is postponed somewhere in society.* This postponement of consumption may be voluntary, involuntary or State-induced. Voluntary self-denial occurs when we postpone present consumption quite deliberately, perhaps to save resources for bad times ahead, or to pursue some long-term policy aimed at capital formation. Involuntary savings occur when someone else prevents us from enjoying our full consumption. This may happen when there is overcharging by entrepreneurs in favourable positions. Gambling dens, which are usually considered as antisocial, might be justified on the grounds that they remove funds from the pockets of those who clearly do not know what to do with their money and put it into the pockets of others who will invest it in solid enterprises. State-induced savings are effected by taxation. If, as a matter of Government policy, income is taxed away to reduce personal consumption these funds will be available for capital formation. Taxes may be imposed on the rich to help the poor. Such taxation will not help capital formation at all, for it encourages consumption.

(b) *Savings release resources to support workers engaged in the creation of capital assets.* It is the postponement of current consumption (savings) which enables unproductive workers to be supported. The word 'unproductive' is used here to mean 'unproductive of consumer goods', because the end product of these workers will be a capital asset. This capital asset will make available a bigger flow of consumer goods eventually.

(c) *The saving made must not merely be hoarded, but must be 'invested',* i.e. used to support the workers engaged in producing the capital assets required. As there is always some risk involved in this type of activity, the savings which have been invested may, or may not, yield a future increased flow of consumer goods. The process of investment is carried out directly by the entrepreneur who sets up in business using his own savings as capital to support himself while he creates the capital assets he requires. It is carried out indirectly when a person who wishes to save invests his money with an institutional investor (such as a bank, building society or unit trust) which records the loan made to it and then makes the savings available to an entrepreneur in search of funds. The claims of the individual who saves the money against current consumption are handed on to the entrepreneur who intends to build a factory, or dig a mine, or create some other producer good. Self-denial on the part of the saver makes possible capital formation by the borrower.

(d) *Not all the new assets created represent an increase in capital.* The capital formation of any country in a given year does not all represent an advance in national wealth. Some of the new capital assets created will merely be replacing old assets which have become obsolete or have depreciated to the point where they must be scrapped. The term **net capital formation** is used to signify that portion of created assets which is in excess of depreciation in the period under review. If Britain builds 300 000 houses per year but pulls down 200 000 older properties in slum-clearance schemes the net capital formation is 100 000 houses.

3.4.2
Capital consumption

Where the net capital formation is a negative quantity, because less new assets are created than old assets are retired from production, we may say the nation is *living on its capital or consuming its capital.* This often happens in war-time, when heavy destruction of capital assets may occur at a time when replacement is particularly difficult because able-bodied men are away fighting. The slow recovery of Britain after World War II was partly due to heavy consumption of capital during that period. Not only was serious destruction of capital experienced but also heavy debts were incurred with overseas countries. The repayment of these debts reduced net capital formation in the years 1945–55.

Every nation must take care to maintain its capital and attempt to increase it. As populations rise, larger supplies of capital are needed to maintain existing living standards. Since most people expect their standard of living to improve year by year, it is essential that a positive net capital formation be achieved.

3.4.3
Credit creation

The description given above about the ways in which capital is accumulated and capital formation is achieved by postponing consumption elsewhere in the economy is a rather simplified view of the provision of capital. It is still largely true for the budding entrepreneur seeking to start a new business, as countless new firms set up every year can bear witness, but it omits the part played by 'credit creation' in providing capital for established firms, and for the most promising new enterprises. In one recent case the takeover of an international company for a figure in excess of £1.5 billion was achieved by a new company with a capital of only £2. Just how this is possible remains to be seen. Credit creation is a process by which the capital available to entrepreneurs is increased by bankers to a level far above that achievable by postponed consumption. It is explained in detail later in this book (see Chapter 28) together with the problems of 'keeping in step', which prevents banks from getting into financial difficulties by excessive creation of capital. The two terms 'capital creation' and 'credit creation' are synonymous, because, in accountancy, capital is always recorded on the credit side (the right hand side) of an account and consequently to create capital is to create credit entries on the books of any firm.

3.5
Is the entrepreneur a factor of production?

At one time the activities of entrepreneurs were considered to be so different from those of other humans that entrepreneurs were regarded as a separate factor of production. They provided 'enterprise', which was essential to the productive process. The development of the limited-liability company as the chief type of business unit has led to a careful examination of the activities of entrepreneurs, for in this form of organisation different persons perform different activities, which were formerly performed by the sole proprietor, or partners.

The activities undertaken by an entrepreneur are as follows:

(a) *Ownership*. The early entrepreneur was the source of the capital of the enterprise, which he had accumulated by postponing consumption. In placing that claim against the goods and services available at the disposal of the business he ran the risk that the business would prove to be a failure. The function of ownership is to carry risk: to bear the uncertainties of business life.

(b) *Management*. Early entrepreneurs, and sole traders or partners today who control their own businesses, work in the business. They make the major business decisions: what to produce, in which quantities, whom to employ, when and where to market the output, whether to expand or contract the activities of the firm, etc. In the limited-liability company such activities are performed by the board of directors, who are not the owners of the company (except that they must hold some shares).

Today we regard the two activities in the typical firm (the limited-liability company) as having been largely separated from one another. The difference is between 'the entrepreneurs' and 'the entrepreneurial function'.

The **entrepreneurs** are the *owners* of the business, who contribute the capital and *bear the risks of uncertainties in business life*. They may be sole traders, partners, limited partners or shareholders.

The **entrepreneurial function** is the *control and management of an enterprise*. It adjusts the enterprise to the dynamic situation in which it is being conducted, coordinating factors to achieve the maximum return on capital invested by the owners. It is a special type of human labour, increasingly performed not by sole traders and partners with personal interest in the affairs of the firm but by professional managers who may also own a few shares. The increasingly complex industrial structure of advanced societies throws up a whole career structure of management and junior management, taking an active share in the entrepreneurial function but quite divorced from true ownership of the business.

Enterprise is therefore no longer generally regarded by economists as a fourth factor of production, even though countless old-style entrepreneurs may be observed running their sole-trader or partnership business and wielding powerful influence in many private limited companies. The public limited company is of such overwhelming importance that it justifies regarding the entrepreneurial function as one performed by ordinary labour, not a special type of labour.

3.6 Combining the factors of production

The entrepreneurial function of management is to maximise the return on capital invested. In order to do this, management combines the factors of land, labour and capital in what it considers to be the best possible way. It then observes the achievements of the resources used, and makes adjustments if necessary. Some possibility exists of **substitution between factors**, replacing an expensive factor by a cheaper one, for example, but complete substitution of one factor by another is usually impossible. Suppose that land prices are high. The management may increase the proportion of capital to land, so that capital-intensive use of the land is achieved. In rural areas it may mean the use of battery systems for producing poultry and eggs; in London it means building tower blocks of flats instead of bungalows.

In employing resources the management will measure the factors in terms of cost, to achieve the most economical input of factors. Factor costs are dealt with in detail later, but the names given to the rewards paid to factors are

Factor	*Rewards paid to the factor (factor cost)*
Land	Commercial rent
Labour	Wages (salaries has the same meaning)
Capital	Interest (paid to the owner for surrendering his claims to current consumption)
	Profit (paid to compensate the owner for the risk he runs)

3.7 The environmental closed cycle of production

We live in a world which is a closed environment, except for occasional space-shots and interplanetary probes. The resources that nature provides or has provided in the past are the source of raw materials, energy and capital goods. The sole sources of labour are the human populations born into the various societies around the world, supplemented by such mechanical contrivances and robots as we can devise. Everything that we use returns to the environment eventually, either as exhaust gases, wasted heat and energy, waste products or eventual scrap. The archaeologist digging in the ruins of ancient cities merely recovers discarded artefacts from the production of earlier eras. Today's cigarette end is tomorrow's artefact.

Viewed in this way, production presents us with a range of economic problems. We may list the more obvious ones as follows:

1 To preserve scarce resources as far as possible by using them efficiently, achieving the maximum output from the minimum input of raw materials, energy and effort. The conservation of non-renewable

resources is particularly important. Thus economists might ask whether we should continue to burn coal – a source of many important chemicals – to obtain energy, when renewable resources like wind power and wave power are hardly used at all to generate power. Unlike the individual entrepreneur, who historically has made use of whatever resources came to hand, however extravagant their use might be, governments and other resource-allocating bodies should take a broader view.

2 To recycle waste products so far as possible.

3 To ensure that waste products are rendered harmless, and returned to the environment in such a way that they do not impose social costs on the community in general, or do harm to future generations as yet unborn.

4 To monitor the ecological impact of production to prevent harmful effects on the biosphere in which we all live. In this respect the fears that have been expressed about the excessive consumption of fossil fuels, which raise the level of carbon dioxide in the atmosphere to raise world temperatures and perhaps melt the polar ice caps, illustrate the sort of problem. The creation of smokeless zones is a similar attempt to ensure that the environment is not marred by waste gases, while institutes of hydrology monitor water quality and devise river management programmes.

5 To use **cost-benefit analysis** to evaluate the probable economic effects of pursuing production in particular directions to seek the maximisation of benefits and the minimisation of costs. Cost-benefit analysis is explained later in this section (see page 36).

It is impossible in *Economics Made Simple* to give a wide review of these 'closed-cycle' considerations in the use of resources. A few examples are given below, but the reader is urged to acquire a broad background by reading widely in such journals as the *Economist, National Geographic, New Society, New Scientist* and *Scientific American*. The points listed below may open up fields of enquiry for students.

3.7.1

The management of scarce non-renewable resources

There is a great need for responsible authorities, i.e. Government departments, quangos (quasi-autonomous non-governmental organisations), development authorities, etc., to supervise scarce non-renewable resources. This particularly applies to minerals whose known reserves are reaching danger level, which may be cornered by aggressive multinationals; for example, chromium, cobalt, manganese and vanadium are metals which some nations feel should be stockpiled for economic as well as strategic reasons. Coal, which is not in short supply but is non-renewable, and might be of much greater use to our great-grandchildren than it is to us, could largely be replaced as a fuel by the renewable resource wood. Wood, in developed countries, is being considerably wasted today, while non-renewable gas and oil are being used to heat homes. One of the problems is that vested interests exist in every area where governments might interfere in the national (or even the international) interest. Thus to close mines for the benefit of future generations will not be viewed by the present generation of miners as desirable; to cut back oil production to conserve resources does not meet with the approval of the oil-producing countries since it threatens present prosperity, and fishermen with nets loaded with herrings resent being required to put the fish back into the sea.

While conservation of scarce resources is essential, the discovery of further resources is also important. Such investigations as the Earth

Resources Satellite Programme, the investigation of deep-sea mining and alternative energy programmes offer important opportunities to ensure economic development for the future. The alternative energy programme in particular seeks to replace the use of oil and natural gas as sources of energy (leaving them as sources of chemicals). Instead we shall make use of the inexhaustible resources of solar energy, wind power, wave power, geo-thermal energy and – if the environmental problems can be overcome – atomic energy.

3.7.2 Recycling waste products

Generally speaking, any industrial process results in a main product, or in several joint products which were the purpose of the activity. There is then left a residue of material which should so far as possible be utilised. Perhaps not all production processes can be as efficient as the Chicago stock yards which claim that they use every part of the pig except the grunt. It may be possible to use the waste to produce a by-product, or to use it again for the original process. Thus after stamping out coins from sheet metal a mint simply melts down the balance of the material from which the coins have been pressed to give a further sheet for subsequent use. Efficient design may reduce waste, as when the fashion designer makes a matching pocket out of pieces left after cutting out the main garment.

Waste products can be recycled in many ways. Bottles may be returned to bottle banks, waste paper can be stripped of its printers' ink and repulped, tin cans can be pressed and bailed, obsolete motor vehicles can be crushed, frozen to very low temperatures at which the metal becomes brittle and will break on hammering. The ferrous material is extracted with magnets and the non-ferrous material re-smelted. Such activities are not always profitable, and hence may be best carried on by official bodies who can assume the risks on the projects in the early years, and reap the benefits once a viable scheme of recycling activities has been developed.

3.7.3 The pollution problem

Many waste products are harmful, and it costs money to make them safe. There is a great temptation to entrepreneurs simply to dispose of the waste without any attempt to render it safe. This has been the cause of enormous misery in the past from atmospheric pollution, disfiguring slag heaps, acid rain, etc. The effect is for costs to fall as social costs upon the general public. It is a world-wide problem and the United Nations has set up UNEP, the United Nations Environment Programme, to monitor the environment globally. It is a problem not only for free-enterprise communities, where profit-seeking entrepreneurs heap social costs on the community. There are major problems in Eastern Europe with polluted, acidic atmospheres caused by excessive industrial development. State-run industries and bureaucratic planning bodies insusceptible to influence by ordinary people have polluted rivers and the atmosphere and (it is rumoured) even caused atomic explosions by careless dumping. The European Union is conducting massive investigations into the presence of heavy metals, nitrates, nitrites and other chemicals in water, root crops, etc., and into sewage pollution of beaches and estuaries. The UK now has a *Deposit of Poisonous Wastes Act* which makes it illegal to dump poisonous materials, and a *Health and Safety at Work Act* which requires employers to provide a safe system of work. The United Nations Foods and Agriculture Organisation monitors the impact of pesticides on food products.

3.7.4
Cost-benefit analysis in ecology

How much weight to give to ecological considerations in any economy is a difficult question. It varies from society to society, from time to time and from area to area. Thus a developing country with a starving population is entirely preoccupied with the economic problems of providing food, shelter and clothing, and once these have been provided the ability to provide a living for its citizens by their own efforts in a social climate where self-respect can be maintained. For more advanced societies the quality of life is influenced greatly by ecological factors, but it may depend on the solution of quite different problems. Let us take water quality as a well-documented example. There are two methods of ensuring a potable supply of water. One is to control the emissions of highly poisonous or unpleasant substances at every point where they are likely to occur. The EU has 1500 such named pollutants, and the cost of controlling emissions can be enormously expensive. The other method is the water-quality method, which seeks to establish what is the quality of any given stretch of water and what must be done to clean it up to potable quality. The UK prefers the latter method – but its rivers are short, and all flow into the sea where the natural processes tend to deposit pollutants as sediments. Holland, at the far end of major networks flowing all the way from the Alps – where traditionally Swiss housewives have cast their waste water into the river with the admonition 'A present for the Austrians' – prefers that nations higher up the river should control emissions strictly. This means that the costs are very high, since polluters must install the best equipment available to control their emissions. No doubt the benefits are also great, but are they justified by the cost? Sedimentation would reduce pollutant levels – though sediments are likely to be scoured up at times of massive storms. Dilution can reduce the impact of pollutants, plants can remove them and improve water quality. Automatic telemetering of rivers is enabling corrective measures to be taken to restore water quality, etc. Major projects on the Bedford Ouse, the Thames and other waterways now make it possible to sample river quality night and day and build in automatic improvements by oxidising the water and influencing river flows. These measures are highly cost-effective, giving great benefits for relatively small inputs of resources.

3.8
Summary of Chapter 3

1 Production is achieved by the combination of land, labour and capital in the creation of goods and services.

2 Land as a factor means the resources made available by Nature. To some extent these are free gifts by Nature to mankind. Every enterprise must have a geographical location. The early economists noticed that land was subject to the Law of Diminishing Returns, but this law is today held to apply to all factors, not exclusively to land.

3 Labour is the human factor, and depends upon the working population available, its quality and suitability for the types of activity proposed.

4 Capital is a claim against the resources of goods and services available to mankind. It has to be accumulated by a reduction in current consumption, and makes possible the creation of producer goods and social assets of all sorts. These assets then enable even greater production of consumer goods and services in the succeeding period.

5 The entrepreneur is today regarded as the owner of a firm. The entrepreneurial functions of management control and coordination of business activities are regarded as being performed by labour today. The typical modern business unit, the limited-liability company, displays this separation between ownership and management.

6   In combining the factors of production, substitution between factors is possible to some extent. Management aims at the best possible combination of factors.

7   The natural environment constitutes a closed-cycle of conditions within which all human activity must take place. We have a closed cycle of production, with raw materials taken from the environment for use by society, and returning eventually to nature.

8   Some resources are renewable and others are not. These finite resources must eventually become scarce, and need to be conserved as much as possible.

9   The results of production activities include potentially harmful pollutants, such as poisons, waste gases, waste energy, etc. These can have harmful effects unless carefully monitored and controlled.

Exercises Set 3

1   What factors would be controlled and manipulated by a retired sea captain using his life savings to run an inn in freehold premises near a major port?

2   Suggest how the following might save labour by using capital: (*a*) a cotton plantation manager; (*b*) a sugar refiner; (*c*) a garage proprietor: (*d*) the board of governors of a college; (*e*) the chief accountant of a multiple-shop organisation.

3   Which types of 'land' are used by the following entrepreneurs: (*a*) a grain farmer; (*b*) a cattle rancher; (*c*) a chemical engineer in an oil refinery; (*d*) a frozen fish-finger manufacturer; (*e*) a manufacturer of neon tubes?

4   List the likely 'capital goods' employed by: (*a*) a gold-mining company; (*b*) an electric-shaver assembly firm; (*c*) a trawler operator; (*d*) a bespoke tailor; (*e*) a hire purchase finance company.

5   Discuss the law of diminishing returns as it applies to the following factors in the given situations; (*a*) land – used for market gardening; (*b*) labour – one man employed to repair watches; (*c*) capital – a machine for filling milk bottles.

6   What do we understand by an 'entrepreneur' today? Who performs this function in the following cases: (*a*) a sole trader; (*b*) a partnership; (*c*) a public limited company?

7   To some extent all factors are interchangeable. Explain, giving examples drawn from primary, secondary, and tertiary production.

8   Distinguish between specific and non-specific assets. The liquidator of a company is appointed to sell off the assets to pay the creditors. What will be the effect on his activities of a high degree of specificity in the assets?

9   An American company has a choice between setting up a factory in Belgium or Turkey. Discuss the likely labour situations facing them in these two countries, and the probable advantages and disadvantages of each.

10   'The sole purpose of capital is to exploit working people' – European Trade Unionist. 'We would welcome capital investments from any country on terms fair to both parties' – African politician. Discuss the accumulation of capital, referring in your answer to the different attitudes displayed by these two spokesmen.

11   Distinguish between renewable resources and non-renewable resources. Give five examples of each.

12   How might non-renewable sources of energy be replaced by renewable resources of energy? What should we then do with the non-renewable resources we have not used?

13 What is the point of recycling waste products? What is the impact of recycling upon (*a*) scarce resources, (*b*) resources in plentiful supply, (*c*) industries in the 'resource-supply' fields, and (*d*) manufacturing industries?

4   The types of business unit

4.1
Introduction

A business is a unit of organisation carrying on some productive activity resulting in the creation of goods or services to satisfy wants. These types of business unit show a progression from small-scale businesses, often run by sole traders or partnerships, to large-scale enterprises of national and even international importance. Since the accumulation of capital is a difficult process, at first the scale of operations must be small. As the profits made are reinvested in the enterprise it grows, and growth accelerates as the years go by. Finally, its manifest success makes investment in the firm attractive to outsiders as well.

The size of the business therefore reflects the amount of capital invested. Differences between the various units reflect: (*a*) the ownership of the capital concerned; (*b*) the control of the conduct of the enterprise; (*c*) the accountability of the controllers to the investors, in so far as they are different people; (*d*) the division of the profits.

4.2
Types of business unit

Business units in Britain may be divided into three main groups: **private enterprises, non-profitmaking units**, and **public enterprises**. A full list includes:

Private enterprises
     Sole traders
     Partnerships
     Limited partnerships
     Private limited companies
     Public limited companies
     Holding companies (a more advanced type of public company)

Non-profitmaking units
     Clubs of many sorts
     Co-operative societies

Public enterprises
     Municipal undertakings
     Quasi-autonomous non-governmental organisations (quangos)
     Autonomous public corporations
     Central government institutions

Readers in other countries may find the British pattern of enterprises slightly different from their own.

Ownership is the key to the difference between these three types of undertaking. Private enterprises are owned and operated by certain clearly identified people, who are also entitled to the rewards of the enterprise. Non-profitmaking groups exist in order to confer benefits on the members which are outside the commercial activities of the unit. Profit is a mere incidental, but any surplus is shared among the membership. With public-enterprise units, the enterprise is socially owned and operated, possibly on a commercial basis, but with the intention of supplying goods and services at reasonable prices for the benefit of the whole community.

4.3 Sole-trader enterprises

A sole trader is a person who enters business on his own account, contributing the capital to start the enterprise, labouring in it with or without the assistance of employees, and receiving as his reward the proceeds of the venture. The advantages are as follows:

(a) No formal procedures are required to set up in business. A licence must be obtained for certain classes of business and, if the business trades under any other name than the true name of the proprietor, the name and address of the owner must be displayed at the business premises and on the business stationery. This notice must be in a statutory form as laid down in the Business Names Act 1985.

(b) Independence is a chief feature of these businesses. Having no one to consult, the sole trader can put his plans into effect quickly.

(c) Personal supervision ensures effective operation at all times. Customers are known to the proprietor, who can cater for their tastes and avoid bad debts by a personal assessment of credit-worthiness; employees are under personal supervision; waste is avoided.

(d) Expansion need be pressed only to the point where the market is adequately supplied. In isolated areas this makes the sole trader the effective business unit.

(e) He is accountable only to himself and (apart from the taxation authorities) need reveal the state of his business to no one.

The disadvantages include:

(a) Long working hours and little time off for vacations.

(b) Sickness can lead to business difficulties.

(c) The proprietor has 'unlimited liability', which means that he is personally liable to the full extent of his private wealth for the debts of the business. Insolvency may mean the sale of his house and home to pay the creditors.

(d) Expansion is usually possible only by ploughing back the profits of a business as further capital. The sole trader may be able to borrow from a bank, or privately, but he is not allowed to borrow from the public. He may take a partner, but this means a loss of independence. He can keep this independence if he takes a 'limited partner', but these are not easy to find in present conditions of high taxation.

(e) The business is part of the estate of the proprietor at his death, and if inheritance tax applies it may be necessary to sell the business to realise funds in order to pay it.

(f) Like most small-scale enterprises, it will be a high-cost enterprise, because the degree of specialisation is usually small.

4.3.1 Vulnerability of the sole trader

From 1945 to 1975 there was a general decline in the number of sole trader enterprises – a tendency which has been reduced recently by official encouragement for the establishment of small firms. However, it is still largely true that every improvement in transport and communication exposes the local shop and the local factory to a blast of competition from larger and more efficient enterprises. One owner of a small factory complained that when trade is booming he cannot find the raw materials at a price that pays him to manufacture, and when trade is bad he cannot find a customer for his product. Sole traders are therefore of less importance today than formerly, but in one respect they are still of considerable value. Despite the high proportion of new ideas and new products which are discovered by the research departments of large-scale organisations, a significant contribution is still made by the small-scale entrepreneur. Inspired individuals still come up with completely new ideas. One has only to think of Frank Whittle's jet engine, Christopher Cockerell's hovercraft or Sinclair Research Ltd's computers to realise that the age of the individual entrepreneur is not yet past entirely. Economists call such enterprises **nodal points** in the economy. A 'nodal point' is a biological term meaning a 'growth' point. Some of the most significant growth points in recent years have developed in small industries. It is these nodal points which official agencies such as The Small Firms Service and the local Enterprise Agencies are seeking to encourage in the present climate of high unemployment.

4.4 Partnerships

In seeking to achieve larger scale, a sole trader may consider entering into partnership.

4.4.1 Why take a partner?

There are several reasons why sole traders combine together to form partnerships. The chief advantages are:

(a) Increased capital, permitting the business to expand more rapidly than is possible by the 'ploughing back' of profits earned.
(b) The responsibility of control no longer rests with one person. This makes possible holidays and free week-ends, and reduces the worry the sole trader experiences in times of ill health.
(c) Wider experience is brought to the firm, and some degree of specialisation is possible; this is particularly true of professional partnerships. A physician and a surgeon may form a partnership; or lawyers with experience in different fields – divorce, criminal law, commercial law – may combine to offer a more comprehensive service to the public.
(d) Very often a young man teams up with an older man. The young man has his health and strength; his partner has the capital and the experience. Together they make a satisfactory team.
(e) The affairs of the business are still private.

4.4.2 Disadvantages of a partnership

(a) The partners still have unlimited liability for the debts of the business.
(b) Each partner must consult the other and consider his views every time a decision has to be made.
(c) The partnership is adversely affected by the death of a partner, whose share may be withdrawn to pay the beneficiaries. It is therefore desirable for each partner to take out life assurance to provide a lump-sum benefit in the event of the other partner's death.

The partnership is particularly suitable for professional people, such as doctors, lawyers and accountants. It is also suitable for small-scale enterprises of all sorts, in retail trade, manufacturing, agriculture and horticulture, road haulage and local wholesaling.

**4.5
Limited
partnerships**

The law affecting partnerships was modified in 1907 by the Limited Partnership Act. This Act permits a partnership to be formed between an active partner or partners and one or more 'sleeping' partners who are accorded the privilege of **limited liability**.

**4.5.1
The privilege of
limited liability**

Where a person has funds available for the promotion of business activity, but does not wish himself to take any part in the conduct of the business or the management of the firm, it seems unfair to require him to carry the burden of unlimited liability which attaches to sole traders or partners. The principle of limited liability holds that such a person should be liable to the extent of the capital he has contributed, but no further than this. The limitation of liability in this way unlocks savings which would otherwise merely be hoarded by their owners, and releases them to play a productive part in the industrial and commercial fields.

In the early days of the Industrial Revolution people who contributed capital to industrial firms were held to be full partners, and many lost their homes when speculative projects collapsed and the partners were required to contribute to pay the debts of the firms concerned. Only in 1855, when the increasing demands for capital met resistance from savers who had already seen others suffer hardship through no fault of their own, did Parliament sanction limited liability for shareholders.

The 1907 Act sanctioned limited liability for partners with capital to contribute, provided that there was at least one partner, the **general partner**, who did assume unlimited liability for the affairs of the business, and provided that the limited partner took no part in the management of the firm. The reader should notice that the division between 'ownership' and the entrepreneurial functions of management control begins to appear at this point.

Some of the risks of the enterprise are now being borne by partners who are statutorily forbidden to take any part in the conduct of its affairs.

**4.6
The private limited
company and the
public limited
company**

These two types of business unit are very closely connected, and both are controlled by the Companies Acts, 1985–9. They have recently been brought even closer together by the removal of the exemption clauses which had previously made the exempt private company so attractive a form of business organisation. Before considering these points let us look at the formation of such a company.

**4.6.1
Floating a company**

Since the year 1980 the promoters of both public and private companies need find only one other person prepared to join with him/her as **members**. They sign a **Memorandum of Association**; a document which governs the relationship of the company with the external world. Its seven main clauses are as follows:

(*a*) The name of the company, ending with the word 'Limited' (private companies), or with the words 'Public Limited Company' (or the Welsh equivalent). Under the 1985 Act a few companies pursuing socially desirable activities in the promotion of commerce, the arts, science, religion, charitable or professional aims as non-profitmaking bodies are exempt from using the word 'limited' in the name. The word 'limited' is a warning to those doing business with the company that the shareholders have limited liability. Many people think a company is more reliable to deal with than a sole trader or partnership, but this is not necessarily so.

(b) The address of its registered office.

(c) The objects of the company. This states what the company will do when it is established, and forms the legal basis for its activities. It will have to keep its activities within the fields specified, or the courts may rule them *ultra vires* (outside the powers). This is a protection to the shareholders. Suppose I invested £50 000 in a company that was to develop a revolutionary type of aero engine, which I believed has a great future. I suddenly discover that the directors are using my money to buy sugar which happens to be rising on world markets. I would naturally feel that this was not the purpose for which I had subscribed my capital, and would be able to obtain an injunction restraining the directors from using my money in an *ultra vires* way.

(d) A statement that the liability of the members is limited.

(e) The amount of share capital to be issued, and the types of share.

(f) An undertaking by the signatories that they desire to be formed into a company registered under the Acts, and to undertake to purchase the number of shares against their names.

(g) By the 1985 Act a seventh rule required that the names, addresses, etc., of the first director (or directors) and the first company secretary shall be stated in a prescribed form. This statement must be signed by the other members and contain the consents of the director(s) and secretary.

Having drawn up and signed the Memorandum of Association, the directors usually then draw up detailed **Articles of Association**, which control the internal affairs of the company. Such matters as the procedure to be followed at meetings, the duties of the managing director, the borrowing powers that may be exercised, and so on are considered and agreed. A set of modal articles, called Table A, is printed in the Acts. These articles will be effective and binding on all companies issuing shares, unless the company's articles specifically invalidate them on some point.

4.6.2 Registration of the company

The promoters of the company may now proceed to register the company under the Acts. They present to the **Registrar of Companies** the Memorandum of Association; the Articles of Association; a statement of the nominal capital, on which a tax of £1 per cent is payable; a list of directors and their written consents and promises to take up shares; and a statutory declaration that the Company Acts have been complied with.

If all is in order, the Registrar will issue a **Certificate of Incorporation**, which bestows upon the company a separate legal personality. The company may now do all legal things that an ordinary person can do: for example, it may own land and property, employ people, sue and be sued in the courts, etc. Before it may begin trading, however, it must secure the capital it needs. With a private company this will largely be contributed by the founders, anyway. With a public company it must be obtained from the public, either directly or indirectly through the institutional investors.

4.6.3
Classes of shares

People with savings to spare have to be tempted to invest in an enterprise; hence the wide variety of shares and bonds offered to them. Some people want a high return on their capital, and to obtain it are prepared to run some risk. Others want security for their savings, even though the rate of interest is lower. Security is particularly difficult to ensure in inflationary times. For instance, savings in Government Securities are absolutely secure; if you leave them in for fifty years you will receive £1 back for every £1 invested, but if that £1 will only buy goods worth 20 new pence, because of **inflation** over the years, you have really lost money on the investment. We say that the **nominal value** (nominal means 'in name only') has remained the same, but the **real value** (in terms of what it will purchase) has declined.

A full explanation of the types of share is given in *Commerce Made Simple*, but for readers unfamiliar with the main points a comparative table is shown on page 47. A further comparative table on pages 48–9 deals with the main aspects of private-enterprise units. Study these tables now.

4.6.4
Certificate of trading

Before a public company can begin to trade it must secure a **Certificate of Trading**. This is issued by the Registrar of Companies, when registration is finally completed by lodging with him the following documents:

(*a*) A statement that the minimum capital has been subscribed.
(*b*) A statement that the directors have paid for their shares.
(*c*) A statutory declaration that the Companies Acts have been complied with.

There are two meanings to the term '**minimum capital**'. Under the 1985 Act (s. 118) a Public Limited Company must have at least the minimum authorised capital of £50 000 (this may be modified by Statutory Instrument). The other meaning refers to that amount of capital stated in the prospectus as being the minimum which, in the directors' opinion, is necessary for the success of the enterprise. If this minimum is not reached all the capital collected must be returned to the shareholders. Directors can ensure successful commencement of trading if they have the issue underwritten by financiers prepared to buy shares should the public not do so.

4.6.5
How a company is formed and financed

Figure 4.1 shows how most public companies are formed. Starting in a small way, often as a family business and operating as a private company, they expand to the point where they can fulfil the strict requirements of the Stock Exchange Council.

When permission to deal in a company's shares is accorded by the Stock Exchange Council the public will be invited to subscribe for shares. The new capital thus made available enables the firm to expand its activities and achieve the advantages of large-scale production.

Invitations to the public to subscribe for shares are made in a **prospectus**, which is a full and frank account of the history of the company to date, its profit record, and every detail likely to be of interest to an investor trying to assess his risks in making an application for shares.

This prospectus must be registered with the Registrar of Companies before the public are invited to subscribe.

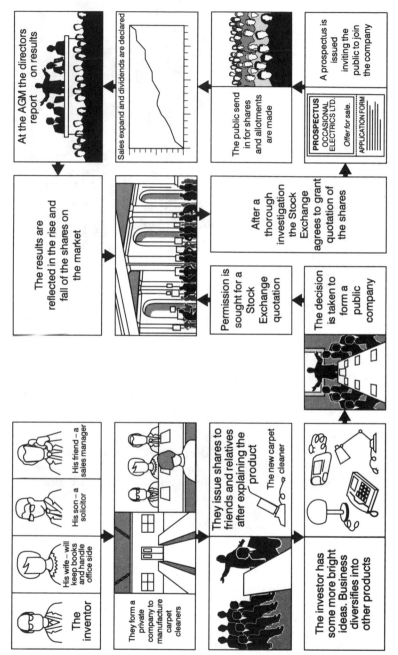

Figure 4.1 The formation of a company

Figure 4.2 The Rochdale Pioneers' historic store as it was in 1844

4.7 Non-profitmaking units

A certain number of business units are non-profitmaking clubs and societies. They are formed to confer on their members certain benefits in the way of club facilities, discount trading or value for money. Such clubs and societies often make profits on the year's trading, but these are not profits in the normal commercial meaning of the word. They really represent over-payments by the members for the services they have received, and are usually called 'surpluses'. Examples of such business units are the Working Men's Clubs of the north of England and the co-operative societies.

4.7.1 Co-operative retail societies

The first successful 'Co-op' store was founded in 1844 in Toad Lane, Rochdale, by 28 weavers nowadays remembered as the 'Rochdale Pioneers'. The idea was to buy foodstuffs at wholesale prices and sell them (to members only) at market price. Profits were divided among members in proportion to the value of their purchases. The share-out (dividend) took place twice a year. By 1845 there were 74 members, the turnover was £710, the profit £22.

The Co-operative movement spread rapidly. Societies were set up in towns all over the UK. In 1862 the members voted to set up a wholesale organisation, the Co-operative Wholesale Society. This society not only supplied the retail societies like any ordinary wholesaler but also ran factories, farms, transport services and even tea gardens to provide everything the retail societies needed. The retail societies joined the wholesale society in exactly the same way as the ordinary members joined the retail society. All the profits of the Co-operative Wholesale Society are shared among the member retail societies, and all the profits of the retail societies are shared among the members. Thus in the end all the profits return to the members of the retail societies, whose purchasing power actually keeps the Co-operative movement going. However, these days the cumbersome distribution of profits to members by a special dividend day every six months has been discontinued and other systems (Co-op stamps for example) have been developed.

Table 4.1 Comparison of different types of share

Type of investment	Reward earned	Degree of risk	Who buys them	Who issues them
Ordinary shares	Equal share of profits, hence nickname 'equity shares'	Carry the main risk	(a) Well-to-do investors who want big returns. (b) Institutional investors, for a balanced portfolio. (c) People interested in capital gains, rather than revenue profits	Private and public companies
Deferred ordinary shares (founder's shares)	Share of profits after ordinary shares have had some (say 10%) profit	Same as ordinary shares	They are taken by the vendor of a business when he sells it, as a sign of confidence in its future	Public companies chiefly, but also private companies
Preference shares	Definite rate of dividend (say 7%), but only if profits are made	Less than ordinary shares as they *usually* have a prior right to repayment	Investors seeking security rather than large dividends	Public and private companies
Cumulative preference shares	As above, but if profits are not earned in one year the dividend accumulates and is not lost	As above	As above	As above
Participating preference shares	After taking the fixed rate (say 7%) these shares earn extra dividend if the Ordinary shares get more than 7%	As above	As above	As above
Debentures (loans to companies: debentures are not really shares)	Fixed rate of interest (say 6%), payable whether profits are made or not	Very small	Timid people wanting a secure investment	Public and private companies, if permitted by their Articles

Table 4.2 Comparision of private-enterprise units

	Aspect	Sole trader	Partnership	Limited partnership
1	Name of firm	Any name provided it is either the proprietor's true name or their names, or the true names and addresses are displayed under the Business Names Act, 1985		
2	How formed	By commencing business without formality except (1) above	By agreement, which may be oral or written; limited partnerships must be registered	
3	Control of the firm	Proprietor has full control	Every partner is entitled to manage	Only the general partner(s) can manage the business
4	Liability for debts	Liable to the limits of personal wealth	They are jointly and severally liable for all the debts and torts of the business	General partners fully liable; limited partners not liable beyond the capital contributed
5	Relationship between owner and business	The business is the owner, or owners, and has no separate legal existence		The business is the same as the general partners; the limited partner is not the business
6	Membership of firm	One	Two or more	Two or more
7	General powers	At will	At will, subject to agreement; if no agreement, Partnership Act 1890 applies	
8	Transfer of ownership	By sale of 'goodwill'	Only with unanimous consent	
9	Controlling Acts	None	Partnership Act 1890	Limited Partnership Act, 1907
10	Disbanding of firm	At will or by bankruptcy	Firm may go bankrupt or be dissolved by notice or mutual consent	
11	Advantages	Independence. Personal control of staff and granting of credit. Decisions acted upon at once	Increased capital. Days off and holidays possible. Wider experience of partners. Privacy of affairs	Limited liability for some partners. Larger capital
12	Disadvantages	Long hours. No holidays. Illness affects conduct of business. Unlimited liability. Small capital.	Unlimited liability. Death or retirement ends firm. Profits must be shared	Unlimited liability for the general partners. Also as for partnerships

4.7.2
Producer co-operatives

Since the 1960s a new type of business unit, the producer co-operative, has appeared. Registered under the Industrial and Provident Societies Acts 1965–8 and generally part of the Industrial Common Ownership Movement (ICOM) these co-operatives are owned and controlled by their

Table 4.2 Comparison of private-enterprise units (continued)

	Private limited companies	Public limited companies
1	The registered name, registered under the Companies Acts 1985–9 Names for private companies end in the word 'Limited	Names for public companies end in the words 'Public Limited Company'
2	By registration under the Companies Acts, with due legal formality	
3	Directors control the company. Members have no control at all, but may elect new Board at the Annual General Meeting if they wish to do so	
4	Limited liability for all members – only liable to the limit of capital contributed	
5	The business is a separate legal personality from the members	
6	Minimum two; no maximum under 1985 Act	
7	As laid down in Memorandum of Association and Articles of Association	
8	Shares may only be transferred with consent of fellow shareholders	Shares are freely transferable
9	Companies Acts, 1985–9	
10	Company may go into voluntary or compulsory liquidation	
11	Limited liability Death of shareholders does not affect the firm Capital can be collected from any number of members Privacy to some extent on affairs	Limited liability Death of shareholders does not affect the firm Very large capital can be collected
12	Publication now required, but since November 1986 turnover need not be revealed unless it exceeds £8 million	Full public knowledge of affairs. Minimum capital for a public company, by s. 118 of the 1985 Act, is £50 000

members. All employees have a right to be members and to have one vote when decisions are made, but outsiders may not be members. Outside capital, where employed, is regarded as loan stock. Managers are usually appointed for about five years, to ensure reasonable continuity.

4.8
The public-enterprise sector of the economy

In the UK, after recent bouts of privatisation, about 60 per cent of the economy and about two thirds of the commerce are conducted by the private enterprise firms already described. The remainder of the activities of the economy are conducted by socially owned enterprises. Some, like the Army, Navy and Air Force, are clearly the sort of institutions that the State itself should control. Others have tended to be performed by the State because they are non-profitmaking, and as such are unlikely to be attractive to businessmen. Such activities as education, medical care and sanitation are best operated as socially provided amenities for the benefit of all citizens.

In the industrial and commercial fields certain goods and services are by their nature monopolies. Among these **natural monopolies** are gas, electricity and water supply. The capital costs of such enterprises are too great for competition to be possible. We do not install three sets of gas pipes into our houses in order to be able to enjoy Jones's, Smith's or Robinson's gas according to which is the 'best buy' this morning.

Transport is another natural monopoly. It would be uneconomic to run two railway lines from London to Reading, or two different sets of half-empty buses along a country road. At one time it was thought that all such natural monopolies should be run as socially-owned enterprises, in the interests of the whole nation. Most of them were nationalised in the years after the war, in a series of nationalisation acts. However, in many cases, even though they were given the status of independent corporations, with only nominal control by central government, the size and complexity of such industries proved them difficult to run in this way. In particular, shortage of capital – it being subject to control by a Government pre-occupied with other matters – meant that development tended to be piecemeal. The case for and against nationalised enterprises is stated below, but a major feature of Government policies in the last 20 years has been the privatisation of many of these industries. A description of some of the effects is given later in the book (see pages 360–2).

4.8.1
The case for public enterprises

(a) They provide socially necessary facilities like education and sanitation which, being unprofitable, are unlikely to be provided by private enterprise.

(b) They are appropriate for running industries which are a natural monopoly, such as railways.

(c) Capital can be provided by taxation and rate assessment, as well as by borrowing, with government guarantees about interest and repayments. This is useful where profits are unlikely for some time, as with airlines.

(d) The provision of services without a principal emphasis on profitmaking renders the goods or service cheaper than otherwise they would be. This amounts to a social subsidy enjoyed by domestic and business consumers.

(e) The large-scale operations performed enable greater use to be made of the economies of scale. Local undertakings cannot do this. The best example is electricity supply.

(f) Sometimes competition is wasteful, and leads to reduced safety standards and 'cut-throat' price cutting. This was a feature of industries like road-haulage, where unscrupulous hauliers operated vehicles with insufficient maintenance and ignored rules about driving hours, loading, etc. Nationalised industries can be kept within the regulations more easily than free-enterprise firms.

(g) Where government policy requires clear lines of control in financial affairs, the existence of a national bank is desirable.

(h) Where labour relations are utterly embittered, as they were in coal mining in Britain in the years before nationalisation, nothing but a complete clean sweep will revitalise the industry. (The fact that 50 years later the vast majority of the pits have now been closed is a sad reflection of the fact that even a nationalised industry cannot resist the tide of change in industry as new materials, sources of energy and technologies replace out-moded ones.)

4.8.2
Disadvantages of public enterprises

(a) There is a conflict between economy of operation and adequacy of service which it is difficult to reconcile. For example, the public will demand as perfect a service as possible, but will complain loudly if they have to pay too much for it. Powerful vested interests, like the trade unions representing particular groups of workers, may conduct campaigns to influence development along non-economic lines. In the UK critics of railway modernisation have pointed out that money was mis-spent to preserve a system which was being progressively deserted by traffic in favour of road haulage. Comparable expenditure on roads would have promoted the efficiency of the economy far more.

(b) Dis-economies of scale occur, particularly if the enterprise is very large or closely controlled by local or central government. This involves an excessive degree of caution on the part of managers fearful of being blamed for innovations they otherwise would introduce. This disadvantage may be simply the result of choosing the wrong sort of business structure for the industry.

(c) Politicians and councillors may know little of business, and may influence the enterprises along unbusinesslike paths.

(d) Waste is sometimes not discouraged, since losses are borne by the ratepayers or taxpayers.

(e) If political repercussions are likely, or if the enterprise is subject to political or parochial pressures, it may not develop in the best way for the industry.

(f) State-operated services often have the opportunity to discriminate against privately owned firms in the same line of business.

These theoretical advantages and disadvantages have been modified in the light of experience over the years in the UK. On the whole the disadvantages increase as the strong position of those entrenched behind a monopoly position (powerful trade unions and self-satisfied managers) has increased. Privatisation has recently ended some of their privileges, and a leaner, more efficient industry has resulted in almost all cases. Privatisation is described in greater detail later (see pages 360–2).

4.8.3
Municipal undertakings

Commercial enterprises run by borough and county councils include such units as municipal swimming baths, bus services, piers and seaside entertainments, theatres and community centres. The capital costs are usually borne by borrowing against the general security of Local Authority funds. The idea is to price the facilities to the public at such a figure as to recover both the operating costs and the interest and capital repayments during the lifetime of the asset.

4.8.4
Quasi-autonomous
non-governmental
organisations

Many activities in a sophisticated society are controversial and subject to pressure from various groups with conflicting views. One way of resolving the problems is to appoint a committee of interested parties representing all facets, who will make recommendations. They have a limited authority to act, but are not quite autonomous – ministers usually have powers of veto on proposals, and frequently recommendations are shelved for lack of funds, or other reasons. The acronym **Quango** came to be applied to these organisations, and some concern has arisen over their proliferation into every type of business and social activity. Reporting to the Nolan Committee on Standards in Public Life, David Hunt, the Minister for Public Service seemed unperturbed that 42 600 places on 2000 Quangos, all filled by government appointees, were meeting in secret with no need to open their meetings to the public, or to the National Audit Office or the Audit Commission, and no codes of practice for guidance. Small wonder that reports of corruption were rife, and that patronage was being exercised on a grand scale.

4.8.5
Autonomous public
corporations

The major nationalised industries left today (1996) in the UK are the Atomic Energy Authority, the Post Office and certain parts of British Rail now re-designated as a variety of companies awaiting privatisation. Other nationalised services, such as the National Health Service are being subjected to a variety of privatisation experiments aimed at reducing the monolithic structure of the service by breaking it up into a series of local 'trusts'. Until 1979 the nationalised industries were run as autonomous public corporations, originally formed by the expropriation of the assets of the major private firms in the industry concerned. The original shareholders were compensated by the issue of gilt-edged securities (Government backed securities) which they were free to retain or dispose of as they preferred. The industry was then operated under powers conferred on a Board by Act of Parliament and was expected to run as a business venture, earning enough profit to pay the interest on the gilt-edged securities issued to finance the takeover. While nominally an independent body an appropriate minister of state actually controlled general policy in the industry, but not the day-to-day detail.

4.8.6
Organisation and
control of public
enterprises

No hard-and-fast rules about the organisation and control of these enterprises was laid down, since every enterprise was controlled by its Act of Parliament, which aimed at devising the organisation most suited to the particular industry. The most general features were as follows:

(a) The industry had been set up to operate as a commercial business without day-to-day Parliamentary control of its activities. Any type of Civil Service organisation was deemed to be too slow-moving for the conduct of what was essentially an industrial undertaking.

(b) Taking one year with another, the business was expected to be economically self-sufficient. The phrase 'taking one year with another' meant that rates and charges to the public were to be such as to achieve an overall cover of expenses, but a loss in a particular year was not important if subsequent years would recoup the loss. This was not always the case, especially where very heavy initial debts were taken on to pay compensation to former owners. In these cases Parliament was simply forced to free the industry from debt by writing off the losses to the Exchequer.

(c) Parliamentary control of the few industries still in the public sector is achieved by:

   (i) The annual publication of accounts, which are scrutinised by the Public Accounts Committee.

   (ii) An annual debate. One day of Parliamentary business in each session is given up to a debate on the industry's affairs. In fact, these days are not always used for their true purpose, for by tradition the Opposition has the right to choose some other topic of business if it is felt that there is little cause for criticism of the industry.

   (iii) The appointment of a Minister to assume general control of policy; he/she has no right to query day-to-day administrative matters.

(d) Parliament usually sets up a Consumers' Council of interested parties to represent the consumer and raise questions about the service and its charges. There are no shareholders able to vote the Board out of control, though the Minister may remove the senior officials. Security of office promotes a proper career structure within the industry and ensures a regular supply of qualified and experienced personnel for senior posts.

4.8.7 Nationalisation in Britain

British Overseas Airways Corporation (BOAC), set up in 1940, was the first public corporation of the type which came to be known as the 'Nationalised Industries'. After World War II the Labour Government was elected on the programme which included large measures of nationalisation, and the following industries and services were nationalised:

(a) The Bank of England (1946).

(b) The coal industry – under the National Coal Board (1947).

(c) Civil airways – under British European Airways Corporation (1946).

(d) The electricity industry – under the Electricity Council. Below the Council a Central Electricity Generating Board generated electricity, and sold it to twelve Area Boards for distribution and supply, e.g. the Eastern Electricity Board (1948).

(e) The gas industry – under the National Gas Council and with twelve Area Boards, e.g. the North Thames Gas Board (1949).

(f) Transport – under the British Transport Commission (1947). This proved to be such an enormous undertaking, with 900 000 employees (more than any other employer in the country), that it was eventually partially denationalised and considerably decentralised in later Acts.

(g) The iron and steel industry – under the Iron and Steel Corporation (1951). This was later denationalised, but renationalised in 1967 under the British Steel Corporation.

(h) The National Health Service, which is rather a different form of organisation, was set up in 1948.

(i) In 1976 the British National Oil Corporation took control of the nationalised part of the North Sea oil and gas industries.

(j) British Aerospace and British Shipbuilders were nationalised in 1977 under the Labour Government of that year.

A discussion of how some of these industries came to be privatised in the 1980s is to be found on pages 360–2.

**4.8.8
Central Government
institutions**

The modern economy provides not only goods but services, and does so through a money system. The economy is intricate, and simple solutions are rarely possible to complex problems. Many solutions are quite impracticable without governmental supervision, for someone has to 'hold the ring' in the general, public interest. Huge areas of economic activity come under the direct influence, and even control, of Ministries, who have supervisory powers, Thus the Department of Trade and Industry is in charge of industrial and commercial policy, the promotion of enterprise and competition, the protection of consumers and investors, industrial innovation, the problems of the inner cities and regional development problems, international trade policies, company law, insolvency and many other matters.

**4.9
Summary of
Chapter 4**

1 Business units may be small-scale, medium-scale or large-scale undertakings.
2 Differences between the forms of business organisation reflect differences between: (*a*) the capital contributed; (*b*) the ownership of that capital; (*c*) the control of the enterprise, and (*d*) the accountability of the controllers to the owners.
3 Sole-trader enterprises are very numerous, but are vulnerable to competition from low-cost large-scale firms. Some of them represent valuable growth points in the industrial structure of the nation.
4 Partnerships offer advantages to small-scale entrepreneurs, but still suffer from the defects of unlimited liability.
5 Limited partnerships permit investors or retired partners to provide capital for firms without the added risk of unlimited liability, but there must be at least one general partner who is liable to the limit of his personal wealth.
6 Private and public limited companies permit the collection of large sums of capital from shareholders who are protected by having limited liability.
7 Non-profit making organisations play some part in business life, particularly the cooperative movement in retail trade and in producer cooperatives.
8 The nationalised undertaking or public corporation played an important part in the economies of many countries in the half century that followed the ending of World War II. More recently large parts of the nationalised industries have been privatised in most countries to restore their competitiveness and enhance their wealth-creating activities.

Exercises Set 4

1 Alan Grant is a sole trader operating a roadside garage. His main areas of trade are: (*a*) petrol and oil sales; (*b*) spare parts and accessories; (*c*) routine servicing and testing of vehicles; (*d*) major repairs to damaged vehicles. Suggest the ways in which he could change the form of his business so as to provide: (i) more capital; (ii) less worry; (iii) more leisure.
2 Discuss the possible reasons why most countries have a nationalised railway system but road haulage is often run by private enterprise.
3 There are 8500 public limited companies in Great Britain but 450 000 private limited companies. What are the reasons for this great disparity?

4 Discuss why there is such a wide variety of shares and debentures available. Which types are likely to prove attractive to: (*a*) a widow, aged 55, wishing to invest a £10 000 life insurance payment received on the death of her husband; (*b*) a millionaire, looking for a big yield; (*c*) a trade union investing sickness contributions from members?

5 Discuss the advantages to independent bus operators of a cooperative organisation. Consider particularly the fields of activity where it would be most beneficial.

6 Consider (*a*) the advantages and (*b*) the disadvantages of limited liability. Your viewpoints should include those of: (*a*) entrepreneurs; (*b*) investors; (*c*) creditors; and (*d*) society as a whole.

7 What are the main forms of business units in private enterprise? Which form would most likely be found operating a chain of grocery shops? Give your reasons.

8 Describe the powers and responsibilities of a public corporation. How does Parliament control such corporations?

9 Explain the difference between debentures and shares. In your answer bring out the attractions of these two types of investment to those who buy them.

10 In Great Britain nationalisation has occurred in different industries in different ways. For instance, the railways were nationalised after many years of private operation. The airlines were nationalised after only a few years of private operation. The Atomic Energy Authority was set up as a nationalised body immediately atomic power became a practical proposition. Suggest reasons for the very different treatment accorded these industries. What is their position today?

11 What are the chief differences between a private limited company and a public limited company?

12 'Penniless inventors search in vain for someone to finance development of their inventions, while prosperous companies are deluged with funds whenever they invite the public to subscribe.' Explain why this is so.

13 What are the disadvantages of a one-man business? Why do so many continue to exist?

14 What is privatiation? What arguments can be put forward to justify the privatisation of an organisation like British Telecom? Do the same arguments apply in the privatisation of a body such as Her Majesty's Customs and Excise Department?

15 What part can a Minister such as the President of the Board of Trade (in charge of the Department of Trade and Industry) play in the affairs of (a) public limited companies (b) public corporations and (c) Quangos?

5   The scale of production

5.1
The plant, the firm and the industry

One of the obvious features of the modern production scene is the existence of large-scale firms. The word 'scale' means size. There are usually advantages to be gained by increasing the size of the business; such advantages are called **economies of scale**. In discussing scale in this context we must distinguish between production units or plants, firms and industries.

Plants are production units devoted to the creation of a particular utility, or group of utilities. Such a unit will have a distinct geographical site and a distinct output, or range of outputs, in the form of goods or services.

Firms are business units exerting ownership over one or more plants. They may be sole traders, partnerships, limited partnerships, private limited companies, public limited companies or public corporations. The production units they own may be in one particular industry, or they may have diversified so that they are engaged in a number of different industries.

An **industry** consists of a group of firms producing similar goods or services for a particular market. They will generally be in competition with one another, but occasionally are found to be cooperating. The complex pattern of industry today defies precise definition. Official definitions embrace groups of industrial and commercial firms which appear to have a mutual bond of interest. These bonds justify the name 'industry'. The major branches of industry in Britain, for example, are set out in the Census of Production Table given on page 21.

5.2
Size of production units

Each production unit, or plant, will have an ideal size. What decides the ideal size varies. It may be that technological factors – the technical processes of production – are the dominant considerations. Technical factors make their impact on the supply side, since they usually involve some increase or reduction in costs which affects the profitability of the plant. Oil-cracking towers, for example, have an economic optimum size. In some industries the market may be the dominant factor. Market factors operate on the demand side, dictating the size of the plant by restricting its growth to the point where the supply satisfies the demand for the goods or service concerned. With some industries technical and market influences may be equally important.

(a)   *The nature of the processes involved in production.* The technology to be used in the plant often decides the scale of the production unit. For example, chemical processes often require large indivisible units of capital which are economic only if operated at certain levels of output. In other industries the capital unit is quite small, and the size of a production unit can therefore also be small. Examples of these two contrasting scales of production are the modern oil refinery, which consists of a complex of interdependent capital units of great size, and the clothing factory, whose capital units consist of relatively small items like sewing machines and pressers.

(*b*) *Increased scope for the division of labour.* The more specialised the production system, the greater the scale of the enterprise and the number of machines or men required.

In the motor-vehicle industry, besides large-scale units which stamp out whole parts of vehicles in a single process, the multifarious activities of many individuals are joined into a continuous process by the 'belt' system of production. Such activities become possible only if the scale of production is large, since they depend upon the fullest use of the division of labour.

(*c*) *The 'lowest common multiple' principle.* Where there are components entering into a product, the major components often dictate the scale of production. If component *A* is made on a machine which can produce 10 units per hour, while the other major component *B* is produced at a rate of 6 units per hour, the lowest common multiple is 30 units per hour. If the management provides three machines for component *A* and five machines for component *B*, then all machines will be kept busy at an output of 30 units per hour. Where there are many components, it is not possible to arrange that every machine is kept busy all the time; the components which are produced very quickly are made in batches and have to be stored until required. Nevertheless the entrepreneur will try to achieve the best possible rate of utilisation for all machines purchased.

5.2.1
Market factors

Where the market is limited, the size of the production unit will be small. The specialist firm, using small-scale methods of production, can supply the demand for many items which are not in popular use. Where goods are in wide demand or are essentials for everyday life, large-scale methods of production will have been devised to satisfy the market. The situation is not static in this respect, and items of specialist interest today may be in widespread demand tomorrow.

5.3
Economies of scale

The economies of scale may be divided into **internal economies** and **external economies**. Internal economies arise within the firm itself. External economies arise in the locality, where ancillary firms and services contribute to the efficient conduct of its operations.

5.3.1
Internal economies of scale

The chief internal economies of scale come under six headings: technical, administrative, financial, marketing, research and welfare

Technical economies arise from the increased use of specialisation and from mechanisation, automation and computerisation. Of particular interest is the more economic combination of factors that large-scale operation makes possible. A 44-tonne truck with a driver and mate is a more economic combination of labour and capital than a 5-tonne truck and driver. A hedging machine will serve a 500-acre farm as easily as a 50-acre farm. Capital tied up in stocks of both raw materials and finished goods need not be increased in proportion as firms grow. This is particularly true of slow-moving items in warehousing, where a minimum stock will serve a large firm supplying many retailers quite as easily as a small firm.

Computerisation offers enormous advantages in the technical field, with computer aided design (CAD), computerised layout and planning of sites and production units and electronic data interchange (EDI) to give instantaneous links between offices, plants, cost centres and suppliers. Bar coding on warehoused products enables goods to be located anywhere in a system and to be immediately available when required, the computer remembering where it is stored and retrieving it in a few seconds.

Administrative economies. There are many administrative economies to be achieved in large-scale firms. Doubled output in the factory does not necessitate two factory managers. It need not mean twice the paper-work; invoices may simply deal with larger quantities. When firms grow larger the specialist skills of particular managers are used to greater effect, and more sophisticated decision-making techniques may be introduced. Probably the administrative field is one of the last areas left where major economies of scale can now be achieved, since firms have brought manufacture and distribution to a fine art.

Financial economies. Many large-scale firms find it easy to borrow money at favourable rates of interest. They can usually offer collateral security, such as title deeds to property and mortgages on fixed assets or stocks. They can often afford fire appliances and security guards, so that they obtain favourable insurance rates, or they may even act as their own insurers, setting aside funds for contingencies. Their 'public company' status attracts investors, who willingly subscribe capital, often paying a premium on shares or debentures for the privilege of becoming members or creditors.

Marketing economies. In recent years competition between firms has led to very efficient use of manufacturing and financial resources. Competition has not been pressed so heavily in the marketing field. Considerable economies are now being achieved in distribution by the optimum siting of depots and warehouses, the elimination of small orders, the cash-and-carry principle, careful calculation of re-order points, etc. Where large-scale firms operate marketing agencies handling an assortment of products, they achieve economies because marketing costs are increased less than proportionately for each new product carried.

The biggest advance in marketing techniques in recent years is the change to customer-driven marketing, where the sale of a product at a supermarket check-out automatically re-orders that particular unit. The computer not only meets the customer's needs by recording the sale on the till receipt and adding it to the customer's bill but also feeds the loss of stock to the warehouse, orders a replacement for delivery next day, checks the available stock level to see if it is approaching the re-order point and orders a further batch of supplies when it becomes necessary.

Research economies. The competitive position of many firms depends on their ability to keep ahead of rivals in the range and quality of their products. Research not only reveals new products, new methods of work, and new markets: it results in more efficient use of present resources, waste products, etc. Large-scale firms can usually afford research departments, since the cost can be spread more thinly over the larger volume of production.

Welfare economies. Welfare concerns the health, living conditions, and recreation of staff. Large firms which can offer attractive conditions, recreational facilities and pension schemes are attractive to labour. Such firms can choose the best-quality applicants, and offer a chain of promotion prospects which reduces labour turnover. Such attractive employment is not available elsewhere.

**5.3.2
External economies
of scale**

Surrounding any firm is a locality which soon reacts to the firm's arrival in the area. Sometimes the siting of the firm will depend on favourable arrangements made with local authorities to provide suitable facilities, housing, water supplies, sanitation and health facilities, training courses at local colleges, etc. Entrepreneurs in related fields or in service industries likely to be needed will make approaches offering goods and services. Labour will seek employment, and may undertake special training when it hears of vacancies. The six types of economies already discussed may equally be achieved externally.

External technical economies are particularly important. They involve the sub-contracting to local firms of ancillary activities of particular aspects of the firm's work. This may result in a more perfect division of labour. Technical components in the motor-vehicle industry are often produced by this type of sub-contractor.

An entrepreneur, about to set up in a particular industry, would be ill advised to site his factory in an area remote from similar firms. To do so would be to reject deliberately any opportunity of achieving external technical economies. This is one reason why Government policies aimed at directing industries to areas where unemployment is high often meet opposition from entrepreneurs fearful of being out of touch with the rest of the industry.

An important aspect of external technical economies today is the development known as JIT (just-in-time). JIT holds that a firm will operate most effectively if everything it needs arrives 'just-in-time' when it is needed. There is really no point in raw materials, components, etc. arriving at the supplier's convenience, and having to be taken into store, checked and tallied and provided with a location in a warehouse, only to be requisitioned, given out checked and tallied as soon as they are required. If the suppliers is told what number of components are required, where they are to be delivered and at what time (and to present an invoice on delivery which will be paid within, say, seven days) the whole tone of the organisation is raised. Instead of a vast buying department ordering supplies, the person on the shop floor, knowing how many units are to be built tomorrow, keys into a computer terminal the requirements from each supplier, the time, place, etc. The orders move by EDI (electronic data interchange) direct to the supplier's terminal and arrangements are made for delivery next day – while the supplier's production department will be alerted to replace the stock so that supplies do not run out. Just-in-time saves millions of pounds in building warehouse facilities, keeping stores records, deterioration and theft of components and other supplies. The external firms soon realise that their prosperity depends on meeting the customer's demands, not dictating to the customer how to arrange their affairs. A daily order, delivered within 24 hours and paid for within seven days is an attractive proposition in a competitive world, and a supplier who does not appreciate it will find that others soon replace him/her.

External administrative, financial and marketing economies. The growth of local tertiary services is of enormous importance to large-scale firms. Specialist mailing agencies, advertising agencies and employment bureaux; local banking, security and insurance services; haulage, warehousing and freight-forwarding firms; chambers of trade and even organised markets spring into existence.

Welfare, training and research economies. The locality is where the firm's employees will live. The provision of housing, educational, and recreational services makes for a contented, trained and stable labour force. Financial contributions to local facilities are less expensive than the private provision of these for employees' use only, and cooperation with other firms can promote research facilities at lower cost.

5.4
Diseconomies of scale

While there are many economies of scale, large size is also a disadvantage in some respects. As the output increases, the tertiary problems of distribution and marketing increase. Advertising expenses may rise, discounts may need to be larger if customers are to be found and export trade involves extra costs. Relations between management and employees become increasingly impersonal, with a long chain of command which discourages enthusiasm. It becomes increasingly difficult to achieve a consensus of opinion, so decision-making is deferred; and when decisions are made they lose effectiveness in the more remote parts of the organisation.

Even the external economies of scale can prove disadvantageous if large firms experience setbacks due to changes in world taste or fashion. The associated secondary and tertiary firms in the locality are dependent on the prosperity of their chief customers. A whole locality may quickly become a depressed area. Some structural unemployment (see pages 67–8) is inevitable, anyway, in industries affected by changes of taste or fashion.

5.5
The optimum firm

Where a firm is operating at a scale which gives it the lowest unit cost possible it is said to be operating at the optimum. It is almost impossible to know when the optimum level has been achieved, and in practice entrepreneurs work on subjective hunches of where the optimum is. In an increasingly involved technological world few products are the result of one process, but are an assembly of components. The optimum level of production of one component is unlikely to be the same as that for another. Sometimes this difficulty can be overcome by batch production of parts, a single department producing two or three components in rotation, where each batch is sufficient to carry the factory through a period of future output. The question of costs is dealt with more fully in Chapter 8.

In a particular industry there may be two or three optima. For instance, some relatively low-level division of labour may be open to small-scale firms who, using this technology, can achieve a certain optimum position. By changing to a more highly capitalised form of production they may be able to reach new levels of efficiency. Firms of this type will be found clustering around a second optimum size. There may even be one or two very large firms at a third higher level. The continued existence of the less efficient firms must reflect some separation of the markets which enables them to survive. The bigger, more efficient firms, have their competitive potential reduced by distribution and warehousing costs, so that pockets of enterprise at a lower technological level can survive.

Even when the enterprise is operating at or near the optimum, various influences are at work to erode its position. For instance, depreciation of equipment gradually turns a low-cost firm into a high-cost firm. Changes of technology bring the same effect about more rapidly as obsolescence ensues. Changes in the availability and price of factors render present combinations less efficient and change the optimum arrangement in favour of newer firms entering the industry.

5.6
Small-scale business units

Despite the dominance of very large-scale firms in most industries, a very large number of small-scale firms continue to exist. There are a number of reasons for this including the **small size of the market**. This has already been referred to on page 19. Where demand is not great, the division of labour to intensify output is pointless. When Henry Ford was about to set up in business he seriously considered watch production. From his early youth he had been fascinated by chains of gear wheels and had repaired clocks and watches for friends and neighbours. Concluding that the demand would be insufficient for a full system of mass production, he turned his attention instead to motor cars. Of course, today mass production of watches does take place, but only because a general increase in the standard of living has raised the demand for watches since that time. In an isolated community we often find a general shop selling everything: groceries, drapery, footwear, ironmongery, etc. The market for each of these groups of commodities is insufficient to support a specialist retail outlet.

Personal service. Where the enterprise offers personal service, large-scale operation simply cannot be achieved. The hairdresser who employs assistants to perform certain activities like washing hair, preparing customers for styling, etc., is still limited as far as the scale of the business is concerned by the number of customers to whom personal attention can be given. Too fleeting a visit from the proprietor will send customers elsewhere.

'Exclusive' products. In some businesses, like the fashion trades and interior decorating exclusive creations which are the work of particular artists or designers are the bases of the enterprise. Complete standardisation or mass production is quite impossible in such businesses.

Psychological factors. Independence of the proprietor is an important reason why some businesses remain small. Where growth can be achieved only by the sacrifice of independence, taking partners, or borrowing from banks or finance houses, the owner may well feel that peace of mind is worth more than extra profits. Sometimes the same results can be achieved by cooperation with other independent operators, pooling resources and sharing marketing facilities.

5.7 The advantages and disadvantages of small-scale production

The advantages may be listed as follows:

(a) *Effectiveness of decisions.* Proprietors have all matters under their personal supervision and can put decisions into effect at once. Time consuming procedures such as are used in large-scale enterprises, where authority has to be obtained before effective action can be taken, are eliminated. Personal supervision ensures that the work proceeds with maximum speed.

(b) *Personal control promotes goodwill and reduces risks.* Where the proprietor has the affairs of the business under continual supervision it is possible to ensure that the service given is of a high standard. Frequently the proprietor lives on the premises and is conveniently placed to control situations such as the late arrival of supplies after normal business hours, or special requests by valued customers. Because the proprietor personally sanctions credit, bad debts are reduced.

(c) *Employer-employee relations.* The proprietor's relations with employees are personal, so the employees are encouraged to be efficient and are not tempted to take advantage of an absentee owner. The owner's understanding of the personal problems of staff encourage staff loyalty, mutual consideration and respect.

The disadvantages are:

(a) *The division of labour will be small.* Resources will therefore be uneconomically used. The most efficient factor combinations, particularly of labour and capital, can be achieved only in large enterprises. It follows that only certain types of business or businesses catering for small localities will not face competition from more efficient units.

(b) *The personal abilities of the entrepreneur decide the scale of the business.* These abilities may be affected by ill health or absences caused by domestic problems.

(c) *The proprietor will be personally responsible for the debts of the business* to the full extent of the assets available. Liability is unlimited, unless it is decided to convert the enterprise into a limited liability company.

5.8 Combination of business units

Under this heading we are concerned with the present trend of large units absorbing small businesses. In the past, all business began in a small way because of the necessity to accumulate capital. Nowadays, in a wealthy nation, firms can actually start off as large-scale enterprises, provided that enough interested people (shareholders) can be found to furnish the capital. Many of these shareholders are insurance companies, banks and investment companies. Such firms are called **institutional investors**. They collect savings from the general public, investing them wisely for the mutual benefit of all parties.

Today there is a growing tendency to increase the size of businesses in nearly all trades, manufacturing, building, wholesale and retail. Because the advantages of large-scale projects are so great, there is a tendency for small businesses to grow into bigger businesses, and for them to be **absorbed** by the bigger firms. There is also a tendency for firms to **amalgamate** to form a bigger firm, and there is a tendency for similar firms to cooperate with one another for good reasons (greater economies) or bad reasons (price fixing). Such associations are called 'cartels' (from a German word), or 'trusts' (an American word). On the whole, the domination of an entire industry by one firm is probably undesirable, because it leads to monopoly profits. In many countries such huge firms are banned altogether, but in Britain they have been controlled fairly effectively by legal methods. The difficulty is to prevent the huge firm abusing its power while at the same time encouraging efficiency by allowing firms to reach the optimum size.

In the United Kingdom the official definition of a monopoly is a firm that has at least 25 per cent of an entire industry under its control. Such a company may be referred to the Monopolies and Mergers Commission by the Director General of Fair Trading. The Commission will then report whether its activities are deemed to be conducted in a way which is not contrary to the public interest.

If we try to increase size we may do so either horizontally or vertically. **Vertical Integration** tries to control all the stages of a particular product. Examples are found in many industries. In the shoe industry some firms make the shoes, distribute them, and sell them in their own retail shops. Some tea firms own tea estates, process tea in their own factories, import it, blend it, package it and deliver it to the shopkeeper. Some oil companies own oilfields, tankers, refineries, delivery vehicles and garages where the refined products are sold. Further good examples of vertical integration are to be found in the brewing and motor-vehicle industries. Frequently a major brewery will jealously guard its water supply against pollution; it will buy its barley and hops, if not from its own farms, at least from accredited suppliers; it will manufacture, wholesale and transport its branded products, and retail them in 'tied' houses. In the automobile industry there are many specialist manu-facturers producing components but the major elements of the assembly process – the body-building, upholstering, power-unit assembly and vehicle assembly plants – are controlled by the parent company, which also licenses sole agencies in the retail trade.

Horizontal Integration is where firms try to control all aspects at one level. For example, wholesalers try to gain control of wider and wider areas; multiple shops take over small businesses all over the country; and chain stores set up branches in every town.

Limited companies may achieve either horizontal or vertical integration by 'holding' other companies (see below).

Lateral Integration is the amalgamation of firms using similar techniques to produce similar products. A maker of pressure gauges may absorb a thermometer manufacturer and make both products in future.

**5.8.1
Holding companies**

Where a company has acquired control of another company by the purchase of 51 per cent of its voting shares, it is said to be a **holding company**. This is one way of building up a large-scale business and it takes advantage of specialisation within an industry. For example, where in years gone by a motor vehicle manufacturing company may have found it convenient to allow a specialist firm to supply it with particular components, a growth in the size of its own business may make it desirable to bring the subsidiary firm within its own direct control. By purchasing 51 per cent of the voting shares, control can be secured and the subsidiary company brought within the direct influence of the parent company.

The integration may permit the smaller company to preserve its goodwill while sharing in the large-scale benefits: research, technical, marketing and welfare economies achieved by the parent firm. The parent firm can gather under its wing subsidiaries in the raw-material, transport, component-supply, marketing, advertising and research fields; this will ensure that it is never starved of raw materials, components or markets. Here we have an example of *vertical integration*: integration from top to bottom of an industry. The same process enables a holding company to diversify into other areas outside its major field, and thus avoid disaster if its major industry should experience a recession. This is called **diversification**.

**5.9
Returns to scale**

We have already seen that the adjustment of factors in combination with one another results in increasing or decreasing returns. The law of diminishing returns refers to the effect on output in the short-run of adjustments of a variable factor when it is in combination with a fixed factor.

'Returns to scale' refers to the returns achieved when an existing combination of factors is increased so as to change the scale of the enterprise. In these circumstances the proportions of all the factors of production can be altered, and the output may increase in the same proportions as the scale, showing that constant returns to scale have been achieved. Alternatively, output may increase more, or less, than proportionately: in these two cases we have increasing returns to scale or decreasing returns to scale. Decreasing returns to scale is a fairly rare occurrence; constant returns to scale occurs more frequently in real life, and increasing returns is the most usual of the three.

5.10 Summary of Chapter 5

1 Plants are units for production; firms are business units which own plants; industries are groups of firms with a common interest in the provision of a particular class of goods or services.

2 The size of business units depends on technical factors connected with production or on the market for the product.

3 The economies of scale may be internal or external to the firm. Internal economies include technical, administrative, financial, marketing, research and welfare economies. External economies accrue to a firm because of its connections with the other firms and institutions in the locality.

4 Diseconomies of scale arise from excessive size and decreased personal interest in the enterprise by management and staff.

5 The optimum firm is that firm which is able to achieve minimum average cost per unit of output.

6 Small-scale production continues to exist for technical, marketing or psychological reasons.

7 Large-scale production is likely to achieve economies. This leads to amalgamations, or to absorption of small firms by outright purchase or as subsidiaries of a holding company. Integration may be vertical or horizontal.

8 When an increase in the size of a production unit results in a more than proportional increase in output we have increasing returns to scale.

Exercises Set 5

1 What is meant by 'the economies of scale'? Illustrate your answer by reference to a local industry with which you are familiar.

2 What financial economies are likely to be achieved by a large-scale firm which a small firm would be unable to enjoy?

3 Discuss the most sutiable size of business unit for the following enterprises, giving reasons for your choice in each case: (*a*) cement manufacture; (*b*) coastal fishing; (*c*) a bakery; (*d*) electricity generation; (*e*) aircraft manufacture; (*f*) legal advice on bankruptcy procedures; (*g*) hosiery manufacture.

4 Discuss from the point of view of a customer who requires an electric point to be installed in her home, the advantages and disadvantages in each case of asking (*a*) a local electrician, (b) a privatised electricity company, to do the job.

5 Discuss the technical economies likely to be achieved in: (*a*) large-scale agriculture (refer to wheat or other staple crop grown locally); (*b*) light engineering (refer to the manufacture of domestic consumer durables such as electric hair-dryers, shavers, toasters or radio and television receivers).

6 Considering your own locality, decide what external economies might be enjoyed by a manufacturer moving into the area. What further inducements might a forward-looking local authority offer to an industrialist to encourage him to set up a plant in the area?

7 'You say I am in business to make money; I know I am in business to make shoes' (a footwear manufacturer). What might be the effect of this attitude on the scale of his enterprise?

8 Discuss the merits and demerits of small-scale business from the point of view of the employee.

9 What is meant by 'the optimum firm'? How can an entrepreneur bring his firm to the optimum position, and what influences are at work to erode the position when it has been achieved?

10 Is it ever likely that the small-scale business will completely disappear? Justify your answer.
11 Is it true to say that the typical firm in advanced economies is large, even though there are a great many small firms? Explain fully.
12 Distinguish between internal and external economies of scale, with particular reference to manufacturing firms.

6   The location of production

6.1
The theory of location

A firm will locate its production units on sites which are convenient and economical. Since the aim of an entrepreneur who is acting rationally is to maximise profits, he will pick that site which enables him to produce at the lowest average unit cost. If there are two such sites the final decision may rest on some other factor, which may be psychological or may maximise non-economic advantages, like staff access to entertainments, housing or schools.

6.2
Causes of location

Industry tends to be located:

1   Near a source of raw material.
2   Near a source of power.
3   Near a means of transport, e.g. a port, river railway, road, canal, or airport.
4   Near an educated working class or other source of labour.
5   Near a market.
6   Near a centre of commerce, particularly financial institutions.
7   Near a centre of Government.
8   In a suitable climate.
9   In a stable political atmosphere.

The following examples of each type of location should give a general guide to location, but readers are asked to consider their own home areas and countries and decide why the business units near at hand have been sited in their present position.

6.2.1
Closeness to a source of raw material

Generally speaking, raw materials are heavy and expensive to move. The manufacture of bricks in the clay fields north of London is a typical example of location close to a source of raw material. Another is the world's largest hardboard factory near Sao Paulo in Brazil, which is situated near a forest of 16 million eucalyputs trees. Its consumption of timber is equal to the annual growth rate of the forest, so that the source of supply is never exhausted.

Sheffield, the British steel centre, was founded because it was conveniently placed for an iron industry, with local supplies of the three basic raw materials: coal, iron ore and limestone.

6.2.2
Closeness to a source of power

An early example of this cause of location is the migration of the English cotton and woollen industries to towns in the Pennine valleys of Lancashire and Yorkshire. Here the damming of the rivers running off the Pennine hills drove water-mills to provide power for the machinery. Later the invention of the stationary steam engine, which was more powerful, caused the cotton industry to move again to areas where coal was in plentiful supply. Manchester, situated on a coalfield, therefore became the chief centre of the cotton industry.

Another excellent example of location of an industry near a source of power is Kitimat in British Columbia. Here there is a lake high in the Rocky Mountains which, because of its geographical situation, could be one of the world's largest hydroelectric-power sources. Unfortunately it is so remote that heat losses in the cables transmitting power to any civilised area would have made it uneconomic. The problem of utilising this source of electricity was solved by erecting an aluminium smelter and subsidiary industries at Kitimat itself. Aluminium smelting requires vast quantities of electrical power. The lake, which was on the wrong side of the mountains, was reached by tunnelling through, and the power station was built into the rock. The natural outlets from the overflow of the lake were dammed up so that the sole exit for water lies through the power station in its cavern far below.

6.2.3
Closeness to a
method of transport

There are innumerable examples of location of an industry at a suitable point for easy transport. Historical examples are the growth of industrial areas along the banks of the British canals as these were dug during the Industrial Revolution, from 1760 to 1820. The growth of the Potteries is a particularly important example. Later the development of towns on railway lines opened up new areas of the country, and in more modern times we have the development of industrial areas around great motorways. The development of port areas is particularly striking. The growth in size of the ports in the south-east corner of the United Kingdom since this country joined the European Community in 1973 has been very striking. Located directly opposite the continental ports like Rotterdam, Antwerp, Dunquerque, etc., the ports of Shoreham, Folkstone, Dover, Sheerness, Tilbury, Felixstowe and Ipswich have made considerable progress. They have not quite achieved the planned increase envisaged by the MIDAS scheme, which a few years ago proposed to develop a Maritime Industrial Development Area in the region. Rotterdam, in Holland, is a typical example of this type of development. The visitor to modern Rotterdam finds the whole port area covered with a complex of industrial projects. Already sited in an excellent position for serving the industrial might of Western Germany through its river and canal links with the Rhine, these new terminals for grain, oil, iron ore, sulphur and many other commodities make Rotterdam the finest example in the world of location near methods of transport. Unfortunately the disadvantages (serious pollution of the atmosphere) are also only too apparent at times.

6.2.4
Closeness to an
educated work force

Labour is one of the factors of production. Entrepreneurs are therefore likely to site their production units near a source of labour. It is often helpful if the available labour is sophisticated and trained, since this will reduce the amount of in-plant training required. When siting his first plant in Great Britain, Henry Ford was influenced by the new housing areas being set up at Dagenham in Essex. This area represented a supply of educated labour of good quality. There was cheap land available in the marshes nearby, and a large market was available in the London area. The River Thames gave good access for raw materials and made export of finished vehicles easy. Such a combination of advantages led to the erection of the Dagenham plant of the Ford Motor Company.

Human beings become attached to the areas where they are born and brought up, so that many are reluctant to move. One economist has called labour 'the immobile factor'. It is a paradox that the only factor that can move by itself should display an almost characteristic immobility. Often this immobility presents problems when **structural unemployment** occurs.

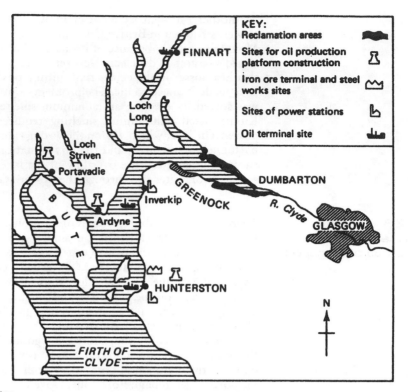

Figure 6.1 The maritime industrial development area at Clydeport

Notes

1 The Clydeport estuary has the finest, natural deep water of any port in the whole of Western Europe. There is a depth of 33 metres of water.

2 The deep-water oil terminal at Finnart can handle the largest oil tankers afloat of up to ½m g.r.t. Large oil tankers regularly lighten at Finnart to enable them to enter other ports in the UK, and in Europe which do not have this deep water. There is an oil pipeline across Scotland to the Grangemouth refinery.

3 The deep-water ore/coal terminal at Hunterston is capable of handling ships up to 350 000 g.r.t. Pending the resolution of the Scottish steel industry's difficulties it is used chiefly as a transhipment port to lighten large ore carriers, and to unload and distribute imported coal.

4 At the Authority's Container Terminal, located at Greenock, the largest container ships afloat or envisaged can be handled at any state of the tide.

5 The deep and sheltered Clyde estuary and adjoining sea locks provide sites ideal for oil platform construction at Hunterston, Ardyne and Portavadie.

6 Freightliner train links and motorway links to the area are fully developed.

7 An oil-fired power station is located at Inverkip, and the power station at Hunterston is atomic powered.

8 Ardrossan, south of Hunterston and just off our map, is the ro-ro (roll-on, roll-off) terminal for ferries to Ireland and the Isle of Arran, and offers substantial break-bulk services for containerised cargo.

Structural unemployment is unemployment caused by a permanent change in demand for a product. For example, Lancashire cotton goods have been in much less demand since the development of synthetic fibres like nylon and Terylene, and also since the growth of cotton mills in overseas territories such as Hong Kong. The resultant decline in the Lancashire cotton industry produced a good deal of unemployment in the area. Other areas have been hit by declines in the demand for British ships and coal. These areas have been given special attention by governments to encourage industries to move to the area in need of redevelopment. Firms find that these development areas offer a pool of good-quality labour, educated in industrial processes and techniques. Such labour is a very valuable asset, and this is one reason why location in a development area may give firms a useful economic advantage over similar firms in more prosperous, and therefore higher-cost, areas.

6.2.5
Closeness to a market

Although raw materials are heavy and awkward to transport, they rarely suffer damage when moved. Today the end product often decides location. If the end product is fragile, or highly polished, or liable to be stolen it may be preferable to produce it near to the eventual market, or close to its biggest markets. This reduces the journey to be made by the majority of the finished product, and thus lessens the risk of damage or pilferage. This explains why household furniture is usually manufactured close to large cities rather than near forests. It also explains the attraction of London as a site for consumer-goods industries. The shift of light manufacturing to the Midlands and south-east during the twentieth century and away from Scotland and the former industrial areas of the north of England is an excellent example of the growth of industrial areas near populations which will consume their products.

Another consideration in the decision to locate near the market is the relative importance of transport costs to the value of the product. If transport costs are high compared with the unit's value – as, for example, with car bodies – such units will be made near the assembly plant. If transport costs are tiny compared with the value of a unit of output – as with transistor radios – transport half across the world will not be too expensive. Singapore's excellent television and video sets are an example.

6.2.6
Closeness to the financial institutions

In Britain changes in taxation policy since World War II have had a profound effect on the financing of industry, which has in turn affected location of industry. The redistribution of income associated with the Welfare State has reduced the personal fortunes of the well-to-do, and raised the levels of income of the mass of the people. This has resulted in an increasing influence of the financial institutions like banks, insurance companies and finance houses. No longer can industry be financed by private individuals. Wealth is shared more evenly, and savings have to be collected in small sums from a mass of people. This makes the institutions which are skilled in collecting such sums (particularly insurance companies, banks, building societies and trade unions) of great importance to anyone seeking capital. The entrepreneur may therefore prefer to locate his business with reasonable access to such institutions. In Britain this played some part in the development of the south-east, with the City of London at its centre. Today, with money transferred more easily than ever before, it is less influential. We are all as close to financial institutions as the nearest computer terminal and modem.

6.2.7
Closeness to the centre of government

Heavy taxation levels increase the proportion of the National Income which is being spent by the government. If the public sector of the economy grows, firms find it advantageous to site their offices and factories near to the centre of government. This again partly explains the heavy concentration of industry in the south-east of England, near Westminster. A more recent example is the growth of Brussels under the influence of the largesse made available by the situation of the offices of the European Union in that city. While this has not resulted in the movement of heavy industries to the area it has resulted in a huge expansion of office activity and a growth of consultancies offering advice on the correct approaches to those seeking access to European institutions, and the contracts becoming available. Policies do change, however, and when governments are aiming to develop or restore depressed areas it is sometimes better to approach the local institutions empowered to assist developers.

6.2.8
In a suitable climate

Sometimes climate has an important part to play. Clearly we cannot grow vines or sugar cane in regions where the sun rarely shines. Humidity is sometimes important: for instance, because threads snap more easily in a dry atmosphere, cotton is manufactured best in damp climates.

6.2.9
In a stable political atmosphere

Capital is scare and capital assets are expensive. They may take years to construct and decades to return the capital invested. Stable political life, absence of revolutions, and freedom from fear of expropriation are prerequisites to heavy capital investment. For this reason industry tends to locate itself in spots where volatile behaviour of political groups is at a minimum. The construction of refineries near oilfields used to be a feature of the oil industry, and large processing plants were built in the Middle East, in Indonesia, and elsewhere. Today there is a much greater tendency to build them in more stable areas, and to transport the crude oil in mammoth tankers to the refinery.

6.3
Industrial inertia

Inertia is the tendency of a natural body to go on doing what it is already doing. It is difficult to overcome the inertia of a stationary boulder, and once we get it on the move it is equally difficult to stop it. The same thing is true of industries; they display 'industrial inertia'. This industrial inertia keeps an industry in a particular area long after the original reasons for its location there have ceased to be important. Many external economies of scale would be lost if the industry moved away from an area where specialist subsidiary firms and local government facilities have been created over the years. More important, the technical knowledge and skill of the local work-force is crucial to the success of the industry.

Sheffield, which is still a world centre for steel production many years after the local supplies of iron ore have been exhausted, is a good example of industrial inertia. It has proved cheaper to import iron ore from Sweden and Spain than to disband the complex of experience, know-how and research which Sheffield offers the British steel industry.

Hollywood is another example of the inertia of an industry. Long after the original reasons (concerning reliable climatic conditions) for location there have ceased to have importance the motion-picture industry persists, despite enormous changes in its techniques and in the requirements of the public. Television, a completely new industry, turns to the old industry in the old place.

A further aspect of inertia is the tendency of huge firms with very large capital assets to persist and develop even when the management is not very dynamic. It becomes difficult for younger and more energetic firms to obtain capital in the face of the great industrial capacity of their well-established rivals.

6.4
The drift to the south-east in Great Britain

During the present century a significant change in the location of industry in Great Britain has occurred under the twin influences of electrification and road transport. This change in location has moved many industries into the Midlands and south-east, and away from the older industrial areas of the North, Scotland and Wales, which as a consequence have become victims of structural unemployment. The inertia which has kept industries like steel centred in the old industrial areas cannot be effective on new industries like aviation, motor-vehicle manufacture, electronics and petrochemicals. Such industries have, until very recently, been free to locate themselves in the optimum positions, and the optimum position has often been near London.

Electricity makes power available to industries throughout the length and breadth of the country at the flick of a switch. This has set industry free from the coalfields, and new industries have not needed to look for power to the old sources of coal and steam.

Road transport has permitted door-to-door delivery of raw materials and finished goods. The increasingly sophisticated products of modern factories are easily damaged or pilfered. Closeness to the market becomes, as we have seen, more important than closeness to raw materials.

A further factor that has shifted the location of industry to the south-east is its greater proximity to the European mainland. With over half of British trade now taking place with the other countries of the European Union the ports of the south-east have grown in importance, while the opening of the Channel Tunnel should also increase the importance of the region. The formerly important ports of Bristol, Liverpool and Glasgow which served world-wide trade in the days of the British Empire became less influential when much of UK trade was Europe-orientated. However, after 20 years or so of diminished prosperity these ports have begun to overcome the problems by huge advances in efficiency. For example shipowners at Liverpool began to realise that these ports still had advantages for trade with the European mainland if the seaward and landward sides of port operations could be improved. By unloading and re-loading ocean going ships in 12 hours by use of containerised traffic, and by turning round long-haul road vehicles in 40 minutes (with guaranteed return loads) containers can be sent on the fast motorway network and through Eurotunnel on special freight trains, into the heart of Europe. In addition the designation of the port as a free trade zone (FTZ) has been very beneficial. Goods may enter the port free of customs duty since they have not 'entered' the UK and are deemed to be, as it were, still on the vessel. This is true even when they leave on a lorry or freight train through the English countryside bound for some destination outside the UK – they are still deemed not to have entered UK, and customs formalities are dispensed with.

6.5 Localisation of production

One defect that is not apparent in south-east England is an excessive 'localisation of industry'. This phrase refers to an excessive concentration in one locality of industries which are interconnected, so that a setback in the main industry causes a general depression in the locality. In south-east England industry is very diverse, and it is rare for diverse industries to experience a depression at the same time. If the furniture industry is quiet the clothing industry or the motor-vehicles industry may be booming.

Excessive localisation occurs because of the advantages of the external economies of scale. Subsidiary industries grow up around the main industry, and service trades grow up around the housing estates associated with all the firms in the area. A modern example of excessive localisation is Aberdeen, which experienced serious difficulties when the oil price collapsed in the mid-1980s. The shake-out in the oil industry adversely affected other industrial and service businesses and the whole area experienced bad times. Like the farmer's wife with all her eggs in one basket, one piece of bad luck can ruin all.

In the second half of the twentieth century Government policies to correct the 'structural unemployment' that results have made a considerable impact upon these local areas of unemployment. The Royal Mint, for example, has been moved to Wales and many other Government offices to areas such as

Tyneside, Liverpool, Lancashire, etc. The general availability of electrical power means that small-scale firms of great variety can be diverted to areas where unemployment is low. The effectiveness of such policies has been somewhat reduced by the general decline in business activity as more and more secondary goods are imported. The consoling thought is that had such policies not been implemented the localised unemployment would now be very severe indeed.

The European Union in general, facing the same sort of difficulties, makes available considerable sums of money to deal with these types of problem, which are called 'regional problems'.

6.6 Summary of Chapter 6

1 Industries are located in places where they can produce at the least possible cost.
2 Important causes of location in earlier times were closeness to a source of raw material and closeness to a coalfield (as a source of steam power). Closeness to a means of transport was also important.
3 Today location is influenced chiefly by closeness to the market; to the institutional investors; to the centre of government, and to transport. Closeness to Europe is beginning to influence location as inter-community trade grows.
4 Industrial inertia often keeps an industry sited in a particular locality long after the original reasons for its location there have ceased to be important.
5 Localisation of industry is the excessive concentration of related firms in one area, so that a depression in a major firm spreads to all the other firms around. This causes hardship as structural unemployment sets in.

Exercises Set 6

1 Consider the capital city of your own country. Draw up a list of reasons why: (*a*) it was originally established where it is; (*b*) what caused industry and commerce to develop it to its present size; (*c*) if it is still growing, what factors continue to make it attractive as a location; and (*d*) if it is declining, why it is no longer attractive as a location.
2 In your own country select two examples of location near each of the following: (*a*) a source of raw material; (*b*) a river; (*c*) the seashore (if available); (*d*) a railway; (*e*) a main road; (*f*) a source of power; (*g*) a centre of government.
3 Rotterdam is now the biggest port in Europe. Consult a map of Europe and suggest why.
4 Discuss the geographical position and the location of industry at any two of the following sites: (*a*) Chicago; (*b*) Southampton; (*c*) Lagos; (*d*) Johannesburg; (*e*) Sydney; (*f*) Liverpool; (*g*) Singapore; (*h*) Hong Kong; (*i*) Cape Town; (*j*) Canberra; (*k*) Auckland; (*l*) Hawaii.
5 Discuss whether industrial inertia has played any part in the continued prosperity of: (*a*) London; (*b*) Bristol; (*c*) the capital of your own country; (*d*) your own local town.
6 The location of industry near power sources is less important today than in former times. Do you agree, or disagree? Give your reasons and examples to support them.
7 To what extent does closeness to the market affect the location of business establishments?
8 How may location affect the costs of a firm?
9 What is industrial inertia? Give examples.

10 Once oil refineries were located near oilfields. Today they are more frequently located near centres of industrial population. Discuss the reasons for this change in policy.

11 It is better to bring the timber to the factory than to take the factory to the timber. Explain the economic argument behind this statement.

Section 3: The Theory of Price Determination

7　Basic ideas of demand

7.1 Definition of demand

If production is undertaken in order to supply the 'wants' of mankind demand must be the most basic idea in economics. Every individual demands goods and services. When all the individual demands are put together the resulting composite demand is what the industry must supply if people are to achieve satisfaction.

In defining 'demand', however, economists cannot equate 'demand' with 'want', because an industry cannot be expected to supply goods and services without payment. In attempting to discover the demand for a particular commodity we only consider demand that is backed by purchasing power. Man's wants are unlimited, but his demand for a particular item is very often limited if the price he must pay is too high.

The demand for goods or services is therefore that quantity of the goods or services which purchasers will be prepared to buy at a given price, in a given period of time.

Note particularly that price is crucial to any discussion about demand. It is meaningless to discuss the demand for motor vehicles unless we know what price range is being considered. The demand for family saloon cars at £7000 each will be very different from the demand for limousines at £90 000 each.

7.2 The conditions of demand

Demand is not fixed, but varies with changing conditions. The demand for silk stockings has been completely altered by the invention of nylon fibre, and the demand for bicycles in advanced nations has been greatly reduced by the development of motor vehicles.

The chief factors affecting demand may be divided into those factors affecting the individual consumer or family of consumers and those factors affecting the total demand of the whole market.

7.2.1 Factors affecting the demand of households

(a) The tastes of the household

Every family is different, and even members of the same family have different tastes and preferences. In most countries populations are not these days homogeneous, but have been formed from mixed racial groups. This is not always obvious if the country has had a long period of settled history, and intermarriage between different racial groups has occurred. All that is left perhaps of originally quite different peoples is a variety of tastes and preferences which have very ancient origins. Superimposed on these ancient patterns of taste are other more modern patterns: religious, social and economic pressures which influence choice in food, clothing, living conditions, entertainment and recreation. These tastes and preferences play some part in deciding the total demand for a commodity or service.

We may therefore demand goods because they satisfy innate wants which we cannot explain but still feel are necessary; or because they are fashionable; or because we have been convinced by advertising that they are desirable. The demand for all such goods will be strong, and the demand for goods which are not to our personal taste, or which are less fashionable or less well promoted, will be weaker.

(b) *The income of the household*	Family income is often decisive as to whether a commodity is demanded or not. Few ordinary households demand light aircraft as a means of personal transport, but a millionaire may keep one available. Many families run a car, some run two cars, and many are resigned to the fact that they will never be in the car-buying income range. Most heads of families know what their families can afford, and buy within quite narrow price bands. Even so-called impulse buying, where consumers buy a thing because they happen to see it, tends to occur within the price range each householder knows to be appropriate for the family.
(c) *The necessity of the commodity, and its alternatives if any*	Some goods are demanded by everyone because they are necessities. We all require food, clothing, shelter, etc. Some goods become necessities because they are habit-forming, like tobacco and alcohol. Where a commodity has alternatives it is not a necessity, but the alternative must be in the same price range. Rolls-Royce cars are not substitutes for small family saloons, and Savile Row suits are not substitutes for ready-made garments as far as the majority of consumers are concerned. Their respective purchasers might each regard the item as a necessity, but the alternative in each case is not only not a necessity, it is not even considered a substitute for the preferred item.
(d) *The price of other goods*	If the price of a commodity is high compared with the price of other goods the demand for it will be relatively weak. If the goods are close substitutes for one another – as, for example, butter and margarine – the price of one will be seriously affected by a reduction in price of its competitor. Even if the goods are not close substitutes for one another, there is usually some competition between them, because the money to be spent represents all the possible alternatives of satisfactions available to the consumer. The young lady who decides against a bottle of perfume and in favour of a pair of new shoes has been influenced by the price of the perfume into thinking that the shoes will yield her greater satisfaction. They are not close substitutes for one another, but they are still in competition.
7.2.2 Factors affecting the total market demand (a) *The size and structure of the population*	If there are many people to be fed, clothed and housed demand will tend to be strong, especially if the population is able to back its 'wants' with purchasing power. The structure of the population will influence demand for particular items. A bulge in the birth-rate for any reason will alter demand as the children born develop through to maturity. In the early years the demand for children's clothes, toys, etc., will be increased. Gradually the increased demand will change to school books and games equipment, later to cosmetics and motor cars. Later still the growing numbers of mature young people of marriageable age may lead to a new bulge in the birth-rate. Finally, an increased demand for wheelchairs and hearing aids may result.
(b) *The aggregate national income and its distribution among the population*	Some societies produce more wealth than others and the distribution of wealth may be different as well. Some are so organised that classes of rich and poor persons appear. Others are organised to achieve greater equality of wealth. A progressive system of taxation, which taxes the rich to help the poor, is often used to achieve greater equality. Market demand

will be stronger in egalitarian societies than in those where obvious inequalities exist, for the mass of the people in egalitarian societies can back their 'wants' with purchasing power. The strong level of demand in Great Britain over the last 50 years reflects the more equitable distribution of wealth that has been achieved since the introduction of the Welfare State. Demand in the United States is strong because it has an enormous national income with reasonably egalitarian distribution. Members of the European Community create slightly less wealth but have more equal wealth distribution meaning demand is again strong. Eastern European countries have egalitarian systems but are poor creators of wealth. The strength of their demand is held back because market forces cannot operate to signal what the ordinary people would like to 'demand'. Students should note that there is a popular misconception that changing over to a market economy is something to do with transport, distribution and getting things into the shops. This is really not the point at all, although we believe this will be the end result of switching to a market economy. What it means when we advocate a market economy is that what the people are wanting to purchase in the shops decides what is manufactured or grown. We do not want central planners trying to guess what the people need. What is demanded in the market guides entrepreneurs as to future production. Goods that don't sell are not produced any more, and effort is switched to other goods and services. The market rules ... OK!

7.2.3
The consumer's scale of preferences

The result of these conditions, often called the determinants of demand, is a **scale of preferences** for each consumer. High on each consumer's scale of preferences come the things needed most, or liked best. Lower on the scale come things the consumer will buy if income permits, once all the more satisfying items have been purchased. The scale of preferences changes with the pressure of daily events. We all know of things we have been meaning to buy for years, but somehow their purchase eludes us because more pressing requirements prevent them reaching the top of our scale of preferences.

7.3
A personal demand schedule

A schedule is a list, and the list of demands for any individual is called an **individual demand schedule**. Table 7.1 shows the demand schedule of such an individual for an everyday requirement like lamb cutlets. This schedule takes for granted that the only thing that has changed to alter

Table 7.1 Mrs Brown's weekly demand for lamb cutlets

Price per unit	Cutlets demanded
1.10	–
1.00	2
0.90	2
0.80	3
0.70	3
0.60	4
0.50	4

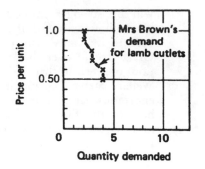

Figure 7.1 An individual demand curve

the demand is the price of the commodity. All other conditions of demand, like family income, or personal taste, or fashion, have not changed. The phrase *ceteris paribus* ('other things being equal') is often used in economics to describe a situation where only one aspect of a situation is deemed to be changing.

Note that Mrs Brown has a relatively small demand for lamb cutlets. There are only two people in the Brown family. When cutlets are expensive they have one each. When cutlets are cheaper Mrs Brown buys Mr Brown an extra cutlet. When they are very cheap she has two herself as well. When displayed graphically, as in Figure 7.1, the line joining the points plotted on the graph is a rather jerky line moving out from the vertical axis of the graph and sloping down towards the right.

Table 7.2 shows three more demand schedules.

What can you guess about the size of Mrs Green's family?

What can you guess about the income of Mrs Gray's family?

What can you guess about Mrs White's family's fondness for lamb cutlets?

Quite apart from the size of Mrs Green's family, would you gather from this schedule that her family are poor or relatively affluent?

Figure 7.2 displays the individual demand schedules for the two families who are requiring some of this product. Once again we notice that the curve slopes downwards towards the right, though once again the motion is rather jerky in the case of Mrs Green's demand curve.

Table 7.2 Three more weekly demand schedules

Price per unit	Mrs Green Cutlets demanded	Mrs Gray Cutlets demanded	Mrs White Cutlets demanded
1.20	4	–	–
1.10	5	–	–
1.00	6	–	–
0.90	6	–	–
0.80	7	–	–
0.70	7	–	–
0.60	8	1	–
0.50	8	2	–

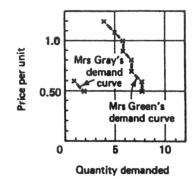

Figure 7.2 Two more individual demand curves

7.4
A composite
demand schedule

If we now imagine the demand schedules for all these individuals added together, and if we add in the families who are demanding legs of lamb, shoulder of lamb, etc. (it would be unrealistic to imagine that only cutlets were being demanded and the rest of the carcases being wasted) we arrive at a **composite demand schedule** or **market demand schedule** for lamb. This demand schedule is given in Table 7.3.

The important point about the composite demand schedule is that, generally speaking, *the quantity demanded of any commodity will increase as the price falls.* This well-known everyday fact is shown quite clearly by the schedule. At a price of 30.00 each the consumers require only 200 000 lambs to be brought to the dinner-table. At a price of 20.00 the article is much better value for money, and as many as 2 000 000 lambs are demanded. Whether any farmers are prepared to supply at that low price is quite another matter, which is discussed on page 95.

Table 7.3 A composite demand schedule

Weekly demand schedule for lamb carcases

Price (in currency units)	Quantity demanded
30.00	200 000
29.00	250 000
28.00	300 000
27.00	500 000
26.00	750 000
25.00	1 000 000
24.00	1 200 000
23.00	1 400 000
22.00	1 600 000
21.00	1 800 000
20.00	2 000 000

Note: As explained in the text, the prices here refer to whole carcases, not the price for cutlets only as in Table 7.1 and 7.2. It would be unrealistic to imagine that the rest of each animal is wasted.

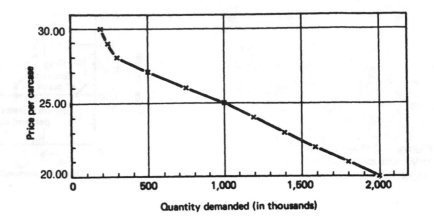

Figure 7.3 A market demand curve for lamb; quantity demanded in thousands of carcases

When graphically presented this information now looks as in Figure 7.3. Notice that the inclusion of millions of different customers has smoothed out the jerky demands of each individual into a smoother curve. This curve slopes downwards towards the right, in line with the rule noticed above that as the price decreases the quantity demanded will increase.

7.5
The general demand curve

For the sake of convenience economists disregard the details of particular demand schedules, although a great deal of research has been carried out on such schedules. In ordinary discussion about likely effects of changes in demand, etc., it is sufficient to use a general diagram which can be varied to envisage different possibilities. The conventional arrangement is to call the vertical axis OY and the horizontal axis OX. The prices and quantities are not marked in with mathematical precision, but are simply assumed to be evenly graduated along the axes from the origin O. The *general demand curve* shown in Figure 7.4 is labelled DD and its general shape conforms to the first 'law' of demand and supply.

The first 'law' of demand and supply states that *the more the price of a commodity is decreased, the greater the quantity that will be demanded.*

Note: It is convenient to use the word 'law' to describe these general observations which appear to be true in many real-life situations. The student of economics should remember that they are not 'laws' in the scientific sense. Economics is an inexact science at best.

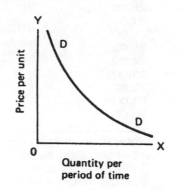

Figure 7.4 The general demand curve

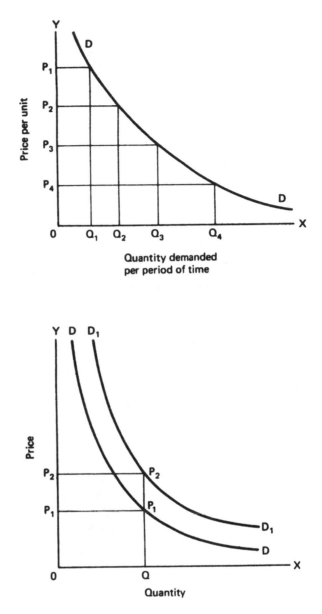

Figure 7.5 Extensions and contractions of demand with changes in price (*see Section 7.6 overleaf*)

Figure 7.6 A change in demand to a new demand curve (i)

Notes
1 Before the change in demand, the demand for a product is shown by curve DD. The quantity that is being made available is Q and the price will be P_1; that price where the demand curve indicates that quantity Q will be purchased.
2 Suppose now that due to a change in taste or fashion demand increases to D_1D_1. Every point in curve D_1D_1 is further from the Y axis than curve DD, indicating that at every price demand is stronger and a greater quantity is being demanded.
3 The effect will be that the product will be in short supply, and price will rise to the level P_2, where the demand curve indicates that the quantity Q will be purchased.
4 Of course this diagram tells us little about the supply, for we have not drawn in any supply curve, other than the fixed quantity, Q. What we can see is the income (price × quantity) OQP_1P_1 (at the old level of demand) and the income (price × quantity) OQP_2P_2 (at the new level of demand). Clearly the suppliers are receiving more income, and if they were making profits before they are making more profits now, but of course we don't know for sure. Since no one who is behaving rationally would bring any supply on to the market until there were prospects of profitability, presumably they were making profits at prices of P_1 per unit of output, so now they are doing very nicely, thank you. One has only to think of the demand for any good which becomes widly popular, from hula-hoops to royal hairstyles, to appreciate the change in income to suppliers when demand moves to a new demand curve. The supply side is considered later in Chapter 8.

7.6
Extensions and contractions of demand

From a demand curve of the sort shown in Figure 7.4 it is possible to read off an infinite number of demands at various prices, which makes it possible to discuss demand quite fully. For instance, in Figure 7.5 we can read off for prices P_1, P_2, P_3 and P_4 the quantities demanded, which are Q_1, Q_2, Q_3 and Q_4. Clearly at each of these prices a different quantity has been demanded, so we could say that the demand has changed. However, in economics the phrase 'a change of demand' has a quite different meaning. This phrase is used to describe a change to a new demand curve, so that at every price a different quantity will be demanded.

We therefore refer to changes in demand along an existing demand curve as extensions or contractions of demand. Although economists do talk loosely about demand 'changing', readers are urged to use the better terms 'extending' or 'contracting' unless they mean the sort of change illustrated in Figure 7.6. Here we really *do* have a change of demand at every price. This type of change is not responding to price alterations on the market, but is responding to some more fundamental change, such as a change in taste or fashion or a change in income. In the last 30 years in Great Britain an enormous change in the demand for motor cars has occurred, due largely to a change in income. More people can afford cars today. The effects of changes to a new demand curve should now be studied by considering Figures 7.6 and 7.7, and the notes below them.

7.7
Regressive demand curves

Some demand curves behave in an unusual fashion. They do not obey the first law of demand given in Section 7.5 above. Instead of continuing progressively along the general demand path, they suddenly turn and become regressive. A regressive demand curve is a demand curve that turns

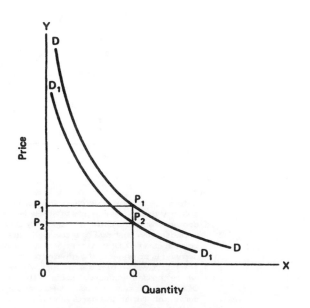

Figure 7.7 A change to a new demand curve (ii)

Notes

1 Once again the initial demand is shown by curve DD, with the quantity Q being purchased at a price P_1. The suppliers receive total income OQP_1P_1.

2 A change in taste or fashion leads to a reduction in demand, the good is less popular and less is demanded at every price. The new demand is shown by D_1D_1.

3 There is a surplus of the commodity on the market and price falls to P_2. The suppliers receive less than before, total income falling to OQP_2P_2. This will lead them to reconsider their supplies, as it may now be unprofitable to supply. This is discussed later. (*Now return to Section 7.7 above.*)

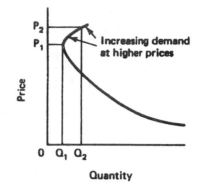

Figure 7.8 Regressive demand curve I: (a) goods of ostentation; (b) expectations of higher prices to come

and starts to go backwards. This exceptional behaviour may occur at either end of the curve.

Regression at the upper end of the curve – goods of ostentation and goods expected to become scarce. Consider the curve shown in Figure 7.8.

At a price of P_1 the quantity demanded is Q_1, a very small quantity. At a higher price P_2 we would expect demand to be even less, but demand for this product is exceptional and it increases when the price is raised. Such goods are called **goods of ostentation**; they are purchased not because of their intrinsic worth but because they are required to emphasise status. There are many levels of status. Retailers often find that cheap costume jewellery on sale at very low prices sells poorly. The same jewellery offered at ten times the price sells quite well. Nobody wants to buy a girl friend a brooch that costs 50 pence: he would lose face if she discovered the price. Yet the same brooch at £5.00 makes a 'worthwhile' gift.

A quite different reason for regressive demand curves of exactly the same shape as above occurs with the **expectation of future price increases**. This is commonly met on the major commodity markets. Dealers fear even higher prices may follow the present increases because world shortages are developing, and press in to buy up whatever supplies are available, even though they are more expensive. Speculative fevers on foreign-exchange markets are particularly common examples of this kind of regressive demand, prices soaring upwards in a frantic attempt to choke off demand, but demand becoming ever stronger as the prices soar.

Regression at the lower end of the curve – Giffen goods and goods expected to become even cheaper. Consider the curve shown in Figure 7.9.

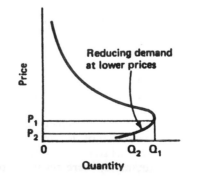

Figure 7.9 Regressive demand curve II: (a) inferior goods or 'Giffen' goods; (b) expectations of even lower prices to come

Here we have a demand curve showing regression at its lower end. This time, despite the reduction in price from P_1 to P_2, the quantity does not increase. The curve turns and goes backwards, indicating a reduced demand despite lower prices. To understand why this occurs we must discuss 'inferior goods' and 'Giffen goods'.

Inferior goods. There are many types of inferior goods. Generally speaking the term applies to the very lowest quality of goods in every branch of merchandise; the type of goods that the very poorest people in any society survive on. The parents of large families know well how long they have to manage with poor clothing of cheap material and unfashionable cut. They know the basic foods that can make cheap nourishing meals for their families, and the cheap furniture with which they must 'get by' until the children grow up. We all aspire to the day when we can forsake such inferior goods and move on into a different satisfaction bracket where better quality clothes, household furnishings, etc. can be enjoyed, now that the children are independent.

However, there are some inferior goods which display a special characteristic; they have regressive demand curves. The best example is bread, which many years ago earned these types of good the name 'Giffen' goods. The economist Sir Robert Giffen, writing in Victorian times, noticed that when wheat was very expensive and bread consequently rose in price, the demand for bread and the consumption of bread actually increased, while when wheat became cheaper, and consequently bread was cheaper, the demand for bread decreased, and consumption of bread declined. When such a commodity forms the staple diet of a large section of the population, a rise in the price of the product (for example from P_2 to P_1 in the diagram (Figure. 7.9) causes them to reduce their standard of living to a bare subsistence on bread, and to increase demand for it. Similarly, when such a population, subsisting on a bare diet of bread, finds that the price of bread is falling to the point that they can afford other food items as well, the demand for the cheaper food does not increase. Instead it decreases, and we have a regressive demand curve. So this type of inferior good is called a 'Giffen good'. The poor English 'peasant', reduced as one writer said 'to a bare diet of bread and cheese, or the poor Irish peasant, surviving on a diet of potatoes 'we eat them, skin and all, over here' made the demand curve for their respective staple diets regressive.

However today the more subtle explanations of demand behaviour recognise that Giffen goods are only a special case of standard demand analysis. The point is that where prices are falling or rising the effects on demand can be divided into two parts, a **substitution effect** and an **income effect**. The normal thing is for the peasant to behave logically and substitute the cheaper goods for other items, when the price falls. Demand therefore tends to increase as the price of the inferior good falls. This **substitution effect** is always positive, it increases the quantity demanded as the poor person substitutes the cheaper good for other products which are not falling in price. However, there begins to creep in an **income effect**, and this income effect is negative as far as the demand for the Giffen good is concerned. The money income of the peasant has not changed, but the real income has increased (i.e. the income in terms of what it will buy). Since the staple diet is now very cheap the peasant can switch to a better diet. The demand for bread declines and the demand for other goods rises, once the negative income effect becomes stronger than the substitution effect and overrides it. By contrast, when the price of a Giffen good rises, the peasant's logical reduction of demand for it is offset by the income effect, which reduces his/her real standard of living to a bare diet of the Giffen good, and consumption (demand) increases when price increases.

An interesting example of regressive demand is the experience of the Co-operative Movement, which has always historically been most prosperous when times were hard and prices and wages low. At such times Co-operative goods, which have always been good-quality products at fair prices, appeal strongly to consumers, and their stores are filled with busy shoppers. In prosperous times, when wages are high and retail trade is booming, the Co-operative Movement tends to do less well. The 'inferior' good, durable and serviceable but lacking style, is less attractive to affluent consumers who buy with less discrimination.

On highly organised commodity markets and stock exchanges it is possible for demand to be regressive when prices are falling, if speculators hold off in expectations of further falls. When the market is 'bearish' speculators not only refuse to buy but actually sell in expectations of buying back later at even lower prices. So, far from strengthening demand, the lower prices have the opposite effect and weaken it still further.

7.8
Choosing a 'basket of goods' – marginal utility as the basis of demand

We now have to consider what governs the choice of the consumer in satisfying his wants. Why does he reject some goods and decide on others? Why do some people find satisfaction in filling their baskets with fruit and bread, while others choose meat and eggs? Why do some pay for piano lessons while others buy motor cycles?

There are several factors that influence every decision, but all are subordinate to the desire to obtain maximum satisfaction. The ability of a good to give satisfaction is called its 'utility'. In thinking about utility we have to distinguish between *total utility* and *marginal utility*.

Total utility is the total satisfaction we derive from the possession of a commodity. Usually total utility will continue to rise as we acquire more and more of the same goods. This would certainly be true, for example, of a collector's acquisition of antiques. It might not be quite so true of a smoker's purchase of cigarettes. There might come a point with many commodities where total utility has reached a maximum and a further supply would be a positive nuisance.

7.8.1
The margin in economics

One of the commonest ideas in economic analysis is the concept of the margin. The word 'margin' means 'edge'; poets talk about 'the margin of the lake', and teachers instruct pupils to draw margins in their exercise books. In economics there are many margins, and they are always very important points because it is at the margin that business decisions are made. For instance, marginal cost is the cost of a unit of production that is just on the edge of current output. If we cut some output it will be that unit which is cut. Similarly, the marginal firm is the firm just about to leave a contracting industry, or the firm that has just entered an expanding industry. Marginal utility is another of these margins.

Marginal utility is the satisfaction we receive from possessing one extra unit of a commodity, or the satisfaction we lose by giving up one unit. Shall I buy another shirt? The satisfaction I shall derive from it is its marginal utility to me. I am weighing the marginal satisfaction of the shirt against the satisfaction of having the money for the shirt instead – the money representing everything else that I could have instead. This is an example of choice, and as we have already said, choice is fundamental to economic life. If I decide on the shirt it is because the marginal utility to me of a shirt is high. If I decide on some other alternative, perhaps a textbook or a visit to the theatre, it

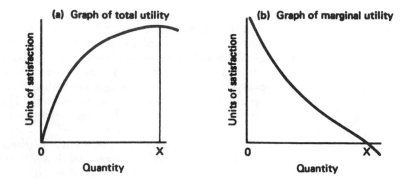

Figure 7.10 Total utility and marginal utility measured in units of satisfaction

Notes
1 Total utility continues to rise, but reaches a maximum where the commodity is such that there is an absolute limit beyond which marginal utility is negative.
2 Marginal utility begins to fall away at once, as soon as we have the first unit. From then on each successive unit gives less and less satisfaction. At point X the marginal satisfaction to be gained is zero, and total utility is at a maximum. Any further purchases of this commodity would now be irrational, for there is no sense in buying goods when the further supply will only be a nuisance, and leave us more dissatisfied.

is because the marginal utility of the shirt to me is low. Business decisions are always marginal decisions. A million housewives every day weigh up the marginal utilities to them of another tin of soup, or packet of tea or pound of sugar. Desirable goods beckon from every counter and every catalogue, but only when an item's marginal utility to the consumer exceeds the marginal utility of the income that must be given up to obtain them is a bargain struck.

Marginal utility diminishes as total utility rises. If marginal utility is the extra satisfaction to be derived from a further unit of a commodity it is clear it will not be the same for every unit obtained. Smokers are on record as saying that the first cigarette of the day is the most satisfying. Subsequent cigarettes have a smaller marginal utility, and even the veteran chain-smoker finds himself indifferent to the eighty-first cigarette of the day. The housewife buying bread certainly needs a loaf or two. She is less enthusiastic about the third loaf, and positively embarrassed by the twentieth, for she cannot either carry it home or use it before it goes stale. Clearly the marginal utility of the twentieth loaf may even be negative.

If we imagine some unit in which we can measure utility, say 'units of satisfaction', we can illustrate marginal utility and total utility diagrammatically as shown in Figure 7.10.

7.8.2
'Free goods' and 'marginal utility'

Some goods are completely free of cost, and some goods are so cheap that they are almost free of cost. For example, air is free, and it is unlikely that anyone will ever be able to monopolise the air and insist on us paying for a breath of it. In many countries water is in sufficient supply for it to be provided at very nominal charges. In such circumstances consumers become very careless about the quantity of water they use, for once the small bill has been paid they can use as much as they like. This attitude is completely changed when the water is metered and the charge is based upon the quantity used.

The marginal-utility curve for such a free commodity is shown in Figure 7.11.

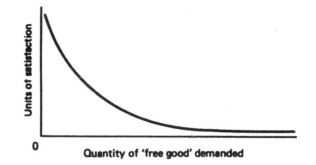

Figure 7.11 The marginal-utility curve of free goods

Note
The marginal-utility curve does not cut the X axis because the marginal utility of the goods never becomes negative. However, the marginal utility does become very low indeed, so that the commodity is almost wasted. The housewife who leaves the garden hose running throughout a long summer afternoon so that the children can cool themselves under the sprinkler is getting very little utility from a great quantity of water.

**7.8.3
Conclusions about the selection of a 'basket of goods'**

Consumers who are basing their choice of a basket of goods on the utility (i.e. satisfaction) they can obtain, will try to achieve the maximum satisfaction possible. This leads to two conclusions.

(a) They will push their consumption of free goods to the maximum possible position, continuing to demand supplies even when the marginal utility has become very low indeed. A good example of this occurred in Britain when no charge was made for prescriptions under the National Health Service. Families had large supplies of drugs like penicillin and other antibiotics which had been given to the family during illness. On a recurrence of the illness further supplies were demanded, even though some of the old supplies were still available. It was free, so demand continued strong even though the utility of the

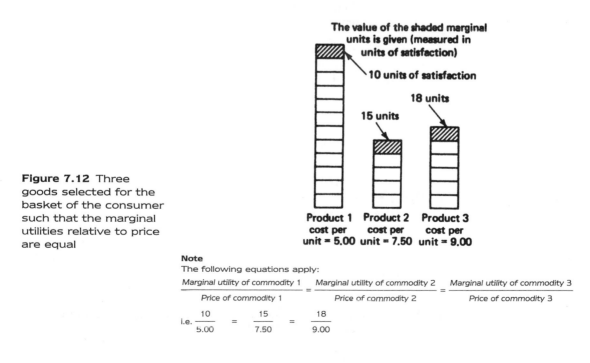

Figure 7.12 Three goods selected for the basket of the consumer such that the marginal utilities relative to price are equal

Note
The following equations apply:

$$\frac{\text{Marginal utility of commodity 1}}{\text{Price of commodity 1}} = \frac{\text{Marginal utility of commodity 2}}{\text{Price of commodity 2}} = \frac{\text{Marginal utility of commodity 3}}{\text{Price of commodity 3}}$$

$$\text{i.e.} \quad \frac{10}{5.00} = \frac{15}{7.50} = \frac{18}{9.00}$$

extra supply was very low. Eventually a prescription charge had to be imposed to reduce the nation's drug bill.

(*b*) They will balance the marginal utilities of the goods they are thinking of buying against their prices. Eventually, when maximum satisfaction has been achieved the ratios of the marginal utilities of all the goods to their prices will be equal. This is illustrated in Figure 7.12.

In this situation a consumer cannot increase the satisfaction experienced. If it is decided to give up one unit of Commodity 3, this will release 9.00 currency units for other purchases, but satisfaction of 18 units will be lost. If the 9.00 is spent on Commodity 2 it will buy (9.00/7.50) = 1.20 units. At 15 units of satisfaction the results will be 18 units of satisfaction from the extra supply of Commodity 2. However, because marginal utility declines as quantity increases, the next unit of Commodity 2 will not yield 15 units of satisfaction but a little less. The consumer therefore achieves less than 18 units of satisfaction and has therefore not increased the satisfaction enjoyed. The same result arises from the purchase of 9.00 worth of Commodity 1.

A more modern approach to the problem of choosing a basket of goods is called the 'Revealed Preference Theory'. This is discussed in Section 13.4.

**7.9
Summary of
Chapter 7**

1 The demand for a commodity or service is that quantity of it which consumers are prepared to buy at a given price in a given period of time.
2 Every consumer subconsciously has a personal demand schedule for each class of goods, which reflects individual attitudes and inclinations.
3 These individual demand schedules can be collected together into a composite demand schedule.
4 From such composite demand schedules we can draw a demand curve for the product.
5 This demand curve slopes down towards the right because it displays the general tendency of consumers to demand more when the price is low.
6 In certain situations and for certain products, demand curves can be regressive, i.e. they turn back on themselves.
7 In choosing a selection of goods and services the consumer is motivated by a desire to achieve maximum satisfaction.
8 In achieving maximum satisfaction the consumer will balance the marginal utilities of goods against their prices, one with another. Marginal utility is the satisfaction derived from a further unit of a commodity by a consumer who already has some of that commodity.

Exercises Set 7

1 Define 'demand'. Distinguish 'demand' from 'want', and illustrate by reference to demand in India and the USA.
2 Suggest reasons why Mrs Brown's demand for bread may be very different from Mrs Smith's. (In this type of question a superficial answer is usually insufficient. Students are urged to think of several factors likely to affect demand.)
3 What is the first 'law' of demand and supply? Illustrate it graphically, indicating different levels of demand along the curve drawn.
4 What is a regressive demand curve? How can a regressive demand curve for 'Giffen' goods be explained?

5 'Copper is cheap. I will buy some immediately' (speculator). 'Copper is cheap, I will sell copper at once' (same speculator on another occasion). Discuss the difference in attitudes displayed.

6 'In ordinary everyday decisions marginal utility is more important than total utility.' Explain, using the demand for breakfast cereals as an example.

7 'Total utility usually rises, marginal utility always falls.' Is this statement true or largely true? Explain.

8 Explain how a housewife decides on a selection of goods for the family.

9 What are 'free' goods? Why is the marginal utility of most free goods small in everyday life? Do we, then, cease to demand them? Explain.

10 When a housewife's selection of goods is complete the marginal utilities of the goods selected relative to their prices will all be equal. Explain.

8   Basic ideas of supply

8.1
Definition of supply

The responses that entrepreneurs make to the demands of consumers bring on to the market a wide variety of goods and services. The total quantity of a good, or service, made available to the general public as a result of the business decisions of the entrepreneurs in the industry is called the **supply** of that good, or service. We may therefore define supply as follows: *the supply of a commodity or service is that quantity of it which entrepreneurs are prepared to make available at a given price, in a given period of time.*

As with demand, we must notice that the price is crucial to any discussion of supply. There is no such thing as the supply of family cars *per se*. It is the supply at £7 000 each or £90 000 each which can be estimated and discussed. In deciding what quantity to supply, each entrepreneur will be influenced by a number of factors, discussed in Section 8.2 below.

8.2
Factors affecting supply

The chief factors affecting supply are: (*a*) the price of the commodity, and (*b*) the conditions of supply. Under (*b*) we may particularly note: (i) the costs of production; (ii) the state of technological development; (iii) natural influences, and abnormal political influences.

The price of the commodity. The price of the commodity affects the prospects of profitability of an enterprise. Every entrepreneur is assumed in economics to be engaged in production in order to achieve maximum profit. Of course this is not universally true, and there are other explanations of the behaviour of firms. The owner of a business will usually hope to achieve a normal return on capital invested, or there is no incentive at all to stay in the industry. The owner will hope to do rather better than this in actual fact, and will attempt to operate at the best level possible. Good prospects of profitability will encourage entrepreneurs to come in and produce the supplies required. They will expand production until output reaches such a level that profit is at a maximum.

The conditions of supply: (i) costs of production. The costs of production are of such importance that a whole profession is engaged in calculating and controlling them. The cost accountant distinguishes between two major sets of costs, **fixed costs** and **variable costs**, but the specialised vocabulary used in a full discussion of costs is very extensive. A simple chart of costs is given in Table 8.1 below.

The conditions of supply: (ii) the state of technological development. Not only does an advanced technology reduce unit costs by achieving the economies of scale but without it the production of even a single unit may be impossible. When the early pioneers of the motor car built their first models it was necessary to cut each component for the gear-box by hand. They started with rods of steel and brass, and sheets of wrought iron, and built the whole vehicle.

The elementary level of motor-vehicle technology prevented any appreciable supply from coming onto the market. The more advanced the technology, the greater the flood of supplies that pours onto the market.

Table 8.1 A simple chart of costs

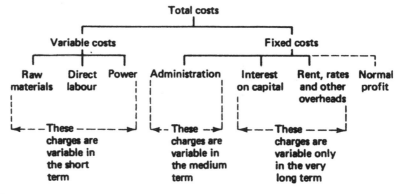

Notes
1 *Variable costs* are costs that vary with the volume of output; if we double the output of furniture, for example, we must use twice as much wood, more labour, etc.
2 *Fixed costs* do not vary with output; for example, rent is the same whatever the output produced.
3 *Normal profit*. To an accountant profit is the difference between costs and selling price, but economists include *normal profit* as an element of cost. This is very helpful, because it draws attention to the entrepreneur's desire for profit. If a firm cannot achieve a reasonable return on capital invested the entrepreneur will leave the industry – in other words, the costs the business *must* cover include normal profit.
4 *Variability in the short run, the medium run and the long run*. This is important in understanding the decisions made by entrepreneurs, but cannot be fully discussed at this point. *Variable costs* can be reduced at once by cutting back production and dismissing workers. Such harsh treatment of workers is becoming less easy in advanced societies where trade unions are strong. *Administrative costs* can be reduced in a rather longer time by dismissing employees on monthly contracts, or by giving 'golden handshakes' to those with longer contracts of service. Other *fixed costs* cannot be reduced so easily, and may involve finding a buyer for factory premises or paying lump sums for the privilege of surrendering a lease.

The conditions of supply: (iii) natural influences and abnormal political influences. Supply is particularly subject to external influences, which may disrupt either the actual output itself or the distribution system moving the supplies to the point of consumption. Hurricanes, tornadoes, hail, frost snow and drought disrupt output. Similarly, war, fire, strikes, and civil unrest prevent the normal activities of production. All these things interrupt transport by rail, road, sea and air.

A further type of political activity is government interference with the market. For instance, taxation may cause demand to change and thus make output unprofitable, or it may simply reduce the profitability of some enterprises below normal. Normal profit is that profit which is just sufficient to retain a firm in the industry but is not sufficient to attract a firm outside the industry to enter. When taxation is imposed the high-cost firms in an industry may find that profit falls below this normal return on capital invested. Such firms will leave the industry and supply will be reduced.

For any given firm the prospects of profitability and the conditions of supply dictate production policy. What the entrepreneur decides to produce in the prevailing conditions leads to an individual supply schedule.

8.3
Individual supply
schedules

There are millions of consumers demanding products, but the number of suppliers is much smaller. Sometimes there is only one supplier, called in economics a **monopolist**. Sometimes there are two or three main suppliers only, as in the British detergent industry, where two great combines dominate the scene. This situation is called **oligopoly** (from the Greek *oligoi* meaning 'few'). The commonest situation is where there are many suppliers

Table 8.2 Two individual supply schedules

Price per unit	Number of animals supplied weekly	
	A. Smallholder	A. Bigboy Ltd
30.00	500	10 000
29.00	450	9 000
28.00	250	8 000
27.00	100	7 000
26.00	–	6 000
25.00	–	5 000
24.00	–	4 000
23.00	–	3 500
22.00	–	3 000
21.00	–	–
20.00	–	–

Notes

1 A Smallholder is a high-cost producer who cannot supply any animals at a price below 27.00.
2 The limited company is a low-cost producer; perhaps because it achieves economies of scale, or is more favourably situated.
3 Unlike a demand schedule, where consumers demand more when the price is low, suppliers offer to supply *less* when the price is low. The higher the price, the greater the quantity that is brought to market.
4 Neither of these producers can suddenly increase supplies of lambs. It takes time for flocks to be bred. What they can do is to send existing animals to market if the price is right, or retain them on the farm until prices improve.

competing with one another. Sometimes we talk about **perfect competition**. A full discussion of what economists mean by **perfect competition** is given on pages 100–2. As a rule some imperfections exist in the market, usually because goods have been 'branded' to make them artificially different from similar goods. This situation is called **imperfect competition** or **monopolistic competition**.

In considering demand we discussed the demand schedules of certain housewives for lamb cutlets, and eventually of the whole body of consumers for lamb carcases. We must now consider the **individual supply schedules** of some suppliers of lambs, i.e. some farmers who raise sheep for wool and meat.

Just as consumers vary in their preferences for goods, suppliers vary in their ability to supply. Some, because they are better situated, or more skilful, are low-cost producers, while others are high-cost producers.

Examples of high-cost and low-cost producers are illustrated in Table 8.2

When these schedules are drawn as individual supply curves the result is as shown in Figure. 8.1.

8.4
A composite supply schedule

If we now imagine that the supply schedules of all the suppliers in the industry have been added together we find that the supply schedule of the industry looks like Table 8.3. This illustrates a very important aspect of supply, which is known as the second 'law' of demand and supply.

The second 'law' of demand and supply states that *the higher the price, the greater the quantity that is supplied.*

The reader is advised to consider every such table in this book carefully. Can you visualise the industry clearly? At a price of 20.00 only

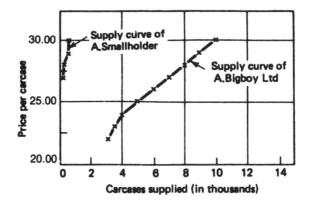

Figure 8.1 Two individual supply curves

the most efficient farmers are bringing their animals to market. They are such low-cost producers that even at a price of 20.00 they can make a profit. As the prices rise more and more inefficient producers are able to make a profit, and bring their flocks in to market. The higher the world prices for lamb, the more producers will join the industry. The lower the prices, the more producers will leave the industry and either give up farming altogether or change over to some aspect of it more lucrative than sheep-raising.

Graphically presented this information appears as shown in Figure 8.2.

Notice that this supply curve slopes upwards towards the right. This is because the quantity supplied rises as the price rises – exactly the opposite of what happens with the demand curves shown in Figures 7.3 and 7.4.

8.5
A general supply curve

Once again we do not bother in theoretical discussions with the actual shape of supply curves for particular industries. Instead, as with demand, we use the **general supply curve** as a basis for discussion. Its characteristics are that uniform graduations are assumed along both axes, and the curve obeys the second 'law' of demand and supply, in other words, it indicates increased supplies coming on to the market as prices rise. This curve is shown in Figure 8.3.

Table 8.3 A composite supply schedule

Price per unit	Animal supplied weekly by whole industry
30.00	2 000 000
29.00	1 800 000
28.00	1 600 000
27.00	1 400 000
26.00	1 200 000
25.00	1 000 000
24.00	800 000
23.00	700 000
22.00	600 000
21.00	500 000
20.00	400 000

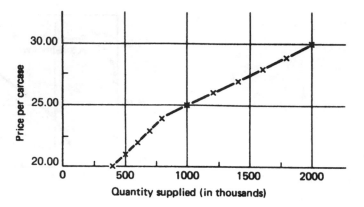

Figure 8.2 The supply curve for lamb

8.6
Extensions, contractions and changes in supply

Once again we must distinguish between extensions and contractions of supply, on the one hand, and changes in supply, on the other. The term 'extension of supply' refers to an increased supply coming on to the market due to the attraction of higher prices being offered there. When the farmer decides to market his lambs, because prices have risen and will now yield him a profit, there is no 'change' in supply as far as economists are concerned. Similarly, when supply contracts under the influence of falling prices there is only a movement along the same supply curve. These extensions and contractions of supply are illustrated in Figure 8.4.

To an economist a change means a change causing a new curve altogether. Such a change must be due to a change in the conditions of supply: perhaps a change in the techniques of production, or some natural or political event which interferes with the supply of the commodity. All such changes result in either a larger or a smaller supply coming on to the market at every price. This produces a new supply curve, as shown in Figure 8.5.

8.7
Regressive supply curves

The regressive type of curve shown in certain cases of demand is not very common with supply. However, a good example is afforded by the supply curve for labour. This is often regressive when very high wages are being paid since workers can then earn sufficient to provide for their families in

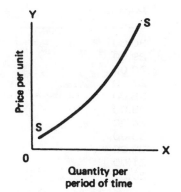

Figure 8.3 The general supply curve

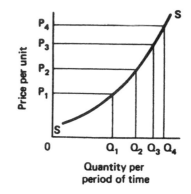

Figure 8.4 Extensions and contractions (but *not* changes) of supply

shorter working periods. Consequently absenteeism grows, especially if the work is hard and unpleasant. In Great Britain absenteeism in the coal mines became a serious problem when higher wages for workers at the coal face meant that men could take greater leisure periods without reducing their standards of living. As income rises, the marginal utility of income falls and

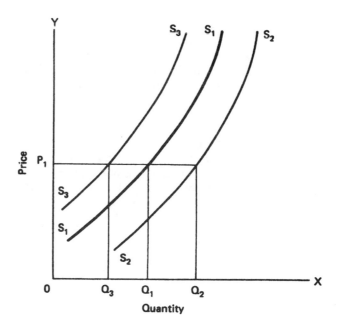

Figure 8.5 An increase (decrease) in supply

Notes

1 Initially the conditions of supply are such that the supply curve is S_1S_1. At a price of P_1 a quantity Q_1 is supplied.

2 An increase in supply could result from lower costs of production, or improved technology, or a reduction in taxation, or favourable natural conditions which increase output without increasing cost.

3 At every price increased supplies are available as shown by the curve S_2S_2. At a price of P_1 quantity supplied rises from Q_1 to Q_2.

4 A decrease in supply could result from higher costs of production, declining efficiency, increased taxation, removal of a subsidy or some natural or man-made interruption to supplies.

5 When supply decreases to S_3S_3 the quantity supplied to the market at every price falls, and at a price of P_1 only Q_3 is available.

6 Although the supply lines have been drawn parallel to one another in this case there is no reason why this should necessarily be so and it could be that the reason for the increase (decrease) operated differently at some price levels than at others.

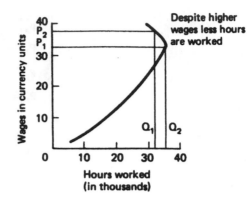

Figure 8.6 The regressive supply curve of labour

Note
At P_1 the wages paid are sufficient to call forth 35 000 hours of work per week at a particular coalfield. At P_2 the extra wages result not in an increased supply of labour but a decreased supply as absenteeism reduces the total hours worked.

the marginal utility of leisure rises; especially where work is dangerous and unpleasant. Figure 8.6 illustrates the supply of such labour.

8.8
Deciding to supply – marginal cost and marginal revenue as the basis of the firm's output

Just as consumers make decisions to demand goods or services, entrepreneurs make decisions to supply them. The decision to demand is based on the marginal utility of the good to the consumer, as already explained in Section 7.8. The decision to supply is based on the relationship between the marginal cost and the marginal revenue. We must now define these terms, and note a number of interesting points about each.

8.8.1
Marginal cost

Marginal cost is the addition to total costs incurred in producing one extra unit of production – the marginal unit. Once again decisions are being made at the margin. It is not a question of whether I shall produce 100 000 cars or none but whether I shall produce 100 000 or 95 000; or will perhaps 105 000 be best. Table 8.4 suggests some imaginary figures for a business whose fixed costs are £100.00. Variable costs start off at £50.00 for the first unit, but are less for the second unit and even less for the third. This is because economies of scale are being achieved. After the third item the variable costs begin to rise more and more rapidly. This means that the *marginal* cost of each unit is going up fast – diseconomies of scale are beginning to creep in. Consider the notes below the Table, and the relationship between marginal cost and average cost.

8.8.2
The relationship between marginal cost and average cost

It is important to understand the relationship between marginal cost and average cost. The marginal cost is the cost of the last unit to be produced. It is therefore the vital thing that controls average cost. If the marginal cost is lower than the average cost the average cost will fall. If the marginal cost is greater than the average cost, then the new average cost – now that one extra unit has been included – will rise. A simple illustration of this is the effect on the average age of any group of the arrival of one more member. Suppose a class of night-school students has an average age of 19 years. If they are joined by one new class member (the marginal student) aged 17 years, the age of this student being lower than average, will reduce the average age of

Table 8.4 Marginal cost and average cost (£)

Output	Fixed costs	Variable costs	Total costs	Average cost per unit	Marginal costs of the extra unit
0	100	–	100	–	–
1	100	50	150	150	50
2	100	90	190	95	40
3	100	128	228	76	38
4	100	176	276	69	48
5	100	240	340	68	64
6	100	320	420	70	80
7	100	418	518	74	98
8	100	540	640	80	122
9	100	674	774	86	134

Notes
1 Fixed costs, as their name implies, are constant.
2 Variable costs, the costs of raw materials, direct labour, power, etc., increase as output rises, but not in a constant way, because of increasing returns to scale and then decreasing returns to scale.
3 The alterations to variable costs are the marginal costs of successive extra units. Notice that they decrease from £50 to £38 under the influence of the economies of scale, but then begin to rise as diminishing returns set in.
4 Average costs per unit fall from £150 to £68, but then being to rise. The reader should note that marginal cost starts to rise before average cost, which continues to fall as long as marginal cost is below average cost.

the class. If the new arrival is a mature student aged 42 this higher-than-average age will increase the average age of the class.

Returning to the effect on average cost of changes in marginal cost, we can see the result in Table 8.4. As long as marginal cost is less than average cost, the average falls with every new unit. As soon as marginal cost becomes higher than average cost, i.e. at £80.00 for the sixth unit of production, the average cost starts to rise. It must do, because the high cost of that extra unit drags up the whole average. This is shown graphically in Figure 8.7.

8.8.3
Marginal revenue

We are still not quite ready to understand at what point the entrepreneur decides to stop supplying his goods or service. This is because we do not yet know what **marginal revenue** is. Even when we have defined marginal

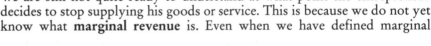

Figure 8.7 Average-and marginal-cost curves

Notes
1 As long as marginal cost is lower than average cost, average cost is falling.
2 As soon as marginal cost rises above average cost it drags the average cost up with it.
3 Therefore the marginal-cost curve always cuts the average-cost curve at its lowest point.

revenue, we have to look at the different types of market situation before we can fully understand it.

Marginal revenue is defined as *the increase in total revenue to be achieved by supplying one further unit of a commodity.*

One might think that this would be the same as the price for which the unit is sold, but in fact this is often not the case. To explain why, we must consider the market situation in which suppliers and consumers meet.

**8.8.4
Markets in
economics**

A market is a place where buyers and sellers are in contact with one another to fix prices. There are many types of market. The highly organised commodity markets and financial markets of the City of London are as near as one can get in real life to the perfect market which economists like to imagine and discuss. By contrast, a thief who is trying to dispose of a stolen ring does so on a very imperfect market. He cannot offer it openly in the market-place in case someone informs the police. Any potential buyer becomes a threat if the thief refuses to sell the ring at the price offered. The illegality of his transaction is what makes his market imperfect, but there are many legal market situations which are imperfect. What is a **perfect market?**

A perfect market is one which displays the following characteristics:

(*a*) a large number of buyers and sellers, none of whom dominate the market;
(*b*) a homogeneous commodity, so that buyers are indifferent from whom they buy;
(*c*) an absence of friction in the market;
(*d*) perfect knowledge in the market;
(*e*) no one receiving preferential treatment.

(*a*) *There must be a larger number of buyers and sellers, none of whom dominates the market.* If there are a large number of buyers and sellers competition on the market will be strong. In perfect market conditions no producer is so large that he can raise the price by withholding his supplies, and no consumer is so important that he can lower the price by refusing to buy. As examples of markets with large numbers of buyers and sellers, we may quote the London Stock Exchange and Lloyd's. The former has hundreds of dealer-brokers and market makers trading; Lloyd's has 6000 underwriters and over 200 firms of brokers selling and buying insurance.

(*b*) *The commodity dealt in must be homogeneous.* In other words each unit of the product must be exactly like every other unit. This is sometimes easy to achieve, and sometimes quite impossible. With silver, for example, on the Sliver Bullion Market in London contracts are made for silver which is 0.999 fine, i.e. 999 parts per thousand pure silver. On the Wool Futures Market in Sydney, Australia such perfection is impossible for sheep are temperamental creatures and the quality of the fleece varies with every animal. Trading is based on the New Zealand cross-bred wool contract, a standard type of wool. The price may need to be adjusted if the wool actually delivered is above, or below, standard. Wool is not a homogeneous commodity; silver is, or can be refined until it is.

This homogeneity of the product makes both buyers and sellers indifferent with whom they conclude a contract. No one's 0.999 fine silver is different from anyone else's 0.999 fine silver. A share in Imperial Chemical Industries from one market-maker is as good as the

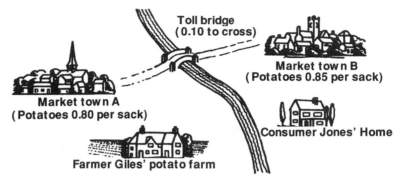

Figure 8.8 Friction in the market

Notes

1 The toll bridge charges 0.10 for each sack of potatoes crossing. It is the 'friction' in this market.

2 Farmer Giles, if there was an absence of friction in the market, would take his potatoes to town B and sell them at 0.85 per sack. Because he will have to cross the bridge and pay 0.10 per sack, his earnings from the market in town B would be cut to 0.75 per sack. He will instead sell them in town A for only 0.80 per sack.

3 Consumer Jones would like to buy his potatoes in town A at 0.80 per sack. To cross the bridge will cost him 0.10 per sack, making 0.90 altogether. He is therefore forced to pay 0.85 at town B.

same share from any other market-maker. Price becomes the only reason for changing suppliers.

(c) *There must be an absence of friction in the market.* Friction, in science, is a force that reduces the efficiency of a machine. Friction in a market similarly reduces the efficient fixing of prices. Figure 8.8 shows friction in the market for potatoes in two market towns, *A* and *B*.

Any such friction reduces the perfection of the market. Transport costs are a typical example of friction in the market. Tariffs are another, while trade-union restrictive practices reduce perfection in the market for labour.

(d) *Perfect knowledge must exist in the market.* In certain of the London Commodity Markets dealing is by 'open outcry'. Everyone dealing in the market knows the prices being asked, for he can hear them. Such perfect knowledge is rare. The housewife, shopping in her local supermarket, has not the time to tour round comparing prices for groceries. By contrast, when she buys furniture or something expensive and long lasting she may 'shop around' for several weeks before she finally decides what to buy. This improves her knowledge of the prices being charged by different firms.

(e) *There must be no preferential treatment for any particular class of buyers or sellers.* Discrimination against one buyer in favour of another reduces the perfection of a market. In times of shortage shopkeepers who keep goods in short supply 'under the counter' for special customers are displaying discrimination. Discrimination is not always unjustified – businessmen are entitled to look after their best customers – but if it does exist it results in prices being different in the imperfect market from what they would be in more perfectly competitive circumstances.

The perfect market has only one price. If a market is perfect there can be only one price for each good. If there were two prices buyers would rush to buy at the lower price, forcing the price up; sellers would rush to sell at the higher price, thus lowering it. Before we can look fully at these market operations we must finally clarify the supply position. This section is about the decision to supply. The crucial point in that decision is the marginal revenue to be received.

Imperfect markets. A full discussion of these is given in Chapter 12. At present we must return to our supplier, and the marginal revenue which he will earn by the output decision he makes.

8.8.5 Marginal revenue in perfect competition

In a perfect market there are many buyers and sellers, none of whom is such a large dealer that he can influence price. This means that for any given producer the price is fixed at market price. We are not quite ready to see how market price is decided; this is discussed in Section 9.3, but if we accept the idea of a price fixed as the result of the interaction of supply and demand we can see that this price will prevail all over the market, because the market is perfect. Nothing any producer can personally do will affect the price, and for every unit that he sells he will receive a **marginal revenue** of the market price. If the price of a family motor car is £7500 he will receive £7500 for every one he makes, including the marginal unit. We can therefore make the following statement: in perfect competition

price = marginal revenue = average revenue.

Now consider the diagram in Figure 8.9 and the notes below it.

8.8.6 Conclusions about decisions to supply

The decisions of entrepreneurs about the quantity of goods to be supplied are subjective decisions based on personal estimates of the marginal costs of their products. Even the best accountant can only guess what is the cost of a particular unit, but he does his best to supply the board of his company with as accurate a view as possible of the current situation.

In perfect competition the entrepreneur produces until the marginal-cost curve cuts the marginal-revenue line. In other types of market, where some element of monopoly enters, the entrepreneur will still produce to the point where marginal cost equals marginal revenue, but the marginal revenue will not be the same as the price. This is explained more fully in Chapter 12.

The total quantity supplied to the market helps decide the market price, and it is this determination of price which is examined in the next chapter.

8.9 Summary of Chapter 8

1 The supply of a commodity or service is that quantity which entrepreneurs are prepared to make available at a certain price, in a given period of time.
2 Supply is affected by the costs of production, by the general level of technological development, and by the prospects of profitability.
3 Generally speaking, the higher the price, the greater the quantity of goods that is supplied.
4 Regressive supply curves are not common, but the supply curve of the factor labour is often regressive when high wages are being paid, because then the marginal utility of leisure rises.
5 Marginal cost is the addition to total costs incurred by producing one further unit of output.
6 Marginal revenue is the additional revenue achieved by the sale of one further unit of output. In perfect competition it is the same as the sale price of the article.
7 A supplier stops production when marginal cost rises to equal marginal revenue. Beyond that point he loses money on every extra unit.

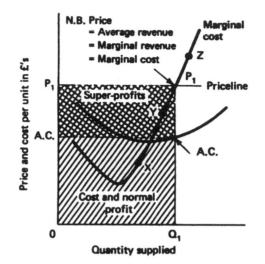

Figure 8.9 Deciding what quantity to supply in perfect competition

Notes

1 We are considering *one* supplier only in this diagram.
2 For this supplier, price is fixed at market price, P_1.
3 This supplier is a low-cost firm, because its average costs are well below market price. The supplier is therefore going to make some very useful temporary profits.
4 Consider the point X on the marginal-cost curve. At this point the marginal cost is £X, but the supplier will receive £P_1 for the sale of this unit. This will be a profitable unit.
5 At point Y the marginal unit is costing £Y, but the supplier will receive £P_1 for its sale, so that this will again be profitable, but not as profitable as the unit costing £X.
6 At point Z the marginal unit costs £Z, but the supplier receives only £P_1. This will mean the supplier loses money on it.
7 It follows that an entrepreneur will stop production when marginal cost becomes equal to marginal revenue. The next unit will lose money.
8 We can therefore say that for every producer in perfect competition at the point where production ought to cease

Price = Average revenue = Marginal revenue = Marginal cost

9 This producer is receiving OQ_1 P_1P_1 of income. Average costs at this output are found where the quantity line cuts the average-cost curve, i.e. at A.C.
10 The area shaded in single hatching (O, Q_1, A.C., A.C.) is the income received to cover costs + normal profit, so that this income includes a reasonable return on invested capital.
11 The area shaded in double hatching, i.e. A.C., P_1, P_1, A.C., is the income received over and above normal costs and profits; we will call this 'super-profit' for the moment. We can thus see that this entrepreneur is doing very nicely.
12 However, the entrepreneur cannot hope to enjoy these super-profits for long. Freedom of entry will mean that competitors will join the industry, supplying goods which will lead to price reductions, and super-profits will be competed away from the supplier as price is lowered to A.C. and even lower. This situation is explained more fully in Figure 9.7, later.
13 Note that the gap between average cost and average revenue is greatest at the point where the marginal cost curve cuts the average cost curve. However, this is not the point where the entrepreneur will cease production. He can still make even more profit if he continues to produce, even though he is now making a less than maximum margin of profit on each unit. He only ceases to make profits when marginal costs are greater than marginal revenue (in this case price P_1). At that point production will cease. (*Now return to page 102, Section 8.8.6.*)

Exercises Set 8

1 Define 'supply'. What motivates an entrepreneur to supply a commodity or service?
2 Distinguish between fixed costs and variable costs, illustrating your answer by reference to any manufacturing industry with which you are familiar.
3 What is 'normal profit'? What justification is there for regarding normal profit as a cost of production?
4 'Mass production lowers average costs by dividing fixed costs between large numbers of units of output.' Discuss this statement, saying whether you agree with it or not.

5 'Millions of people demand goods. Only a few thousand supply them. That is why demand schedules and supply schedules look so different.' Illustrate the differences by drawing up an imaginary demand schedule and supply schedule for tea, or cheese.

6 What is a regressive supply curve? Under what circumstances is supply likely to be regressive?

7 Copy this diagram (Figure 8.10) and then label it fully.

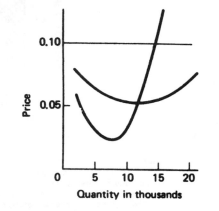

Figure 8.10

Now answer these questions:

(a) Is this a diagram of a high-cost producer or a low-cost producer?

(b) Estimate the output of this supplier.

(c) Will this supplier make normal profits, or more than normal profits, or less than normal profits?

(d) Is this industry likely to increase in size, decrease in size or stay at its present size?

8 Write short notes about each of the following: (a) an extension of supply; (b) a change in supply; (c) the shape of a supply curve; (d) regressive supply.

9 How does an entrepreneur in perfectly competitive situations decide what output to produce? Illustrate your answer with a diagram.

10 What is marginal cost? What is average cost? What is the relationship between them?

11 What is marginal revenue? What is average revenue? When are they the same?

12 What is a perfect market? Do they exist in real life? Give examples of: (a) near-perfect markets; (b) imperfect markets.

13 'Perfect knowledge is impossible in markets unless they are highly organised.' What is 'perfect knowledge' and how can an organised market ensure that knowledge is perfect?

14 Discuss the likely frictions in the market for wool.

15 Why is a market of significant importance in free-enterprise societies? In your answer suggest the important features of a free market.

9 How price is decided in perfect markets

9.1
Equilibrium in the markets

In perfect or perfectly competitive markets prices are fixed in an atmosphere of **pure competition**. This is a theoretical concept in the minds of economists rather than a real-life situation, but it is helpful to consider the forces at work in a situation free from any restrictions on the movements of goods, customers or suppliers. The extent to which real-life forces then modify market patterns can be followed. In any case some public markets are very nearly perfectly competitive. In such markets the price adjusts upwards or downwards to achieve a balance, or **equilibrium**, between the goods coming in for sale and those being requested by purchasers. Demand and supply react on one another until a position of stable equilibrium is reached where the quantities of goods demanded exactly equal the quantities supplied. The price at which goods are changing hands varies with supply and demand. If the supply exceeds demand at the start of the day prices will fall. This may discourage some of the suppliers, who will withdraw from the market, and at the same time it will encourage consumers, who will increase their demands. A twin force is therefore at work to achieve equilibrium, and establish a **market price** which equates demand and supply.

We can best see how this occurs by comparing the demand and supply schedules already discussed in Tables 7.3 and 8.3.

9.2
Demand and supply schedules in equilibrium

These schedules are given together in Table 9.1.

As already noted, when price is high the quantity demanded is small, but the quantity offered by suppliers is great. As price falls the quantity demanded increases, but the quantity offered by suppliers is reduced, since

Table 9.1 Demand and supply in equilibrium

Price in currency units	Weekly demand by consumers	Weekly supply by producers
30.00	200 000	2 000 000
29.00	250 000	1 800 000
28.00	300 000	1 600 000
27.00	500 000	1 400 000
26.00	750 000	1 200 000
25.00	1 000 000	1 000 000
24.00	1 200 000	800 000
23.00	1 400 000	700 000
22.00	1 600 000	600 000
21.00	1 800 000	500 000
20.00	2 000 000	400 000

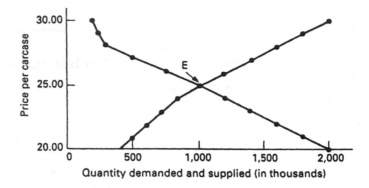

Figure 9.1 Equilibrium price in the market for lamb

Notes

1 Demand for lamb is weak when the price is high and great when the price is low.
2 Supply of lamb is small when the price is low and large when the price is high.
3 At E the demand and supply are in equilibrium, at 1 000 000 carcases being brought to market. At this price there are just enough animals being brought to the market to satisfy the demand. All will find a buyer and the market will be cleared.

the least efficient suppliers cannot offer the goods at the lower prices. Equilibrium is reached in this example at a price of £25.00 per carcass, when one million animals are demanded by consumers and supplied by producers. This illustrates the third 'law' of demand and supply, which states that '*Price adjusts to that level which equates demand and supply.*' The intersection of the demand and supply curves is illustrated in Figure 9.1, which is an amalgamation of Figures 7.3 and 8.2.

9.3 Diagrammatic presentation of equilibrium price

A general diagram illustrating the determination of price at the point where demand and supply are equal is given in Figure 9.2.

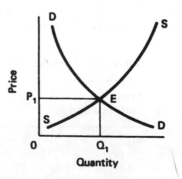

Figure 9.2 The determination of equilibrium price

Notes

1 Demand is small when the price is high, and great when the price is low.
2 Supply is great when the price is high, and small when the price is low.
3 At E (equilibrium) the demand curve and supply curve intersect.
4 At this point E, demand and supply are in equilibrium, at a price which is satisfactory to both. Above this equilibrium price suppliers are prepared to supply, but consumers are not prepared to demand. Below this equilibrium price consumers are prepared to demand, but suppliers are unwilling to supply. Only at this price are both parties willing to fulfil their side of the bargain, and the market will be cleared.
5 The price P_1 is called *equilibrium price or market price.* It is that price which equates supply and demand.

9.4
Changes in price under the influence of changes in demand and supply

Changes in the conditions of demand result in a completely different demand curve for a product. Changes in the conditions of supply similarly result in a completely new supply curve. Such changes result in more, or less, goods being demanded, or supplied, at every price. When such changes occur they result in a change in market price, for the equilibrium position described in Figure 9.2. is disturbed. There are four possible disturbances:

(*a*)   an increase in demand;
(*b*)   a decrease in demand;
(*c*)   an increase in supply;
(*d*)   a decrease in supply.

A close study of the four cases illustrates equilibrium price very clearly. The reader should follow through the development in each case so as to be quite clear how the market regulates price to achieve equilibrium. Before doing so there is one further point to note: the responsiveness of demand and supply to changes in price are different.

9.4.1
The responsiveness of supply and demand to changes in price

Demand is very responsive to price changes because consumers are able to adjust their demands quickly. A momentary calculation of the utilities involved, a quick decision, and the housewife presses in to buy the most desirable commodity available. Supply cannot possibly react in this way. At the very least, the entrepreneur has to replan his activities and switch to a new product. In many cases he has to erect a new factory, or plant fields or dig mines before he can produce any output. This means that there is always a time-lag when demand changes before supply can adjust itself. When supply changes, the reactions of customers demanding the product are almost immediate.

The reader is now urged to consider Figures 9.3–9.6 and the notes below them, bearing in mind that in each case the changes result from a change in

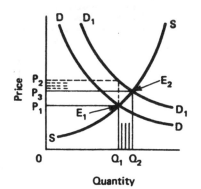

Figure 9.3 Effect on price of an increase in demand

Notes
1   Due to some change in the conditions of demand, perhaps a change of taste or fashion, or a change of income, demand has altered from DD to D_1D_1.
2   Supply cannot react at once because entrepreneurs have to modify plans. There is therefore a shortage and price rises steeply to P_2, the point where a supply of Q_1 cuts the new demand curve. Entrepreneurs supplying the goods are now making excellent profits.
3   Under the influence of these profits, firms expand output and supply begins to creep up from Q_1 to Q_2.
4   As supply extends the price falls from P_2 to P_3.
5   The new equilibrium price of P_3 is established at E_2, where the old supply (which has *extended* to E_2) cuts the new demand curve, which has *changed* to D_1D_1.
6   *Conclusion*: an increase in demand raises price and eventually increases the quantity supplied by the industry.

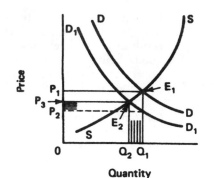

Figure 9.4 Effect on price of a decrease in demand

Notes
1 Due to some change, perhaps of taste or fashion, demand has decreased from DD to D_1D_1.
2 Entrepreneurs supplying the commodity cannot immediately cease production of it, and as a result there is too great a supply for the demand. Price falls drastically to P_2. Some entrepreneurs at this price are making losses.
3 Under the influence of these losses, entrepreneurs reduce production, and supply falls from Q_1 to Q_2.
4 As the supply contracts price begins to recover and creeps up from P_2 to P_3.
5 The new equilibrium price P_3 is decided where the old supply curve (supply having *contracted*) cuts the new demand curve D_1D_1.
6 *Conclusion*: a decrease in demand lowers the price and eventually leads to a decreased supply from the industry.

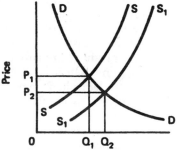

Figure 9.5 Effect on price of an increase in supply

Notes
1 For some reason, perhaps a change in the techniques of production, supply has changed from SS to S_1S_1.
2 The increased supply causes a surplus on the market, and price falls.
3 Due to the swift reactions of consumers, demand extends to take up the new supply at the price P_2.
4 *Conclusion*: an increased supply causes a fall in price and an increase in the quantity demanded.

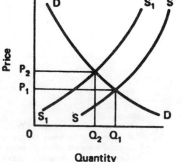

Figure 9.6 Effect on price of a decrease in supply

Notes
1 For some reason decreased supplies are available: perhaps a war has interfered with the output in a country which has previously been a major supplier.
2 The decreased supply causes a shortage, and price rises.
3 Consumers react quickly and the demand contracts to Q_2, achieving equilibrium at the new price P_2.
4 *Conclusion*: a decreased supply causes an increased price and a decrease in the quantity demanded.

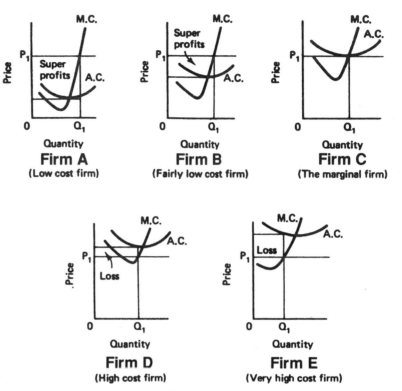

Figure 9.7 Five firms in the same industry (see Sections 9.5 and 9.6 overleaf)

Notes

1 These five firms are all supplying in the same market. They range from a very low-cost firm (Firm A) to a very high-cost firm (Firm E).

2 Firm A is like the firm already discussed in Figure 8.9, making super-profits because it is a low-cost firm with modern, highly productive plant.

3 Firm B is not as efficient as Firm A, but it is still making more than normal profit. It is operating closer to optimum production. Optimum production is production where average cost is at a minimum. (See Firm C.)

4 Firm C would be the marginal firm in an ordinary competitive industry, but, as will be seen below, this industry is unusual because it has 'specific assets' which are of no use in other industries. Firm C is making normal profit and is operating at the optimum, i.e. minimum average cost.

5 Firm D is a firm that is looking for a way out of the industry. It looks as if it is making losses, but this might not actually be true – it might just be making less than normal profits. In other words, its capital could be better used elsewhere. Why doesn't it get out? It would like to leave, but it can't, because its assets are no use in any other industry.

6 Firm E is really making losses, and it would go if it possibly could. It looks as if this industry must have *very* specific assets. This is explained in Figure 9.8.

7 In the short run even a competitive industry can have high-cost firms and low-costs firms. In the imaginary case of *perfect competition*, especially in the long run, all firms like D and E will leave the industry. Firms like A and B will have their super-profits competed away from them. All firms will be like Firm C, the marginal firm. For the marginal firm in perfect competition, we can say that

Price = Average revenue = Marginal revenue = Marginal cost = Average cost.

The firm will be working at the optimum level with average cost at the minimum. (*Now return to the main text at Section 9.7.*)

the *conditions of demand* or the *conditions of supply.* They show respectively:

(*a*) The effect on price of an increase in demand (Figure 9.3).
(*b*) The effect on price of a decrease in demand (Figure 9.4).
(*c*) The effect on price of an increase in supply (Figure 9.5).
(*d*) The effect on price of a decrease in supply (Figure 9.6).

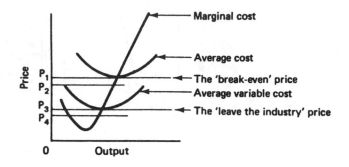

Figure 9.8 Leaving the industry – let the specific assets rust

Notes

1 At P_1 the firm is making normal profits: it is the marginal firm.
2 At prices below P_1 the firm is making less than normal profits. Suppose it receives a price of P_2 when it is paying costs of P_1. It is definitely now earning a less-than-normal return on capital invested, and ought to leave the industry.
3 If we examine the costs at P_1 we find that these costs are made up of *Fixed costs + Variable costs + Profit*. The fixed costs have already been suffered (the entrepreneur has already built the factory, installed the plant, etc.); indeed, some accountants describe these costs as **sunk costs** because they have already been sunk into the business.
   The variable costs are payments for wages, raw materials, etc., incurred with each unit of output. These are shown in the diagram by the Average Variable Cost curve.
   As long as price is above average variable cost, it will pay the entrepreneur to keep production going. At the price P_2 for each unit of production sold the firm receives: (*a*) everything it spends on variable costs, plus (*b*) something towards 'sunk' costs or 'fixed' costs. It is still worthwhile producing.
4 At price P_3 the firm is receiving back its variable costs, but nothing more.
5 Suppose prices drops below P_3, say to P_4. The entrepreneur will now be paying for wages and raw materials a price of P_3, but will receive back less than P_3 for the goods produced. Clearly this is ridiculous: it would be throwing good money after bad. The only thing to do here is to put the plant into mothballs and shut down. P_3 is therefore the 'leave-the-industry' price, even for an entrepreneur with very specific assets. The only thing to do is to wait for better times to return. (*Now turn back to the main text at Section 9.8.*)

9.5 The demand curve for the firm and for the industry

In passing it is usual at this point to mention a difficulty that arises for the student in reconciling the concepts of the demand curve for the industry and the demand curve for the firm in competitive conditions. The demand curve for the industry is a downward-sloping demand curve, as shown in Figure 9.2. The demand curve for the individual firm is horizontal, as shown in Figure 9.7 for example, where the price line from P_1 is the demand curve. The explanation is that, by definition, in perfect competition no one firm is large enough to influence price in the market. What one firm brings to market will immediately be purchased at market price.

Imagine a firm with 1 000 units to dispose of entering a market where total demand is for 10 000 000 units. The firm will have no difficulty disposing of its entire output, because perfect knowledge exists in the market and market price is established at that point where both suppliers and demanders are prepared to deal, because the price is right for both groups. Hence the demand curve for the firm's product is horizontal at market price.

9.6 The effect of price on firms in competitive industries

In Figure 8.9 we looked closely at a firm producing for a perfect market, and said that this firm would produce that output which maximised its profit. In order to do so it would stop production when marginal cost equalled marginal revenue. We also saw that, for a firm in a perfectly competitive market, the marginal revenue and the average revenue are equal to price. No firm can do anything about price – there are so many buyers and sellers that any given firm wields no influence at all on price.

Now consider five firms all producing for the same market. Their situation is illustrated in Figure 9.7.

9.7
When will a firm with specific assets leave the industry?

In the notes to Figure 9.7 it was stated that where a firm has 'specific assets', that is assets which are of little use in any other industry, it is difficult for that firm to leave the industry. There are many examples of firms with this type of asset. A catalytic cracking tower is not of much use outside the oil industry. Much of the point of a methane carrier built to carry compressed gas at very low temperatures will be lost if we use it to carry wheat at ordinary temperatures.

Similarly, a coffee bush cannot be converted to yield tea if there is a slump in world demand for coffee. At what point will such a producer cease production and leave the industry? The answer is that *a producer with specific assets leaves the industry when the price will not even cover average variable costs.* Figure 9.8. explains why. (See page 110.)

9.8
Summary of the 'laws' of demand and supply

1 Generally speaking, the quantity demanded increases as price falls.
2 Generally speaking, the quantity supplied increases as price rises.
3 Equilibrium price is that price which equates demand and supply.
4 An increased demand raises price, and also calls forth an extension of supply.
5 A decreased demand lowers price, and also brings about a contraction of supply.
6 An increased supply lowers market price, and causes an extension of demand.
7 A decreased supply raises market price, and causes a contraction of demand.

9.9
Summary of Chapter 9

1 Price is decided under perfect competition by the interaction of demand and supply.
2 Market price is that price which equates demand and supply, so that the quantity of goods supplied by producers exactly equals the quantity demanded by consumers.
3 Other things being equal, an increase in demand or a decrease in supply leads to a rise in price.
4 Similarly, a decrease in demand or an increase in supply leads to a fall in price.
5 In competitive conditions, in the long run, all firms tend to be marginal firms making normal profits and producing at the optimum (minimum average cost) level.
6 Where a firm has specific assets, it cannot leave the industry if price levels fall to the point where it is making less-than-normal returns on capital invested. Such a firm continues in production until price falls below average variable cost, when it shuts the plant down and waits for better times.

Exercises Set 9

1 Fill in the missing words in the sentences below:

(*a*) The price of a commodity rises when – is supplied.
(*b*) The price of a commodity rises when – is demanded.
(*c*) The price of a commodity falls either because – is supplied or because – is demanded, or both.
(*d*) In a competitive market, price is established where demand and supply are in – .
(*e*) A change in supply is caused by a change in the – of supply.

(f) An extension of supply results from an – in –.
(g) A change in demand is caused by a change in the – of demand.
(h) A contraction of demand results from an – in price.

2 Write about half a dozen lines on each of the following: (a) a demand schedule; (b) a supply schedule; (c) a graph showing a demand curve and a supply curve; (d) equilibrium price.

3 What are the 'laws' of supply and demand? Why do we write the word 'laws' in inverted commas?

4 What is equilibrium price? Consider in your answer the example of tomatoes on sale at Covent Garden Market in London: (a) in August; (b) in December. Account for any difference in the prices observed.

5 Why does the price of lettuces fluctuate more than the price of tinned soup?

6 Discuss the likely effect of: (a) a good harvest on the price of wheat; (b) a sudden frost on the price of autumn flowers; (c) a change to automation in the electronics industry on the price of television sets; (d) rising family income on the price of cars.
   Illustrate your answers with diagrams.

7 'In this industry once you have set up in production you cannot turn back. All you can do is keep production going and hope prices will be large enough to make it all worth while.'
   What sort of industry do you think this speaker was describing? Outline the problems of such an industry as far as price is concerned.

8 'United States' stockpiling for strategic reserves has virtually ceased. This has eased the markets for most primary products.'
   Discuss the likely effects on: (a) the price of copper; (b) the supply of magnesium; (c) the demand from Zambia for British manufactured goods (Zambia is a large copper producer).

9 'For the marginal firm in perfect competition average cost, marginal cost, average revenue, marginal revenue and price are all equal.' Explain, with the help of a diagram.

10 The prices of shares fluctuate daily. The prices of motor-vehicle accessories are more stable. Explain why.

Elasticity of demand and supply

**10.1
Definition of
elasticity**

The 'elastic' used in clothes extends and contracts under the influence of forces applied to it. Demand and supply similarly extend and contract under the influence of such forces as changes in price. It is often useful to know the degree of extension or contraction that will follow a given price change. For instance, a Finance Minister who is about to impose a tax of 10 per cent on some commodity with a view to raising revenue would like to know in advance the probable contraction in demand that his new tax will inevitably cause. The extension and contraction of demand and supply with changes in price has been termed the 'price elasticity of demand and supply'.

Price elasticity of demand is the responsiveness of the quantity demanded of a particular good to a small change in its price.

Price elasticity of supply is the responsiveness of the quantity supplied of a particular good to a small change in its price.

Since responsiveness changes at different points along most demand curves, price elasticity always refers to particular points along the curve– which is the same as saying it refers to a particular price. Thus the elasticity of demand for a commodity at £1.00 per unit might be different from its elasticity of demand at £0.50 per unit.

Elasticity of demand and elasticity of supply are relative measures, not absolute measures. Measuring change in absolute terms is not very helpful. As an example, if we lower the price of petrol by 1 per cent and as a result sell 40 000 litres more per week, this absolute figure sounds impressive. If we then compare it with weekly sales of 40 million litres we see that sales actually only rose by 0.1 per cent. The percentage figure gives us a much better idea of what really happened – an insignificant increase in business as a result of the price cut.

The usual formula for discovering price elasticities is

$$\text{\textit{Price elasticity of demand (or supply)}}$$

$$= \frac{\textit{Percentage change in quantity demanded (or supplied)}}{\textit{Percentage change in price}}$$

Besides price elasticity of demand it is possible to have **income elasticity of demand,** i.e. the responsiveness of demand to changes in income; and **population elasticity of demand,** i.e. the responsiveness of demand to changes in population. We also have **cross elasticities**, where a change in the *price* of one commodity produces changes in the *demand* for another.

Besides price elasticity of supply it is possible to have *factor cost* elasticity of supply, the responsiveness of supply to changes in factor prices.

**10.2
The price elasticity
of demand**

The price elasticity of demand is the responsiveness of the quantity demanded of a particular good to a small change in its price. If demand responds more than proportionately to a change in price the demand is said to be **elastic;** if it responds less than proportionately to a change in price it is said to be **inelastic**. Consider the following examples:

(a) Housewives demand potatoes every day, and regard them as a staple diet for the family. Suppose potato prices rise by 10 per cent. Will this cut back demand by 10 per cent? It is unlikely, it might even increase demand, for potatoes are inferior goods.

$$\frac{\textit{Percentage change in demand}}{\textit{Percentage change in price}} = \frac{\text{say} -1\%}{+ 10\%} = -\frac{1}{10} = -0.1$$

Hence the response of the quantity demanded to the change in price of the good is inelastic, i.e. a less than proportional response.

(b) The price of beef rises by 10 per cent. Will housewives cut back on their purchases of beef? Probably they will, for there are several good substitutes, such as lamb and pork. Suppose the demand drops by 25 per cent:

$$\textit{Elasticity} = \frac{-25\%}{+10\%} = -2\tfrac{1}{2}$$

The demand for beef is therefore elastic, i.e. a more than proportional response.

(c) The price of lettuces rises by 10 per cent and demand falls by 10 per cent.

$$\textit{Elasticity} = \frac{-10\%}{+10\%} = -1$$

The demand for lettuces is said to show **unitary elasticity**, i.e. the response is exactly proportional to the change in price.

The price elasticity of demand is nearly always negative, i.e. quantity falls as price rises, and quantity rises as price falls. By convention we disregard the minus signs, so in the above examples we would refer to the elasticities as 0.1, 2½ and 1 respectively.

10.3
Five typical cases of price elasticity of demand

It is difficult to be precise about elasticity without using mathematical terms which are beyond the scope of *Economics Made Simple*. Of the multitude of possible elasticities, the five most common cases are:

(a) infinite elasticity of demand with respect to price;
(b) zero elasticity of demand with respect to price;
(c) unitary elasticity of demand with respect to price;
(d) fairly elastic demand with respect to price;
(e) fairly inelastic demand with respect to price.

Let us first look at the limits of elasticity. These limits (infinite elasticity and zero elasticity) are illustrated and described in Figure 10.1.

10.3.1
Unitary elasticity

Midway between these two limits lies the case of unitary elasticity, where the responsiveness of demand is exactly proportional to a change in price. Figure 10.2 shows such a curve (see opposite).

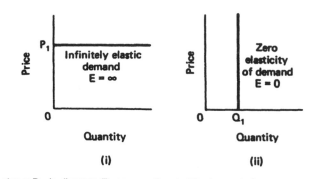

Figure 10.1 (i) Infinite elasticity of demand, i.e. E = ∞; (ii) Zero elasticity of demand, i.e. E = 0

Notes

1 At prices above P_1, in diagram (i), no quantity at all is demanded.

2 As the price falls to P_1, quantity increases to infinite demand.

3 This seems to be a highly theoretical situation, and it is chiefly to be regarded as a mathematical limit: elasticity can go no farther than infinity. It is, however, highly realistic if we think of the demand in perfectly competitive markets for the supplies of a single producer. If the market price is P_1 for 'Hoover' shares and I offer them for a little less than P_1 I shall immediately dispose of my entire supply.

4 By contrast, in diagram (ii) the quantity demanded does not change at all: there is absolutely zero response to any change in price, however great. The demand curve is a vertical straight line.

5 Again this is a highly theoretical situation, for it is difficult to imagine such a commodity. The demand for some things, for example, habit-forming drugs, is very inelastic. Addicts have been known to beg, borrow, steal, and even murder for the price of a shot of heroin. Demand does not change, however high the price.

These three cases are peculiar in that in each of them the whole curve shown has constant elasticity, either infinite elasticity, zero elasticity or unitary elasticity. These are not the only occasions when these measures of elasticity occur, they are simply interesting special cases. We shall see (in Figure 10.5) that any straight-line demand curve displays points where the responsiveness of demand is infinite, unitary and zero, respectively.

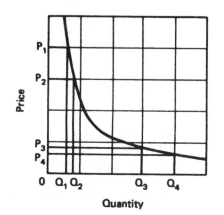

Figure 10.2 Unitary elasticity, $E = 1$

Notes

1 Here we must remember that it is the relative changes that are important. As we move down the price axis, equal absolute changes become relatively more and more significant. As we move along the quantity axis, equal relative changes have to be bigger and bigger in absolute terms. From P_1 to P_2 is a $33\frac{1}{3}$ per cent change in price; from Q_1 to Q_2 is a $33\frac{1}{3}$ per cent change in quantity. From P_3 to P_4 is also a $33\frac{1}{3}$ per cent change in price, while at this point a $33\frac{1}{3}$ per cent change in quantity requires demand to shift from Q_3 to Q_4.

2 It is often said that the slope of a demand curve gives an indication of the elasticity. But in this diagram elasticity is unitary everywhere (i.e. demand is changing proportionately to price all the way along the curve), even though the gradient of the graph varies from almost vertical to almost horizontal.

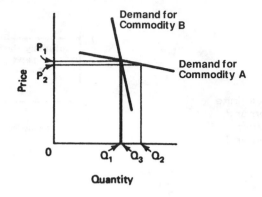

Figure 10.3 Demand curves with different elasticities at a given price

Notes

1 At a price of P_1 the quantity demanded of both goods is Q_1. This coincidence is purely fortuitous, for the demands for these goods are quite unrelated: they might be, for example, the demand for beef (Commodity A) and cigarettes (Commodity B).

2 Imagine a small change in price, say a reduction of 5 per cent, to P_2.

3 In the case of Commodity A the quantity demanded would change more than proportionately to Q_2 (it looks about a 25 per cent change). Therefore

$$Elasticity = \frac{25\%}{5\%} = 5$$

4 In the case of Commodity B the change, to Q_3, is less than proportional (say $2\frac{1}{2}$ per cent). Therefore

$$Elasticity = \frac{2\frac{1}{2}\%}{5\%} = \frac{1}{2}$$

5 It follows that where two demand curves pass through the same point the more gradually sloping curve is the more elastic of the two at this point. Remember that apart from the special cases already mentioned curves are not of constant elasticity all the way along the curve. Elasticity varies at every point, but at the point mentioned the curve for Commodity A is more elastic than the curve for Commodity B.

6 The numerical values of elasticity for points where demand is elastic must lie between 1 and infinity. In note (3) above the value is 5, which *is* a number between 1 and infinity.

7 The numerical values of elasticity for points where demand is inelastic must lie between 1 and zero. In note (4) above the value is $\frac{1}{2}$, which *is* a number between 1 and zero. (*Now return to Section 10.4.*)

**10.3.2
Fairly elastic and
fairly inelastic
demand**

Consider the demand curves shown in Figure 10.3 (see above) which intersect at the price P_1. These demand curves are not related in any way, but both goods can be bought at price P_1. What is the elasticity of such curves? The notes below Figure 10.3 explain their elasticity.

**10.3.3
Demand curves with
constant elasticity**

We cannot as a general rule talk about the elasticity of demand curves, for these are only three curves that have constant elasticity. They are:

(*a*) The perfectly elastic curve, Figure 10.1 (i), whose elasticity is infinite.

(*b*) The perfectly inelastic curve, Figure 10.1 (ii), whose elasticity is zero.

(*c*) The curve with unitary elasticity (Figure 10.2), whose elasticity is 1.

Other curves have different elasticities at each point along the curve, even though the absolute changes might appear to be regular. This is illustrated by the demand schedule and graph of Figure 10.4 and the calculations below it.

The typical straight-line demand curve is shown in Figure 10.5. It can be established mathematically that the elasticity along this curve varies from infinity at the price axis to zero at the quantity axis (see opposite).

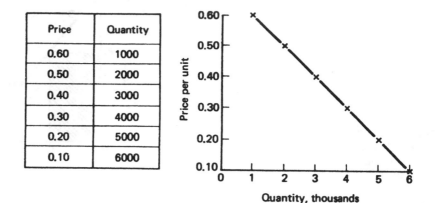

Price	Quantity
0.60	1000
0.50	2000
0.40	3000
0.30	4000
0.20	5000
0.10	6000

Figure 10.4 A demand schedule and its demand curve

Notes

What is the elasticity of demand at price of 0.40? If we are envisaging a decrease in price we have

$$\text{Elasticity} = \frac{\text{\% change in quantity demanded}}{\text{\% change in price}} = \frac{\dfrac{1{,}000}{3{,}000} \times 100}{\dfrac{0.10}{0.40} \times 100} = \frac{33\frac{1}{3}\%}{25\%} = 1.3$$

which represents a fairly elastic demand, whereas at a price of 0.20 the figures are

$$\text{Elasticity} = \frac{\dfrac{1{,}000}{5{,}000} \times 100}{\dfrac{0.10}{0.20} \times 100} = \frac{20\%}{50\%} = 0.4$$

which represents a fairly inelastic demand.

10.4
Total revenue and the elasticity of demand

To an entrepreneur the amount spent by consumers on his product is the total revenue that will accrue to him by his activities. It can be found by multiplying price by the quantity sold, so that at any point on a demand curve the total revenue earned is represented by the rectangle price × quantity, which is the area OQ_1DP_1 in Figure 10.6.

Entrepreneurs are interested in the total revenue, and the effect upon total revenue of changes in price. If an entrepreneur cuts price, will it lower total revenue? This depends on the elasticity of demand at this point. If demand is elastic, so that quantity sold increases more than proportionately, total revenue will rise. If demand is inelastic it will not pay to cut price, for a cut in price will reduce the amount spent by the public on the product.

In Figure 10.7 a straight-line curve (whose elasticity varies from infinity at the price axis to zero at the quantity axis, as explained earlier) is used to demonstrate the change in total income caused by a change in price.

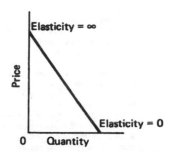

Figure 10.5 A straight-line demand curve

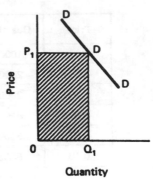

Figure 10.6 Total revenue of an entrepreneur or an industry

10.5
What determines the elasticity of demand?

The elasticity of demand depends chiefly on the availability of substitutes for the goods concerned. If there are no close substitutes for a commodity, demand for it will be inelastic, since customers will be forced to buy it if they want that particular class of satisfaction. Thus while the demand for cabbage is elastic, since there are many other vegetables, the demand for tobacco is relatively inelastic, since there are no close substitutes for tobacco. A shortage of close substitutes is a particular feature of goods that are habit-forming, like tobacco and alcohol, the demand for which tends therefore to be inelastic.

The other main factor affecting the elasticity of demand is the relative importance of the price of the goods to our total income. Where a commodity represents a very tiny fraction of total income, demand for it will be inelastic.

The satisfaction to be derived from a box of matches or a newspaper is great relative to its cost, so that demand will be unresponsive to price changes.

The student might like to assess the elasticity of demand for various everyday products, in the following way. Make a list of twenty items used or

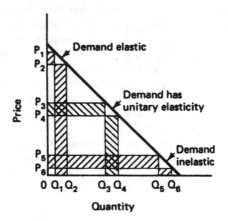

Figure 10.7 Changes of total revenue with price changes

Notes

1 A change from P_1 to P_2, where demand is elastic, results in a greater total income. The shaded area of extra income is greater than the shaded area of lost income, as quantity changes from Q_1 to Q_2.

2 A change from P_5 to P_6, where demand is inelastic, results in a decreased total income. The shaded area of income lost is greater than the shaded area of income gained as demand extends from Q_5 to Q_6.

3 Clearly somewhere between an infinitely elastic demand and a demand which has zero elasticity there lies a point where elasticity is unity. With a straight-line curve this point lies half-way along the curve.

4 Wherever the point of unitary elasticity lies, a change at that point will not alter total revenue, for the shaded area of revenue lost by the decreasing price equals the shaded area of revenue gained from the increased quantity sold. This can be seen in a change from P_3 to P_4. (Now return to Section 10.5.)

enjoyed since dawn of the present day, and consider what the elasticity of demand would be for each item if prices rose by 10 per cent.

Although it is sometimes said that the demand for luxuries is elastic and the demand for necessities is inelastic, this statement is not necessarily valid. Thus luxuries having no near substitutes, like diamond engagement rings, are usually in inelastic demand, while necessities like brown bread are inelastic demand, for there are dozens of similar products available on the shelves of supermarkets as substitutes.

10.6
The importance of elasticity of demand

There are a number of business decisions which are affected by the elasticity of demand. It is not easy to predict what the elasticity of demand is at any particular price, for the evidence available is usually slight. For example, a businessman may know what current sales are at current prices, and he may know that there are few close substitutes for his product. This may lead him to think that if he raises price, demand will prove to be inelastic, so that the change in sales will be less than proportional. But there is no guarantee that his decision is the right one. Since elasticity is different at every price, he may discover to his chagrin that the price increase was the last straw as far as his customers were concerned and that as a result sales fell more than proportionately.

Important decisions affected by elasticities include the following:

10.6.1
Price-fixing by a monopolist

The monopolist wishes to set such prices as will yield the maximum revenue. If we refer to Figure 10.7 again we see that when the demand is inelastic it will pay the monopolist to raise prices. Suppose comfortable profits can be made at a price of P_5. Profits can be raised if the price is raised towards P_4. When prices rise past P_3, however, demand will become elastic, and from that point on increased prices will be less profitable. The monopolist will therefore find it profitable to restrict output and force prices up but only to the point where the demand for the good becomes elastic.

10.6.2
Taxation policy of a chancellor

Taxes are imposed for a variety of reasons. The raising of revenue is one common aim, but the discouragement of undesirable industrial development is another.

If a Chancellor wishes to raise revenue he must tax goods which are in inelastic demand. Since there are no close substitutes for these goods, consumers will be unable to avoid the tax by reducing purchases of the goods. Taxes on tobacco, wines and spirits, and on tea have always been good revenue raisers in the UK. There are no close substitutes for any of these products, though the non-smoking teetotal citizen will avoid tax on the first two. Petrol tax has also been a very prolific source of revenue.

If a Chancellor wishes to influence what he deems to be undesirable developments he may do so by imposing taxation. The extent to which the policy succeeds will depend on the elasticity of demand, as where a tax to cut demand fails to do so and only produces extra revenue for the Chancellor.

10.6.3
Devaluation or depreciation of the currency

Manipulation of the currency is discouraged today. Briefly, to devalue or depreciate the currency is to lower it in value against all other currencies. This enables foreigners to buy our exports more easily, for they become cheaper, while at the same time foreign goods become more expensive to our own citizens. This should improve the balance of payments position, by increasing exports and reducing imports. The elasticity of demand for exports and imports may affect the success of this policy. If the demand for exports is elastic, so that even though each unit of exports sold brings in less foreign currency the extra demand more than offsets this, foreign earnings will increase. If the demand for exports is inelastic with respect to price the policy will be worse than useless, for the volume of exports will not increase, and those sold will bring in less earnings than before. There are similar effects on imports.

10.7 Income elasticity of demand

Income elasticity of demand is the responsiveness of demand to changes in income, and is found by the formula

Income elasticity of demand

$$= \frac{\textit{Percentage change in the quantity demanded of good X}}{\textit{Percentage change in aggregate income}}$$

Income elasticity of demand is very important in planning both industrial and social requirements. In Great Britain, for example, people seem to expect that their incomes will double every 25 years. In order to achieve such an increase in incomes the national income must grow, at a compound rate, by 2½ per cent per year. In other countries much more rapid rates of growth are being achieved, though the actual volume of goods being produced is not so large. Readers will remember that the volume of real goods needed to secure a 10 per cent increase in a country with a low standard of living is smaller than the volume needed to produce a 2½ per cent increase in a wealthy, developed country. It all depends on the size of the base from which the countries start. The best we can say is that a developing country with a 10 per cent growth rate will eventually overhaul a developed country with a 2½ per cent growth rate, but it will still take a considerable time.

When incomes rise people do not merely increase their demands for the goods they consumed formerly, but change to new products. They may enrich their lives by more varied diets, or more sophisticated consumer goods. Entrepreneurs and governments must predict these requirements, and form opinions as to the likely elasticities of demand for various goods and services as incomes rise.

Consider a rise in incomes of 10 per cent, which leads to the following changes in demand for the five commodities shown in Table 10.1 (See opposite).

Generally speaking, the demand for inferior goods has negative elasticity as incomes rise, while the demand for consumer durables and tertiary services rises more than proportionately with rising incomes.

10.8 Cross elasticity of demand

Sometimes it is helpful to know the changes in demand for a commodity that is likely to follow a change in the price of some other commodity. This is particularly true where the goods are substitutes for one another, or are complementary goods. For example, a change in the price of butter might cause a large change in the demand for margarine, while a change in the price of petrol might influence the demand for new motor vehicles.

Table 10.1 Income elasticity of demand

Effect on demand of a 10% increase in income	Commodity				
	A	B	C	D	E
Change in demand	Fall of 10%	No change	Rise of 1%	Rise of 10%	Rise of 50%
% Change in quantity	−10	0	1	10	50
% Change in income	10	10	10	10	10
Value of elasticity	−1	0	0.1	1	5
Income elasticity of demand	Negative income elasticity	Zero income elasticity	Inelastic demand with respect to income	Unitary income elasticity	Elastic demand with respect to income

(After studying this table return to Section 10.8 on page 120.)

The responsiveness of demand for one commodity to changes in the price of another commodity is called the cross elasticity of demand. The formula is:

$$Cross\ elasticity\ of\ demand =$$

$$\frac{Percentage\ change\ in\ quantity\ demanded\ of\ commodity\ X}{Percentage\ change\ in\ the\ price\ of\ commodity\ Y}$$

10.9
The price elasticity of supply

This is the responsiveness of supply to changes in price. Once again it is found by the formula

$$Price\ elasticity\ of\ supply =$$

$$\frac{Percentage\ change\ in\ quantity\ of\ good\ X}{Percentage\ change\ in\ price\ of\ good\ X}$$

10.9.1
Supply curves with constant elasticity

Once again perfectly elastic supply is a straight line, parallel to the X axis, while zero elasticity (supply completely unresponsive to price) is a straight line parallel to the price axis.

Perfectly elastic supply is rather improbable in real life, it indicates that at prices below P_1 suppliers are not prepared to supply at all, but at the price of P_1 they are prepared to supply any quantity required.

A supplier motivated by non-economic motives might behave this way, for example, if as a matter of principle he would not supply below the 'fair' price, nor charge more than the item was 'worth' even when demand was strong.

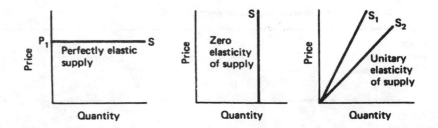

Figure 10.8 Supply curves with constant elasticity

Supply with zero elasticity is quite common in real life; the paintings of Rembrandt have zero elasticity of supply and sell on the market for whatever price they will fetch.

Unitary elasticity of supply is a special case. Every straight-line supply curve passing through the origin must have unitary elasticity. Quantity supplied must change proportionately to price if the 'curve' is to be both straight and through the origin.

10.9.2
When will supply be elastic (i.e. responsive to changes in price)?

Supply will be elastic (elasticity greater than 1) in the following cases:

(*a*) Where an entrepreneur or group of entrepreneurs produce for several different markets and can divert suppliers to the market offering the best rewards.

(*b*) Where the assets producing the good are non-specific. Thus an entrepreneur producing a variety of products with non-specific assets can turn production over easily from less profitable lines to more profitable ones. Similarly, a manufacturer with non-specific assets can leave an industry or enter an industry easily, but a manufacturer with specific assets must remain in production so long as there is any advantage from doing so (see Figure 9.8).

In both these cases an increase in price will quickly attract supplies into the market, while a decrease in price will drive supplies away, or discourage the supplier so that he reduces output.

10.9.3
Time and the elasticity of supply

Time has a great effect on the elasticity of supply. In the short run the supply of many items is inelastic. For instance, milk production cannot be raised until cows are brought into calf. Apple trees take several years to grow and tea gardens even longer. To build a new factory is not the work of a week or so, but may take years to design and equip. The effect of this time-lag on prices is illustrated in the next section.

10.10
Price fluctuations and price elasticity of demand and supply

Fluctuations in price are a source of much inconvenience both to producers and to consumers. In the market economies (as distinct from the planned economies) of the world the development of highly organised markets is an attempt to smooth out fluctuations in price. Chapter 11 is devoted to a full discussion of these matters.

Generally speaking, the prices of primary products fluctuate more than prices of secondary products. Not only are the agricultural products susceptible to interruptions of supply due to bad weather, crop diseases, etc., but all primary products tend to be carried long distances to the market, so that they are peculiarly susceptible to delays due to strikes, wars, or rumours

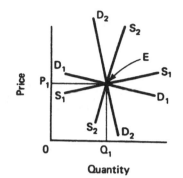

Figure 10.9 Demand
and supply curves with
different elasticities

Note: At the price P_1 the demand curve D_1 is more elastic than the demand curve D_2, and
the supply curve S_1 is more elastic than the supply curve S_2.

of wars. Diversion of shipping, for example, due to the closure of the Suez
Canal changed the pattern of supply for many products and led to a dramatic
growth in the size of oil-tankers and other bulk carriers.

Fluctuations in price are difficult to illustrate because of the ease with
which wrong ideas about elasticity can be conveyed. Readers are apt to
forget that elasticity refers only to a particular price: it is *not* constant all the
way along a demand curve or a supply curve, except in those special cases
already described of infinite elasticity, unitary elasticity and zero elasticity.

To avoid confusion, Figure 10.9 has been drawn showing two demand
curves and two supply curves meeting at a point. The diagram has then been
split into four parts, to illustrate the effect of four possible cases which cause
prices to fluctuate. These cases are:

(*a*) a change in demand, supply being elastic;
(*b*) a change in demand, supply being inelastic;

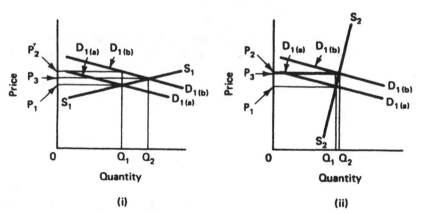

Figure 10.10 Elasticity
of supply and change of
demand: (i) supply
elastic; (ii) supply
inelastic

Notes
1 Demand is elastic at this point, like D_1 in Figure 10.9.
2 The result of an increase in demand in Figure 10.10 (i) is that price rises to P_2. Supply
   adjusts easily to the changed demand, turning out the increased quantity required. Price
   falls to P_3, with only a small final increase in price.
3 The result of an increase in demand in Figure 10.10 (ii) is that supply adjusts with difficulty
   to the changed demand. The price rises to P_2 and eventually settles at P_3 – a large price
   increase is necessary to encourage suppliers, because supply is inelastic.
4 The reader should work out on a piece of scrap paper what would have happened in each
   case if: (*a*) demand had decreased, instead of increased; (*b*) demand, instead of being
   elastic at this point like D_1 in Figure 10.9, had been inelastic like D_2 in Figure 10.9. (*Now
   see Figure 10.11 and page 124*)

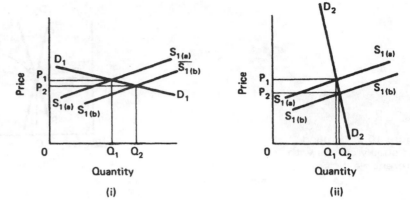

Figure 10.11 Elasticity of demand and change in supply: (i) demand elastic; (ii) demand inelastic

Notes

1 Supply is elastic at this point as in S_1 in Figure 10.9.
2 The result of an increased willingness to supply is that demand, in Figure 10.11 (i), extends rapidly to consume the increased supply offered. Price falls only slightly, and the increase in goods supplied is large.
3 The result of an increased willingness to supply in Figure 10.11 (ii) is that demand extends only slightly, price falls a good deal, and the extra quantity supplied is small.
4 The reader should again work out the effects of: (a) a decrease in supplies offered by producers; (b) the changes that would have resulted had the supply at this point, instead of being elastic as in S_1, been inelastic as in S_2 in Figure 10.9.

(c)   a change in supply, demand being elastic;
(d)   a change in supply, demand being inelastic.

Figure 10.10 shows the effect of a change of demand, when supply is elastic or inelastic, on the price of the commodity being demanded. (see page 123.)

Figure 10.11 (see above) shows the effect of a change in supply when demand is elastic, or inelastic, on the price of the commodity being demanded.

10.11 Summary of Chapter 10

1   Price elasticity of demand is defined as the responsiveness of the quantity demanded of a particular good to a small change in its price.
2   It is found by the formula:

$$\frac{\textit{Percentage change in quantity demanded of good X}}{\textit{Percentage change in price of good X}}$$

3   There are three demand curves with constant elasticity: the infinitely elastic curve, the unitarily elastic curve, and the curve with zero elasticity.
4   All other demand curves have elasticities which change along the curve. For such curves elasticity refers to a particular point on the curve, i.e. to a particular price.
5   Total revenue to the producer (i.e. total expenditure by the consumer) depends upon sales volume and price. Elasticity affects volume sold and has a great influence on total revenue.
6   Price elasticity of demand chiefly depends on the availability of close substitutes.
7   Price elasticity of supply is defined as the responsiveness of the quantity supplied to changes in price. Its formula is similar to that given in note (2) above.

8   Prices fluctuate widely if supply or demand are inelastic.
9   Prices are stable if supply or demand are elastic.
10 Primary producers suffer more from fluctuating prices than secondary producers.
11 Besides price elasticity of demand and supply, income elasticity of demand is also of interest.

Exercises Set 10

1   Define elasticity of demand. A refrigerator priced at £100.00 on the market is selling 1000 models per week. When the price is cut to £95.00 the sales increase to 1750 models per week. What was the elasticity of demand at a price of £100.00?

2   A motor car retailing at 4500 currency units is bringing in a total revenue of 45 000 000 per month. When the price is lowered to 4275 the total revenue increases to 49 500 000. What is the elasticity of demand at 4500?

3   Why are percentage changes more useful than absolute changes when comparing the effects of price movements? Illustrate your answer by reference to the elasticity of demand for two products, A and B, whose prices are cut by 10 per cent. Each improves its sales by 5 units per week. A had previous average weekly sales of 10 units, B had previously been selling 100 units per week on average.

4   In a perfect market the demand for the output of a single producer is infinitely elastic. Explain.

5   What is the relationship between the elasticity of demand and the total expenditure on a commodity by the consuming public?

6   Explain the term 'price elasticity of demand' and discuss its relevance to the taxation policy of a Finance Minister.

7   'It is no good cutting the price of our rail tickets,' said the accountant, 'the elasticities are against us in these affluent times.' What elasticities was he referring to? How were they operating against the railway company?

8   Draw and label fully: (*a*) an infinitely elastic demand curve; (*b*) a supply curve of zero elasticity; (*c*) a curve of unitarily elastic demand.

11   Competitive markets – the institutions where price is decided

11.1 Definition

A market is defined as a place where buyers and sellers are in contact with one another to fix prices.

This contact may be established directly, e.g. where retailers buy supplies at the wholesale produce markets, such as Convent Garden or Billingsgate: or indirectly through specialists, such as the broker-dealers and committed market-makers on the London Stock Exchange. Physical presence in the market is not necessary; indeed, the Foreign Exchange Market is largely conducted by computerised links.

Generally speaking, the major markets are such specialised affairs, and dealings are conducted in such large quantities, that the general public is ill equipped to deal upon them. For instance, the minimum contract for wheat on London's Baltic Exchange is 100 tonnes and the minimum contract for sugar is 50 tonnes on the London Sugar Futures Market. Such markets are called **highly organised markets,** and only experts may deal on them.

While absolute perfection in the market is difficult to achieve, some of these institutions come very close to the perfect competition imagined in theoretical economics, and equilibrium price is established in conditions where perfect knowledge of the market and complete absence of friction exist. A full list of these institutions as far as the UK is concerned is given below. Overseas readers are urged to consider the institutions of their own countries, and to decide how comparable they are with British institutions.

11.2 Competitive markets in Great Britain

A full list of these markets includes:

11.2.1 Commodity markets

(a) The London Metal Exchange in Plantation House, Fenchurch Street, where copper, tin, lead and zinc are bought and sold.

(b) Tea Services (London) Ltd in Sir John Lyon House, Upper Thames St.

(c) The London FOX (the Futures and Options Exchange), Commodity Quay, St Katherine's Dock. This new exchange resulted from the re-launch of a well-established group of commodity markets, The London Commodity Exchange, in new premises at St Katherine's Dock. London FOX offers futures and options contracts for cocoa, coffee, raw sugar, white sugar, potatoes, soya beans, wheat, barley, pigs, lamb and freight.

(d) The Uncut Diamond Market run in co-operation with the Diamond Corporation of South Africa.

(e) The London Bullion Market, under the auspices of the London Bullion Market Association. This organisation was set up in 1987 after the Bank of England – newly appointed as supervisor of the wholesale bullion market – made it clear that it preferred to deal with a single body for gold and silver. The two existing markets, the London Gold Market and the London Silver Market, accordingly amalgamated.

(f) The International Petroleum Exchange of London Ltd. There are 70 'Floor' seats in the Exchange at which representatives of the 46 'Floor Members' trade. Anyone, whether a member or not, can trade through the Floor Members.

11.2.2 **Financial markets**	(a) The Stock Exchange in Throgmorton Street. (b) The Discount Market, centred around Lombard Street and Cornhill. (c) The Foreign Exchange Market, now freed from control after 40 years, where bankers exchange pounds for foreign currencies. (d) The Eurocurrency Market and the Eurobond Market are markets where currencies which have escaped from their own territories can be borrowed by financiers. (e) The 'money market' is the market for short-term money. Like (d) above it has no real market-place, but is conducted over the telephone. (f) The Insurance Market centred around Lloyd's. (g) The Baltic Exchange in St Mary Axe, where shipping and air freight space can be chartered or hired. (h) LIFFE – the London International Financial Futures and Options Exchange. This exchange in new premises near Cannon Street railway station in the heart of London, has 420 trading booths and a 'Trading Floor' of 25 000 square feet. The trading booths have 450 dealer board consoles and there are 750 Information Display System colour screens so everyone can see the prices being quoted.

There are some 20 futures and options contracts which enable investors to protect themselves against changes in interest rates, and adverse movements in shares and bonds. Some 9 million contracts were made in the month of September 1992 alone, and on the single day of Wednesday 16 September 1992 the Exchange handled 886 110 futures and options contracts worth £254 000 million. This was the day the United Kingdom left the Exchange Rate Mechanism (ERM) and gives some idea of the huge amounts of money on the move that day.

11.2.3 **Wholesale produce markets**	These are very widespread, but the London ones are famous and attract produce from a wide area. They are: (a) Convent Garden, the fruit and vegetable market. This market has now been moved to a location outside central London, at Nine Elms. (b) Spitalfields, the fruit and vegetable market, now moved to Temple Mill in Hackney Marshes, from the original East End site. (c) Smithfield, the meat market. (d) Billingsgate, the fish market, now at West India Dock.
11.3 **Methods of dealing**	The methods of dealing in the commodity markets vary greatly because they are the result of a century or more of trading in the particular commodities concerned. To some extent the method is affected by the commodity itself.

Where a product has, or can be given, a uniform standard quality, dealings are made much easier, because the dealers know with certainly what they are buying and selling. For example, on the London Metal Exchange the commodities dealt in are called Standard Copper, Standard Tin, etc. The quality of these products can be scientifically tested and established.

Tea, on the other hand, is insusceptible to standardisation. The quality varies not only from growing area to growing area but also seasonal differences in rainfall, etc., make the product different from year to year in the same area. Even on a given bush the leaves vary from poor to top quality. Similarly, no two sheep give wool that is alike: some sheep are contented and docile, with a good fleece, while others are temperamental and grow a poor-quality fleece. Products such as tea and wool must therefore be sampled by the buyers before they can decide on a fair price.

In particular, if a commodity can be standardised so that dealers know with certainty what they are buying and selling it makes possible a 'futures' market.

Crossbred wool growers and users are continually looking for protection schemes to shield them from the effects of these inherent price risks, and futures trading is designed to provide an opportunity to insure their forward commitments, caused particularly by the time-span required for wool to pass through the various processes before it becomes a fully manufactured product.

As is common to most futures contracts trade operators use the market principally for hedging or for price risk protection and normally do not permit contracts to reach maturity. History has shown that fulfilment by physical delivery on futures markets has rarely exceeded 2 per cent of the contracts traded. Dealers buy and sell their futures contracts on the market, but the actual sales and deliveries are made on the 'spot' market – where the wool can actually be seen and delivered. The process is explained later (see page 136).

There are four main areas which are common to all futures markets and make trading possible. They are:

1   Standardisation of contract terms
2   Centralised trading
3   Clearing, and
4   Margining.

11.3.1
Standardisation of contract terms

A futures contract has been defined as 'an agreement to buy or sell a standard quantity of a commodity, of a prescribed quality, at a specified date in the future at a price established at the time the bargain is struck'. The parties must know exactly what they are agreeing to – hence the need for a standard product, both as to the amount contracted for and the quality concerned. The date the bargain is to take effect is also clear, so the only point at issue is the price, and when the price is agreed they have a firm bargain, and are bound to honour it.

11.3.2
Centralised trading

If bargains are to be made in a proper competitive manner, and the behaviour of the parties is to be upright and fair, we need an organised, centralised market to which all traders can come, at agreed times. There has traditionally always been a ring, or a 'floor' of a building where bargains can be struck (though to help traders sort out their books it has usually been the case that a certain amount of after-hours 'kerb-side' trading outside the trading ring has taken place). Today it is common for computerised trading to take place using screen displays which are accessible to all traders, and where bargains can be struck 'screen to screen'. The computer is central to this electronic 'trading floor' and deals are made through the electronic system.

11.3.3 Clearing

The term 'clearing' means that some central clearing house must ensure that all bargains are honoured. Usually the central clearing house assumes the role of principal to all transactions – i.e. it becomes the seller to every buyer and the buyer to every seller. This ensures that every contract is correctly performed according to the rules of the market concerned. This places the Clearing House at a considerable risk and to ensure it is able to honour all the bargains, it requires the parties to pay in 'margins'.

11.3.4 Margining

A margin is a sum of money believed to be enough to cover the risk (i.e. the chance that the price will move against one party or the other). The 'initial margin' is fairly large, but this deposit is repayable when the bargain is closed out, or when a trader – by selling a contract to someone else – ceases to be interested. It also earns interest in some markets.

Suppose a trader has put down an 'initial margin' but the price moves against him/her. A 'variation margin' will now be called for to cover the extra risk. These potential losses (or, of course, the price could move the other way to cause a potential profit) are settled every day with the clearing house. Finally the contract will be closed out when the date for fulfilment arrives.

In general, if a commodity can be standardised so that dealers know with certainty what they are buying and selling, it makes possible a 'futures' market. Futures markets are particularly useful in reducing the risks of business life (see page 136). The chief types of dealing are:

(*a*)   Auction sales
(*b*)   Ring trading or pit trading
(*c*)   Challenging
(*d*)   Private treaty
(*e*)   A special case – diamonds

(a) Auction sales

Auction sales occur where the product is not susceptible to standardisation. It must be sampled beforehand if the buyers are to decide a fair price. At the London Tea Auctions in the Tea Trade Centre the buying brokers sit round in tiered seats while the brokers representing the tea growers in India, etc., mount the rostrum to auction their lots. The buying brokers know which particular lots they require and have decided the limits of prices to which they will go. The highest bid wins, but sellers may specify a reserve price below which they will not sell.

(b) Ring trading or pit trading

Ring trading is a method of trading used at the Metal Exchange and the Sugar Exchange in Mark Lane. The name originates from the use of a chalk ring on the floor in years gone by to separate the buyers from the sellers.

In the Metal Exchange the ring now consists of a circle of curved benches, and there are 40 members who take their seats at 12 noon for the first of the three daily sessions. Dealings are allowed for five minutes only in each metal, and are started by the Secretary of the Exchange with the hanging up of a notice bearing the name of the metal to be dealt in and the appropriate words; for example 'Tin, ladies and gentlemen, tin'. Members with tin to sell shout their offers, and those wishing to buy approach the seated sellers. Clerks standing behind make a note of the deals concluded. After five minutes the notice is changed, and the cry 'Copper, ladies and gentlemen, copper' is heard.

Besides these open-market periods when trading takes place in a very public way, private contracts are concluded outside market hours between dealers who wish to get their books straight or to complete unfilled orders. This may be done in the centre of the Metal Exchange floor, in private offices or by telephone.

In the Raw Sugar Market buyers and sellers meet inside a marked area of the floor to make binding contracts by open outcry. Sugar prices fluctuate widely because sugar is a vital food used in many food-processing factories as well as in ordinary households. Changes in the world-wide situation may cause demand to rise suddenly. Entry into the EC has caused some difficulties, since European beet sugar is replacing cane sugar to a considerable extent. Readers might like to see the list of countries interested in deals in raw cane sugar on the Raw Sugar Futures Market at 'London Fox. It reads: Australia, Argentina, Barbados, Belize, Brazil, Colombia, Costa Rica, Cuba, the Dominican Republic, El Salvador, Ecuador, Fiji, French Antilles, Guyana, Guatemala, Honduras, India, Jamaica, Malawi, Mauritius, Mexico, Mozambique, Nicaragua, Peru, the Philippines, Reunion, South Africa, Swaziland, Taiwan, Thailand, Trinidad, the United States of America and Zimbabwe. Notice how many of these are Third World countries, some of them entirely dependent on their sales of raw sugar.

One of the sugar markets at London Fox, the White Sugar Futures Market, is operated with electronic trading, screen to screen, and does not use open outcry.

Open outcry is very widely used at these markets as the traditional competitive way of trading. At London Fox open outcry is the rule for the cocoa, coffee, soyabean, pigmeat, barley, wheat, potatoes, lamb, raw sugar and BIFFEX markets. The BIFFEX market is the Baltic Freight Index Market used for buying space on ships at a future date to hedge against possible increases in freight charges.

Pit trading At the International Petroleum Exchange of London the trading is carried out in 'pits' by open outcry. A pit is a marked circular area on the trading floor of the Exchange, where traders must stand while executing futures trades. Bids and offers are shouted across the pits. All 'Floor' traders have to pass a series of examinations before they are allowed to trade in the pits. This ensures a high level of competence and experience on the floor.

There are five main contracts (see Table 11.1 on page 132) but other contracts are available and although a new contract usually takes some time to attract enough participants to be viable, in the long term the Exchange is growing in influence. It is looking particularly at out-of-hours electronic trading since petroleum is of world-wide interest and 24-hour trading is already taking place.

In the Coffee Market, Mark Lane, a similar trading method is used. It is called 'open outcry' on the floor of the market, and calls are made four times a day at 10.45 a.m., 12.30 p.m., 2.45 p.m. and 4.50 p.m. The wide range of qualities and varieties on offer in world coffee markets makes 'trading in actuals' a complex operation, and dependent entirely on the sellers and buyers honouring their contracts. For instance, if the grade, size, roast or 'cup' of a consignment of coffee proves to be different from the original sample, disputes can and do arise. There is no arbitration body to decide such disputes, probably because no one has more knowledge of the product than the dealers themselves.

(c) Challenging

The London gold and silver bullion markets are less boisterous, because the number of dealers authorised to deal in these metals is limited. The half-dozen brokers sit around a small table and challenge one another until a firm price is agreed. This is said to be the price at which gold has been 'fixed' for the day, and the room where the brokers sit is therefore called the 'Gold Fixing Room'.

Whether a perfect market can be said to exist when the number of buyers and sellers is limited to half a dozen is debatable. To the extent that they are speaking on behalf of most of the users of these metals, it probably approaches perfection.

(d) Private treaty

Private treaty is the method used by the dealers on the Stock Exchange, the Baltic Exchange, the Foreign Exchange Market, the Corn Exchange and the Insurance Markets. In the Copra Market the business is done mainly in the offices of the firms themselves. In the General Produce Market private treaty now fixes the price of most of the bargains. In the Rubber Market the floor of the house is used to conduct business, but it is by private treaty and not open outcry. Private 'treaty' means private discussion of the price to be paid. Despite the fact that the bargains they strike are private contracts between the parties, fierce competition exists in these markets.

(e) Diamond market

Some 85 per cent of all newly mined rough gem and industrial diamonds are sold through the London based Central Selling Organisation (CSO), whose companies sort, value and sell rough diamonds to the world's major diamond cutting centres and industries. Companies within the CSO enter into agreements with the various diamond producers to purchase their entire output. In times when certain categories (there are over 2000 of them) are in excess of demand, the CSO will hold them in reserve and offer them for sale only at a rate at which world markets can absorb them. This has created price stability for diamonds, confidence in the diamond industry and ensured that the producers do not have to worry about fluctuation in demand.

When the diamonds reach the CSO in London they are sorted and valued according to size, colour, shape and quality before they can be sold. Industrial diamonds are sold through Industrial Distributors (Sales) on a day-to-day basis to meet the demands of modern industry. Gem diamonds are sold at the ten annual sights held by The Diamond Trading Company. The Company's customers are advised of the sights and send in their requirements which are equated against present stocks. They will then come to London to inspect their diamonds, although they cannot argue about the price of the diamonds except in the case of a large stone. The customer can refuse to take the entire parcel but cannot merely take any particular part of it; however, should an error in valuation occur this would be rectified.

In Hatton Garden, close to the CSO offices, there are many traders in diamonds both rough and polished. There, diamonds are available in much smaller quantities than those supplied by the CSO.

At the time of writing (1995) the diamond market is going through a difficult time. The reason is that the unsettled state of some countries in Africa has brought large numbers of 'illicit' diamonds onto the markets. The danger is that these diamonds will flood the market to such an extent that those who hold diamonds, whether dealers or members of the general public (we have all heard that diamonds are a girl's best friend), may find that prices fall seriously and reduce the value of their holdings. The Central Selling Organisation is doing its best to buy up these diamonds at fair prices (for it knows how poor are some of the diggers trying to market them). Whether its resources are large enough to buy up the illicit stores remains to be seen, but it is under severe pressure at the moment.

Most of the diamonds are re-exported and are an important foreign exchange earner for the UK.

Details of some of the main markets are given in Table 11.1.

Table 11.1 British terminal markets

Market	Minimum contract	Price quoted in
London FOX (Futures and Options Exchange)		
Cocoa Futures	10 tonnes	£ per tonne
Cocoa Trade Options	10 tonnes	£ per tonne
Robusta Coffee Futures	5 tonnes	$ per tonne
Coffee Traded Options	5 tonnes	$ per tonne
Raw Sugar Futures	50 tonnes	$ per tonne
Raw Sugar Traded Options	50 tonnes	$ per tonne
White Sugar Futures	50 tonnes	$ per tonne
White Sugar Traded Options	50 tonnes	$ per tonne
Potato Futures	20 tonnes	£ per tonne
Potato Traded Options	20 tonnes	£ per tonne
Wheat Futures	100 tonnes	£ per tonne
Wheat Traded Options	20 tonnes	£ per tonne
Barley Futures	100 tonnes	£ per tonne
Barley Traded Options	100 tonnes	£ per tonne
Soyabean Meal Futures	20 tonnes	£ per tonne
Soyabean Meal Traded Options	20 tonnes	£ per tonne
Pig Futures	3250 kg	pence per kg
Pig Traded Options	3250 kg	pence per kg
Lamb Futures	2000 kg	pence per kg
Biffex Futures	BF Index	£10 per point
Biffex Traded Options	BF Index	£10 per point
London Metal Exchange		
Copper Market	25 tonnes	£ per tonne
Tin Market	5 tonnes	£ per tonne
Zinc Market	25 tonnes	£ per tonne
Lead Market	25 tonnes	£ per tonne
International Petroleum Exchange		
Brent Crude Oil Futures	1000 barrels	$ per barrel
Brent Crude Oil Traded Options	(42 000 US gallons)	$ per barrel
Gas Oil Futures	100 tonnes	$ per tonne
Gas Oil Traded Options	100 tonnes	$ per tonne
Unleaded Gasoline Futures	100 tonnes	$ per tonne

11.4
Specialists who promote perfection in the markets

The specialists who operate on highly organised markets fulfil a variety of functions. Their range of activities is wide, and no general description can hope to give a clear picture of a particular market or a particular transaction.

11.4.1
Merchant functions

Where a dealer buys and sells on his own account, as a principal to the transaction and not as an agent, he is performing the merchanting function. The commodity belongs to him, to be resold at a profit at some future time. Whether or not he actually takes possession before reselling depends on the trading period in the market. In some situations, like the fruit and vegetable markets, physical possession of the goods is commonplace; in other markets the vast majority of the items dealt in are not handled physically by the dealers.

11.4.2
Agent functions

Some dealers act only as intermediaries between the producer and the retailer, selling the goods on a commission basis. Such dealers are called **agents**. Strictly speaking, an agent is anyone who does something on behalf of another. In commerce we call them 'mercantile agents'. A mercantile agent is defined in the Factors Act of 1889 as a person 'having in the customary course of his business as an agent the authority either to sell goods, or to consign goods for the purpose of sale, or to buy goods, or to raise money on the security of goods'.

The two most important types of mercantile agent are **brokers** and **factors**. The difference between them is a difference in the extent to which they handle goods.

(a) Brokers' functions

Brokers merely sell the goods for their principals: delivery of the goods sold is left to be arranged later, for the broker does not have them in his possession. A broker knows the field of activities and the correct procedures to follow. He knows who is short of a particular commodity and who has (or will have) supplies available. His function is to bring buyer and seller together at an economical price for both. Mutual benefit is the essence of contracts, and brokers are agents who arrange contracts for the benefit of their principals. Thus stockbrokers buy and sell shares at the best market price available. Lloyd's brokers buy insurance for their clients from underwriters at the lowest premiums possible, while shipbrokers negotiate on the Baltic Exchange to sell space on ships and aircraft to cargo owners trying to move their goods.

(b) Factors' functions

The factor (unlike the broker) is in possession of the goods. He sells the goods for his principal, delivers them up to the buyer for payment, and renders an account (less his commission) for the sums due.

11.5
Speculators and the commodity markets

A chief feature of highly organised markets is the development of speculative functions. Practically all dealers on the market engage in speculation at some time or another, and some dealers specialise in these activities. The historical development of this function is interesting.

In any productive process there are a number of activities to be undertaken. Formerly these were all done by one firm. For instance, in the early days of the cotton trade, merchants went to America, bought cotton,

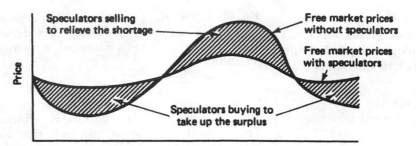

Figure 11.1 Damping out fluctuations with speculation

Notes to Figure 11.1

1 The natural tendency of all primary products is to have periods of market activity ranging from 'slumps' to 'booms', with low prices in slumps and high prices in booms. The free market prices are therefore shown in the diagram as the wilder fluctuations, from very low prices to very high prices.

2 If the speculators buy when prices are low (storing the product temporarily until it can command a better price) they strengthen demand in what would otherwise be a slump period, and keep prices up (which benefits the primary producer).

3 When there is a shortage of the product, and prices rise, the speculator releases the stored commodity onto the market and takes his/her profits. This reduces the 'boom', relieving the shortage, and keeping prices down a bit, to the benefit of the secondary producers needing the raw material concerned.

4 Students should now understand why the speculator (so frequently referred to by unthinking people as a 'profiteer') feels aggrieved when accused of 'creating a shortage'. Speculators do not create shortages. They are the only people who are relieving the shortage when prices are high, and are helping to prevent prices going through the roof. The fact that they make profits is not their fault – it is the high demand that is causing the profits. They accept them gratefully (and pay taxes on them) because they need resources to buy more supplies when the next slump makes it possible to do so. Do not abuse the speculators! If you envy them their profits, join in. It is a competitive market, and anyone may join who is prepared to run risks.

arranged export procedures, shipped the cotton to Lancashire, running the risks of its physical loss or damage and the economic risks of changes in its price, paid import duties and finally manufactured it.

Gradually these functions were split away from one another. The shipowner, for example, appeared as a specialist functionary, and the insurance underwriters assumed the risks of physical loss of the cargo. With the development of the highly organised markets the speculator appeared. His function is to carry risks through time so that the manufacturers can make contracts involving the future manufacture of finished goods in the face of fluctuating raw-material prices. If raw-material prices fluctuate, and on page 122 we have seen that they do fluctuate because of the inelastic nature of both supply and demand, then a manufacturer's contracts and tenders could be seriously upset. By assuming these risks, the speculator performs a useful function (see Figure 11.1).

11.5.1
How speculation works

The purely speculative activity depends on the prediction of future prices based on informed opinion. It cannot arise in situations where price control over a commodity is established by a state trading organisation. For example, at one time a London Shellac Market operated. Shellac at that time was used in large quantities to make gramophone records. When the Indian government stepped in to fix prices the traders were sold whatever they required at a fixed price, however large the quantities they ordered. Speculators could not therefore make a profit by buying when prices were low and selling when prices rose higher. The market could not operate and was forced to close. Today Shellac is of less importance in world trade since other materials are now used for records and discs.

Table 11.2 How speculation works

Present time	Action of speculator	Effect of speculation	Future time	Action of speculator	Effect of speculation
Supplies abundant		Supplies cleared from market	Supplies short		Shortage relieved
Demand weak		Demand strengthened	Demand strong (as predicted by speculator)		Demand satisfied
	Buys supplies and holds as stock			Releases stocks and takes his profits	
Price low		Prices firmer to benefit of primary producers who therefore do not let specific assets waste away	Prices high		Prices eased to benefit of secondary producers who therefore do not let specific assets waste away

Suppose the speculator expects a future rise in prices. His activities are outlined in Table 11.2. To follow this table properly students should read straight down the first column, then the second column, etc. In Table 11.2 the references to specific assets (assets which are only of use in one particular industry and if demand in that industry is weak the specific assets will be abandoned, or left to deteriorate) may be illustrated as follows:

(a) Primary producers

Weak demand for primary products may result in the eventual destruction of coffee plantations, return of rubber plantations to the jungle, abandonment of uneconomic mines, etc. The speculators' activities mean such actions are no longer necessary, and the very reverse may occur: new plantations may be laid out with the most modern methods being used.

(b) Secondary producers

Faced with high prices for raw materials, the factory owners may reduce activity to less than optimum levels, or may even close down plant. The release of speculative stocks lowers price and enables plant to continue in use, or even be expanded and improved.

11.6 'Spot' markets and 'futures' markets

Markets which deal in goods for prompt delivery are called **'spot' markets** because the goods are there on the spot and can be delivered as soon as payment is made. This is true of tea, raw wool, gold and diamonds.

11.6.1 Futures markets

'Futures' markets, or terminal markets, are markets where the goods being bought and sold are not available yet, but will become available in the future. It is of the greatest importance that 'futures' prices should be firm, both to the buyer and the seller. Since an understanding of 'futures' is essential to our study of markets, let us see why the buyer of copper, or tin, or rubber needs to have firm prices for his goods, even though he does not want them for three months, or six months.

11.6.2
The importance of 'futures' prices

(a) To the buyer

Imagine a manufacturer who is submitting a tender for the supply of copper piping, radiators and boilers for a heating installation. The job is to be carried out in July, but tenders must be submitted by March 1. In deciding his price for the job the manufacturer will need to know his raw-material prices. However, these fluctuate day by day. Today's price will not do for the basis of the contract, unless the manufacturer can actually buy the copper today and keep it. This would tie up his capital and present him with storage problems. If he can find someone who will sell him 'future' copper, for delivery in July at a firm price, he will be able to submit his tender. That tender will include a profit on the contract. Should the price of copper rise above his 'future' price it will not affect him. The supplier will still have to supply at the agreed price. Should the price of copper fall, the buyer will have to honour his agreement, even though he could buy more cheaply on the open market. This will not worry the buyer, because he will still earn a reasonable profit from the contract.

(b) To the seller

Suppose the supplier of the copper mentioned above is the selling organisation of a nationalised industry in Zambia. The industry has wages to pay, development to finance, transport and processing charges to be met. It will feel happier if some at least of its eventual output is sold already. To sell 'futures' at firm prices gives the industry a guaranteed market for some of its output. The chief worry facing producers is the prospect of a fall in the world price of their goods. If the 'bottom falls out of the market' the producers may face serious losses. It is for this reason that they are willing to accommodate buyers anxious to insure against a rise in price.

A futures contract is essentially a transaction between two parties who require to cover themselves against opposite risks, one fearing a rise in price, the other a fall.

11.7
Hedges – shelter from the bitter economic winds

The buyers and sellers mentioned above are willing to buy and sell 'futures' at firm prices so that some of the risk is taken out of their specialist trades. It is inconvenient, however, for them to look for one another, for they are busy with their proper occupations. This is where the speculator, whose proper occupation is to bear the risks of price fluctuations, plays his part. The buyer of copper and the seller of copper make their contracts with the speculator. Such contracts are called 'hedging' contracts. There are many different types of 'hedges', but all are designed to protect the contracting party against some business risk. Examples are:

(a) A selling hedge

In January a wool grower with an expected clip of 63 bales of wool which he expects to shear in April–May considers covering himself for the price of his wool. He works out his costs of production and the margin of profit needed and sees that he needs to get at least 425 cents per kilo clean. He sees

Table 11.3 How hedging works

Selling hedge		Buying hedge	
Futures	Physical	Futures	Physical
January Sells three May Futures contracts @ 430 cents per kg clean	No transaction	*January* Buys three May Futures contracts @ 430 cents per kg	Tenders for future delivery at 440 cents per kg
April No transaction	Shears sheep	*April* No transaction	No transaction
May Buys three contracts @ 415 cents (profit 15 cents per kg)	Sells wools at 415 cents	*May* Sells three contracts @ 415 cents (loss 15 cents per kg)	Buys wool at 415 and delivers it at 440 as agreed (profit 25 cents per kg)
Total earned 430 cents per kg		Total earned 10 cents per kg (25–15 = 10)	

that the May futures price is trading at 430 cents, and sells three contracts of 21 kilos each.

In May the price has fallen to 415 cents. He sells his wool on the open market at this price and also buys back three futures contracts which are now trading at 415 cents. He is therefore paid 15 cents per kilo on these contracts – he sold three at 430 and bought three at 415. The result is that he receives altogether 415 cents per kilo on the sale of his wool plus 15 cents per kilo on the hedging contract i.e. 430 cents altogether. This is what he hoped to get originally.

(b) A buying hedge

A wool merchant is asked to tender for the supply of 63 bales of wool to a manufacturer in May. The current price is 440 cents per kilo. He sees that the May futures price is 430 cents per kilo, and decides to tender for the delivery in May at 440 cents per kilo, a profit of 10 cents per kilo. The tender is accepted. There is no point in buying the wool now (at 440 cents) and paying storage charges and interest on the money tied up in it. Instead he buys 3 futures contracts (21 bales per contract) at 430 cents per kilo. In May the price has fallen to 415 cents per kilo. He buys the wool on the open market at 415 cents per kilo and delivers it to the manufacturer at 440 cents per kilo as promised. The profit is therefore 25 cents per kilo, but he now has to undo his futures contract. He does this by selling 3 contracts at 415 cents per kilo – a loss of 15 cents per kilo. So the final result is that he makes a profit of only 10 cents per kilo – which is the 'fair' profit he hoped to get out of the contract. What actually happened on these two hedging contracts is shown in Table 11.3 above.

**11.7.1
Settling futures
contracts**

The vast majority of futures contracts are not pressed to maturity. The manufacturer who has hedged disposes of the hedge if and when the risk run on his normal contract comes to an end. By selling the futures contract he liquidates it without physical delivery of the commodity having to take place. Despite the high probability that the contracts will never come to maturity, the risk is always there and the market traders are alert to the need to preserve their good names by ensuring that deals are honoured.

Terminal contracts are therefore registered with the London Produce Clearing House, on standard forms provided by the Clearing House and in accordance with the rules of the Terminal Market concerned. Both buyers and sellers are required to lodge with the Clearing House a deposit which is held until the contract is liquidated. If the price moves against either party, so that the deposit would not be great enough to buy him out of his difficulty, he must increase the deposit by paying in a 'margin', which is reclaimed if prices recover in his favour.

Like all clearing houses, the London Produce Clearing House eliminates intermediate buyers and sellers to establish who is finally dealing with whom. These actual contracting parties will be involved in the final settlement.

11.8
The economic status of speculation

One of the most difficult subjects facing the student of economics is the status of the speculator. Is the speculator a valuable member of the community, shouldering burdens others are unwilling to bear? Or is he a secret manipulator, creating market situations which will be profitable to his firm? Let us consider the points for and against speculation.

11.8.1
Points in favour of speculative activities

Middlemen are to be found in various fields of activity; many of the functions they perform are beneficial to the community, and would have to be performed by someone even if the middleman did not exist. These functions include:

(a) The holding of stocks

This is a highly specialised activity. It involves carrying goods through time, against the ravages of Nature, their own inherent vices and the criminal or negligent activities of human beings. Nature attacks with microbes, insect pests, vermin, damp, desiccation, fading by sunlight, electrolytic action and in many other ways. Inherent vices include chemical decomposition, disease and death of livestock, susceptibility to spontaneous combustion, etc. Accidental damage, negligence, and various types of theft are the commonest human causes of loss of stock values.

(b) The breaking of bulk and the marketing of goods

These two activities go hand in hand. The middleman often removes from the manufacturer the burden of marketing his goods. He often handles the transport side of the operation. He buys in bulk, and breaks the consignments down to the needs of the eventual retailer. By dealing with many manufacturers he presents a variety of goods which retailers can select, so that the total volume of transactions; is reduced. One-hundred retailers dealing personally with 100 manufacturers requires 10 000 transactions. The middleman can reduce this to a mere 200 transactions; 100 between the retailers and the middleman, 100 between the middleman and the manufacturers.

(c) The carrying of risks

Speculators in many fields carry risks which the ordinary manufacturer or private citizen is unwilling to bear. That these risks are serious ones can be seen by the onerous qualifications for entry to the organised markets. A member of Lloyd's requires a personal fortune of £75 000 before entering, and his affairs are then subject to a compulsory audit of the utmost stringency every year. Unlimited liability is also a feature of many of these institutions. The carrying of speculative risks promotes business activity generally, benefiting not only the parties making use of the facilities but also the general public. The level of employment is raised by the greater confidence businessmen have that enterprises will be profitable. The increased scale of business thus made possible, means cheaper goods for everyone.

(d) Speculation is a specialist function

If specialisation is a good thing in general (remember Adam Smith found it to be the source of the wealth of nations), then the performance of risk-carrying functions by specialists is *prima facie* desirable. We have seen that in perfect or near-perfect markets the operations of these specialists provides a residue of dealers so essential to the creation of a market at all. There must be someone always willing to buy, or willing to sell, if the ordinary members of the public are to be able to obtain supplies when they require them, or dispose of surpluses when they have them to spare. Such activities are in the interests of all.

(e) Speculative profits are the result of high prices, not the cause of high prices

When a speculator makes profits it is because the ordinary movement of supply and demand has caused prices to rise. In these circumstance his accumulated stocks can be disposed of at more than normal profits. He is not the cause of the shortage, but the only person trying to relieve it. In the process of doing so he hopes to earn good profits which compensate him for losses on other transactions. Since speculation is a competitive business, free entry to those envious of the profits earned is available – but only of course to those who can meet the financial entry requirements.

These are the defences put up by speculators to justify their activities, and there is a good deal of truth in them. We could unhesitatingly support these claims if in fact speculators always acted absolutely honourably.

**11.8.2
Points against speculative activities**

(a) Market responses are speculator-induced

The fact is that speculators do, to some extent, influence the market. In particular, many of the responses of the market are induced by speculators for their own advantage. The 'bear' who sells stocks in expectation of a fall in price induces the very response that he is hoping for. The sales he makes force market price down, and create a pattern of nervousness on the market which is to the disadvantage of the general public if personal circumstances force them to sell at this time. The 'bear' who buys back what he originally sold at a cheaper price has profited at the expense of an 'innocent' victim of market forces. It is made worse by the fact that the 'bear' may not have had any shares to sell in the first place. There is something unsavoury about a system in which a person is able to profit by selling shares he does not own to the detriment of a genuine investor. Similarly, there is something unsavoury about a 'stag', who does not want to invest in a company, applying for a large number of shares in the hopes of selling them at a quick profit. He may get a big allotment of shares, while a genuine investor is refused any shares because his application is too small.

(b) The market must follow the least scrupulous speculator

Even when strict codes of conduct are laid down and everyone is paying lip service to the maintenance of high professional standards of behaviour, the market is powerless when external forces or the pressure of events are mounting. In some recent foreign-exchange crises this has been apparent. International pressures have been pushing the revaluation and devaluation of currencies in certain directions. There is always someone with less scruples, or more to lose, than the next man. When this happens the flood barriers are down and speculative pressure mounts to promote the very events which are considered undesirable. To be left behind in such a race is to court disaster. It is difficult for the individual speculator to go against the main stream of activity. Indeed, he must often join in and swim with the current to preserve his financial position. Only a central bank with virtually limitless resources can hope to swim against the tide.

Today the worst abuses of speculation have been contained and controlled in most countries – partly by legislation, partly by taxation aimed at creaming off super-profits for the benefit of the mass of the people, and finally by a proper sense of self-discipline and the establishment of codes of conduct. At the same time the borderline between legitimate protection of one's own financial position and activity to take advantage of the market is a fine one about which it is difficult for a panel of investigators to agree. In the last analysis the choice lies between a free-enterprise society and a controlled economy.

**11.9
OPEC and similar groupings**

Reference has already been made to the collapse of the London Shellac Trading Association which ceased to trade when shellac became the subject of price control in India. Markets of this type can only function where there is a free play of market forces and those buying and selling on the market can take advantage of a surplus to stock up for future sales when the product is in short supply. When the world's producers co-operate together to fix prices in a cartel such as OPEC (the Organisation of Petroleum Exporting Countries), free markets in the commodity concerned are seriously hampered. Any over-production is stockpiled in national reserves, and speculators are unable to play any part in the system.

**11.10
Summary of Chapter 11**

1 A market is a place where buyers and sellers are in contact with one another to fix prices.
2 A wide variety of highly organised markets exists to fix prices for the major commodities of the world. There are similar markets for insurance, sea and air cargo space, money and stocks and shares.
3 The methods of dealing in these markets are designed to promote perfection in the market by ensuring homogeneity of products, common knowledge of prices, and elimination of friction and discriminatory dealings. The number of buyers and sellers is large, to promote competition.
4 The specialists in these markets have expert knowledge and large resources; they operate within a code of conduct which is designed to promote fair dealing on behalf of the general public. In particular, the activities of speculators on these markets, while generally beneficial and a major buttress of economic activity, must be supervised by codes of behaviour or legislation.

Exercises Set 11

1 What is a highly organised market? What is a perfect market? Discuss whether (*a*) the Stock Exchange or (*b*) the London Metal Exchange fits both descriptions.

2 'A free market in diamonds is desirable.' Discuss the implications of this statement for: (*a*) a Sierra Leone citizen working diamonds outside the control of his government; (*b*) a diamond producer inside the present controlled arrangements; (*c*) a retired actress reluctantly having to sell diamonds given to her when she was 'the toast of London'.

3 How does a 'futures' market help the manufacturer in his pursuit of ordinary business?

4 Speculators are less active in a market where the goods on sale are insusceptible to standardisation. Why is this? Give examples of both types of market.

5 What do you understand by 'hedging'? What is the effect of a hedging contract taken out by a manufacturer who feared a fall in prices, if in fact prices rise?

6 'Speculators reduce fluctuations in market prices.' 'Speculators exacerbate fluctuations in the market, so that frenzied selling, or frenzied buying occurs.' Are both these statements true? Explain each of them.

7 What is meant by a 'minimum contract'? How would such a minimum prevent an ordinary person from dealing on a market?

8 Market price is determined by the interaction of demand and supply. Explain how this would take place in a market conducted by 'open outcry'. Can it also be true of markets conducted by 'private treaty'?

9 'A perfect market has many buyers and sellers. The general public may not deal with underwriters at Lloyd's. Therefore Lloyd's is not a perfect market.' Do you agree? Discuss these statements.

10 'Middlemen perform functions others prefer not to perform.' What are these functions? Are they necessary, and what rewards do middlemen receive?

12   Monopoly, oligopoly and monopolistic competition

12.1
What is monopoly?

Monopoly means supply by only one person or firm. It can exist only where the product being supplied has no close substitutes and the supplier, for some reason, is able to exclude other firms from producing it.

It may arise in the following ways:

(a) Personal supply by a specialist or talented individual. Examples are concert violinists, hair stylists, and fashion designers.

(b) Supply under patent right or copyright. Legal force is given to the rights of inventors, authors and composers to enjoy for some period of time the fruits of their labours.

(c) Natural monopolies: control of natural resources such as coal mines, oil wells or mineral deposits; or the control of expensive capital assets which it is socially undesirable to duplicate. It is uneconomic to take water into houses through several pipelines for the sake of competition in the industry, or to lay two railway lines between towns when one is adequate for the traffic.

(d) Monopoly through the economies of scale. When a large-scale enterprise dominates an industry it is difficult for competitors to enter that industry, for to do so they must be comparable in scale with the efficient firm already established. From Adam Smith onwards classical economists have held that monopoly was *prima facie* bad, and the uncontrolled behaviour of monopolists did much to support this view. The early canal and railway companies were notorious for their exploitation of the travelling and freight-forwarding public, and in more recent times when the first commercial television companies were formed in Great Britain extremely high returns on capital invested were achieved by some companies. The denigration of monopolists can be carried too far, however. Even if monopolists are in a position to exploit their monopoly, they do not always do so, as was proved in the case of cement rings, and in most countries reasonable controls have effectively restrained those who do. The first thing to notice about monopolists is that they are subject to the authority of the consumer.

12.2
Monopolists are subject to the authority of the consumer

A monopolist can dictate either price or quantity, but not both. One half of the decisions to be made will still rest with the consumer. Thus a monopolist who decides to produce a new type of family car may say that he is prepared to market it at a price of £8000.00. It will be up to the body of consumers to say how many they are prepared to buy at that price. Alternatively, he may decide to make 100 000 models of the car. In that case consumer demand will decide what price to pay, let us imagine £5600.00. What the monopolist cannot usually do is say, 'I will make 100 000 cars and you will buy them at £8000.00.' He is still subject to the authority of the consumer, even if he is a monopolist. The exception to this rule is where the goods or services concerned have no close substitutes, and must be purchased by the consumers.

12.3
The demand curve and marginal-revenue curve of a monopolist

In pure competition the demand curve for an *individual* supplier is a line parallel to the X axis, for it is an infinitely elastic demand. If an *individual* supplier in perfect competition cuts his price, however slightly, he will be inundated with orders, since his output is trifling compared with the demand of the market. The monopolist is not so fortunate. He can sell more only if he cuts the price successively with each increased volume of output, so the demand curve (price line) slopes down towards the right.

For example, a monopolist supplying 10 units at £1.00 each earns a total revenue of £10.00. If he increases output to 11 units, but has to cut the price to £0.99 each he will now earn 11 × £0.99 = £10.89. The extra unit has resulted in an extra revenue of £0.89, although it was sold at £0.99. This is because £0.01 was lost on each of the 10 units sold previously. The marginal revenue of a monopolist is therefore less than the average revenue per unit.

Because he is the only supplier of his product, the monopolist's demand curve is a market demand curve. We would therefore expect it to slope downwards to the right as explained above. The marginal-revenue curve slopes down to the right even more steeply, for, as the example shows, the marginal revenue is less than the price at which the items are sold. Figure 12.1 illustrates the situation graphically.

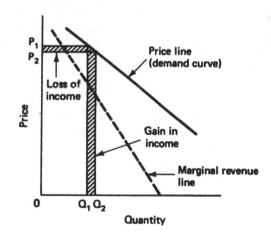

Figure 12.1 The marginal revenue of a monopolist

Notes

1 At P_1 the monopolist sells Q_1 articles.
2 If he increases output by one unit to Q_2 he will receive a lower price because of the downward-sloping demand curve.
3 The whole quantity, Q_2 will be sold at the price, P_2, bringing in an average revenue of P_2 to the monopolist.
4 The marginal revenue (i.e. the increase in total revenue to the monopolist from the sale of the extra unit) is not P_2, but P_2 less the loss in income sustained because of the lower price on all the other units.
5 The reader should now work out for himself the effect on a monopolist's total revenue in the following cases.

   (a) A decision to increase output from 100 to 101 units, if price has to be lowered from £1.00 to £0.99 per unit.
   (b) A decision to increase output of video machines from 10 000 to 15 000 if the price has to be lowered from £250 to £220 each. Calculate what each extra video machine actually earns the monopolist.

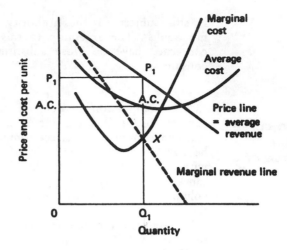

Figure 12.2 Price determination in monopoly conditions (*before studying Figure 12.2 read Section 12.4*)

Notes

1 As already explained in Figure 12.1, the average revenue line is a market demand curve, sloping downwards to the right, but the marginal revenue cuve is a much steeper curve sloping down towards the right. Marginal revenue is much less than average revenue.

2 The marginal-cost curve cuts the marginal-revenue curve at x, and well below the price line. Output ceases at this point with an output of OQ_1.

3 Price will be decided by the point where a line from Q_1 parallel to the price axis cuts the price line, at price P_1P_1.

4 The entrepreneur will earn revenue of $OQ_1P_1P_1$ at a cost (including normal profit) of OQ_1, A.C., A.C. He is therefore earning super-profits of A.C., P_1, P_1, A.C. *BUT these super-profits will not be competed away, as they would in competitive conditions, because the lucky man/woman is a monopolist. (Now return to Section 12.5.)*

12.4
Where will a monopolist cease production, and hence determine price?

Once again production will cease at the point where marginal cost equals marginal revenue, but the situation under monopoly is quite different from the situation already described on page 109 under perfect competition. Figure 12.2 illustrates the situation.

12.5
The monopolist and the elasticity of demand

On page 118 we saw that when demand is elastic it may pay a firm to increase output, since total revenue will rise. When demand is inelastic a reduction in output will force price up, and raise total revenue. It follows that a monopolist, the sole supplier of his commodity can raise prices to exploit his monopoly when the demand for the goods is inelastic. If the good has no close substitutes so that people must buy it or if it is a habit-forming substance, they will be unable to reduce demand when prices rise. Restriction of supplies in this case may force prices up to the benefit of the monopolist.

Total revenue is not the only factor affecting the output of a monopolist, of course; costs also decide whether one output is more profitable than another. If a monopolist can reduce supplies and force prices up, without at the same time raising unit costs, he will find it profitable to do so.

12.6
What is oligopoly?

Oligopoly is a situation where there are only a few firms operating in an industry. Oligopoly approaches monopoly, and may be described as competition among the few. Usually it is extremely difficult for new entrants to join the industry, because of the high capital cost involved. Typical examples are the oil, cement and detergent industries.

The chief features of oligopoly may be listed as follows:

(a) Each firm produces a significant portion of the total output of the industry. This contrasts with the situation in pure competition, where each firm only produces a tiny fraction of total output and is incapable of influencing prices by varying its output. With oligopoly a firm can influence market price by supplying more, or less.

(b) Factor inputs are greatly influenced by the power of the oligopolists. Suppliers of raw materials have only a few firms to supply, and hesitate to offend a major customer. Skilled labour has only a few employment opportunities, and is more specific than other labour.

(c) Retaliatory action by major competitors makes price-output decisions by oligopolists subject to considerations of what the other firms will do. There is a major incentive to form 'cartels' – the firms forming a 'ring' to preserve their own positions by mutually agreed output, price and marketing arrangements. These reduce competition, exclude entry to the industry, share up the market and ensure 'adequate' profit levels. While this may not be against the public interest, it is highly likely that abuses will creep into such arrangements and some states have enacted anti-trust (anti-cartel) legislation. In the United Kingdom a Monopolies and Mergers Commission exists to control such situations.

12.7
Oligopoly and the kinked demand curve

Profits under oligopoly will tend to be higher than profits under competitive conditions, but the profit made by any particular firm will depend upon its own cost structure. High-cost firms will be making less profit than low-cost firms, but this lower profit will still be greater than 'normal profit' in a competitive industry. The demand curve for any particular firm has a characteristic kink at the 'agreed' price. This is illustrated in Figure 12.3.

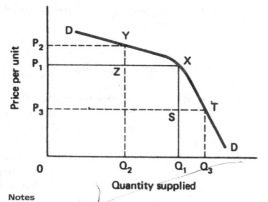

Figure 12.3 A 'kinked' demand curve in oligopoly

Notes

1 The kink in the demand curve occurs at the agreed price of P_1, where this particular firm produces output of Q_1.

2 Any attempt to vary price from the agreed price will result in a lower total income, and since profit is the difference between this firm's total income and its costs, this will mean less profit.

3 Consider what happens if prices are raised above P_1 to P_2. Other firms will not raise their prices and this firm will lose market share to its competitors. Sales will be reduced to Q_2, resulting in a loss of income of Q_1Q_2ZX offset by a gain in income of P_1P_2YZ. The net result is lower total income – in other words, demand is elastic with respect to price above P_1.

4 If prices are cut below P_1 the other firms will follow the price cutter down to preserve market share. The extra revenue gained (Q_1Q_3TS) will be less than the revenue lost by reducing the price (P_1P_3SX). In other words, demand is inelastic with respect to price because of the retaliatory action of the other firms in the industry.

5 The conclusion is that there is no incentive to change prices in oligopoly, and the 'fair' price agreed on by the ring of suppliers will be stable until by mutual agreement, either open or tacit, they decide to change prices.

**12.8
What is
monopolistic
competition?**

Today in all advanced nations the characteristic structure of industry is a concentration of power in large-scale industries which display some tendency to monopolise activities in their fields. Examples of pure monopoly tend to be rather rare in democratic societies, for it is difficult for the monopolist firm to resist legislative attempts to curb its power. Oligopoly is more common than monopoly, and in an attempt to bring cartels and 'rings' under control, the official British definition of a monopoly is a situation where a firm controls at least 25 per cent of the output of an industry. Thus many oligopolists would be classified by this definition as monopolists. In the British detergent industry the Monopolies and Mergers Commission found that two firms had 94 per cent of the market and a third firm had almost all the remaining 6 per cent.

More widespread than oligopoly is the situation know as monopolistic competition. Here elements of monopoly exist alongside elements of competition. The industry consists of several firms making almost identical products, each an almost perfect substitute for the other. The small differences between them may be real or imaginary. Usually there is some subtle difference which enables the product to be 'branded' with a brand name which makes it different from similar products. Examples of brands which do represent real differences may be found in foods like jam and marmalade, prepared from special recipes.

Sometimes the differentiation is justified by the service provided. For example, dried fruits like currants and sultanas are washed, cleaned and packed in convenient and attractive packaging. Salt is supplied in convenient packs, with an additive to make it 'run' freely, and with a pourer which is designed to prevent it spilling. In patent medicines subtle differences between products can be contrived, as in the various products, basically aspirin, which act as analgesics. More artificial is the difference between 'pink' and 'blue' paraffin.

**12.9
The characteristics
of monopolistic
competition**

The chief characteristics are as follows:

(a) *The product is not homogeneous*, but differentiated by 'brand names' into a number of 'different' products, each of which is not quite a perfect substitute for the other. Because the products are 'different' the producers can charge different prices and still sell the dearer items. The elasticity of demand for different brands is reduced, that is, the demand is less responsive to price changes because some buyers are convinced a particular brand is better and worth the extra money. Even so, the demand curve is not very inelastic. When the price is slightly higher than the price of competitive brands customers will continue to buy their favourite brand, and demand will be inelastic. The farther apart the prices move, the greater the elasticity of the highly priced alternative, or the greater the advertising costs of maintaining inelasticity of demand. Either way the supplier is losing his super-profits.

(b) *There are several suppliers and entry to the industry is still possible*. The number of suppliers is still sufficiently great for quite severe competition between products. In industries where large-scale operation is essential for technical reasons oligopoly is the usual structure of the industry. In industries with less specific assets where entry is easy and scale is smaller monopolistic competition will be the usual form. In the fashion trades, in groceries, in footwear, electronics, plastics, etc., branding of goods seeks to secure some measure of 'monopoly' in a fiercely competitive industry.

(c) *Heavy expenditure on advertising.* This is a feature of brand promotion. There are two kinds of advertising: informative advertising and persuasive advertising. Informative advertising makes clear the availability of the product, its uses and advantages, its price, quality and terms of sale. There can be no serious objection to informative advertising. In a specialist world we are all too busy to investigate product for ourselves. The variety of our lives is enhanced by being informed about products which would otherwise escape our attention.

Persuasive advertising does not just inform, it uses subtle techniques to persuade, and even delude, the public into buying. At best it is unnecessary. It may be misleading, wasteful, and even harmful if it makes antisocial behaviour appear desirable.

The reason why advertising is such an important feature in monopolistic competition is that firms are not content to take market prices as fixed and uncontrollable (whereas the individual firm in perfect markets has to). Because of the differentiation between products they are able to some extent to vary prices to maximise profits. In other words, they have some of the advantages of monopolists who can reduce output and force prices up so long as the demand for the product is inelastic.

Example. Certain goods are in great demand at festival times of the year. The housewife must have them whatever the price. The demand therefore is inelastic. If sellers of such goods raise prices at these times they will make excellent profits. After the festival is over housewives will not demand the same goods nearly so much, but they may do if the price is low. In other words, the demand is elastic. The entrepreneur who lowers prices will sell the product, but not quite so profitably.

We therefore find retailers following policies aimed at maximising profits: lowering prices when demand is elastic and raising them when demand is inelastic. At one time the advertising emphasises the low price; at the festival time it emphasises the product's appropriateness for the festival.

12.10 Determination of prices under monopolistic competition

In perfect competition the low-cost firm enjoys super-profits in the short run, but in the long run new firms entering the industry will lower the prices and compete away these super-profits. With monopoly conditions the monopolist is able to maintain the short-run position into the long term because new firms can be prevented from entering the industry. With monopolistic competition the supplier of branded goods cannot prevent new firms entering the industry, but they cannot enter it and use the same brand name. The decision of a supplier about the output to be produced is illustrated in Figures 12.4 and 12.5. Before considering these the reader should note that, as with monopoly, the demand curve for a supplier in monopolistic competition slopes down towards the right. It is a market-demand curve, and the supplier can increase sales only by lowering price.

It follows that marginal revenue is again less than price, and the short-run position of a firm in monopolistic competition is therefore similar to a firm in monopoly conditions.

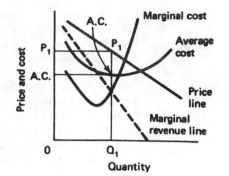

Figure 12.4 The short-run position of a supplier in monopolistic competition

Notes

1 The supplier in Figure 12.4 is making super-profits with his brand equal to A.C., P_1, P_1, A.C.
2 New firms will be attracted into the industry, selling the same goods in a differentiated form. The new supplier or suppliers will have to be aggressive in advertising and pricing policies if they are to make inroads on the market in the established brand, and to the extent that they are successful there will be a change in the conditions of demand (see page 77).
3 The demand curve for the supplier of the established brand will move to the left, a decrease in demand.
4 The marginal-revenue line will also move to the left, and some of the entrepreneur's super-profits will be competed away.
5 Sooner or later the competition of other brands may move the demand curve so far to the left that all the super-profits will be competed away. At this point the price line will just be touching the average cost curve. The ultimate position, at which entry to the industry by other competitors will cease, is illustrated in Figure 12.5.

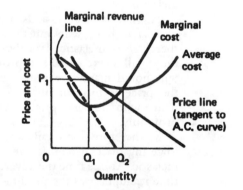

Figure 12.5 The long-run position of a supplier under monopolistic competition

Notes

1 The demand curve has moved, owing to the changed conditions of demand, so far to the left that it has become tangential to (only just touching) the average-cost curve.
2 At this point all super-profits will have been competed away and the firm would be left making normal profits only. Consequently in monopolistic competition the firm's aim is to maintain brand image and consumer loyalty by an endless succession of innovations to keep the branded product 'different' and desirable.
3 There is excess capacity in the industry; the supplier could increase output to the optimum level of minimum average cost at OQ_2 and decrease unit costs by doing so, but the marginal revenue would decrease *even more*, leaving him worse off. It is therefore a feature of monopolistic competition that excess capacity exists in the industry in the long run.

12.11 Conclusions about monopolistic competition

Increasingly monopolistic competition is becoming the characteristic feature of free-enterprise market economies as far as the consumer is concerned. While perfectly competitive markets persist to facilitate the bulk handling of primary commodities, fewer and fewer of such primary products reach the ultimate consumer. The preparation of foods in hygienic pre-packed branded forms, the elimination of personal service in retail trade, the increased standardisation of products, and the indifference of affluent people to minor price differences all give monopolistic competition great advantages as a method of production. We should note the following points:

(a) *The aim of the competitive monopolist is always to preserve his monopoly position.* The final position of the supplier shown in Figure 12.5 with all the super-profits competed away is plainly a situation to be avoided at all costs. If a supplier does get to that position the point of branding will have been lost. The solution is to find an endless succession of real, or imaginary, improvements in the product. This may mean the addition of unnecessary foam to household cleaners, or a change in the length of cigarettes and cigars or the endless redesigning of external trimmings on motor vehicles to make them 'new' models. This otherwise pointless activity puts off for a further few months, or years, the time when a product loses its appeal to the consumer.

At the same time it may lead to genuine improvements which are beneficial to the public. New types of tyres, braking systems, better lighting, and design features which improve safety, economy of operation, comfort and convenience have been introduced by motor-vehicle manufacturers as part of the process of presenting an old vehicle in a new form.

(b) *The industry will usually be operating at less than the optimum.* This is the same as saying that there will always be excess capacity in the industry. It would be possible, but it would not be profitable, to lower the unit cost. This excess capacity must not be exaggerated though. It is at its greatest when the firms are in such strong competition that they have reached the situation shown in Figure 12.5. If the entrepreneur is active in differentiating his product the demand curve for his product will not move so far to the left, and he will be able to operate nearer the optimum while still enjoying super-profits.

(c) *Non-price competition must be a feature of monopolistic competition.* If the only requirement for high sales was that the goods should be cheap, i.e. value for money, then price competition would be the usual form of competition. Unfortunately a certain amount of informative advertising is indispensable, and some persuasive advertising inevitably follows, The cost of laying down production lines is so great that it is essential to exert every effort to recoup these costs with a reasonable return on capital invested as well. This can be achieved only by varying the demand for one's product by successful advertising.

12.12 Summary of Chapter 12

1 Monopoly means supply by only one person or firm. The commodity must have no close substitutes, and the monopolist must be able to exclude other firms from its production.

2 Monopolists are still subject to the authority of the consumer, for they cannot compel the public to buy the quantity manufactured at the monopoly price. Consumers may elect to do without the goods altogether unless they are essential to life itself.

3 The demand curve for a monopolist's product slopes downwards to the right, like any market-demand curve.

4 The marginal revenue of a monopolist is always less than the average revenue earned.

5 The monopolist will never exceed that output where marginal cost equals marginal revenue. At this price super-profits will be made which will not be competed away because other firms can be excluded from the industry.

6   It will often pay a monopolist to raise prices and reduce output to the point where the demand for the product becomes elastic.

7   Oligopoly is production by a few major firms in an industry. Pricing policy is influenced by the chances of retaliatory action, and there is a tendency for cartels or rings to form to fix prices and share up the market.

8   The characteristic feature of oligopoly is the kinked demand curve for a firm's products. It will not pay a firm to move away from the agreed price-output arrangement.

9   The official definition of a monopolist also covers many oligopolists. Monopoly is held *prima facie* to exist when one firm controls more than 25 per cent of an industry's output.

10   Monopolistic competition is a situation where elements of monopoly exist alongside competition from other firms. This is the situation where 'branded' articles are being sold. Advertising is used to differentiate between products which are basically similar and therefore in competition with one another.

11   In the long run, monopoly profits would all be competed away by rivals entering the industry in monopolistic competition. The supplier's aim is to avoid this situation by 'new' versions of his product. This is often achieved by packaging or altering the exterior appearance of the product, while its basic structure is left the same.

Exercises Set 12

1   What is monopoly? In what different ways may monopoly arise? In what circumstances can monopolists dictate both prices and output?

2   'The price line for a monopolist slopes downwards towards the right. The price line for a firm in pure competition is horizontal.' Explain. Now explain what would be the marginal revenue in each case.

3   How is price determined in pure competition and under monopoly conditions? Illustrate your answer with fully labelled diagrams.

4   The monopolist will find it profitable to restrict output as long as the demand for his product is inelastic. Discuss.

5   What is monopolistic competition? In your answer refer to any industries you know which operate in these conditions.

6   'Advertising promotes prosperity.' 'Advertising is wasteful.' Discuss these alternative views.

7   'The purpose of advertising is to alter the demand curves for products, so that they continue to earn super-profits.' Explain.

8   'In the short run suppliers under monopolistic competition are monopolists. In the long run they are the marginal firms in competitive industries.' Explain, with diagrams, the short-run and long-run positions of suppliers under monopolistic competition.

9   'The monopolist cannot sell his product at any price he likes.' Comment on this statement, bringing out the way in which prices of goods supplied by monopolists are decided.

10   What is meant by the term 'excess capacity in an industry'? Why is this capacity not used?

11   What is oligopoly? Why is it such a common form of market structure? In your answer refer to typical industries where oligopoly is usually found.

12   What is a 'kinked' demand curve? Explain why stable marketing, price and output arrangements are a feature of oligopoly.

13   'There is always one fool who cuts prices!' What is the significance of this statement made by an oligopolist?

14 What is the official British definition of monopoly, which entitles the situation in an industry to be referred to the Monopolies and Mergers Commission? What sort of firms would be caught by this definition?

13   Further aspects of demand and supply

13.1 Introduction

By its very nature this chapter is bound to be fragmentary. A variety of topics is introduced. These cannot be more than thumbnail sketches of the investigations into demand and supply, and the various theories developed by a number of economists over the years.

13.2 Interrelated demands

13.2.1 Joint, complementary or derived demand

Sometimes two commodities may be so related that the demand for one affects the demand for the other. They may be in **joint demand**, with one commodity complementing, i.e. completing, the other. Common examples of goods in joint or complementary demand are knives and forks, strawberries and cream, whisky and soda or bread and butter. Sometimes the joint nature of the demand is a **derived demand**, one of the commodities being a dominant commodity, the demand for which calls forth a demand for the second commodity. The motor car is strongly demanded, but as it will not run without petrol, the demand for petrol is derived from the demand for motor cars.

Joint, complementary, and derived demands are similar, in that an increase in the demand for one product leads to an increase in the demand for the other. What effect such a change in demand has on the price of the commodities depends on the conditions of supply. In Figure 13.1 the supply curves have been drawn at different slopes to indicate different elasticities, but readers are reminded that slope is *not* the same as elasticity. (*Study Figure 13.1 now.*)

The reader is now invited to think for himself what would be the effect on the price of petrol of a change in the conditions of demand for motor vehicles. Suppose a change in subsidies to public transport has caused a considerable increase in demand for motor cars, and also for petrol. What will be the effect of this on the price of motor vehicles and petrol? We will imagine the supply of motor vehicles can be increased fairly easily, but the supply of petrol is inelastic.

Derived demand – a special case. A special case of derived demand is the demand for the factors of production, which is derived from the demand for 'utilities' to satisfy 'wants'. If entrepreneurs are to produce, they must have land, labour and capital. The demand of the motor-car manufacturers for land, premises, plant and machinery, raw materials, labour and power is derived from the need to produce motor vehicles to satisfy the strong demand for them.

13.2.2 Competitive demand of substitutes

Sometimes one commodity is a substitute for another, and an increased demand for one will lead to a reduction in demand for the other. An obvious example is margarine, which is a substitute for butter. Similarly, modern artificial fibres are excellent substitutes for natural fibres. An increased use of fluffy synthetic fibres will lead to a decline in the demand for wool. The

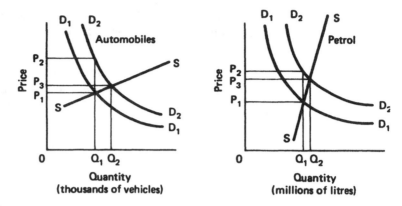

Figure 13.1 Joint demand: motor cars and petrol

Notes

1 The change from D_1 to D_2 represents a similar proportional increase over D_1 in each case.

2 For the purpose of this example, vehicles are imagined to be in elastic supply but the supply of petrol is inelastic. Consequently, the change in demand affects the price of the two goods differently.

3 Both products eventually settle at a price of P_3 and a quantity of Q_2. Because of the different elasticities of supply the price of vehicles rises by one-ninth, but the price of petrol increases by about half.

effect is the opposite of the situation with joint demand: the increase in demand for one commodity reduces the demand for the substitute. In Figure 13.2 the conditions of supply have been assumed to be similar.

**13.2.3
Competitive demand
– the need to choose**

Substitution takes place not only when the qualities of the substitute are almost identical with those of the goods it replaces but also when the purchase of one commodity prevents the purchase of the other. To this extent all goods are in competitive demand, and especially where a particular product is expensive. The family buying its first motor car finds it must give up many other items it previously enjoyed, and a young couple with a large mortgage may postpone temporarily having a family.

This type of competitive demand affects the total demand for any particular class of goods, and explains why prosperity in particular industries is often accompanied by a decline in business elsewhere. It

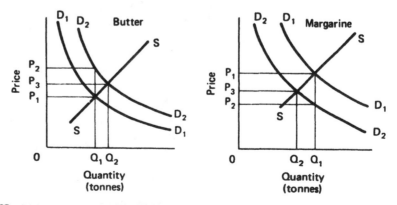

Figure 13.2 Competitive demand: butter and margarine

Notes

1 Owing to some change in the conditions of demand (for example, a change in consumer's aggregate income) butter is more strongly demanded. The price of butter rises from P_1 to P_2, settling at P_3 as the quantity supplied extends from Q_1 to Q_2.

2 Margarine is now not demanded so strongly, since butter has been substituted for it. Price falls from P_1 to P_2, but recovers to P_3 as supply contracts from Q_1 to Q_2.

illustrates again the idea of 'opportunity cost': that having selected one opportunity, the other opportunities which we might have chosen are lost to us.

13.2.4
Composite demand

Many commodities are non-specific, that is they may be used for a variety of purposes. Steel may be used to build ships, lay railways, store fuel oil, make consumer durables like washing machines and refrigerators, or form the framework of hospitals, hotels and office blocks. The demand for steel is the sum of all these varied demands. Such a demand is said to be a **composite demand**.

13.3
Interrelated supply

13.3.1
Joint supply

Some products are in joint supply, that is, one cannot be produced without the other. We cannot increase the supply of hides without producing beef, or the supply of wool without increasing mutton. In the extraction of petrol from crude oil profitable disposal of the many by-products is essential if costs of the main process are to be reduced. By skilful use of petrochemical technology, the oil industry uses the majority of its derivatives, but not without affecting the price of any commodities with which they compete.

Simple cases of joint supply, like petrol and heating oil, may be illustrated as in Figure 13.3.

13.3.2
Competitive supply – choice of output

The supply of certain goods follows naturally from circumstances beyond man's control. A Canadian fur-trapper, for example, cannot suddenly decide to grow bananas or coffee beans. More often we choose what we will produce, and to this extent the alternative outputs are in competitive supply.

If we plough up grazing land to sow wheat the supply of milk and beef will be reduced, while that of wheat increases. In manufacture entrepreneurs choose between different products; in service trades they make different facilities available.

On a broader view, the competition between entrepreneurs for factors (land, labour and capital) makes choice essential. We must choose not only

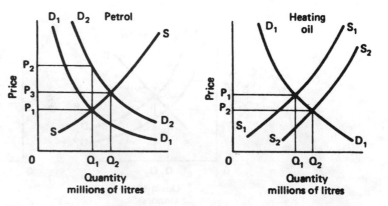

Figure 13.3 Joint supply: petrol and heating oil

Notes

1 A change in demand for motor cars increases the demand for petrol. Demand moves from $D_1 D_1$ to $D_2 D_2$ and price increses to P_2. Supply extends to Q_2 and price settles to P_3.

2 The increased output of petrol throws more heating oil on the market. The supply of heating oil therefore changes from $S_1 S_1$ to $S_2 S_2$, but there has been no increase in demand. This means that the price of heating oil must fall to P_2. As it does so, demand extends to use the extra output.

between individual products but also between broad alternative policies. Shall we have more material goods or more leisure, more education or more food, more travel or more defence? Since the factors we possess are limited, we cannot have everything.

13.4
The revealed
preference theory

This theory holds that the preferences which a household has already revealed will give a clue to its behaviour when prices change, and explain what quantity or range of quantities it will demand in the new situation. This readjustment to a new basket of goods can be explained by dividing the effect of the price change into two different parts: the **substitution effect** and the **income effect**. The substitution effect will encourage the household to substitute the cheaper commodity for other goods if a fall in price has occurred; or other goods for the dearer commodity if the price has risen.

The income effect arises because a change in the price of goods always affects the **real incomes** of households, i.e. their income in terms of what can be bought with their money. A fall in prices increases real incomes, and a rise in prices reduces real incomes.

It can be shown that the substitution effect is always 'non-negative', by which is meant that it always does what is expected. It leads a household to buy more of a cheaper product, and can never lead it to buy less. It leads a household to buy less of a dearer commodity, and can never lead it to buy more.

The income effect, by contrast, may be positive or negative. When real incomes rise we tend to buy more of most commodities, but with some commodities increased income will enable us to change our way of life, alter our diet, etc., so that less of some goods are now demanded. These are the so-called 'Giffen goods' (see page 85). Figure 13.4 explains the theory in non-mathematical terms.

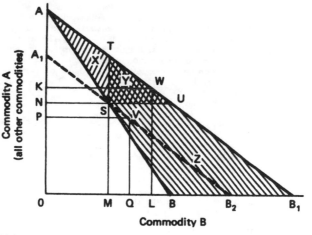

Figure 13.4 The substitution effect and the income effect of a change in price

Notes
1 Commodity A represents all other commodities except Commodity B.
2 The household under consideration can buy any combination of A and B which it likes. It can buy anywhere inside the triangle AOB, but it cannot move beyond the line AB, which is the limit of combinations of Commodity B and all other commodities which this household can afford. This line is therefore called the household's budget line. If it bought OB of Commodity B its entire budget would be spent and it could buy no other goods at all. If it bought OA it would spend its entire income on other goods and not buy any of Commodity B at all. Let us imagine it buys at the point S on AB, i.e. OM of Commodity B and ON of all other goods.
3 When the price of B falls the household is now able to buy a larger basket of goods, its real income has risen because all the possible points in the shaded area are now available to it as alternatives. To get maximum satisfaction it should move to some point on AB₁, its new budget line. But which point will it choose?

4 First notice that in the shaded area X it will only be getting smaller quantities of Commodity B than OM. It is unlikely to choose to change its purchases to any point between A and T, because it has already revealed a preference for having OM of Commodity B, even when it was expensive. Now it is cheap it will, if it is behaving logically, buy more of Commodity B because it will substitute Commodity B for other goods. The only thing that could make it move its purchases into the shaded area X would be if the increased real income led to a *negative income effect*, i.e. if Commodity OB were a 'Giffen good' and no longer attracted this household since it had become more affluent.

5 Similarly, in the shaded area Z, purchases include larger quantities of Commodity B, but smaller quantities of other goods. The household will therefore be unlikely to choose any point on the budget line between U and B_1, for it has already revealed a preference for having ON of other goods. Only if the substitution effect was very strong indeed, leading to a large increase in consumption of Commodity B, or if the income effect was so excessively positive that other goods were abandoned from a desire to purchase Commodity B (which would therefore be 'goods of ostentation') would a family shift its purchases to such a point.

6 The most likely position is somewhere between T and U.

7 To see the *substitution effect* we must imagine that there is no income effect at all, which involves imagining that as real income rises (due to the fall in price of B), money income is reduced to keep the household only as well off as it was before. This involves sliding the budget line AB_1 parallel to itself until it passes through the original preference point S. The household is now able to afford the basket of goods it was buying previously. But will this now be a sensible basket of goods, or should it rearrange its purchases somewhere along the dotted line A_1B_2? Clearly anywhere between A_1 and S would not be sensible, since it involves less of Commodity B than its already revealed preference, and Commodity B is now cheaper. The household, if it is acting logically, will purchase more of Commodity B. It will therefore move somewhere along the dotted line SB_2. Let us suppose it moves to the point V, substituting a quantity MQ of Commodity B for other goods, which are reduced to OP. MQ is the *substitution effect* on this family's demand for Commodity B.

8 However, in fact the real income of the family has risen, and it is really able to afford baskets of goods on the budget line AB_1. The most likely place for it to choose is a point between T and U. This point will be W, found by sliding the new budget line A_1B_2 and the point V out to its proper position again at AB_1. We now have the household enjoying OL units of Commodity B and OK units of other commodities. QL units of Commodity B is the *income effect*.

9 Remember that had the income effect been negative, as it would have been for a poor family subsisting on inferior goods, the income effect could have moved demand for Commodity B down to lower levels, somewhere between T and W, leaving the household enjoying a more satisfying basket of goods.

10 It follows that for most goods the demand curve will slope downwards to the right, since the substitution effect will increase demand for the commodity as it becomes cheaper, and so will the income effect, if the income elasticity of the commodity is greater than zero. If the income elasticity of the commodity is negative, then the income effect will counteract the substitution effect, and if it is sufficiently great to cancel out the substitution effect altogether the household will be seen to buy less of Commodity B, which must therefore be a 'Giffen good'. The demand curve in such a case will be regressive.

11 To conclude, in this example we have:

    (a) a substitution effect of MQ extra units of Commodity B being purchased;

    (b) a positive income effect of QL extra units of Commodity B being purchased; and an extra amount NK of other goods;

    (c) a total extra consumption of ML units of Commodity B and NK units extra of other goods. (*The reader should now return to Section 13.5 in the main text*)

13.5
Price controls

The price mechanism decides what goods shall be produced and to whom they shall be supplied. It is a self-regulating mechanism which calls on to the market supplies large enough to satisfy the demand. If all markets were perfectly free the price mechanism would be a very satisfactory system for distributing 'scarce' supplies among consumers. The fact is, however, that not all markets are perfectly free. Many goods are put on the market that would not be demanded at all if people were left alone. Such goods have to be forced on buyers by persuasive advertising. Critics of the price mechanism hold that the creation of artificial 'wants' in this way is undesirable, and diverts scarce resources, which could be more usefully employed in other ways, into the production of unnecessary goods. Other sources of complaint against the price mechanism are the anti-social overtones of a system which is incapable of responding to anything but

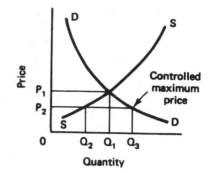

Figure 13.5 Maximum price controlled: rationing

Notes
1 Market price is P_1 and the quantity supplied is Q_1.
2 For some reason, perhaps because the C is a basic food in wartime and the market mechanism is enabling the rich to eat while the poor starve, the Government fixes a maximum price of P_2.
3 At this price quantity Q_2 is distributed by the suppliers, but the people would like to buy quantity Q_3. This means that there is a serious shortage. Unscrupulous shopkeepers will keep supplies under the counter for favoured customers.
4 The only fair way to solve the problem is to introduce a rationing system.

demand and supply. If addicts demand heroin the market will supply it; but Society ought to have a say in such matters.

In real life, governments and legislative bodies interfere a good deal in the free play of the price mechanism, and manipulate the market to achieve desirable social ends. The weapons used are taxation, which raises effective prices; subsidies which lower effective prices, and price controls, which dictate maximum and minimum prices. The first two are discussed in Chapter 29. The last, sometimes called physical controls, have interesting side effects, and are illustrated in Figures 13.5 and 13.6.

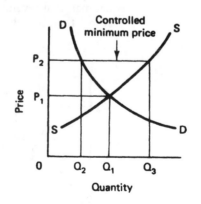

Figure 13.6 Minimum price controlled: state stockpiling

Notes
1 Market price is P_1 and quantity supplied is Q_1.
2 For some reason, usually to guarantee farm incomes, the government decrees that prices cannot fall below P_2.
3 At this price people only wish to buy Q_2 of the Commodity, but suppliers insist on turning out Q_3.
4 Since the public will not buy the commodity, the government has to do so, and vast stockpiles of food and raw materials are built up which have been purchased with taxpayers' money. Sometimes quite ridiculous situations develop, with hungry people unfed while granaries are bursting. The US has at times been in great difficulties because of such stocks, and has had to adopt the 'soil bank' scheme. This pays farmers when they *don't* produce, leaving the ground to gain in fertility by lying fallow. The European Union countries similarly from time to time have huge reserves of farm products, butter mountains and wine lakes. To save storage costs farmers are paid to 'set aside' land.

13.6
Market price and normal price

Sometimes these two terms are confused, and as they relate to very similar situations, it is as well to clarify their meaning. Prices are fixed in the market by the interaction of the forces of supply and demand. Both the quantity demanded and the quantity supplied are affected by the price, and are brought into balance at the equilibrium price.

Market price refers to the short-term equilibrium price decided from day to day in the market-place as a result of short-term influences. Where conditions are stable, i.e. the conditions of demand and supply are not changing, the industry settles down to a point where supply and demand are nicely matched. For example, if on the demand side the prices of other goods are not changing particularly, or the income of buyers is stable, or changes in the number of buyers and their scales of preference are not great, then the entrepreneurs will produce what is necessary to meet demand. On the supply side, the entrepreneurs must not be faced with changes in the conditions of supply; international prices of raw materials must be steady and wages and interest rates reasonably stable too. If short-term fluctuations are not exerting much influence the industry settles down to the point where the supply is nicely adjusted to demand, and the rate at which the commodity is consumed exactly equals the rate at which it is produced. Price will now be stable, and this long-run equilibrium price is called **normal price**.

13.7
Supply curves

13.7.1
The supply curve of a single firm in a perfectly competitive market

We have already established the following rules:

(a) No firm will produce at all unless its total revenue exceeds its total variable cost. This is because it will prefer to shut down and produce nothing. That way it suffers losses equal to its total fixed costs. To produce at prices so low that total revenue does not even cover total variable cost would be to add variable losses to fixed losses.

(b) It will pay a firm to produce that output where marginal cost rises to equal marginal revenue. At any point before this the marginal unit will cost less than its sale price, and will therefore be profitable.

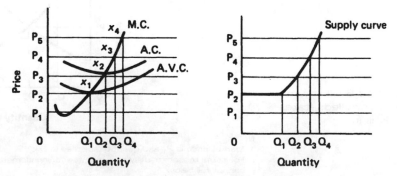

Figure 13.7 The supply curve of an individual firm in a competitive market

Notes
1 At a price of P_2 with an output of Q_1 the total revenue $(OQ_1x_1P_2)$ exactly equals the total variable cost $(OQ_1x_1P_2)$. A firm that is not already in the industry would not come in at this point because it would be losing its fixed costs. A firm already in the industry, but closed down because of low prices, would now find it worthwhile to start up production.
2 At each successive price P_3, P_4, P_5 the firm is prepared to supply more, i.e. Q_2, Q_3, Q_4, because it will be profitable to supply until the marginal cost rises to equal the marginal revenue, i.e. the price per unit.
3 For the individual firm in a competitive industry the supply curve is the same as the marginal-cost curve above the minimum average variable cost.

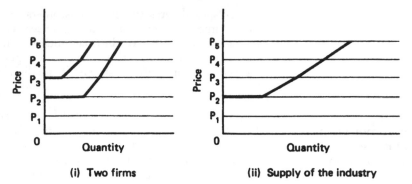

Figure 13.8 The supply curve of an industry in a competitive market

(i) Two firms   **(ii) Supply of the industry**

Notes

1 The individual supply curves of two firms are shown in (i) above. Of course, in real life there would be many such firms.

2 The supply curve of the industry is the horizontal addition of the outputs of all the firms. Two firms' outputs have been added in (ii) above, but in practice there would be many such firms, whose outputs (supplies) are decided by the shape of their marginal-cost curves (above minimum average variable cost).

If we now consider Figure 13.7 we see that the supply curve is the same as the marginal-cost curve once it has risen above average variable cost.

13.7.2 The supply curve of a competitive industry

An industry consists of low-cost firms, medium-cost firms, and high-cost firms. At low prices only the low-cost firms will supply; as prices rise medium-cost firms will find it possible to produce at a profit and will start up, while at very high prices even the high-cost firms come in with some supplies to the market. The supply for a competitive industry must be the sum of the quantities supplied by the individual firms. Taking the supply curve in Figure 13.7 as an example, and adding a second firm with higher costs as in Figure 13.8, the supply curve of this two-firm industry is the horizontal addition of the individual supplies.

13.7.3 Is there a supply curve under monopoly conditions?

A supply curve is essentially a pictorial representation of the quantities of goods supplied by the industry at certain prices. In monopoly conditions the sole supplier is not bound by any automatic relationship between supply and price, indeed, he is able to manipulate price by varying supply if the goods he produces are in inelastic demand. The supply is therefore subject to the whim of the supplier. While he still equates marginal cost to marginal revenue, and will therefore never produce a unit if it means a decline in total profit, he is able to choose how much he will produce. Of course, he will choose to maximise total profits usually, so that he will produce that output which equates marginal cost and marginal revenue, but he may settle for less than maximum total profits if he likes.

It follows that there is no unique relationship between price and supply under monopoly conditions, i.e. there is no relationship which follows automatically from a change in demand.

13.8 Discriminating monopoly

Sometimes a monopolist can sell the same product at different prices to different customers. For example, a suit sold in a well-to-do area may fetch a better price than a similar suit sold in a less fashionable area. Cement manufacturers often sell bulk cement at a very much lower price than they sell to retail customers, even though the sacks are identical. Railways often charge special rates to certain customers or charge the traffic what it will bear. Surgeons often supply the same services free to poor patients as they charge expensively to the accounts of rich patients. Obviously price discrimination cannot take place under perfect market conditions; some element of monopoly must exist if the discrimination is to succeed.

13.8.1
Consumer surplus and price discrimination

In perfect competition there is only one market and only one market price for each product. In monopoly, oligopoly and monopolistic competition there is no single market to which everyone has free access. Customers do not have perfect knowledge of the market and those prepared to pay more can be charged more. If an item costs £1.00 in a competitive market and some buyers, purchasing at this price, would have been prepared to pay more – say £1.50 or £2.00 or even £10.00 – then they are said to enjoy a *consumer's surplus* of satisfaction.

Clearly a consumer's surplus represents a loss to the suppliers. If they could strike a bargain with every customer, and get that customer to pay what the commodity is worth to him, instead of the market price, they would improve their profits. This can be done when it is possible to sell to different customers at different prices.

In order to do this the following conditions must be fulfilled:

(*a*) *It must be possible to keep the 'markets' apart.* Sometimes markets are separated by physical barriers like frontiers. Sometimes they are separated by high transport costs, so that it will not benefit a consumer to buy in the remote market, even though prices there are cheaper. Sometimes contractual separation may be achieved, by requiring the customer supplied at the cheap price to enter into an agreement not to resell to anyone at less than the open-market price. Such restrictive practices have to be registered under the Restrictive Trade Practices Act as far as Great Britain is concerned, but are not prohibited if they are found to be in the public interest.

(*b*) *The elasticity of demand in the two markets must be different.* There will be no point in offering two different prices if the elasticity of demand of the two groups of customers is the same. It is the refusal of the favoured customer to buy unless terms are made favourable to him that makes the monopolist offer the cheaper rate. In other words, the favoured customer has a more elastic demand than the unfavoured customer. For example, a large industrial user of gas might make special arrangements for a preferential rate in return for using this fuel rather than coal or oil. Cheap-rate electricity at off-peak hours for domestic heating attracts householders into installing electrical storage heaters rather than other heaters using alternative fuels.

The result of these discriminating policies is a larger volume of output, which reduces the excess capacity in the monopolist's undertaking and brings him nearer to the optimum position at which a competitive industry works.

The discriminating monopolist now has the problem of equating the marginal cost of his entire output with a marginal revenue made up of two parts: the marginal revenue to be earned from the consumers in the normal market (called Market I in Figure 13.9), and the marginal revenue to be earned from the privileged customers (Market II in Figure 13.9). Of course, there could be several such privileged customers. The results are shown in Figure 13.9.

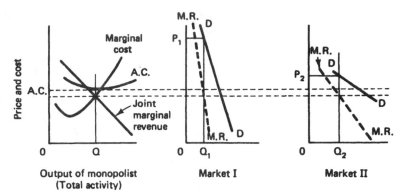

Figure 13.9 The output of a monopolist when discrimination is possible

Output of monopolist (Total activity)   **Market I**   **Market II**

Notes

1 The entrepreneur expands output until marginal cost equals total marginal revenue.
2 That level of cost is carried over into Markets I and II, and in each case cuts the marginal revenue lines 1 and 2 at points which indicate outputs of Q_1 and Q_2.
3 As a result, OQ_1 of the output will be sold at price P_1; output OQ_2 will be sold at a price of OP_2.
4 The monopolist is making super-profits in each case, but more in Market I than in Market II. His discrimination in favour of the market where demand is more elastic depends upon his ability to keep the two markets separate.

13.9 Summary of Chapter 13

1 Joint or complementary demand occurs when two goods are used or consumed together, e.g. bread and butter.
2 Derived demand occurs when the use of one of the two goods which are in joint demand follows the use of the other; e.g. petrol is demanded by motorists for their cars.
3 A special case of derived demand is the demand for factors, which are demanded because of the demand for 'utilities' to satisfy 'wants'.
4 Competitive demand occurs when goods are substitutes for one another; e.g. butter and margarine.
5 Since household incomes are limited, all goods and services are in competitive demand with one another, and the housewife must exercise choice between them.
6 Where the price of a commodity changes, the household will vary its purchases to take account of the change in price. The change in demand can be divided into two parts: a substitution effect and an income effect. The substitution effect is always non-negative; the income effect may be positive or negative.
7 Price controls interfere with the market. Maximum prices lead to a shortage of goods, which means that rationing must be introduced. Minimum prices lead to excessive supply, with the need for government purchase of the surplus.
8 Market price is the short-term equilibrium price on the market. Normal price is the long-term equilibrium price achieved when an industry has settled down in stable conditions of demand and supply.

Exercises Set 13

1 What are the likely effects of a rise in the price of wool on the following: (*a*) the price of Harris Tweed; (*b*) the price of blankets; (*c*) the price of mutton; (*d*) the demand for fluffy synthetic fibres; (*e*) the price of sheepskins; (*f*) Australian incomes?
2 Explain why a rise in the price of cars might lead to a fall in the price of petrol. Refer in your answer to the specific nature of the assets used in oil refineries.
3 What would you expect to be the effect of an increase in the demand for

hides on: (*a*) the price of beef; (*b*) the price of pork; (*c*) the price of plastic handbags; (*d*) the price of wool; (*e*) the price of shoes; (*f*) the rent of grazing land.

4 'An increase in the price of petrol makes paraffin cheaper.' Do you agree? Support your answer with reasoned economic argument and diagrams.

5 'When a commodity becomes cheaper it effectively raises the real incomes of all who use it.' Explain what the author of this remark meant. What changes in expenditure may reasonably be expected as a result of the reduction of the price of goods in strong demand?

6 What is the effect on (*a*) farm outputs, and (*b*) taxation, of a decision never to allow the price of wheat to fall below 2 dollars per bushel.

7 What disturbances in the market will be caused by a Government decision to keep food prices low by a maximum-price policy?

8 Why does the electricity supply industry offer different rates to different classes of consumer? How can they prevent the markets mixing?

9 'Do not worry, madam, your son's operation will be performed free. Miss Jones, double the bill you typed out this morning for Sir Joshua's son, will you?' Explain the economic implications of these two sentences, spoken by a leading surgeon.

10 In what circumstances is it (*a*) practicable, and (*b*) profitable, for a firm to practise differential charging?

Section 4: Exchanging the Fruits of Production

14 Exchange and money

14.1 Specialisation and exchange

Specialisation and **exchange** have been described as opposite sides of the same coin. Every economy depends on specialisation, and in advanced economies specialisation is fully developed by automation and computerisation to produce a flood of 'surplus' goods. By 'surplus' we mean surplus to the requirements of the particular group who produced the output under consideration. This group of producers then wishes to trade its surplus output with other workers who have produced surpluses in *their* particular fields of activity. In a similar way some of these workers will wish to exchange some of their surplus goods for personal services, since not all specialists produce an end product. The personal services rendered by employees in tertiary production have also to be 'paid for' by surrendering to them some of the goods produced in primary and secondary production. We must now examine the problems of exchange.

Even the very start of such an examination of exchanges is blurred by the intricate nature of advanced economies. Readers will immediately think of objections to the statements in the previous paragraph. How can one talk about workers in the petroleum industry exchanging the surplus petrol they manufacture with the employees in the building industry? The petrol belongs to the owners of the oil refinery, and the surplus houses erected are the property of the developers who organised the project. These objections are very real, and yet they do not destroy what has been said. Because of an ancient economic device called 'the money system', the basic exchanges which are taking place are hidden by a 'money veil'. The main purpose of this chapter is to examine how 'the money system' works. Before doing so we must consider exchanges arranged without a money system.

14.2 Exchange by barter

Until a full money system has been developed, trade is usually carried on by barter. This is the exchange of goods directly for other goods, and it presents quite serious problems to the parties trading. These problems are not a real handicap when trading is an unusual event, for example in simple tribal societies practising autarky (self-sufficiency). To people growing their own food, keeping their own cattle and weaving their own cloth, the occasional bartering activity can usually be resolved fairly easily. The purchase of a knife or an axe, at an annual fair, or from the visiting pedlar, is an event to which due time can be given.

Trade is not the only activity of mankind, however. Marriage and revenge are older practices still and appear to have played a considerable part in the development of money. Bride-price and blood-price are ancient institutions, and are often reported among primitive people. Compensation for a man's death is a sum equivalent to what his father paid as bride-price for the dead man's mother a generation before. These two activities, and barter, are matters to which due time can be given, especially by peoples largely self sufficient in ordinary bread-and-butter matters.

When we live in a community where specialisation is the rule, so that every single thing we need has to be obtained by exchange, the difficulties of barter become so onerous that a 'money' system has to be developed.

Even today it is sometimes necessary to use barter. The collapse of a currency system, such as occurred in Germany at the end of World War II, meant that barter took place on an extensive scale, and eventually cigarettes acted as money. Bartering agreements at national level have also been arranged between some of the countries of the former communist bloc in Eastern Europe and Western nations in the last few years. A variety of specialists have come forward in this sort of reciprocal trading to ease the problems of barter. Thus a Western supplier who agrees to supply computers to a former Comecon country may be promised part of the purchase price in hard currency and the rest in shoes manufactured in the country concerned. If he can find a specialist prepared to take the shoes off him at a reasonable price and find a market for them, the trade can go ahead.

14.2.1
The disadvantages of barter

The disadvantages of barter are (a) the need for a coincidence of wants, (b) the difficulty of deciding equal values, and (c) the indivisibility of large items.

(a) *The necessity for a coincidence of wants.* It is impossible to barter unless A has what B wants, and A wants what B has. Sometimes this difficulty can be overcome by holding one half of the transaction over until a later time, but this requires trust and a sense of honouring obligations. It is made easier if the respective parties can read and write, so that the debt can be recorded. The records of citizens of the early United States include many such entries. Independence had ended the use of British currency before the United States was ready to provide a dollar system. 'I owe Nathanial Hawke 1 coil of rope length 20 yards', runs a typical entry.

(b) *The difficulty of deciding equal values.* Even when each party wants what the other has it does not follow they can agree on a fair exchange. Is a decorated pot worth a plump hen? A good deal of time can be wasted sorting out such equations of value.

(c) *The indivisibility of large items.* If a cow is worth two sacks of wheat, what is one sack of wheat worth? Once again we may need to carry over part of the transaction to a later period of time. This is not very easy even in a settled community; with nomadic peoples it is very difficult indeed.

For these reasons the barter system is discarded by societies which develop beyond autarky to more specialised methods of production. For such peoples a money system is essential.

14.3
The functions of money

Money is (a) a medium of exchange, (b) a measure of value, (c) a store of value, (d) a standard for deferred payments and (e) it facilitates one-way payments.

14.3.1
A medium of exchange

This is the chief function of money. It overcomes the need for a coincidence of wants, since everyone 'wants' money, which represents a claim against any goods or services which will yield satisfaction. It does follow, though, that money must be generally acceptable. In earlier times this general acceptability was achieved by using metals which were themselves valuable:

the coinage metals gold, silver and copper. Today all coins are 'token' money only, that is they are acceptable because we all agree to accept them as being worth a certain claim against goods and services. This general acceptability is supported by a declaration by the law-making body that the tokens do constitute 'legal tender'.

14.3.2
A measure of value

This function overcomes the difficulty of equating a decorated pot with a plump hen. We exchange the hen for what is agreed to be a fair quantity of money – now called the price of the hen. We then see whether it is sufficient money to buy a decorated pot. If it is not, we must save the price of the hen until we have enough other money to put with it to buy the pot. Thus the money is also useful as a store of value.

14.3.3
A store of value

This store of value can also help us to overcome the disadvantage of barter, that some items are indivisible. The farmer with only one sack of wheat cannot buy half a cow, but he can save up the money he has obtained in exchange for his wheat in the hope that before long he will be able to afford a cow.

The use of money as a store of value only applies when individuals are storing it; a whole nation could not do so. Robinson Crusoe on his island found a box of gold coins which proved useless to him until he returned to civilisation. If a whole nation stored up its money and then retired simultaneously they would all starve for lack of current production. Money is only a claim against the real goods and services which have utility. It is of no use unless the wealth is being created which yields satisfaction of wants.

14.3.4
A standard for deferred payments

Money is a useful unit of account, and accounts are records of debts to a business. It follows that the money system provides a standard for deferred payments, enabling us to record debts and eventually collect them either in one payment or in a series of payments on the instalment method. It is important here, however, that the value of money is stable over reasonably lengthy periods of time.

14.3.5
One-way payments

Some payments are not made in exchange for goods or services directly enjoyed. The benefits of peaceful existence, freedom from riot and civil disturbance are enjoyed in return for one-way payments called taxes, or rates if they are levied locally. Such one-way payments are inconvenient without a money system. In the Middle Ages the Court of England moved around the country, consuming the taxes in kind levied on the shires of England. As a result the King's Council, the forerunner of Parliament, was sometimes to be found elsewhere than at Westminster, and some famous Acts bear the names of towns where they were enacted. The Provisions of Oxford, 1258, is a well known example.

14.4
Exchanging surpluses through the money system

Exchange is essential if indirect production is a general feature of the economy. The surpluses produced by specialisation have to be exchanged if all are to enjoy a balanced diet and adequate satisfaction of other needs.

Figure 14.1 illustrates the part money plays in promoting these exchanges. Everyone, rich or poor, strong or weak, contributes in some way to the

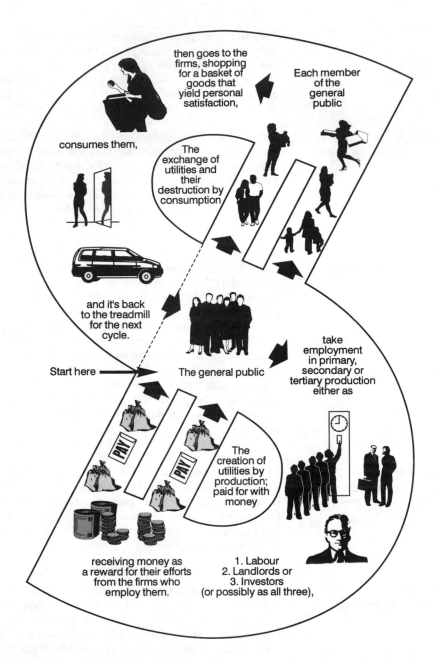

then goes to the firms, shopping for a basket of goods that yield personal satisfaction,

Each member of the general public

consumes them,

The exchange of utilities and their destruction by consumption

and it's back to the treadmill for the next cycle.

Start here →

The general public

take employment in primary, secondary or tertiary production either as

The creation of utilities by production; paid for with money

PAY

PAY

receiving money as a reward for their efforts from the firms who employ them.

1. Labour
2. Landlords or
3. Investors
(or possibly as all three),

Figure 14.1 The money system

production process. It may be by work of a skilled, semi-skilled or unskilled nature, or by displaying entrepreneurial ability. It may be by a person providing natural resources which for some reason he controls, or by providing capital he has accumulated. In other words the **factors of production** are put to work, and rewarded by a money payment. The rewards paid to these factors are discussed in the next few chapters; they are paid to, and received by, every member of society. There are no exceptions, but special arrangements have to be made for that tiny section of the population who are unable to work, such as the chronically sick, the aged and infirm. A few unscrupulous or anti-social elements may also obtain support by fair means or foul. Everyone receives some share of the **national**

income. Whether it is a fair share or not is discussed later. Here we are concerned only with *what* happens. Each of these individuals then purchases a 'basket of goods and services' to his personal taste and satisfaction.

A simple illustration of the process is the purchase of a packet of tea by a housewife whose husband is a minor clerk in a Government department. He has been performing his useful, but routine, services on behalf of – let us say – the Ministry of Agriculture and Fisheries. His duties concern the licensing of slaughter-houses and the supervision of their sanitation (a matter of public concern), for which he receives an average wage. His wife uses some of this wage to purchase a packet of tea which was grown in Sri Lanka on a plantation financed by joint British-Sri Lankan capital. It was shipped to the UK in a box lined with metal foil produced in Canada from ore smelted at Kitimat, in British Columbia. The transport was in a British liner manned by an Indian crew. The cargo was auctioned at the London tea auctions, and purchased by a blender who eventually packed it in cartons made from pulp produced in Labrador. The blender then wholesaled the tea to the retailer who sold it to the housewife.

At the time of the purchase the housewife's sole thought was that she had enough money for the tea, but would have to postpone until pay day the tin of instant coffee she had also hoped to purchase. Yet, behind the veil of money that obscured what was really going on, an army of people all over the world in a hundred specialised occupations were attending to her needs in return for her husband's supervision of the sanitary arrangements in British slaughter-houses.

14.5
The characteristics of money

Money must be (*a*) generally acceptable, and stable in value, (*b*) durable and rustproof, (*c*) difficult to imitate, (*d*) portable, and (*e*) divisible into small units.

14.5.1
General acceptability

This has already been referred to on page 166. There is no difficulty where coins have an intrinsic value of their own; but when that is the case, debasement of the currency may occur if people are tempted to clip precious metal from the edges of coins. Where coins are merely 'token money', i.e. the metal in the coin is worth less than the coin's so-called value, general acceptability is a matter of confidence in the coinage. Where devaluation of a currency is threatened, foreigners are unwilling to accept the coinage or notes of the country in question because they have no confidence that such tokens will keep the value they are supposed to have.

Often new coins are not popular with the public, who take some time to accept the idea of an unusual shape or new metal. The British public resisted the 50-pence piece when it was first introduced in place of the ten shilling note. Similarly Scottish bank-notes, although acceptable throughout Britain, are so rarely seen by English and Welsh shopkeepers that the production of one in a supermarket is sure to cause delay while managers are consulted.

14.5.2
Durability

Coins and notes are expensive to produce. Most coins have a life of about 50 years, whereas notes last about three months. As a result the UK changed over to 50 pence and £1 coins in place of paper notes of the same value. It is also important that the metal used should not react chemically with the air, or with water. Such 'rusting' would reduce the life of the coin, and its value if it had intrinsic value. The noble metals, gold, silver and copper are good in this respect, though silver tarnishes and copper does oxidise slowly. Aluminium alloys, being light and therefore portable, are widely used for coinage, but are less durable than cupronickel.

14.5.3
Ease of imitation

Where coinage or notes are imitated, the coiner or forger obtains a claim against the available consumer goods and services. But the counterfeiter is clearly not entitled to such a claim, for he has not himself joined in any useful productive activity at all. The money system is designed to make exchanges easier between the producers of useful goods and services. Any outsider, any non-producer, who shares in the wealth created must therefore do so at the expense of honest workers who have contributed real wealth to the pool of utilities created. Counterfeiting is most likely to occur when token money is in daily use. It has sometimes been used as an instrument of policy. During World War II vast quantities of £1 and £5 notes were manufactured by the Germans with a view to undermining the British economy. Every effort has to be made to make coins and notes difficult to imitate. Suppliers of special paper for bank-notes are strictly controlled and the destruction of dirty notes is carefully supervised.

14.5.4
Portability

Money must be portable. One of the disadvantages of gold for coins is that it is so heavy. Notes are a great improvement in this respect.

14.5.6
Divisibility

It is highly desirable that money should be capable of paying for the smallest transactions of everyday life. This is only possible if small units of money are available, which provides another reason why token coins have replaced coins of intrinsic value. The impossibility of making gold coins small enough to be worth a penny led to the use of copper and even less valuable metals. It has been suggested that coins should be made of plastic, which is light, durable and very cheap. The ease with which they might be imitated is the major drawback here.

14.6
Types of money

Originally money was in the form of coins, made from the coinage metals, copper, silver and gold. The face value of the coins and their real value were the same. If the kings who issued coins debased them, i.e. mixed inferior metals with the coinage metals, merchants simply reduced the value of the coins in their transactions. They also weighed coins if they feared they had been 'clipped'.

Gresham's law. This law, incorrectly attributed to Sir Thomas Gresham, the Elizabethan finance minister charged with the task of restoring confidence in the currency after Henry VIII's debasement of it, states that *bad money drives out good.* If debased coins are issued of a nominal value greater than their intrinsic value as metal, it will pay anyone with one of the older coins to melt it down and use the metal to buy more than the same quantity of debased coins. No doubt this is not easy for everyone to do, especially if there are penalties for tampering with the coinage, but there is some truth in the 'law', which like most economic laws is not an inevitable occurrence but refers to something that tends to happen. When people become sufficiently mature financially to recognise that money is merely a medium of exchange, the token nature of money becomes so generally recognised that attempts to profit in this way are less frequent.

The chief types of money in use today are:

(*a*) *Token coins*. These are coins made from metals whose real value is less than the face value of the coin. Because they are generally acceptable and because they are given the validity of 'legal tender', they enable exchange to take place on a basis of confidence in the currency. *Legal tender* is any method of payment which we are forced by law to accept as adequate settlement of a debt. All token money, whether coins or notes, is designated by the sovereign body – in the case of the United Kingdom the 'Queen in Parliament' – as being legal tender to a certain amount. Thus bronze coinage is legal tender to 20 pence, the 5p 10p and 20p coins are legal tender to a value of £5 and 50p coins to £10. £1 coins and all notes are legal tender to any amount. Thus if we pay for a £7600 car in notes or in £1 coins the garage dealer cannot object – it is a legal tender. If we tried to pay in pennies he/she would not accept the money.

To 'tender' payment is to offer payment. If I owe a debt and offer to pay in a legal tender the other party must accept the payment. If he/she refuses (perhaps because the counting of notes is a laborious job and payment by cheque would be safer and less trouble) I am excused the need to tender again. This does not mean I am let off the debt – it simply means that if the creditor wants the money he/she must now come and ask me for it – and bring a suitcase for all those notes. I tendered payment in a legal way, and need not repeat my attempt to pay.

(*b*) *Paper money*. Printed money is more convenient than coins, being lighter to carry and easier to handle in large quantities. The denominations of notes can be arranged to suit price levels in common use.

(*c*) *Bank deposits*. Deposits at a bank are the same as money. Originally they are paid into the bank in coin or paper by the depositor, or they may be created by the banker in a way which is explained on page 338. These deposits can then be transferred from one person to another by means of cheques. Cheques are not therefore money, but only *orders to pay* money. The quantity of bank deposits transferable today is so great that coins and notes have become the 'small change' of the money system, most big payments being made by cheque. Table 14.1 shows the most recent figures available for the UK.

The whole question of 'money' and the 'stock of money' is extremely complex and it depends to some extent on how we define money as to how

Table 14.1 Money in circulation in Great Britain, December 1993

Form of money	£ millions
Coins and bank notes	17 795
Bank current accounts	35 410
Bank deposit accounts	144 426
Building society savings	197 774
Total	£ 395 405 m

Source: Annual Abstract of Statistics, 1994

much money we conclude is in circulation at any given moment. This is dealt with in detail in Chapter 28 (see pages 344–5).

14.7
Convertible
currencies

In former times when money was either made of precious metals or was in the form of bank-notes which were backed by gold reserves in the banker's vaults, all token money was **convertible**, i.e. it could be exchanged on demand for precious metals. This was the case in the UK before 1914. We were on the gold standard. It is not the case today as far as British citizens are concerned. The promise on Bank of England notes which reads 'I promise to pay the bearer on demand the sum of five pounds' only refers to some alternative paper security – for instance, a Government security or an entry in the National Savings Bank. Gold is now going through a gradual process of demonetisation. Even the International Monetary Fund is selling off one sixth of its gold reserves. Since the abolition of exchange control it is now permissible for British citizens to convert sterling to any other world currency, and to hold gold if they wish to do so. This convertibility of sterling makes foreigners more willing to hold UK currency, and thus facilitates overseas trade.

14.7.1
Fiduciary issues

A fiduciary issue of notes is one not backed by gold, and whose basis is trust (*fiducia* is the Latin word for 'trust'). The Bank Charter Act of 1844 sanctioned a fiduciary issue of £14 million. Mainly on the grounds that at any given time some proportion of the note issue was temporarily out of circulation, it was deemed permissible to issue more notes than the actual value of gold in the reserves. The aim of this move was to finance the maximum volume of trade. Today the fiduciary issue is over £15 000 million; even so, the use of bank deposits transferable by cheques to finance transactions, still leaves Bank of England notes as only the 'small change' of the modern money system.

The large fiduciary issue today reflects the enormous volumes of goods and services produced in an advanced nation like Great Britain. If the note issue was linked to the gold reserves as it once was, the value of gold would have had to rise many times since 1914. This would have benefited those countries in which gold is mined. Modern money systems are backed not by the gold reserves, but by the trust that can be placed in a nation to produce goods and services to honour its obligations to foreign holders of its money. The more goods and services it is able to produce the more notes it is entitled to issue; there is no financial crisis unless falling productivity, strikes, civil disturbances or war threaten to interrupt prompt supplies of goods and services to these foreign creditors.

14.8
The value of money

Money is a medium of exchange and as such is continuously being traded for countless commodities. It is highly desirable that the value of money should remain stable over the years, otherwise its functions cannot be performed properly. This is particularly true of its use as a standard for deferred payments. For example, if money falls in value over the years, a person borrowing money is made better off because the money with which the debt is repaid later is less valuable than the money borrowed. The person from whom the money was borrowed receives back the devalued currency and has therefore lost on the transaction. To overcome this decline in the value of money, interest rates rise in such times, so that those who lend money receive in interest some of the capital losses they are inevitably going to suffer when repayment time comes. Nineteenth-century businessmen earned 2½ per cent on capital. Today many bank loans are being made at about 14 per cent and hire purchase loans are repayable at an effective rate of about 30 per cent (1995)

14.9
An index of prices

Changes in the value of money can be followed by using an index of prices. In preparing such an index, a base date is chosen and a suitable selection of prices is taken on that date and regularly thereafter. It may be necessary to weight the index according to the particular behaviour of the group about which we are hoping to collect evidence. In considering the value of money it is the average householder we have in mind. How has the changing value of money affected him or her? To discover the answer to this question we must first find out the pattern of spending of such a householder. This will involve a survey of the spending habits of a random sample of householders. If 10 per cent of the income of an average householder goes on basic foods, these foods must be weighted in the index to give due influence to this important group of purchases. If the average householder never buys platinum cigarette cases, this commodity need not be included in the calculations that lead to the index.

When a suitable selection of goods has been arrived at, the prices of these goods are noted and the total cost becomes the 'base' point from which the index will be measured. It is usually called 100. Suppose this collection of goods costs £20 in January of one year, but a year later it is costing £21. The index has risen from 100 to 105, since this is a 5 per cent increase. *The real value of money for the average householder has fallen and, unless the household's income has been increased to compensate for the changes in prices, the family's standard of living has been eroded.*

The Index of Retail Prices prepared in Great Britain shows the following changes in recent years:

Retail prices	1974	1975	1980	1985	1990
(January each year)	100	119.9	245.3	359.8	471.4

Clearly the value of £1 to the average householder has fallen considerably over this 16-year period to about one fifth of its 1974 value. Falling values of money are the sign of that major economic problem, inflation. This is dealt with more fully in Chapter 28.

14.10
Summary of
Chapter 14

1　People practising specialised production must exchange their outputs of goods and services with one another.

2　Goods may be bartered for other goods and services, but barter has certain disadvantages. The chief of these are the need for a coincidence of wants, the difficulty of equating values and the indivisibility of large items.

3　Money is a solution to the problems of barter, because each commodity or service can be exchanged for money, which can then be used by the new owner to purchase a balanced supply of utilities.

4　Desirable characteristics of money include general acceptability, portability and cleanliness in handling.

5　The commonest types of money are token coins, notes and bank deposits.

6 Some currencies are convertible into gold; others are not convertible. Willingness to accept non-convertible currencies depends on world confidence in the economies of the countries issuing the money, since it represents a claim on these economies for real goods and services.

7 An issue of notes and token money not backed by gold reserves is called a fiduciary issue, i.e. one based on trust.

8 It is important that the value of money should be held steady if its use as a basis for deferred payments is to be fulfilled properly. The changing value of money can be studied by using an index of prices.

Exercise Set 14

1 Why is specialisation desirable? Why does money become an essential medium of exchange when specialised production is adopted to provide the goods and services needed in a community?

2 Money need not be valuable in itself, so long as it is generally acceptable. Explain.

3 What are the disadvantages of barter? Why are these disadvantages of less importance to primitive people than to advanced nations?

4 Records show that one of the methods used to force primitive people to accept paid employment in mines or factories was to impose taxation on the head of the family. Suggest why this policy succeeded where persuasion had failed.

5 What are the functions of money? Why are these functions less effectively performed if money changes in value?

6 Gold is intrinsically valuable. Token money needs the support of a legislative declaration that it is 'legal tender'. Explain, referring in your answer to the legal tender of your own country.

7 All nations have laws against counterfeiting. What is wrong with counterfeiting, and why does it strike particularly at economies where token money is in use?

8 What is a fiduciary note issue? Why is it possible for the Bank of England to keep such a large fiduciary issue in circulation today?

9 If money falls in value it helps debtors. Explain.

10 An index of wholesale prices for Great Britain shows the following:

1975 = 100; 1977 = 145.6; 1979 = 167.6; 1981 = 193.5; 1983 = 222.0; 1985 = 244.1; 1987 = 275.2; 1989 = 318.5; 1991 = 364.6; 1993 = 374.8

Comment on these figures with regard to the value of money over the period shown. To what extent could these changes have been caused by (a) a rise in overseas prices; (b) a cut in insurance rates; (c) a fall in productivity in certain factories?

15   The distribution of wealth – rewards to factors

**15.1
The importance of
'distribution
theory'**

Adam Smith drew attention in 1776 to the change that had come over production methods in his lifetime. Almost in a generation Britain had become an industrial society. Fortunes were being made in iron works, coal mines, heavy engineering, cotton and woollen manufacture and the pottery industry. Canals, ports, roads, bridges, aqueducts and coastal shipping were opening up areas of the country previously uninhabited. A flood of cotton goods, ironware, brassware, porcelain and china, woollen cloth, knitware, craft and carriages, ships' gear and farm equipment, building material and furniture poured out of the ringing workshops and was forwarded to the four corners of the earth by shippers, insurance brokers, carriers and financiers. Yet amid all this plenty the paradox that puzzled economists, capitalists and workers alike was the enduring poverty of the majority of ordinary people. The book that enquired into *The Nature and the Causes of the Wealth of Nations* had nothing to explain the poverty of the working class. Driven by the Enclosure Acts from the land that had previously sustained them, they fought a hard struggle for survival in the shanty towns and overcrowded slums of industrial cities. The great successors to Adam Smith were Thomas Malthus (1766–1834), David Ricardo (1772–1823) and John Stuart Mill (1806–73). Malthus is chiefly famous for his *Essay on Population*, written in 1798 (see page 195). It was this essay that earned economics the nickname of 'the dismal science'. Ricardo was the first economist to recognise that the poverty of ordinary people was simply due to an unsatisfactory distribution of wealth. John Stuart Mill carried the discussion further, to state quite clearly that this was a matter which man could solve by wise policies. No inevitable natural economic forces were at work to defeat him.

The writings of these two great economists are so much a part of the background of modern economics that it is worth while pausing for a moment to consider their influence.

**15.2
David Ricardo**

David Ricardo (1772–1823) wrote about the distribution of wealth in his *Principles of Political Economy and Taxation*, published in 1817. Writing forty-one years after Adam Smith's *Wealth of Nations*, his picture of the economic scene was painted in dark colours. Darker still were the interpretations placed on his book by readers who found its gloomier phrases suited to their own moods. Reaction to the revolution in France, to the unrest after the Napoleonic wars, and the continued existence of poverty despite wealth had made Britain's leaders hostile to any pressure for reform. They seized on Ricardo's wages theory (see page 196), ignored its hopeful and optimistic phrases, and repeated its gloomy forebodings about the inevitability of future poverty.

This brilliant son of a Dutch Jewish stockbroker was a financial genius who specialised in foreign exchange. Estranged from his family because of his marriage to a Quaker, Ricardo was reduced to poverty. Borrowing from friends he quickly amassed a huge fortune and turned his leisured activities towards the study of economics, currency and politics. The main feature of his *Principles* was the emphasis he placed on the distribution of wealth, which John Stuart Mill was to develop.

He is most famous for his definition of rent as 'that portion of the produce of the earth which is paid to the landlord for the use of the original and indestructible powers of the soil'. Ricardo here is quite clear that money is not of any real importance in the payment of rent. The landlord does not want money for the use of his land, but a portion of the produce of the earth: meat and fish, and bread and wine and manufactured goods. We can all accept this lucid and straightforward definition.

Ricardo died suddenly at the age of 51, in 1823. The genuineness of his concern for the evils of the existing system, and his acute statements on economic principles have been obscured by their misrepresentation by others. Along with Malthus he came to be regarded as one who held a gloomy view of the prospects for ordinary people. His definition of rent survives in popular knowledge as clear and meaningful.

What followed from it was not so easy to understand, but it was to become a major point in the theory of distribution which unlocked many riddles that puzzled economists. This was the concept of 'economic rent' (see page 182).

15.3
John Stuart Mill

John Stuart Mill (1806–73) was a boy genius whose father, James Mill, was a follower of Jeremy Bentham, the practical philosopher of the Industrial Revolution. His father took personal care of the boy's education from an early age. He began to learn Greek when he was only three, and Latin shortly after. At the age of twelve his studies included philosophy, political economy and logic. By the age of 16 he had founded the Utilitarian Society, whose members supported Jeremy Bentham's political theory of 'utility'. This theory held that the standard by which we must judge all the actions of men, institutions and Governments was the yardstick of human happiness. The action that promoted the well-being and happiness of the greatest number of people was the right one. It is an idea that still commands widespread respect.

Mill did not overthrow the ideas of Adam Smith, Ricardo or Malthus. He moved their ideas on a short step in a more optimistic direction. He agreed with them that production of wealth was a bitter process, subject to harsh, inexorable laws like competition. 'But,' he says in his *Principles of Political Economy*, 'it is not so with the Distribution of Wealth. That is a matter of human institution solely. The things once there, mankind, individually or collectively, can do with them as they like.'

And, no doubt, what mankind did with the wealth they had created was to be judged from the standpoint of the greatest good to the greatest number. It was an idea that shook a sleeping world awake, and led eventually to the type of managed prosperity which has been such a feature of the second half of the twentieth century.

Mill defined economics as 'the practical science of the production and distribution of wealth'. Not only must man produce wealth, he must distribute it more reasonably. Too great a believer in the advantages of competition to advocate Government intervention himself, Mill sowed the seeds of State interference on many 'exceptional' grounds. One of these was that he thought the State should introduce compulsory education; another was that the State should compel factory owners to obey the legislation

Parliament had enacted, even though it raised costs. He died in 1873, during Gladstone's great Parliament of 1868–74, when a burst of legislative activity on education, public health, electoral law, control of corruption and control of monopolies was passing through the British Parliament.

15.4 Rewards to factors

The money system involves two equal and opposite flows, which are shown diagrammatically in Figure 15.1

These flows will be discussed more fully in later chapters, but the flow from firms to individuals is the one that interests us at present. It is in this flow of money incomes from firms to individuals that the distribution of wealth is made.

Note, first, that the entire proceeds after tax of the activities of firms are given to individuals, who are the owners of the factors employed. The landlord receives his **rent**, the worker his **wages**, the investor his **interest** and **profits**. The flows into industry consist initially of capital flows; these are paid out to landlords and workers in the form of rent and wages for the initial creation of capital assets like buildings, machinery and fixtures. Later a different form of flow into the firms takes place: the capital flow is replaced by current-account flows, i.e. payments for the goods and services supplied by the firms once production has started. These inputs are again paid out to the landlords for continued use of their land and to the workers for their labour – but this time not to construction workers but to a different class of labour employed in the production activities of the firm. Now, too, the investors of capital begin to draw rewards for their efforts: interest payments as a reward for postponing their personal consumption while the firms constructed the plants; profits as a reward for running the risks of the enterprise. The entire receipts are paid out to individuals. What, the astute reader will ask, about profits which are not redistributed to the shareholders, but are 'ploughed back' into the firm? Of course all such amounts are paid out to more construction workers to extend the plant and layout of the firm, returning eventually as even bigger profits, or even more growth.

Profit is the residual balance of the activities of firms. The amount of this residue of profit depends on the extent to which the other payments to factors can be increased or decreased. For example, if rent is raised, profits will be lowered; if wages are forced up, profits will be forced down; if interest rates are lowered, profits will be higher. It also varies with the price that can be obtained for the goods and services sold by the firms.

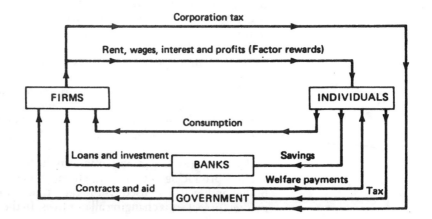

Figure 15.1 Flows round the money system

The enduring confrontation between workers and entrepreneurs arises from the conflict of interests that exists between them. Today, when we regard entrepreneurs as only another class of labour, it seems peculiar that there should be a conflict: but in fact labour is not a homogeneous commodity, for it is split into many different grades. The loyalty of entrepreneurs to the profit motive is linked to their activity as agents for the investing public. Their rewards, and continuation as agents, depends to some extent on their success in achieving good profit records.

The distribution of wealth therefore depends on the willingness of entrepreneurs, in their capacities as agents of the investing public, to concede an increased share of the fruits of production to landlords and workers. The extent to which they are prepared to do so is explained by the **marginal-productivity theory of factor prices**. Alternatively, the ability of landlords and labour to compel entrepreneurs to yield a larger share of the fruits of production enters the 'distribution' picture. When workers are strong, or occupy a bottle-neck position where they can easily interrupt production, concessions will be forced from entrepreneurs which amount to a change in the distribution of wealth.

15.5
The market for factors

A market is a place where buyers and sellers are in contact with one another to fix prices. Just as markets exist for the purchase and sale of commodities, a market may be said to exist for the purchase and sale of factors. There is the 'capital market' where financiers willing to make loans are to be found by those wishing to borrow money. There are estate agents and property dealers with premises, sites, farms and mines available if the price is right. There are employment bureaux and labour exchanges willing to find jobs for workers and workers for jobs.

The entrepreneurs enter these markets in order to purchase factors. Like all consumers they are price conscious and the basis of their activities is their estimate of the likely productivity to be achieved by employing a factor. As usual in economics it is not a question of an absolute choice between having labour or not having labour. All productive activities require some labour. The choice is a marginal one. Shall I have more labour and less land and capital, or more land and less labour and capital, etc.? The basis of his/her demand for factors is the entrepreneur's estimate of their marginal productivity.

The marginal productivity of a factor is defined as *the increase in total revenue to be derived from the employment of one extra unit of the factor.*

On the supply side the individuals offering land, labour or capital are concerned to achieve the best price possible for their services. Once again it is usual for economists to consider a perfect market, where free flows of factors take place to the point in the market where the best rewards are being offered. David Ricardo, writing at a time when some of the factor markets were much more perfect than they are today, observed that

> *Whilst every man is free to employ his capital where he pleases, he will naturally seek for it that employment which is most advantageous; he will naturally be dissatisfied with a profit of 10 per cent if by removing his capital he can obtain a profit of 15 per cent.*

Today there are many imperfections in the factor markets, but even against the friction-producing activities of strong trade unions, powerful professional bodies and well-organised employers' trade associations the free play of the market for factors is changing all our lives. In the UK in the past 15 years (since the Conservative election victory of 1979) a revolution has taken place in the factor markets. When politicians talk about the freeplay of the market they don't just mean the market where the householder is buying the day's food for the family, and as choice is exercised in the market place the entrepreneurs are being told what to buy or what to make. They mean free play in the markets for factors as well. Countless workers who thought they were secure in career jobs for life have seen the fruits of 200 years of trade union struggle swept away in 15 years. Employers who once had to convince doubtful shop stewards of the merits of a restructuring programme have been assisted to adopt a more 'hire and fire' policy. However cushioned the workers have been by helpful social policies, unemployment relief, retraining programmes, etc., the fact is that almost every month some new 'cushion' is removed and the free play of market forces in the factor markets gets harder to bear.

15.6
The demand for factors – a derived demand

The price of a factor is fixed like all other prices by demand for, and supply of, the factor. Factors are demanded by entrepreneurs, and this demand is a derived demand which arises not because the factors are wanted for themselves, but for what they can create in the way of 'utilities' to satisfy 'wants'. It follows that if a unit of a factor is going to provide more in the way of created 'utilities' than its cost to the entrepreneur, he will buy it; if it is not going to create as much wealth as it costs, it will not be purchased by the entrepreneur.

It is for the entrepreneur to demand factors according to his ideas of what will achieve the 'optimum' firm for him. He plans the enterprise, mixing his factors according to the dearness or cheapness of each. If labour is dear he will use more machines, i.e. more capital. The demand for factors is derived from the demand for the goods and services factors can make available

15.7
The marginal-productivity theory of factor prices – the demand side

The marginal-productivity theory attempts to explain how factor rewards, i.e. the prices of factors, are decided. It assumes perfect competition in the market for factors, and looks at the market from both sides. There is the point of view of the buyers of factors: the demand side. It is this point of view that gives the theory its name. The other point of view is that of the suppliers of the factors: the landlords, workers and investors. These, the theory holds, obey the rule of **maximum net advantage** moving to the point where the best rewards are offered.

Let us look at the demand side first. The marginal-productivity theory of factor prices says that a factor will be rewarded well, or ill, according to the contribution that it makes to the total product, or revenue, of the firm. The theory is concerned with *the addition to output and income of the firm resulting from the employment of an additional unit of the factor.* The marginal unit of the factor is the unit the entrepreneur has just hired, in an expanding industry; or is about to discard in a contracting industry.

The increase in output is often called the **marginal physical product,** and the increase in income the **marginal revenue product.**

The imaginary figures given in Table 15.1 illustrate the marginal physical products and marginal revenue products of successive employees taken on by a firm in perfect competition. In these circumstances wages are fixed at the market price for that particular class of labour, so that there is nothing the entrepreneur can do to alter wages. His personal demands are very tiny compared to total demand. Figure 15.2 shows the same information in diagrammatic form. Table 15.1, Figure 15.2 and the notes below it should now be studied.

Table 15.1 Marginal physical product and marginal revenue product in perfect competition

Number of men	Units of output	Marginal physical product (i.e. output of extra man)	Marginal revenue product (i.e. extra man's output in money terms)	Wages
1	5	5	£300	£240
2	12	7	£420	£240
3	22	10	£600	£240
4	33	11	£660	£240
5	43	10	£600	£240
6	50	7	£420	£240
7	55	5	£300	£240
8	59	4	£240	£240
9	62	3	£180	£240
10	64	2	£120	£240

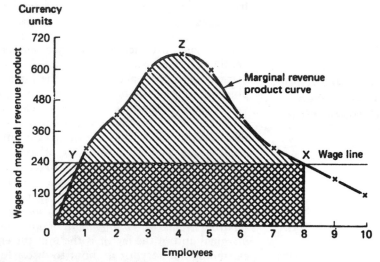

Figure 15.2 Marginal physical product and marginal revenue product in perfect competition

Notes
1 Marginal revenue product increases at first, and reaches a maximum at the point Z when four employees are engaged.
2 The fifth worker produces an increase of 600.00 currency units, which is less than the fourth worker's marginal product but it is still worth while employing him for his wage is only 240.00 currency units.
3 When the marginal revenue product falls below the wage line at the point X (eight workers employed) it is not profitable to employ any more.
4 The total wage is shown by the area 08 X 240 = 1920.00.
5 The total revenue is the shaded area under the curve 0YZX8, and is equal to 3540.00 (the sum of the marginal-revenue products).
6 The reader should note that the rewards to the other factors can also be seen from the diagram. They are the area under the curve YZX minus the area of the triangle 0Y240. (*Now return to the top of page 181.*)

In rather similar ways we can show that the entrepreneur's use of land will depend on the marginal productivity of the land, and his use of capital will depend on the marginal productivity of capital. If the revenue produced by the land is likely to be greater than the cost of the land, the entrepreneur will demand its use; if not he will look elsewhere for land at a cheaper price. If the likely revenue to be earned from the use of capital will exceed the rate of interest (i.e. the charge for borrowing the capital), the entrepreneur will go ahead with the project and borrow the money. If not, he will postpone the project until capital is cheaper.

15.8
The marginal-productivity theory of factor prices – the supply side

From the point of view of the factor owners, their willingness to supply depends on the achievement of *the maximum net advantage* to them. The term *net* advantage involves a deduction from the rewards of the agreement of any losses inevitable in the bargain. These may be monetary losses or non-monetary losses. Many a worker offered employment at higher wages elsewhere does not take it because his wife will not be near her mother, or the children will need to change schools. If the advantages of the bargain outweigh the disadvantages, factors will move between firms and industries. These movements clearly reflect the derived nature of the demand for factors, for it is the elasticity of demand for the ultimate output which controls the ability of the entrepreneur to pass increased factor costs on to the ultimate consumer; and hence his willingness to make concessions. If a change in taste or fashion makes a product highly desirable to consumers the marginal productivity of factors can be maintained even if factor costs rise; the entrepreneur simply raises the price of the product. If a change in taste or fashion makes the product less desirable, the entrepreneur will face a declining marginal revenue product. Any concessions to factors (e.g. wage increases) will mean lower profit margins. The entrepreneur must stand firm and resist any claims for increased rewards to factors.

15.9
Criticisms of the marginal-productivity theory

Although there is obvious truth in the statement that entrepreneurs will not buy a factor if it is going to cost more than it produces, this theory has been much criticised. One criticism is that it is all too theoretical, that entrepreneurs cannot know what any one worker's contribution to revenue is. In fact, of course, they don't; but this does not alter the fact that when the entrepreneur maximises profits he does so by paying the factors no more than they are worth according to the entrepreneurs' views of their likely marginal-revenue products. The theory does not require that the entrepreneurs know with certainty, only that they pay in such a way as to maximise profits. Another criticism is that the theory leads to peculiar conclusions. For example, it might suggest that high wages are the cause of unemployment, because if wages were lower more hands would be taken on. In fact the theory has little to say about the causes of unemployment, which it is generally recognised lie in the region of total monetary demand for goods and services. If the demand for goods and services is generally weak, the derived demand for factors will be weak too. To draw from this the conclusion that lowering wages will raise employment would not necessarily be right, for it would decrease still further the low level of demand that is already causing the difficulty. High wages are perfectly compatible with full employment if productivity is high. A full discussion of this is to be found on pages 326–32.

15.10
The rewards to factors – definitions

The rewards accruing to the factors are termed respectively rent, wages, interest and profit.

- **Rent** is that portion of the produce of the earth which is paid to the landlord for the use of the original and indestructible powers of the soil (David Ricardo).
- **Wages** are that portion of the produce of the earth which is paid to the worker for the use of his labour.
- **Interest** is that portion of the produce of the earth paid to the investor for the postponement of his own consumption, and the placing of his claims against resources at the disposal of the entrepreneurs.
- **Profit** is that portion of the produce of the earth paid to the entrepreneur for bearing the risks of losing his capital. It is a residual amount left after rewarding the other factors. It may, of course, be negative (i.e. a loss).

Early economists found great difficulty in explaining the rewards to factors, and the definitions given here are the result of more than a century of discussion. For example, the poor rewards paid to workers in the coal mines seemed quite out of proportion to the rewards paid to university lecturers or the rewards paid to professional actresses. A major clue to explain these apparently illogical rewards was the doctrine of 'economic rent'. The name is confusing, since it would appear to refer to land only: but although this idea developed from David Ricardo's view of rent, it is now recognised that 'economic rents' are earned by all factors.

15.11
Economic rent – how the idea started

Imagine a country where there is plenty of land, all of good quality and not inhabited by an indigenous people. Some African countries are like this today. There is plenty of good land, and anyone can carve out a smallholding for himself. In these circumstances would anyone pay rent? Of course not, for free land is to be had for the asking. Ricardo said,

> *It is only, then, because land is not unlimited in quantity and uniform in quality, and because in the progress of population, land of an inferior quality or less advantageously situated is called into cultivation, that rent is ever paid for the use of it.*
>
> *When in the progress of society, land of the second degree of fertility is taken into cultivation, rent immediately commences on that of the first quality, and the amount of that rent will depend on the difference in the quality of these two portions of land.*
>
> *When land of the third quality is taken into cultivation, rent immediately commences on the second, and is regulated as before, by the difference in their productive powers. At the same time the rent of the first quality will rise.*

The point here is that land is not uniform in quality, and as population rises more and more marginal land must come into use. The high costs of production on the most marginal land will decide the price of grain. The better land, yielding a higher return, must earn rent. The rent payable on good or conveniently situated land, as distinct from inaccessible marginal land of poor quality, was a payment to the landlord for the use of its peculiar and indestructible powers.

It was at this point that the difficulty arose. A major controversy during the Napoleonic War period until 1815 had been the high rents of farms. These high rents were due to the high prices for corn resulting from the war.

Some politicians, and most ordinary people, blamed the landlords' rents for the high price of bread. Ricardo defended them, proving that the high price of bread was causing the high rents: in other words, *rents were price-determined, not price-determining.*

As this controversy developed, simplification of the argument led to the adoption of two basic premises: (*a*) that land is in short supply, (*b*) it will only grow corn. If it doesn't grow corn, then it will not be used. If it does grow corn, then the rent that it earns is a payment to the factor land over and above what is necessary to keep it in its previous employment, namely lying idle. This rather muddled thinking led to the conclusion that the whole of 'rent' was a surplus payment to landlords for being the fortunate owners of a factor which was in fixed supply and strongly demanded. The stronger the demand, the higher the 'rent'.

The meaning of economic rent, often simply called 'rent', is much wider today, and the idea that rent for land is entirely 'economic rent' has been rejected on the grounds that land does have alternative uses. Vilfredo Pareto, an Italian economist, defined 'rent' as 'a payment to a factor over and above what is necessary to keep it in its present employment'. If a factor, whether it be land, labour or capital, is not sufficiently rewarded in its present occupation, then it will move out to seek a better reward elsewhere. We must therefore pay the factor at least as much as its 'transfer' earnings. **Transfer earnings** are the amount the factor would earn in its best-paid alternative employment. To use an earlier term, transfer earnings are the 'opportunity cost' of the factor.

A few examples may help. Imagine a teacher who has taught in a school for many years and is attached to the village, its people, and her own status in the community. Suppose she earns £200 per week. Would she leave the school if they cut her salary to £175? Probably not. Would she leave at a

Table 15.2 Normal and abnormal rewards to factors

Factor	Normal reward	Economic rent
Land	Commercial rent	'Situation rent'
Labour	Wages	'Rent of ability'
Capital (i) (For foregone consumption)	Interest	–
Capital (ii) (For taking risks)	Profit	'Monopoly rent' or 'super-profits'

Notes

1 Interest does rise above normal sometimes, but because money is 'hot' (able to flow quickly round the system from places where interest is low to places where interest is high) the economic rent it earns is short-lived.

2 Examples of situation rent are the high rents of properties in London's Oxford Street, or Fifth Avenue, New York. Because shoppers in these fashionable areas are prepared to pay high prices, and the number of shop fronts is limited, premises earn more than normal rent. Doctors seeking premises in Harley Street similarly bid up the rents of surgeries in this fashionable area.

3 Rent of ability is the name given to the 'rent' element in wages. There are many examples. A pop singer earning £10 000.00 per week would as willingly sing for £1000.00, and probably a short while before he reached his sudden popularity was doing so for £50. If the best reward he could earn in some other occupation is £100, then £9900 of his earnings is economic rent.

4 When a monopolist, or a supplier of branded goods, earns more than normal profit, the super-profits earned are often referred to as 'monopoly rent'. Normal profit is that portion of profit which just keeps the entrepreneur in the industry. Monopoly rent, like all economic rent, is a payment to the factor capital over and above what is needed to keep it in its present employment.

salary of £150? Possibly not. Would she leave at £125? Well, yes, she might. Then £125 is her transfer earnings, and she is earning £75 'economic rent'.

Consider a baker selling bread and pastries in a country area. He can charge more or less what he likes for cakes, and earns a comfortable living from the business, of, say, £250 per week. A multiple firm starts to operate in the area selling from mobile shops. The baker is forced to cut prices. When his earnings fall to £150 per week he is seriously considering giving up the business. Obviously the other £100 was 'economic rent'.

Table 15.2 shows the normal rewards to factors, and the names given to their particular forms of economic rent (see page 183).

15.12
Rent, quasi-rent and elasticity of supply

If a factor earns more than normal rewards it is often because the free flow of factors around the market is interrupted by some sort of economic friction. The ability of some trade unions to exclude non-members from entering an industry is an example of such friction. It enables the union's members to earn more than normal rewards for their labour. Similar 'rents' may be earned by the fortunate possessors of skills which are in great demand and are either the result of natural talent or long training. Both opera singers and computer programmers are able to command economic rents: the first because their natural talents are rare, the second because the supply of trained personnel is inelastic. Dentists and doctors earn more than normal rewards because of the long training required; labourers are often poorly paid because their skills can be quickly acquired.

In deciding the rewards to factors, elasticity of supply is of great importance. If supply is inelastic, factors will be able to command economic rents, and the more fixed the supply the greater the proportion of the reward paid that will be economic rent. If supply is completely fixed, and no alternative use is possible, the price of the factor depends entirely on the demand. An example is the rent of property in a parade of shops. Such land cannot be returned to corn growing or market gardening, and its price is largely economic rent fixed by the demand for its services as shop property. Figure 15.3 illustrates the change in rent that follows an alteration in demand.

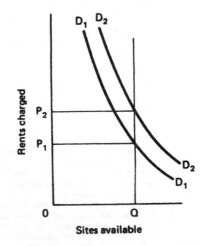

Figure 15.3 Economic rent for shop sites

Notes

1 When demand is D_1D_1 the rent charged is P_1. Probably this rent is 'economic rent' already, because this land has no alternative uses – it is stuck in the middle of a parade of shops.

2 When demand rises to D_2D_2 the rent rises to P_2. Clearly the whole of this increase is 'economic rent', arising from the demand for this type of shop property which is in inelastic supply.

Mark Twain tells an amusing story about the wages of pilots on the Mississippi River steamboats in the nineteenth century. The pilots' union had fixed wages at $240 a month, but in hard times when there were unemployed pilots about, the steamship owners forced down wages because pilots were in elastic supply. One pilot was forced to sign on for $100 a month and promptly took his ship up the centre of the river against the full force of the current. Fearful that fuel supplies would run out, the captain sent his compliments and suggested that better speeds could be achieved if the pilot would steer closer to the bank, where a notoriously slow vessel was overtaking them at the moment. Back went the pilot's compliments to the captain, but he could not be expected to know as much as a man earning $240 a month. The supply of pilots, now that the vessel had left the quayside, was very inelastic indeed, and 30 seconds later the ship was shaving the bushes near the bank, while a pilot on full pay earning his 'fair' share of economic rent was showing the rival steamship what a compound engine could do.

The confusing use of the same word 'rent' to describe things as different as the payment for farm land and the wages of violinists or operatic sopranos, led Alfred Marshall, an eminent Victorian economist, to adopt the term 'quasi-rent' for rent earned by the other factors. The Latin word *quasi* means 'as if', and the term quasi-rent therefore indicates a close connection between these abnormal earnings and situation-rent earned by some types of land. The general acceptance of 'rents' as being a reward to any factor over and above what is necessary to keep it in its present employment has led to a change in the use of the term quasi-rent. It is now often used for temporary rents, which will eventually be eliminated by competition. The fortunate owner of stocks of food at a time when, owing to weather or industrial disputes, an area is cut off by transport dislocations, may earn temporary quasi-rent. Similarly, a shortage of computer programmers may lead to higher salaries being earned temporarily by such workers. These are quasi-rents of ability.

15.13
Are rents price-determining or price-determined?

Ever since Ricardo wrote about rent, discussion has persisted as to whether rents are price-determining or price-determined. Ricardo held that rents are price-determined and not price-determining; in other words that the high price of land was the result of the high price of corn and not the cause of it. The cause of the high price of corn was the shortages due to war and a succession of bad harvests. There is much to be said for this argument. It has already been pointed out in the section on speculation (see page 139) that a speculator selling stored produce at high prices is not the cause of the shortage, but the only person who is doing anything to relieve it. His efforts are not forcing up the price, but tending to reduce it.

By contrast, the high situation-rents paid to landlords in fashionable areas are the result of competition between those in search of property or sites which are in inelastic supply. To the multiple-shop proprietor seeking a site in the West End of London countless sites are available for his particular purpose, even though sites in general are in inelastic supply, so that the whole of the payments he makes are transfer earnings and he certainly includes them in the calculations of the prices he will charge for goods. Such payments therefore form part of the costs of production, and are price-determining. The debate seems likely to continue.

To the extent that rents are the result of the fortunate situation of the individual who benefits, they can be taxed away for the benefit of the general public without the factor being withdrawn from service and without prices being increased. If this is done, the public who have in fact contributed to the rents earned, recoup them through the tax net. It seems highly desirable that this should be so, but it is a political rather than an economic decision.

15.14 Summary of Chapter 15

1 The problem of the continued poverty of masses of people, when wealth was being created in great quantities, led the early economists to turn their attention to the distribution of wealth.
2 The entire proceeds of production flow in the form of money payments to individuals who are either landlords, workers, or investors.
3 The proportions in which the wealth is shared depend on the demand for, and supply of, factors.
4 The demand for factors is a derived demand which arises from the demand for utilities to satisfy wants.
5 The entrepreneurs who demand factors will not pay more for them than the marginal-revenue productivity of the factor.
6 The suppliers of factors, landlords, workers and investors will not supply the factor to any entrepreneur if they can earn a better reward elsewhere, so that factors flow around the factor markets to equalise, in the long run, the net advantage to factor owners.
7 Part of the rewards to factors, which arises when free flow around the markets is interrupted for some reason, is economic rent, a reward paid to any factor which happens for the moment to be in inelastic supply (see page 182 for definitions).

Exercises Set 15

1 'The production of wealth is one thing: distribution of wealth is another.' What is the importance of the distribution of wealth and how is it arranged in market economies?
2 What is rent? What is economic rent? What is quasi-rent?
3 Explain why a miner might earn £200 for a week's work underground, while a television personality earns £10 000 for a two-hour programme.
4 Consider the proportion of earnings which are economic rents in each of the following cases:

   (a) A lady teacher, salary £200 per week, who could never dream of taking up any other vocation.
   (b) A refuse collector earning £120 per week, who is thinking of taking employment as a road-haulage driver, for £200 per week.
   (c) A folk ballad singer earning £1500 per week who used to be a clerk at £80 per week.
   (d) A trade union official, formerly earning £12 000 per annum, chosen by the Prime Minister to be chairman of a nationalised industry at £50 000.00 per annum. He would be prepared to take on the post even for £15 000.
   (e) A midwife earning £150 a week in a British hospital who rejects an offer of a post at a salary equivalent to £200 a week in an American small town.

5 What are transfer earnings? What will be the effect on an entrepreneur who refuses to pay this amount to a skilled employee?
6 Distinguish between 'normal profit' and 'monopoly rent'. Can monopoly rents ever be justified?

7 What is the marginal-productivity theory of wages? How far does it explain wages in the real world?
8 What economic forces help to determine the rewards paid to (*a*) a plot of land in a city centre, (*b*) a talented actress, (*c*) a semi-skilled assembler in an electronics factory?
9 This Table shows the number of shirts made in a factory and the number of staff employed. Copy it out and complete the Table. Each shirt is worth 10 currency units.

Women employed	Output of shirts	Marginal product (in currency units of 1.00)
1	24	
2	54	
3	86	
4	116	
5	140	
6	150	
7	158	

How many women will be employed if wages are (i) 200 (ii) 300 currency units?
10 This table shows the profit earned by a travel agency operating a head office and a number of branches. Each branch costs £20 000 to set up, and a 15 per cent return on capital invested is required. All branches are equally profitable. What is the maximum number of branches that the head office should operate? Copy out and complete the Table.

No. of establishments	Capital used (units of 1.00)	Profit earned (units of 1.00)	Marginal product
Head Office	40,000	8 000	
H.O. + 1 branch	?	11 700	
+ 2 branches	?	15 200	
+ 3 "	?	18 500	
+ 4 "	?	21 600	
+ 5 "	?	23 800	
+ 6 "	?	25 600	
+ 7 "	?	27 000	
+ 8 "	?	28 000	

(*Hint* The decision will be made at the point where the marginal revenue from the branch falls below 15 per cent of the extra capital required to run a branch.)

16 Rewards to factors – rent

16.1
Rent – the reward to land

Some confusion is unavoidable here, since both the word 'rent' and the word 'land' have special meanings in economics. While the commonest meaning of the word 'land' is geographical land, in economics land consists of the resources of the earth made available by Nature. Some of these resources are free goods, like the air and the sunshine. Some are not quite free, but are in abundant supply so that they are relatively cheap, like water and marginal land. Some are in short supply and the fortunate owners of such resources are able to command payments for their use, called rent.

In everyday language, rent is a sum of money paid for the use of landed property. Everyone needs a geographical 'territory', some place that can be called home. We must therefore buy a piece of land and build a house on it, or buy an existing piece of property, or rent a home from someone (called a landlord) who does have such a property surplus to requirements. As we have already seen, the meaning of the word 'rent' has become confused, and the terms economic rent and commercial rent have come into use to differentiate between the special sense in economics and the ordinary commercial meaning. When a tenant pays rent to a landlord, be it a private landlord, a local council, a New Town Development Corporation, or perhaps a Government department, the rent is said to be commercial rent'. We have already seen that in some popular sites the rent payable may also include an element of economic rent.

Where the payment is for use of a deposit of natural resources, such as an iron-ore concentration or a bed of gravel or sand, the rent is usually paid in the form of a royalty per ton of mineral extracted. It is often arranged that the royalty owner will be paid at least a minimum sum per annum for the use of the deposit, whether the mining company manages to extract that quantity or not. When this is the arrangement the minimum payment agreed on is called the **minimum rent**.

The rent of land is decided by the interaction of supply and demand. If demand is strong, or suitable land is in short supply, prices will be high. If demand is weak or land is plentiful, prices will be low.

16.2
The demand for land

The demand for land is derived from the demand for the satisfaction of the basic wants of shelter, territory and agricultural products. Demand is strong when population is rising, and when food production is profitable. It grows stronger when incomes rise and weaker when incomes fall.

Demand for land is said to be 'price-elastic' when it changes more than proportionally with a change in price. The elasticity of demand for land depends on a number of factors. If the demand for the product to be grown or produced is elastic, the demand for land on which to produce it will be elastic too. If the demand for the product is inelastic, the demand for the land is inelastic too, and it will continue to be demanded despite changes in price. The demand for land in fashionable shopping areas is inelastic because it is very unlikely that customers for fashion goods will ever cease to regard shopping in these areas as a desirable and pleasant way to spend their time and money.

Where substitution with other factors is a possibility the entrepreneur will use less of an expensive factor and more of an inexpensive factor. Thus skyscrapers (capital) in New York are built higher and higher, and a year or two ago considerable discussion occurred in the Press as to the desirability of allowing Buckingham Palace to be overlooked by the London Hilton Hotel. If land is expensive, the addition of extra capital may reduce rents to reasonable proportions. The expensive site costs in great cities are reduced by putting taller buildings on them, which are then rented off as apartments.

16.3
The supply of land

Early economists were impressed with the shortage of land, which is limited to what Nature has supplied. As they were mostly British, and the land in Great Britain has been completely owned since Norman times, this view is understandable. Perhaps more important, the influential writings of Thomas Malthus on *Population* had led them to expect an early 'population explosion' which would fill the earth with people. In fact changes in both population and in methods of production have slowed down the complete occupation of land, and only in our own time has this problem begun to look serious. Even today it is more a matter of poisoning the world with effluent than a shortage of land for agricultural or industrial purposes.

For many purposes land is in plentiful supply, and activities such as reclamation from the sea and slum clearance in the centres of large cities are even increasing the supply of land. Despite this, shortages do exist in particular areas, or for particular types of land, and both commercial rent and economic rent are demanded in many situations. A particularly interesting example of land shortage is the situation currently facing the authorities of the Port of Rotterdam, in Holland. Not only is land reclamation an important activity for the port authority, but it is vital that the areas made available should be utilised to the full. Applications for land received from industrial and commercial firms are therefore considered very carefully. Plant density is a crucial element in the decision to grant permission to an industrial user, for only the very intensive industries using bulk-carrier shipping to supply very large plants are likely to be economic in the long run. Other industries can be accommodated in less vital areas farther inland or along the canals linking Holland with the Rhine. One side effect of the concentration of industry in this way is the serious atmospheric pollution which has resulted.

The early economists did not envisage the intensive use of land as we know it today. Extensive agriculture is very wasteful of land, and in times past has ruined in a matter of years the fertility built up by millions of years of natural activity. Intensive agriculture, by contrast, preserves and even enhances the fertility of the soil. Intensive housing reduces the spread of urban areas and offers economies in sanitation and other social assets. This has made possible very dense concentrations of population in such areas as Hong Kong and Singapore. In Britain about 10 per cent of land is urban and about 80 per cent agricultural.

When goods are in demand, a higher price calls forth a larger supply. It is less easy to produce extra supplies of land, but land for a particular purpose, such as housing, can always be obtained at a price, provided that planning authorities do not interfere. The supply of land is inelastic, but the supply of land for a particular purpose is much more elastic, and if intensive use is made of it, whether for agriculture (for instance by using greenhouses) or for housing (by building skyscrapers) or for industry (by using dense plant concentrations), it is probably very elastic indeed.

16.4
The price of land

How much an entrepreneur will pay for the factor land depends on his estimate of the marginal productivity of the land to him. He will not pay more for a cubic yard of sand than he will earn for it from a builder who requires it. He will not pay more for an acre of arable land than he can earn from the best crop he can grow on it. Similarly the landowner will only part with the ownership of a yard of gravel or a ton of ore if he feels that he is being offered a fair price for it. He will only rent an acre of land to a farmer if he feels sure he cannot get a better price for it from some other user of the land. In other words he will always try to obtain the maximum net advantage from the use of his land.

The price of land is fixed as a result of the interaction of supply and demand, the supplier of land attempting to achieve the maximum net advantage from it, and the entrepreneurs demanding it only if its marginal product is likely to exceed the rent payable.

16.5
Elasticity of supply of land – rent of situation

If the price of a commodity rises it will generally call into the market an increased supply of that commodity. If the price of land rises, it may or may not be able to call forth an increased supply of land. For example, an increase in the price being offered by hill farmers may increase the quantity of land available for sheep rearing. An increase in the price of land at the junction of Piccadilly Circus and Haymarket in London cannot produce any increase in the sites in that area. It is this inelasticity of supply which leads to 'economic rent' being paid for land, i.e. 'rent of situation'. Where an entrepreneur is indifferent as to situation he will not pay economic rents, but will set up his enterprise in a cheaper situation elsewhere. Where he is bound to choose a particular site, because the advantages of location outweigh the disadvantages of high cost he will continue to demand land and pay 'situation' rent.

Poor rural land therefore only earns commercial rent; better land earns 'economic rent' as well. For instance, if wheat-growing land is currently fetching £100.00 an acre and entrepreneurs are thinking of planting hop gardens they will have to pay at least the transfer earnings of £100.00 to rent land for hops. If the profitability of hops is such that the demand for land for hops forces up the rent to £140.00 the hop growers as an industry are paying £100.00 as transfer earnings and £40.00 as economic rent.

Urban land, by contrast, is in inelastic supply and its situation is of paramount importance. Whatever the price, its supply cannot be increased, and a large part of its earnings must be 'situation' rent. Entrepreneurs who set up business in fashionable areas cannot avoid paying high prices for land. These high prices are the result of strong demand, and are not a payment for the 'original and indestructible power of the soil'.

16.6
Office rents in the UK

Table 16.1 shows some typical rents in the UK. Rents in the West End of London average £400–440 per square metre: in the prime City of London areas from £600–700 per square metre. As each employee requires about 12 square metres (irrespective of car parking and canteen space) the cost per employee approaches £8000 for accommodation alone, when rent, rates, lighting and heating have been taken into account.

Table 16.1 Rents in the UK, 1988

Place	Average cost per square metre per annum	Approximate annual cost per employee
London	£480	£5560
Bedford	£ 75	£ 900
Norwich	£120	£1440
Leicester	£ 55	£ 660
Southend-on-Sea	£ 85	£1020
Sheffield	£ 90	£1080
Liverpool	£ 70	£ 840
Edinburgh	£155	£1860

16.7 Summary of Chapter 16

1 Land consists of the resources made available by Nature. In most countries rent is charged for land. If the land is a resource the rent payable is often determined as a royalty per ton of the resource extracted.
2 Commercial rent is payment for the use of landed property.
3 The price of land is the result of the interaction of demand and supply.
4 The demand for land is derived from the demand for agricultural and mineral products.
5 If the price of land is high, substitution of other factors may occur. Thus intensive methods may be adopted in agriculture, or high-rise blocks of flats may be erected on sites to spread the cost of land over a large number of apartments.
6 The entrepreneur demands land as long as its marginal product exceeds the cost price, i.e. the rent payable.
7 The landowner will rent out land to the highest bidder, so as to get the maximum advantage from his land.
8 Where land is in inelastic supply, as with urban land in fashionable areas, the strong demand will raise rents so that the land earns 'situation' rent.

Exercises set 16

1 What is land to an economist! Is land a free commodity? Is it fixed in supply?
2 A cinema owner is looking for a site in the heart of a large city. Consider the rent he might have to pay, and discuss whether it is economic rent.
3 Point out the similarities and differences between the following:

(a) the charge to rent a 50-acre farm from an estate owner in a rural area;
(b) the charge to rent a site for a supermarket in a new town;
(c) the charge to rent a television set;
(d) the charge to rent a theatre in London's West End.

4 Explain the following:

(*a*) rent is the price of accommodation;
(*b*) rent is a surplus.

5 Suggest why the opening of a motorway leads to an increase in rents in the areas around access points to the motorway.

6 'The cost of reclaiming this land from the sea is high. We suggest therefore that the location of Wheaty Biscuit Company on this site will be unsatisfactory, in view of the high rents; the site should therefore be reserved either for the James Watt Engineering Co., or the Mogul Oil Co.,' Discuss.

7 'Consult us when you choose your industrial site. Government grants available' (Development Area New Town Corporation). What are the rent implications of this advertisement?

17   Rewards to factors – wages

17.1
Wages – the reward to labour

Labour has been defined as the supply of human resources, both physical and mental, which is available to engage in the production of goods and services. The reward paid for labour is wages, though some prefer the term salaries. To an accountant there is a difference: the term 'salaries' is generally used to designate the pay of office or supervisory staff, and this forms part of overhead expenses rather than part of prime costs. To the economist wages and salaries are merely alternative names for the reward earned by the factor labour.

Labour is not homogeneous, for it is a human resource. Labour may be intelligent or stupid, skilled or unskilled, enthusiastic or work-shy, cooperative or resentful. An industry may have a history of bad labour relations over a long period, so that men are embittered by years of low wages and repressive management. Such was the situation in the mining industry in Great Britain before nationalisation in 1947. By contrast many employees develop such loyalty to their firms that they do not change to more rewarding employment, enjoying instead non-monetary satisfactions.

In these circumstances economic theory can never be precise, and the more extensive the field under discussion the broader the terms we have to use. This chapter draws attention to some of the major influences at work in the determination of wages.

17.2
Wage-rates and earnings

Wage-rates are the price of labour, which entrepreneurs are prepared to pay for the use of a man's physical or mental skills. They may be expressed in units of time: so much an hour, so much a week or month. They may be piece-rates: so much per unit of production. In free competition entrepreneurs would vary the rates they offer according to the marginal net product of the worker. In practice these rates are often the subject of negotiation between the representatives of labour and management, and cannot be varied according to economic theory.

Earnings means the actual sum of money earned. They may be the agreed weekly or monthly wage; or the product of the hourly wage rate and the hours worked; or the product of the piece-rate and the number of pieces produced. A bespoke tailor paid 12.50 per coat who makes seven coats in a week has earnings of 87.50. The following points are of interest when contrasting time-rates and wage-rates.

17.2.1
Time-rates

Time-rates are more satisfactory when:

(*a*) Output cannot be easily measured. For example, in teaching, most professional employments, or police work.
(*b*) The employment itself is the incentive, so that there is no need to devise incentives to higher productivity. This is true in many professional and

near-professional employments, in clerical work of many sorts, and supervision posts in factories.

(c)   Where high speed is impossible, or might be harmful, as in transport services, hospital services, repair work of many sorts.

Sometimes time-rates are unsatisfactory, especially if overtime is regularly worked. There is a temptation to go easy during the day so that plenty of overtime will be available. This means supervision of workers is essential. With time-rates, the work output may become that of the least-willing worker. The energetic and enthusiastic man receives no direct reward for his extra effort, and may even be looked upon as someone who is trying to spoil things for the rest. Such situations are less likely to develop with a piece-work system.

<table>
<tr><td>17.2.2
Piece-rates</td><td>The advantage of piece-rates are:</td></tr>
</table>

(a)   Productivity is raised, because there is no bar to the hard worker earning a reward for his extra effort. The worker is keen to reach work, keen to start work, and reluctant to stop work.
(b)   A different kind of spirit develops, with workers devising new methods of work which raise output.
(c)   Capital costs are lowered, for the machinery is used more intensively so that machine failure precedes obsolescence, and the subsequent re-tooling with modern equipment raises output to new levels.

At the same time piece-work has disadvantages. It turns men into money-making machines, causing them to overwork. It leads to resentment by the less nimble and less efficient of their more active or more successful fellow workers. One remedy is to change to team piece-rates, where the extra product is shared evenly among the team. This reduces friction, but may lower productivity if the more active reduce their efforts now the incentive has gone.

Piece-work causes difficulties when new rates have to be negotiated, and causes unrest when agreements in one field of activity enable workers to earn more than workers in other parts of the plant, or industry. Sometimes piece-work rates are regressive, i.e. less is earned per unit on higher outputs. This reduces the worker's incentive to work hard.

<table>
<tr><td>17.3
**Money wages and
real wages**</td><td>*Money wages* refers to the actual money earned by the worker. *Real wages* refers to the actual 'basket' of goods and services which he can purchase with his money wages. In periods of rising prices workers may be conceded wage increases by employers, but may find that their increased money wages have not enabled them to buy as many goods and services as before. Like Alice in Wonderland, they have to keep running desperately hard just to keep where they are. Conversely, in times of falling prices, workers who are forced to accept a cut in salary may still find themselves better off, because their reduced money incomes have not fallen as much as prices have fallen. When the massive slump between the two world wars lowered prices to very low levels, school-teachers who were forced to take a very serious cut in salary found that in fact they had suffered no real hardship.

The index figures (Jan. 1970 = 100) in Table 17.1 illustrate the changes in the UK in earnings and retail prices.</td></tr>
</table>

Table 17.1 Average earnings and prices, 1970–88

	1970	1974	1978	1982	1984	1986	1988
Average earnings	100	138	246	447	521	587	687
Retail prices	100	142	268	437	482	534	573

Source: Monthly Digest of Statistics (adapted)

Notes
1 Average earnings rose to almost seven times the 1970 figure by 1988.
2 Retail prices rose almost as fast as earnings.
3 It follows that although the average citizen in 1988 earned almost seven times what was earned in 1970, it only purchased about 20 per cent more in actual goods and services.

17.4
Early theories about wages

Reference has already been made to the difficulties early economists experienced in explaining the unequal distribution of wealth and the continuing poverty of the masses of the people. It was the meagre wages of the poor which caused their miserable share of the world's produce, and the economists did little to improve their lot. Economic theory furnished excellent excuses to the capitalist classes for the perpetuation of low wages, and led Thomas Carlyle to call political economy a 'dismal science'. The chief of the excuses for keeping wages low was advanced by Malthus in his *Essay on Population*, which appeared anonymously in 1798. Let us pause to consider its influence.

17.4.1
Thomas Robert Malthus (1766–1834) and the subsistence theory of wages

Thomas Malthus was the son of a country squire, who became a parson for a short while after leaving university where he read mathematics and philosophy. The climate of thought at the time, when the French Revolution had not yet turned ugly and revengeful, was optimistic. Progress was in the air: it was an Age of Reason. Tom Paine's book of that name was just about to appear, and the development and perfection of a better society, with better men to live in it, was optimistically forecast. Malthus was sceptical, and when the mood in France changed, he pondered on the forces acting against the improvement of mankind. He decided that population pressure was the chief cause of poverty, and his *Essay on Population* described, without real evidence of any kind, the 'inevitable' nature of the forces at work.

Briefly, the *Essay on Population* held that population tended to increase in geometrical ratio, e.g. 2–4–8–16–32–64 etc., with world population doubling every twenty-five years. By contrast, land was limited in area and could only be improved by heavy capital investment. The likely improvement in food supplies was at best an arithmetic progression, e.g. 2–4–6–8–10–12. The difference between the two ratios made poverty inevitable unless the passion between the sexes could be controlled. Why, then, had mankind survived thus far? Because natural checks were exerted to redress the balance between population and food supply. These checks were of two sorts. Self-restraint, displayed chiefly by the rich and prosperous, was used to reduce the size of families for fear of poverty or decline in the social scale. Marriage was postponed until later in life, and the size of families was limited voluntarily to maintain the standard of living of the family.

For the poor, with no motive for reducing sexual appetite, nature had devised positive checks. Infant mortality, infanticide, diseases, epidemics, plagues, unwholesome foods, dangerous occupations, and even famine which 'with one mighty blow, levels the population with the food of the world'.

His theories were at once seized upon and expounded by the leaders of society of his time. The spokesmen of the poor reviled the essay and its author, but were powerless to defeat arguments which fitted so well with the established political and economic framework of the times. Why pay higher wages when the only result would be an increase in sexual appetite and a new generation to eat the parents down to the poverty level again? Why envisage safer working conditions, better housing, and better sanitation when these checks and balances were but a natural device to prevent famine from stalking the land? Well might William Cobbett, the radical writer, say 'Parson! I have during my life detested many men; but never anyone as much as you.'

Although respectable opinion took up his arguments, and Malthus himself was much listened to throughout his lifetime, the world has escaped until now the dire calamities he foretold. The opening up of the American prairies, the Ukraine, Australia, New Zealand and Argentina proved capable of supporting mankind for a century or two. Whether Malthus might yet be proved right is a different matter, discussed later in this chapter.

The germ of Malthus's ideas came from the French 'physiocrats' who held that it was in the nature of things that wages could never rise above a bare subsistence level. When wages did for a time rise much above the bare necessities of life, the illusion of prosperity produced larger families, and the severe competition among workers was soon at work to reduce wages again. In a world where child labour was the rule, it was only a few years before the children forced unemployment upon the parents, and all were again reduced to poverty. Such was the **subsistence theory of wages**. The working classes were eventually to prove it wrong. With the gradual growth in the complexity of work and the scale of enterprise, the demand for labour began to exceed the supply. The subsistence theory speaks only of the supply of labour, it does not take any heed of the demand side. As demand grew, labour was able to exact its due rewards. That it had grown bitter in the process was, perhaps, regrettable. Much of that bitterness came from fear of the workhouse – an enduring monument to Malthus's effect upon the times in which he lived.

17.4.2 David Ricardo and the 'wages fund' theory of wages

While chiefly remembered for his ideas on rent (see page 182), Ricardo's theory of wages is also of interest. He held that, like any other commodity, the price of labour depended on supply and demand. On the demand side, the capital available to entrepreneurs was the sole source of payment for the workers, and represented a 'wages fund' from which they could be paid. On the supply side, labour supply depended upon Malthusian arguments about population. The intense competition of labourers one with another, at a time when combinations of workers to withdraw their labour from the market were illegal, kept the price of labour low. The fraction

$$\frac{\textit{Total wages fund (capital available)}}{\textit{Total population}}$$

fixed the wages of working men.

Here was a second theory which was seized upon by the employing classes to justify the continuation of low wages. Despite some optimistic suggestions by Ricardo tending to modify the severity of the 'iron laws of wages' (such as his suggestion that 'subsistence level' might mean different things in different countries), advocates of the theory used it to justify the abolition of the Poor Laws. Even Ricardo argued that any interference with market forces was bad, because it prevented the mass of the people from experiencing that grinding poverty which alone could teach them not to have more young ones. The Poor Law system of that time, devised by the magistrates of Speenhamland in Berkshire, was to levy rates in support of the poor, and to subsidise the wages of low-paid workers by giving them public assistance to support their families. Ricardo's theory holds that such action must be wrong, because in raising rates (i.e. local taxes) from the rich of the neighbourhood, you must reduce their ability to save; and it is the savings of the rich which provide the capital for the wages fund. If you reduce the wages fund there is less for the workers to receive as wages.

Ricardo held that if population could be restrained, so that wages could be increased to the point where workers could enjoy high wages for a few years, the experience of plenty would convince working people how much better prosperity was than large families. Education could not of itself convince people, only that most efficient of educators, experience, both bitter and sweet.

Today we reject the idea that capital is the sole source of wages; there is no 'wages fund' as Ricardo envisaged it. Not only do the banks 'create' capital by multiplying up the savings deposited with them, but the current earnings of firms form part of the rewards to labour. It is not capital alone, but the whole National Income, which is the source of rewards to factors.

Before leaving this section about early theories of wages, it is appropriate to consider the life and writings of one early writer and thinker whose ideas, until very recently, commanded a wide following.

17.4.3
Karl Marx (1818–83) and the 'full fruits of production' theory of wages

Karl Marx was a scholar, philosopher, journalist and revolutionary extraordinary who spent much of his life in dedicated poverty reading in the British Museum library. His impressive series of books, and those of his great collaborator Friedrich Engels, are read more widely today than they were in his own times and have been translated into every language. His fundamental philosophy of 'dialectical materialism' rejects religion and holds that human progress is the result of interacting and opposing forces in the real world. His labour theory of value held that a commodity's worth was directly related to the hours of work that had gone into making it, under the normal conditions of production and with the average degree of skill and intensity prevalent at the time. Because only labour created value, the worker was entitled to the full fruits of production. Those sums distributed as rent, interest and profits, which Marx called surplus values, were stolen from the worker by the capitalist class. He prophesied that the increasing rapacity of the capitalist class and the increasing misery of the masses of the people would inevitably lead to a revolutionary overthrow of the system, in which the capitalists would themselves be expropriated. The socialisation of the means of production, distribution and exchange would restore to the masses the full fruits of their activities.

Marx's enduring appeal lies in the emotional idealism he inspired. To end the more outrageous abuses of early capitalism is today deemed everywhere to be an acceptable aim. That later Capitalism has proved less demanding and rapacious than Marx envisaged is perhaps only a reaction to the widespread support his ideas received. That Communism has proved largely unable to achieve the aims in real life which its founders envisaged is a measure of the weaknesses in Marxian economics. The consumer society is too intricate for central planning, and a dictatorship – even of the proletariat – too chilling to the tender growths of the myriad nodal points of a sophisticated, consumer-orientated society. With no market system to alert producers to what the consumers really need; political considerations entering into every aspect of economic activity; self-centred 'apparatchiks' afraid to make decisions while at the same time skimming the cream off every output and an excessive military and security system directing efforts into non-productive activity, the egalitarian dream has proved equally awful almost everywhere.

17.5
The marginal productivity theory of wages

This theory has already been explained on page 179. It holds that entrepreneurs will only purchase the factor labour when its price (i.e. wages) is less than the marginal product of an additional unit. Labour, on the other hand, moves between various employments to achieve the maximum net personal advantage. Wages, the price of labour, are fixed by the interaction of the demand for labour and the supply of labour.

17.5.1
The demand for labour

We have seen that the demand for each factor is a derived demand, arising from the demand for the goods and services the factor makes available. In the case of labour, this results in a demand curve which slopes off towards the right in the usual way: more labour will be demanded when the price is low, provided that other things remain unchanged. As shown in Figure 15.2 (page 180) the demand curve for labour is the same curve as the marginal-revenue productivity curve. How far out from the origin of the graph will such a curve be? This depends on the marginal productivity of labour, which varies either with the price of the goods or the productivity of the workers. A change in price might occur through a change in demand for the product being considered. If the price of the product increases it will raise the marginal-revenue productivity of labour, and entrepreneurs will be prepared to employ more workers. If the price of the product remains steady but the

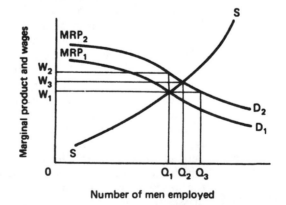

Figure 17.1 The effect on wages and employment of a change in marginal productivity of labour

Notes
1 The marginal-revenue product curve is the same as the demand curve for labour.
2 When the marginal revenue produced rises the curve moves to the right to MRP_2.
3 The possibilities are now as follows:

(a) The present workers Q_1 will earn higher incomes, wages rising to W_2.
(b) If extra workers are able to come in the supply of labour extends to Q_2 and wages rise only to W_3.
(c) If there is unemployment in the trade so that the supply curve is infinitely elastic, employment will increase to Q_3 and the wages would remain at W_1 since the supply curve will be horizontal.

productivity of workers is increased so that costs per unit of output are lowered, this will again raise the marginal revenue produced and will encourage entrepreneurs to employ more workers. Thus a trade union like the Electrical Trades Union might well support an advertising policy encouraging the householder to adopt electrical storage heaters as a method of domestic heating, while at the same time urging its members to abandon some practice which reduces output. The first would shift the demand curve for labour to the right by increasing demand for the product; the second would shift it to the right by making the industry more profitable. Either way the effect is to increase both wages and the number of men employed (see Figure 17.1).

17.5.2
The elasticity of demand for labour

The elasticity of demand for labour is also of great importance in the fixing of wages. If the demand for labour is elastic, entrepreneurs will be able to withdraw easily from the market and it will therefore be difficult for labour to secure wage increases.

 The demand for labour will be elastic when: (*a*) the demand for the final product is elastic; (*b*) the labour can be replaced by other labour; (*c*) other factors (particularly capital) can replace the labour; (*d*) labour costs represent a high proportion of total costs.

(a) Elasticity of demand for labour and the demand for the final product

The supplier who concedes a wage increase must raise prices to the consumer. This means that a smaller supply will be available at every price and a change in the conditions of supply has occurred. The different effects on the sales of products which are in elastic demand, and on those in inelastic demand, is shown in Figure 17.2.

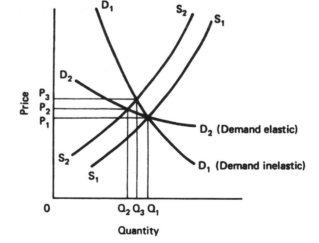

Figure 17.2 The effect of elasticity of demand on sales after a price increase

Notes
1 Owing to an increase in wages the supply curve has moved to the left.
2 The price of the product which is in elastic demand rises a little, and demand contracts a great deal, to Q_2.
3 The price of the product which is in inelastic demand rises a great deal, but demand only contracts a little to Q_3.
4 It follows that a supplier whose product is in elastic demand will resist wage increases more than a supplier whose product is in inelastic demand. If wage increases are forced on him/her the demand for labour will be reduced.

(b) Elasticity of demand for labour which is unskilled

The most likely substitute for any particular class of labour is other labour. It follows that unskilled workers find it difficult to secure wage increases in the face of determined entrepreneurs, for other workers can easily be substituted for them. Provided that the demand for the product they can make is strong, the demand for skilled workers' services will be inelastic. Consequently their bargaining position will be a strong one, since they can always move to a position of greater net personal advantage. Immigrant labour is often unskilled labour, since the most mobile form of labour is peasant labour, moving from peasant communities to towns. This movement of unskilled labour is a feature of present-day populations, not only from the new Commonwealth countries to Great Britain, but from the Mediterranean lands to the Common Market countries, from African villages to the towns, and from the rural areas of South America to the cities of the coastal regions. Some of the opposition to this type of immigration comes from unskilled workers fearing its effect on their standard of living.

(c) Elasticity of demand for labour which can be replaced by machinery

Elastic demand might be found where it was possible to substitute other factors, particularly capital, for labour. Aggressive wages policies by labourers might result in the purchase by contractors of mechanical earth-shifting equipment which reduces the demand for labour considerably. The demand for labour will be more elastic if such aids are cheap. *In purchasing a balanced assortment of factors an entrepreneur will select them until their marginal products relative to their prices are equal.*

(d) Elasticity of demand for labour where labour costs form a high proportion of total costs

In these circumstances any increase in labour costs means a considerable increase in the sale price charged for the ultimate product, and a reduction in profit margins if the demand for the product is at all elastic. The granting of such wage increases will therefore mean serious reductions in the marginal-revenue productivity of labour, and the entrepreneur will therefore reduce demand for it at the higher prices he must now pay.

17.5.3
The supply of labour

The supply of labour depends on several features of the society under discussion. First there is the population structure. Then there are the prevailing customs and laws about education and employment, the willingness of labour to work for the wages and other incentives offered to it and the degree of emigration or immigration permitted.

The **mobility of labour** is an important factor in deciding the supply of labour for particular purposes or particular areas. Labour tends to be most mobile when it is young, or unmarried. It is difficult for labour to flow from one area to another unless housing is made available, and the social costs of providing this may be great. Labour is also very immobile where retraining is required, because the supply can only be increased by fairly long courses of training during which time the worker is non-productive. If mature adults with family responsibilities are to be retrained, for example because their unemployment is *structural* (caused by a change in world demand), the costs will be great. Such retraining is often resisted by workers in the industry for which they are to be trained, since it involves an increase in the supply of their type of skilled labour which results in a reduction of their bargaining power. Such retraining is therefore best directed at growth areas of industry where traditional trade-union practices have not yet appeared.

17.6
The bargaining theory of wages

Some economists argue that the only appropriate theory of wages for the second half of the twentieth century is one that recognises that decisions about wages are made by two groups of monopolists. The organised trade unions are monopolist suppliers of labour; the organised employers are monopsonists. (A monopsonist is a monopoly buyer.) Many products are sold in a situation where there is a buyer's monopoly. For example, only governments usually buy machine guns, so in any given country there is an official monopsonist facing arms suppliers who are in competition with one another. In a particular industry, with well organised trade unions and a strong trade association representing employers, wage bargains are struck between these two organised groups, who are therefore the important operators in the wages market. If we accept that there is some truth in this idea, then we must also recognise that the government is a third important operator on the labour market. First, the government is often holding the economy at a satisfactory level by techniques developed to manage the economy, so that the bargainers can only operate in the climate of market activity which prevails. Secondly, the government has a part to play in preventing the erosion of the standard of living of the unorganised part of the community, the pensioners, the young and the poorly organised workers. Whether it does this by an openly discussed **incomes policy** or by more subtle measures, it is 'holding the ring' for the rest of the people to ensure that neither group of monopolists exploits its position. With a determined Government facing a monopolist, employer control may be sought by appointing a Monopolies Commission (in the UK the current term is Monopolies and Mergers Commission (MMC)) to which all monopolies can be referred for investigation. This will determine whether they are operating against the public interest. Conversely, as we have seen in recent years, a determined government faced with a monopolist trade union can enact legislation to reduce its monopoly powers and the measures it takes to exploit its position. In the UK in recent years 'wildcat' strikes have been ended (all strikes are now subject to ballots in the workplace before they can begin), 'closed shops' have been abolished, secondary picketing (picketing at places not directly related to the dispute) has been outlawed and the power of trade unions has been severely reduced. Here it is helpful to consider what is meant by collective bargaining.

17.6.1
Collective bargaining

Workers are at their most vulnerable when they are not represented by any organisation. They have small reserves and must find employment quickly. They have an imperfect knowledge of the market, and cannot know where to offer their labour for the best reward. If there is surplus labour available workers may compete with one another to their mutual disadvantage and to the benefit of the employer. Workers have therefore formed trade unions to represent them in any bargaining that is to take place. The advantages of collective activity are also appreciated by the entrepreneurs. If wages are agreed throughout the industry, the fierceness of competition is reduced. Rival employers cannot cut costs by cutting wages, and hence price competition is reduced.

17.6.2
Functions of trade unions

From among the varied functions of present-day trade unions we may pick out the following:

● Securing an adequate reward to members for their efforts in the employment concerned. The adequacy of this reward may depend on the extent to which social provision is made for education, health, unemployment relief and sickness benefit: if these are socially provided, the wage demanded will be reduced. If employees have to provide these things themselves they will need a higher level of wages.

- Securing an improvement in working conditions. These include safer systems of work in hazardous employments like mining: provision of special clothing and protective equipment where dirty or dangerous materials are in use; reducing hours of work and extending holiday periods etc.
- The provision of educational, recreational and social amenities. Particular emphasis is placed on adequate training for apprentices and new workers.

Against these advantages of collective bargaining we must list the following objections:

- Collective bargaining is generally speaking inflationary. It gives the most vocal and voluble trade union official an advantage over more staid (and possibly wiser) heads. You cannot force up industrial costs to the benefit of your members if industrialists vote with their feet and leave the industry in droves. Collective bargaining in the United Kingdom's smokestack industries in the 1970s and 1980s led to large sectors of industry going out of business altogether. Every benefit won loads a further cost on industry and raises the price of the product.
- The strongest bargaining tends to take place in areas remote from the market, where market forces cannot introduce practical economics into the discussion. This often means nationalised industries and social services. If the burden becomes too great for the taxpayer, or if the strikes and unrest become endlessly repetitive and amount to a deterioration in the quality of everyday life, there will be a reaction. It has to be admitted that, since time immemorial, some of the rewards for social service have been non-monetary. Privatisation of nationalised industries in the 1980s has led to an increased influence of market forces and a decrease in trade union power.

17.6.3
Conditions favourable to wage increases

Generally speaking, a trade union will be able to obtain concessions from employers which result in wage increase in the following circumstances:

(a) Where the demand for goods is strong, so that the entrepreneurs are likely to be able to pass on the increased wages to the consumer in the form of increased prices. This has an inflationary effect on the economy, giving a cost-push to the inflationary spiral.

(b) Where the increased wages can be justified on the grounds of increased productivity. This means that a promise of higher outputs per worker will be made, so that the increased wages need not cause an increase in prices but can be spread over the larger volume of stock that is manufactured. Such increases in productivity are achieved by abandoning restrictive practices directed against new machinery or new methods of work.

(c) Where too large a labour force exists in the industry. If labour can be persuaded to retire from the industry, taking some sort of severance pay as compensation, the fewer workers left in the industry can then enjoy higher wages. As in (b) above, there is an increase in productivity if the same industry is run with less labour.

(*d*) Where entrepreneurs are earning 'economic rents', and the trade union can bring sufficient force to bear on their employers to make them yield up some of these profits.

(*e*) Where the employer is a low-cost employer, whose low-cost position is being partly achieved by the exploitation of the workers, i.e. by paying them a smaller wage than the marginal net product. In such circumstances there is a strong incentive for the workers to organise, and such an organisation may compel concessions. Workers exploited in this way are sometimes difficult to organise, however. They may be scattered in many small firms, or live in areas where unemployment is abnormally high. They may be immigrants, who do not speak the language, or refugees fearful of deportation.

17.7 'Economic rent' and wages

Labour is very diverse and the rewards paid to workers vary greatly. There is very often some element of economic rent in wages: some payment to the worker over and above what is necessary to keep him in his present employment. This is called 'rent of ability'. Common examples are the high fees earned by professional musicians and vocalists of international reputation. Former trade-union officials appointed to lucrative posts at the head of public corporations are earning economic rents; so are employees in industries with strong trade-union restrictions on the entry of apprentices. Professional bodies who make examinations artificially difficult to pass so that the profession will not become overcrowded secure 'economic rents' for their members; so do shop stewards who negotiate agreements permitting the addition of overtime hours to wage claims, even though the overtime is not in fact worked. It must be admitted that the term 'rent of ability' seems inappropriate in some of these examples. Perhaps a better name is 'scarcity rents'.

17.8 Wages in a 'depression'

Today's pensioners can remember a time in the 1930s when the whole world went through a state of great depression. Today, fortunately, we have not experienced similar hard times, but even a minor depression can feel 'severe' to those who are in the least fortunate positions. It was John Maynard Keynes who showed us how to get out of the severe depression of the 1930s and this is discussed later in this book in the section on 'managed prosperity' (see pages 325–32). What can we say about wages policy in the relatively minor 'depression' of the late 1980s and early 1990s? First, in times of mini-depression it is not easy to raise wages, or even maintain the wages formerly conceded by entrepreneurs. It is a little as Malthus predicted – there are too many people wanting too few jobs and it is easy for entrepreneurs to pick and choose between those who are available. If foreign competition is strong, in a business climate where foreign goods cannot easily be excluded and if technological change is rapid, so that established industries are forced to up-date their techniques and use new methods which require less labour, it is a very difficult task to bring unemployment down.

Wise social policies can do much to alleviate the hardship that results, but in the UK these have had little chance to work, for the whole emphasis in recent years has been on the reduction of benefits, especially in some of the most essential areas – for example in the 16–18 year-old age group. The removal of such people from the welfare system has forced many to rely on family support – but there are many families that break under the strain. Those unable to command an income any other way are forced to work for any price, and as Malthus said, 'force unemployment upon their parents'.

The gap between the employed and the unemployed has grown wider and wider and the increased efficiency in the slimmed-down industries has arisen from more efficient capital, not more skilled labour. The rewards have gone to the captains of industry and the investors of capital, and the cry of 'reduce taxes' prevents the implementation of social policies that should be introduced if social unrest is to be avoided.

17.9
Equal pay legislation

In the UK, under the *Equal Pay Act, 1970*, women are entitled to the same treatment as men as regards wages and other conditions of employment when employed on work of a similar nature, or work graded of equal value under a job evaluation scheme. If a contract of employment does not contain an equality clause it is deemed to do so under the Act, unless the employer can show that the variation between the male and female rewards is genuinely due to a material difference other than a difference of sex.

17.10
Summary of Chapter 17

1 The reward paid to the factor labour is called wages.
2 Wages are often different from earnings, because of the inclusion of payments like overtime money and bonus money.
3 The common ways of calculating earnings are 'time' rates and 'piece' rates.
4 Money wages are not the same as real wages. An increase in money wages will not mean an increased standard of living if prices are rising as fast as incomes.
5 Among early theories of wages, the subsistence theory held that the mass of the people would always be poor because any increase in living standards was counteracted by a rise in population. The wages-fund theory held that taxation of the rich to help the poor was self-defeating; it only reduced the savings of the rich, whose contributions to the fund of capital out of which wages were paid were thereby decreased.
6 Modern theories of wages include the marginal-productivity theory and the bargaining theory. The latter holds that wages are decided by the bargaining of two sets of monopolists: the organised trade unions and the employers' organisations. While this may be true in prosperous times, in times of depression the power of trade unions is eroded by the large numbers of people seeking work at any price, and the free play of market forces drives wages down.
7 'Rent of ability' is the economic rent earned by the factor labour.

Exercises Set 17

1 What are 'wages' to an economist? Distinguish between money wages and real wages.
2 What sorts of employment could best be rewarded by a 'piece-rate' wages system? What are the advantages of piece-rates from the point of view of (*a*) workers, (*b*) entrepreneurs?
3 What is the elasticity of demand for labour? Is the demand for machinists in the garment trades likely to be elastic or inelastic? Give reasons.
4 Discuss whether the supply of labour will be increased or decreased by the following. In each case indicate the likely effect on wages.

   (*a*) The reduction of apprenticeship periods from seven years to five years owing to changed educational achievements prior to the commencement of the apprenticeship.

    (b) Prohibition of immigration from less developed are̶ world.

    (c) Institution of a lump-sum premium on entry to all professi̶ occupations.

    (d) Institution of 'degree entrants only' qualifications for the teaching profession simultaneously with a fully professional scale of rewards to teachers.

    (e) Abandonment of educational entry requirements for lawyers' clerks.

5 'The market for labour is very imperfect, yet competition is fierce.' Discuss.

6 Distinguish between money wages and real wages. If money wages rise by 50 per cent and prices rise by 25 per cent, what increase has the worker achieved in real terms?

7 What do you understand by the Malthusian Doctrine? Why did it have such a profound effect upon the early nineteenth century?

8 Why are wages generally lower in India than in Great Britain?

9 What do you understand by the term mobility of labour? In your answer consider the following cases:

    (a) A French peasant whose farm is suffering from soil erosion who hears of cheap land in Canada.

    (b) A teacher devoted to her pupils in the primary school who is offered a post at a secondary school 300 miles away.

    (c) A skilled engineer offered a post as research technician in a university department at a slightly lower wage than his present one.

    (d) A young machinist of limited intelligence. She has just been praised by her employer for completing a dozen garments without a single reject for the first time since she took employment.

10 What is 'collective bargaining'? What economic circumstances favour the employers in such bargaining?

Rewards to factors – interest

18.1
Interest – the reward to capital

We have already discussed (see page 28) some aspects of capital. In economics the word 'capital' has several meanings. It refers first to **liquid capital**, funds available in money form which are not required for consumption purposes but can be set aside by consumers for the use of entrepreneurs as factor capital, to be engaged in production. **Fixed capital** refers to the solid assets created by the entrepreneurs from some of the liquid capital made available to them. They may be buildings, plant, machinery, furniture, motor vehicles etc. These then become part of either **private capital**, which is a stock of assets owned and controlled by firms or individuals for private purposes, or **social capital**, a stock of assets owned and controlled communally for the benefit or enjoyment of the citizens as a whole. The rest of the liquid capital may be used as **working capital**, to buy stocks and pay wages in the actual production of consumer goods.

Liquid capital is really a claim against the goods and services produced in the previous production period, which the recipient of the money income decides to save. If I earn £180 a week, but my needs are satisfied with an expenditure of £100 per week, the remaining £80 can be saved. I will postpone consuming this further share of the world's goods to which I am entitled, and make it available to any entrepreneur who wishes to borrow it, provided that I feel sure I shall be able to regain it when required, and that he/she will pay me something for postponing my consumption. This payment for postponing consumption is called **interest**.

Interest is the payment made for a loan of liquid capital. It is usually paid at an agreed rate per cent per annum.

The entrepreneur who receives the use of the money then uses it to employ other factors (i.e. land and labour) either to create consumption goods or non-consumption goods, in other words to create capital goods. In this way the liquid capital is turned into fixed capital, a stock of producer goods which will be available in the future for producing an increased supply of consumer goods. Thus liquid capital employed to produce an oil refinery results in an increased supply of petrol for many years to come, while liquid capital used to build a theatre or an opera-house provides entertainment for future generations.

18.2
Collecting capital – the institutional investor

If I decide to save £80 per week, as suggested above, I shall need to feel sure that I can regain my funds at any time should I require them. I may have decided to save for a specific purpose, like a holiday or a new car. I may have simply decided to save in case some unfortunate event occurs, like an illness or an accident. Everyone likes to have some reserves 'against a rainy day'. As very few of us are experienced enough, or have enough time, to judge whether an entrepreneur's schemes are sound or not, it is quite common to leave these problems to a specialist such as a banker. Most ordinary people therefore save money with a bank or building society, where funds are absolutely safe and a reasonable rate of interest is earned, and leave it to the institution to direct it where it is required.

Some of the savings made available each week are used for short-term loans to businessmen, local authorities and government agencies, who for some reason have temporary need of money. People, for example, pay taxes in an uneven way, so that sometimes the government is short of cash, while at other times it has funds to spare. This type of short-term loan is arranged on what is called the 'money market', a general term for many different kinds of financial specialists who supply certain types of loans. There are discount houses, merchant bankers, accepting houses, commercial banks, finance houses, mercantile credit bankers etc.

The rest of the savings made available may go into more permanent forms of loan, which are designed to be used in producing fixed capital assets, like buildings and plant. This more permanent type of investment is handled rather differently by what is called the 'capital market'. This again consists of a number of firms acting in different ways. Some of the commoner types are unit trusts and investment trusts, issuing houses and building societies; the Stock Exchange provides a special market where those who have saved in the past but now wish to regain liquidity may do so by selling their investments for cash.

Since many of these institutions spread their investments and loans over a wide field of industrial and commercial activity, in other words develop *balanced portfolios of investments*, they may be found operating in both the capital market and the money market.

The small saver, by lending money on agreed terms to a bank or building society, or perhaps to an insurance company, achieves a reasonably secure investment without having to bother about the safety of the money saved. The institution to whom the money has been loaned will take on the responsibility of checking the security of the investment. These institutions and their activities are described in Chapter 20.

18.3
The supply of loanable funds

18.3.1
Savings by individuals

The ability of individuals to save varies with their personal incomes and personal situations. Some individuals have a high **propensity to consume**. They may have families to support, or need expensive medical treatment and care. They may have carefree personalities which give no thought to tomorrow, and be prodigal in their behaviour. Others have a high **propensity to save**, counting thrift a great virtue and abhorring waste of economic resources, however trivial. Generally speaking the income of the individual affects his propensity to save. A poor man, earning a wage of £50 per week, will find it difficult to pay his way in the world and may even need welfare payments from the State to help him meet his most elementary needs. He has a high propensity to consume – more than 100 per cent of his earned income. A rich man, earning £1000 per week, may spend £200 on current requirements per week – four times more than the poor man – yet be said to have a low propensity to consume and a high propensity to save, because he is only spending 20 per cent of his income. Clearly the terms 'propensity to consume' and 'propensity to save' are relative terms: they are meaningful only when related to income. The £50 of the 'spendthrift' poor man is much less than the £200 spent by the 'thrifty' rich man.

18.3.2
Savings by corporations or companies

Corporations save on a very large scale, retaining in their business profits which have been earned in the course of their activities. These profits really belong to the shareholders, who might prefer that they should be distributed as dividends, but the distribution of dividends is a matter of company policy. Cautious directors may prefer to retain profits as reserves to meet future contingencies. Sometimes governments require them to do so, and impose a policy of 'dividend restraint'. While it is probably desirable in many cases for firms to retain adequate reserves, so that the business can be expanded, there are disadvantages too. One disadvantage is that the large, well established firm is never short of capital, and its directors may be led to spend these reserves on less essential assets. Splendid executive suites contribute little to higher productivity. If the same funds had been returned to their true owners, the shareholders, they might have been employed more usefully – for example in helping struggling inventors to exploit bright ideas.

18.3.3
Savings by governments

Governments frequently save, sometimes on a grand scale. Since a government is by definition a law-making body employing forces to impose the law upon its citizens, it can impose taxation and compel the payment thereof. This enables it to make people 'save', if it seems desirable to do so, by taxing away their incomes. There are many occasions when the existence of excess spending power in a country's economy is liable to produce an inflationary situation. Such a situation would benefit only a small number of people, and do many people harm. Thus those who owe money in inflationary times do benefit, since they repay in money that has been devalued. Others, who have saved – perhaps for pensions or to lend money out at interest and those who are on fixed incomes suffer because their savings are repaid in devalued currency, or their fixed incomes such as pensions are worth less and less in real terms. Inflation is discussed more fully on pages 335–6.

18.4
The demand for loanable funds

Funds are required by the same three groups that make funds available: individual citizens, corporations or firms, and the government. Individuals and firms are numerous, and some can be saving while others are borrowing. Government agencies are also numerous, and may be carrying out different activities at different times, for example, when the Treasury is busy collecting funds, other departments may be disbursing funds; temporary loans called 'ways and means loans' may then be arranged for particular departments when required.

18.4.1
Individuals

Individuals demand loans for a variety of purposes, of which house purchase and hire purchase of consumer durables (e.g. television sets and motor cars) are the most important. In December 1990 the total loans to individuals in the UK stood at £16 115 million by members of the Finance Houses Association, but the banks also provided considerable funds to customers and retailers for hire purchase business. In August 1990 the banks had over £125 000 million out on loan to individual borrowers for house purchase, hire purchase, and other purposes.

18.4.2
Firms and corporations

Firms and corporations demand funds for both fixed and working capital. The whole prosperity of society is dependent on adequate capital being made available to create the producer goods that are necessary to create the 'utilities' that satisfy 'wants'. In a free-enterprise society the majority of such activities are undertaken by firms and limited companies who appeal to the public, both privately and publicly, for funds. As the classification of bankers' advances (Table 18.1) shows, the banks are active in providing such

Table 18.1 Classification of bankers' loans (Aug 1990)

	£ million	%		£ million	%
Manufacturing			Services		
Food, drink and tobacco	8 232	1.9	Transport and communications	6 784	1.6
Chemicals, etc.	2 551	0.6	Public utilities, national and local		
Metal manufacturing	1 763	0.4	government	1 784	0.4
Engineering, ship-building and vehicles	14 510	3.3	Distribution	27 748	6.3
Other manufacturing	14 368	3.3	Other services	11 087	2.5
Total manufacturing	41 424	9.5	Total services	47 403	10.8
Other production			Financial		
Agriculture, forestry and fishing	7 210	1.6	Institutions	17 995	4.1
Mining and quarrying	2 541	0.6	Leasing	17 838	4.1
Oil, gas and energy	4 400	1.0	Property companies	37 008	8.4
Construction	16 496	3.8	Other financial	65 059	14.9
			Business loans	55 344	12.6
Total other production	30 647	7.0	Total financial	193 244	44.1
Personal					
House purchase	84 244	19.2			
Other personal	40 981	9.4			
Total personal	125 225	28.6	Total advances	£437 943	100.0

Source: *Bank of England Quarterly.* Aug 1990

funds. They had loans out to manufacturing industry of £41 424 million, £30 647 million more to other productive industries like agriculture, mining and construction, over £47 000 million to service industries and almost £200 000 million to financial and property companies. Total bank lending exceeded £437 000 million.

The demand by firms is intensified these days by the pace of technological advance. Research and development generate an increasingly wide variety of products and processes which need to be followed up with capital investment if they are to prove fruitful. Whole ranges of new materials have appeared in the last 30 years, rendering older materials obsolete.

18.4.3 Government and local government

Government and local government demand for funds centres on the need to provide socially desirable assets. The whole infrastructure of town and countryside is of increasing importance as denser populations have to be supported. Sanitation, education and retraining, communications, traffic control etc. have great economic contributions to make. The nationalised industries provide essential services to firms as well as individuals, and the contributions they make to industry may be of crucial importance to economic efficiency. If such industries are starved of capital the effect on the economy may be very serious.

18.5
The rate of interest

It is difficult to give a clear picture of how the rate of interest is decided, for the decision is affected by so many different influences. No theory can explain all aspects of a situation where many people who save behave illogically, or where expert financial manipulators are operating to balance profitable investments against less profitable ones, risky investments against safe ones, sophisticated savers against naive ones, and so on. Even more, the government or the central bank of any country often controls interest rates in an effort to achieve the management of prosperity or the fulfilment of national aspirations. Such activities make absolute nonsense of any sort of 'cast-iron' theory of interest rates.

It is therefore best to look at some of the savers and at some of the borrowers to see what motivates them in their lending or borrowing. First we must note that the primary consideration with most savers is that they need to hold money rather than lock it away in savings. Traditionally, two motives were regarded as explaining why we need to hold money, the *transactions motive* and the *precautionary motive*. Keynes was later to add a third motive, the *speculative motive*, but we will postpone discussion of this until later (see Chapter 27).

(a) The transactions motive

We all have to live, and to purchase our daily bread, or a basket of consumer goods appropriate to our everyday needs. The poorer we are, the more influence the transactions motive has, for our available income is barely enough to provide for our daily needs. We can give little thought to tomorrow (the *precautionary motive*). What little wealth we have we keep in liquid form (i.e. cash) for immediate use in the transactions of everyday life.

(b) The precautionary motive

Money is needed as a reserve against unforeseen events. These emergencies require people to keep their assets in liquid or near-liquid forms. Thus the private citizen leaves certain balances as credits in current accounts in the banks, and the banks, for fear it is demanded suddenly, must be cautious about preserving adequate cash reserves.

These two motives are fairly stable, and do not cause much fluctuation in either the rate of interest or the level of activity in the economy. When these two motives have been satisfied, the person who still has some liquid funds available is now able to consider saving. The following types of savers may be distinguished.

18.5.1
Types of savers

(a) The naïve members of the public

Many simple people save money regularly in quite tiny sums. When they keep it in a stocking hidden under the mattress, this is called 'hoarding', and the money is lost to the economic system. Such claims against the goods produced in the period when the income was earned are not put to use by entrepreneurs, and never become capital at all. If money keeps its value the claims against goods may eventually be enjoyed by the saver, or more likely by his heirs. But if money loses its value the claims may simply be wasted. There is a story of a Polish miser who saved all his life, living frugally and denying himself many essentials. He carried his hoard in a belt around his waist, and lived in fear of robbery. When the Polish currency collapsed at the end of World War II he exchanged his entire hoard for one bread roll.

Even when money is saved in some institution, it does not necessarily follow that it earns a proper rate of interest. For example, many people leave their savings in accounts which are not earning an adequate rate of interest. The best example today is the money left in National Savings Ordinary Accounts, which earns 1.75 per cent per annum – a very low rate of interest. The balances left in the current accounts of commercial banks formerly carried no interest, and gave the banks a very valuable source of profit at no cost. More recently most of the major banks have started paying some interest on current account balances, but at a lower rate than on deposit accounts where the money tends to be left in for longer periods.

(b) More sophisticated individual savers

Less naive savers may decide to invest their savings in a variety of ways, according to the degree of risk run. The saver who wants to avoid any risk at all will place money in **saving accounts**, or **deposit accounts** in banks or building societies. These institutions collect money from savers for the purpose of lending it out to borrowers: they assume virtually all the risks but pay quite reasonable rates of interest to savers. Building societies, for example, pay rates of interest very close to **minimum lending rate**. Minimum lending rate (MLR), formerly called bank rate, is *the rate at which the Bank of England will discount first-class bills of exchange.* It used to be announced formally by the Bank of England every Thursday. This idea was abandoned in 1981, when market forces were left to decide interest rates to some extent, but the Bank of England reserved the right to designate an official rate should the market appear to be drifting into levels of interest rate which were undesirable from the government's point of view. Within a few weeks of the new system starting such a situation did develop and the Bank stepped in to designate a minimum lending rate (but only for 24 hours). This was an overt (open) declaration of MLR, but today the more usual thing is a covert (secret) whisper to any bank that is being over-generous in its lending policies. If a bank is attracting business by low interest rates a quiet phone call from the Bank of England to senior management will convey the Bank's disapproval. Whether MLR is overtly designated, or covertly manipulated it does give institutions some idea of what interest rates are considered desirable by the government.

The commercial banks designate base rates at levels somewhere close to MLR, and then pay something less – say 2 per cent less than base rate to depositors (but often arrange special rates for firms depositing large sums). This is not as good a rate as the building-society rate, but building societies are designed to help house purchasers and are not intended for large investors. There is usually a limit set to the amount that may be invested in such societies.

The more sophisticated saver, then, lending money to such institutions, runs no risk at all and earns a reasonable rate of 'pure' interest.

(c) Sophisticated saving – the institutional investor

Some investors are more prepared to run calculated risks, if the reward to be earned is higher. Other investors, the institutional investors, combine risk-free investments (earning 'pure' interest only) with rather more speculative investments earning higher rates of interest. Such institutions might be ordinary banks, or insurance companies with large pools of premiums collected from the insuring public. From these pools of reserves the relatives of deceased insured persons and the unfortunate members of society who are injured in accidents, or taken ill on holiday, or suffer the loss of premises through fire or flood damage, will be compensated. Trade unions similarly collect subscriptions from members to be used when sickness, unemployment, or industrial disputes arise.

What rates of interest do such institutional investors hope for? The answer is that they hope to achieve a rather better rate of interest than the 'pure' interest rate earned by the ordinary citizen. Their activities are dominated by two opposite motives: the desire to earn a reasonable interest rate and the desire to keep reasonable reserves of liquid assets to meet claims when they arise, e.g. after storms, fires or strikes. The method adopted is the 'balanced-portfolio' method. A balanced portfolio is a collection of shares, debentures and other securities. Some are short-dated (i.e. repayment will take place very soon) but the rate of interest is low; others are medium term, but with a higher rate of interest and some prospect of capital gains; others are long term, or even highly speculative, with a fair degree of risk but also excellent prospects of profitability if all goes well.

<table>
<tr><td>

18.5.2
Short-term and long-term rate of interest

</td><td>

Some of the investments made by sophisticated savers are short-term loans to the discount houses and other specialist operators on the Money Market. 'Short-term' loans are loans made for a period of less than three months, and the rate of interest earned will usually be something less than Bank Rate. They are not therefore very profitable loans, but they have the advantage of being more liquid than long-term loans. Many short-term loans are very short indeed, for instance loans 'at call' are repayable immediately on request. Loans 'at short notice' are usually repayable within one to three days of being asked, though some may be 'seven days' loans. Who uses such short-term loans? The majority are used by firms or government departments temporarily short of funds. Businessmen who are engaged in profitable transactions which will be concluded in the short-term period will often find it profitable to finance the venture on the Money Market by means of a **trade bill**. This is a bill of exchange, an interesting commercial document which gives security for a short-term debt. Those readers who are unfamiliar with trade bills will find a description of their use in *Commerce Made Simple*. A **Treasury Bill** is a similar bill issued by the British Treasury. The Radcliffe Report, which examined various financial institutions at a time when interest rates were in the 6–9 per cent region, found that many businessmen were not at all concerned with the rate of interest they paid, for it represented only a small fraction of the profits made on trade. If a particular transaction, say the purchase of 10 000 tonnes of wheat, is to yield eventually a 40 per cent profit, the manufacturer financing it with a bill of exchange will care little whether it costs him 6, 7, 8 or 9 per cent. The transaction is going to clear a very useful profit margin whatever happens. This is not quite so true of trading today, where the very high interest rates prevailing (say, 20 per cent at times) combine with the depressed profit margins on transactions to make it much more uncertain that a particular transaction will prove profitable.

</td></tr>
</table>

Many savers like to lend on a short-term basis, but many borrowers wish to borrow for longer periods. The rate of interest for long-term borrowing is usually greater because the advantage of early liquidity is lost, and the risks of non-payment of interest, or non-repayment of capital are increased. Banks lend considerable sums to personal borrowers and to firms, taking whatever **collateral security** they can. The title deeds to property, or debentures secured on fixed assets or stocks are acceptable forms of collateral. Interest rates will usually be 2–3 per cent above bank base rate. Such rates of interest may again be of little interest to businessmen making good profit margins, but undoubtedly personal loans to individuals are sensitive to interest rates. High interest rates may cause many persons to postpone purchase of items whose utility has to be weighed against the repayments envisaged.

Hire purchase of consumer durables is usually arranged over at least a full year, often two or three years. The person lending to such borrowers not only has to wait longer than three months, but also has to accept repayment in small sums over the whole of the period. This requires the keeping of records of payments, and perhaps the sending of reminders to slow payers. It also involves considerable risks of non-payment, especially where the asset is worn out before the repayment period is over. Loans of this kind are usually made by specialist firms called **finance houses**. They set up the necessary book-keeping systems and employ specialists in repossession and debt collection. The rate of interest charged is much higher than Bank Rate, and may even be excessive in many cases. It is one of the more speculative fields of loan activity, and is subject to stringent legal control over documentation procedures. Even so, the activities of finance houses are of great importance to poor people needing extended credit periods. Hire-purchase rates of interest are rarely less than 20 per cent, and often exceed 30 per cent, but because of technical procedures in the repayment system rarely appeared to the hire purchaser to be as high as they are. In 1980 a requirement was introduced by the Director General of Fair Trading that every advertisement about credit should carry a bold statement giving the **Annual Percentage Rate (APR)**. This has done much to enable borrowers to compare the interest payable on credit or hire purchase proposals with alternative arrangements for financing the purchase.

Very long-term investment of capital is arranged under a rather different system. The saver, lending his money to the government or to an industrialist, buys bonds or shares which represent a relatively permanent investment in the firm or industry concerned. The liquidity of that capital is lost completely for many years, but can be regained by the investor through the Stock Exchange, which is a market for stocks and shares. By selling the security to another investor, the original investor is restored to a liquid position. This leaves the original fixed capital still in the industrial firm or public enterprise, but its ownership has changed hands at a price that was appropriate for the time when the bargain was struck. All investments earn interest or dividends, but because liquidity is easily regained the rate of interest will be less than hire-purchase interest rates. Dividends do include an element of profit however, so that it is sometimes hard to see exactly what 'pure' interest is being earned on industrial or commercial shares.

We therefore see that interest rates range from about 2 per cent below Minimum Lending Rate on short-term investments to about 30–35 per cent for speculative hire-purchase loans. Most exorbitant rate of interest of all is the moneylenders' rate of 4 per cent per month, controlled by the Consumer Credit Act, 1974. It is difficult to see an economic pattern in these interest rates, but many of them are not truly 'interest' in the economic sense of that word. We must distinguish the following elements in any 'interest' payment:

(a) *'Pure' interest* – payment for postponing consumption and making loanable funds available.
(b) *'Service' charges* – charges by the lender for the trouble of keeping accounts and collecting payments.
(c) *'Profits'* – the rewards for running the risks that interest may not be paid, nor capital repaid, in due course.

Strictly speaking, profits are a separate reward from interest, and if we remove this section (c) from the picture, to be discussed in the next chapter we can simplify the study of interest a good deal.

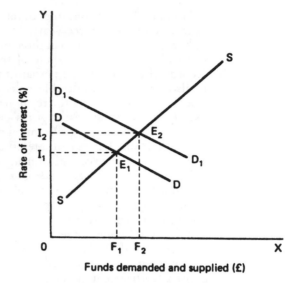

Figure 18.1 The loanable funds theory of interest

Notes
1 Initially the demand for funds and the supply of funds are in equilibrium at the point where the demand curve DD cuts the supply curve SS, and the interest rate is fixed at I_1%.
2 Imagine that the demand for loanable funds then increases to D_1D_1. In normal circumstances this would cause a temporary shortage of funds and interest rates would rise to a level (not shown on the diagram) where the line from F_1 through E_1 meets the new demand curve D_1D_1. This rate of interest would be well above I_2. Such a situation used to arise in earlier days – for example, during the Industrial Revolution – so that the high rates of interest would attract out hoarded funds and the supply of funds would thus extend to E_2, fixing the interest rate finally at I_2.
3 Today the time-lag is so short in the movement of liquid funds that adjustments take place very rapidly, and the supply will extend to E_2 as funds are switched from other employments to meet the increased demand.
4 The rate of interest adjusts to settle at the point where those who wish to lend funds are lending the quantity they wish to lend *at the going rate*, and those who wish to borrow funds are borrowing just the quantity they wish to borrow *at the going rate*.

18.6 The loanable funds theory of interest

Ignoring for the present other influences on interest rates, such as the speculative motive for holding money, and direct governmental or central bank manipulation of the interest rate, we may see from Figure 18.1 how the rate of interest is decided by the demand for, and supply of, loanable funds. As with any other free market situation the price of money (the rate of interest) is decided at the point where the demand for funds and the supply of funds are in equilibrium. The notes below Figure 18.1 explain the position.

18.7 Summary of Chapter 18

1 Interest is the payment made for the loan of liquid capital. It is usually paid at an agreed rate per cent.
2 Since the loan of money is subject to risk, it is usual for these risks to be assumed by specialist firms called institutional investors.
3 Loanable funds may be made available by individuals, firms or governments.
4 The demand for capital is made by different individuals, firms and government agencies.
5 Rates of interest paid vary widely with the naivety or sophistication of lenders and borrowers. Borrowing on short term is cheaper than long-term borrowing.

6 The loanable-funds theory of interest holds that the rate of interest equates the demand for loanable funds with their supply.

7 The supply of money is more volatile than the supply of manufactured goods in a sophisticated society with a fully developed money economy. Consequently there is little time-lag in the money market, and the supply of money reacts almost instantaneously to an increase or decrease in the demand for loanable funds. Scenes of high excitement, frequently shown on our television news bulletins, occur on the various money markets from time to time.

Exercises Set 18

1 What is interest? Who receives it, and why does it vary?

2 'The government has decided to offer a higher rate of interest to regular savers, who are prepared to leave their savings untouched for a period of at least six months.'
Explain the economic justifications for the higher rate of interest mentioned in this announcement.

3 'Initially capital was saved by individuals and used by them to promote their enterprises. Today the functions of saving and investment have been largely separated.' Explain.

4 'Capital is accumulated by self-denial.' 'Capital is a surplus that is not required for everyday purposes.' Discuss the truth of these statements, and their economic implications.

5 Why, at any given time, are there several rates of interest? What kinds of loan earn these different rates?

6 A bank's advances show the following classes of borrower:

Type of borrower	£ million
Manufacturers	4500
Farmers	800
Householders	900
Tertiary services	1500
Foreigners	2300

(a) State: (i) the total of bank advances; (ii) the percentage of total advances going to each class of borrower.

(b) Discuss the likely considerations entering into a banker's decision to lend money to (i) manufacturers, (ii) foreigners.

7 What is a balanced portfolio of investments? Suggest classes of share suitable for a balanced portfolio for a trade union which has to meet the following future commitments: (a) pension funds for members likely to retire in twenty years' time; (b) strike payments to a small number of members in one particular industry where industrial unrest is likely to occur very shortly.

8 What is likely to be the effect of a rise in basic lending rates of 2 per cent on the following?

(a) An industrialist proposing to buy a machine which will reduce labour costs by 40 per cent.

(b) A schoolteacher who has budgeted that he can just afford a holiday in Spain if he borrows £250.00.

(c) A sole trader in a competitive industry who has been considering whether to borrow funds at 8 per cent for a project which will yield him an estimated 12½ per cent.

19 Profit – the reward for bearing uncertainty

19.1 Uncertainty

In controlled economies the State initiates all enterprise, and private enterprise is discouraged. In economies which produce utilities to satisfy the wants of mankind by a free-enterprise system, someone has to take the decisions to produce. Free enterprise is shown by entrepreneurs, who employ and coordinate the factors of production. In simple cases the entrepreneur personally supervises the activities, deciding what to produce and in what quantities, and marketing the eventual output in exchange for money. This involves a variety of risks. There are some risks, called **insurable risks**, which can be predicted with reasonable accuracy. For example, the chances of a hailstorm flattening a wheat crop are known with considerable accuracy, for records have been kept for many years. Similarly the chances that my chimney-stack will be struck by lightning, or that the father of a family will suffer a fatal heart attack can be calculated mathematically. These risks can be covered by insurance.

Other risks, called non-insurable risks, cannot be covered by insurance, for they are insusceptible to statistical calculation. What is the probability that I shall prove to be a good businessman? How likely is it that the furniture I propose to manufacture will prove popular? No insurance company will cover me for these sorts of uncertainty, for there is no accumulated evidence to help it predict the probability that the event will take place. Such uncertainties must be borne by the entrepreneur, and the number of bankruptcy proceedings and winding-up resolutions passed by companies shows that success is by no means certain.

19.2 The risks of business

Enterprise consists in producing goods and services in anticipation of demand. Even where demand is highly probable it is never quite certain, and since modern business situations are dynamic (in other words, they change continuously) the uncertainties of production are increased. Business risks come under three main headings: marketing risks, obsolescence risks and political risks.

19.2.1 Uncertainties in market conditions

An entrepreneur cannot feel entirely confident that his product will sell. Public taste and fashion is unpredictable and the demand for many goods is elastic outside certain price ranges. If an entrepreneur tools up an expensive factory layout only to find that world prices of his raw materials have risen in the meantime, pricing him out of the market, his efforts have been in vain. New products may or may not catch on, and promotion costs can be very high. Good **market research** beforehand should inform the businessman of many predictable influences at work on the market, such as trends in employment, patterns of income, unfavourable reactions of certain age-ranges etc. which might influence his publicity. So enormous are the present-day costs of laying down complex production lines that entrepreneurs dare not be wrong, and have to spend large sums on persuasive advertising to ensure that the product sells.

**19.2.2
Uncertainties due to
rival products and
changes in
technology**

Obsolescence renders an existing piece of equipment uneconomic before it is worn out fully, because more efficient new products replace it. In present dynamic business conditions scientists and technologists produce an unending series of new materials, designs and patterns. There is a well-known saying to the effect that 'if a man builds a better mousetrap, the world will beat a path to his door'. Every nation is engaged in the process of innovation and the rewards are very great. The Atomic Energy Authority, in a development for marketing radioactive products, announced its estimate of the potential market as £1000 million. New techniques constantly improve production methods, to the chagrin of those who have just invested expensively in the old ones. New materials with greater strength, heat resistance, weather-proof qualities, adhesive properties etc. quickly replace traditional materials to the discomfiture of workers and entrepreneurs.

**19.2.3
Financial, legal and
political uncertainties**

This class of risks which businessmen must bear arises from the financial, legal and political framework in which we all live. The national interest must take precedence over personal interests in many cases. Contracts are frequently frustrated by the outbreak of wars, by the declaration that proposed products or services are illegal, by the refusal of financial permission to export capital or buy foreign exchange, by the development of social disorders or withdrawal of labour.

The compensation for running these risks is profit, the second reward to the factor capital. Interest is the other reward to capital, as we have seen in Chapter 18.

**19.3
The reward for
bearing uncertainty**

Profit is the reward paid to the entrepreneur for risking the loss of his capital. We have already discussed the difficulty of deciding who is the entrepreneur in modern advanced economies. There are, of course, many sole traders and partners engaged in small-scale enterprises who still provide their own capital and are entitled to the profits of the enterprise. They also, of course, suffer the losses. We agreed, however, that hundreds of thousands of such small-scale firms are relatively insignificant compared with the 6000 public limited companies in Great Britain alone. One such firm, with several hundred million pounds of capital, probably does as much business every year as all the small-scale enterprises put together.

The degree of concentration in British industry tends to be under-estimated by the general public. For example the *Bolton Report of the Committee of Inquiry on Small Firms* (designated as firms having less than 200 employees) found that small firms formed 94 per cent of all the firms in manufacturing industry, but they only employed 20 per cent of the labour (the 6 per cent of firms who were large employed 80 per cent of industry's labour force). They also produced only 16 per cent of the total output, so that 94 per cent of the firms produced 16 per cent of the output, and the 6 per cent of the firms who were large produced 84 per cent of the output. Unfortunately, the Committee found it impossibly difficult to secure really sound figures of profits made by small firms, so a comparison of profits between the two groups cannot be given.

In large enterprises there are no old-fashioned entrepreneurs, only paid employees who also own a few shares to comply with statutory requirements. The 25 directors of Barclays Bank who held shares in the bank at December 31, 1989 owned between them 227 868 shares out of a total of 1500 million shares. We see therefore that the entrepreneurs of this world-famous bank owned a negligible fraction of its capital; 0.015 per cent to be precise. This is typical of the modern position. Who then are the entrepreneurs? In a property-owning democracy we are all shareholders. Everyone who insures his life, or his car, or his house; every trade unionist who joins a welfare scheme, every pensioner with a few trust units is a shareholder in countless enterprises. The profits from these enterprises, paid for running the risks of losing the capital, provide the insurance funds, pension funds, and welfare funds of our society.

From the economic point of view profit is different from the other rewards to factors. The chief differences are:

(a) *Profit is a residue of business activity.* Unlike rent, interest and wages, it has no certain contractual basis. It is uncertain, depending on the degree of success in predicting demand, and the good fortune of the entrepreneur in not meeting competition, political disturbances, or legal or financial restraints.

(b) *Profit may be negative*, i.e. a loss may be sustained. This is implicit in its residual nature. The loss sustained eats into the contributed capital, reducing the worth of the business to the shareholders who own it.

(c) *Profit fluctuates in dynamic conditions.* When 'boom' times come the entrepreneur is able to make good profits, which rise faster than wages, rent or interest. When a 'slump' arrives the reverse is true. Wages cannot be reduced immediately. Rent is usually tied to a lease with a certain life. Interest is a contractual matter which remains fixed until the contract is discharged. Profits therefore decline as falling demand reduces turnover.

19.4
Elements of profit

Profit to the accountant is the difference between the sale price of an article and its total costs of production, using the word 'production' in its economic meaning to include manufacture, distribution and marketing costs. Economists cannot accept this as the true profit in economic terms, because we include in costs the alternatives foregone. We notice the elements in profit listed below

19.4.1
The wage of the entrepreneur

Where the entrepreneur is just another worker his salary is included in the overhead costs of the enterprise. Thus the fees of part-time directors and the salaries of full-time directors of limited companies are included in the costs charged to the profit-and-loss account when profits are being calculated. Small-scale enterprises where the entrepreneur is self-employed do not include any remuneration for the entrepreneur in these calculations. Thus a shopkeeper whose profits are £15 000 per year could probably be earning £10 000 as the manager of some other retail outlet. He cannot therefore disregard this in his calculations of the value of the enterprise. Deducting this 'alternative cost' from the profits of the enterprise leaves £5000 as his true return from it.

19.4.2
Normal profit

The second element in profit is **normal profit**, already defined as an acceptable return on capital invested (see page 93). Every enterprise must earn a reasonable reward for the capital invested in it, otherwise the capital will leave the industry and go to some alternative employment where the rewards for bearing uncertainties are better. In perfect conditions this free flow of capital will eliminate any element of 'economic rent' in the profits earned by firms, and leave all firms achieving 'normal' profits. In real life this does not quite happen. Some firms have better entrepreneurs than others, who keep ahead of competitors even in the long run. We must therefore recognise a 'rent of ability' as accruing to such entrepreneurs.

Another point is that normal profit is not uniform between industries, because some industries are particularly susceptible to uncertainties and consequently require a higher rate of normal profit to attract capital.

We may therefore recognise in normal profit several elements. First there is the interest element which is not really profit at all. Then there is an element of true profit – the reward for bearing risks – which will be larger in some industries than in others. Finally there is an element of 'rent of ability' earned by the best entrepreneurs.

19.4.3 Quasi-rents

Quasi-rents are abnormal profits over and above normal profit, which are enjoyed by an entrepreneur temporarily because competitors cannot enter the industry. This may be because there is a shortage of skilled workers, or because plant takes time to construct. Quasi-rent is an extra profit earned on factors which happen to be fixed in supply for some reason.

19.4.4 Monopoly rents

These are economic rents enjoyed by entrepreneurs who are able successfully to exclude competitors from the industry. This may be done by patent rights, copyrights, sole ownership of natural resources, or the artificial branding of products.

19.5 The functions of profit in a free-enterprise system

The profit motive is viewed very differently by people of different political and economic persuasions. Some denigrate profit as the 'immoral earnings' of the capitalist class. However true this view was in the early days of capitalism, today nearly everyone lives to some extent on such 'immoral' earnings. Others praise the profit motive as a truly dynamic force in society, which has solved the problem of creating utilities to satisfy wants. Working as it does through the enterprise of individuals, it must lead to disparities of wealth, but there are means of redistributing such disparities. The tax system redresses the inequalities of income continuously, while inheritance tax returns to the public purse much of the wealth to which they have contributed. By arranging to do so at the least painful moment, when the accumulator of the wealth has died, his/her natural resentment is avoided. These matters of policy are more appropriate to the study of applied economics than to the present volume. For our purposes it is sufficient to answer the question: What does profit do in a free-enterprise economy? The main functions of profit may be summarised as follows:

(a) *Profit motivates enterprise.* Enterprise alone produces utilities to satisfy wants. The prospects of profitability encourage men to bear uncertainties. The normal profit is the minimum reward that will keep the entrepreneur working in the industry and prevent transfer to another occupation.

(b) *Profit permits growth.* Not only do people wish to satisfy their elementary wants, they hope to enjoy progressively more sophisticated satisfactions. These require higher and higher levels of industrial and social investment. Profits are the major source of such investment, especially abnormal profits. They can be ploughed back into the same industry, or on distribution to shareholders can be reinvested in new industries. They enable higher rewards to be offered to factors, to encourage them to move to the newer and more profitable industries, away from declining or obsolete trades.

(c) *Profits often indicate efficiency.* Since the general rule is that a firm with low costs is more profitable, the profitability of a firm is some indication of its efficiency. It might equally indicate unscrupulous behaviour, for example by monopolists. In general though, it is profit

Table 19.1 Income, saving and capital formation of UK companies 1970 and 1990 (£ million)

		1970	1990 (at 1970 values)		1990 (at 1990 values)
Total income		7974	14664		150599
Less					
Dividends	1378		2111	21678	
Building Society Int.	–		1970	20234	
Other interest	1274		3414	35066	
		2652	7495		76678
		5322	7169		73621
Less					
Profits due abroad	322		693	7122	
Charitable donations	33		25	271	
UK taxes on profits	1314		2073	21295	
Royalties on oil, etc.	–		67	689	
		1669	2859		29377
Savings (undistributed profits)		3653	4310		44244
Grants, etc.		509	–		–
Capital transfers		–	50		514
Funds available		4162	4360		44758
Less					
Sundry capital items			102	1049	
Increase in stocks			438	4499	
			540		5548
Funds available		4162	3820		39210
Capital formation		3359	6010		61719
Surplus (deficit)		803	(2190)		(22509)

Source: National Blue Book, 1991

Notes

1 Between 1970 and 1990, prices rose by 1027 per cent. Consequently the very large figures for 1990 (in the end column), when expressed at 1970 values, show that over the 21 years growth was in fact very low (just over 1 per cent per annum).

2 The share of profits actually going to shareholders increased only slightly in the 21-year period, whereas interest paid to banks and building societies increased considerably. This illustrates the residual nature of profit, and the niggardly behaviour of directors towards shareholders.

3 In every year (see Blue Book for full figures) new capital formation was made possible entirely by profits (except 1989 and 1990 when there was a deficit). Businesses grew by ploughing back profits, rather than the collection of new capital, but in the last two years they borrowed money to finance new capital formation.

by others that encourages new firms to enter an industry or to imitate the successful firm. Moreover, the competitive power of the low-cost firm eventually drives the high-cost firm out of business. Its resources are transferred elsewhere. By showing where expansion should occur, since profits indicate higher prices caused by strong public demand, they redistribute industry to take account of changes of taste or fashion.

Table 19.1, and the notes below it, show what share of profit made by UK companies was returned to the shareholder, paid out to the banks and other financial institutions as interest and retained for developing the business (undistributed profits). In every year of the period, except 1989 and 1990, the profits retained were sufficient to cover all the capital development carried out.

19.6 Abuse of the profit system

It would be ridiculous to suggest that the profit motive is never abused, and that individualism is bound to operate for the collective good. At the same time the collective good is inseparable from the individual good. It does appear that there is less incentive to reduce costs and practise economy if no personal loss or gain is involved. A sound framework of law can correct the worst abuses of the profit system. The less serious abuses appear to be a price we must pay for freedom.

19.7 Summary of Chapter 19

1 All business activities incur risks. Risks which cannot be covered by insurance must be borne by the entrepreneur.
2 The chief non-insurable risks are market risks, risks of competition due to rival products, risks due to changes in technology, and financial, legal and political risks.
3 Profit is an unusual reward to factors. It is a residual reward; it fluctuates with changing circumstances and it can even be negative, i.e. losses can be made.
4 The elements of profit are entrepreneurial wages, normal profit, quasi-rents and monopoly rents.
5 The function of profit is to reward the factor capital for bearing uncertainties, to redistribute capital to where it is most effective in producing profits and to expand production in the directions most desired by the public so as to maximise satisfactions.
6 Abuses of the profit system are best controlled by legislation, or taxation may be used to redistribute incomes.

Exercises Set 19

1 What is uncertainty? What types of uncertainty must be borne by entrepreneurs?
2 'I am not in business to make profits. I am in business to make shoes.' Discuss these statements critically.
3 'Profit is not contractual like other rewards to factors; it is residual.' Explain.
4 'I created this business using techniques I have patented myself. As a result it has been impossible for others to compete with my products. I earn £20 000 a year, but must expect some change in this when the patents expire in five years' time.' What elements of profit would you discover in an analysis of this entrepreneur's reward? What do you expect will happen when the patents expire?

5 What are monopoly rents? Explain clearly the following aspects of them: (*a*) How they arise; (*b*) whether they are permanent or impermanent; (*c*) what economic factors are at work to keep them reasonable; (*d*) how they may be controlled; (*e*) how they may be recouped for the benefit of ordinary people. (If necessary re-read Chapter 12 on monopoly conditions.)

6 A retail tobacconist tells you that his total profit is £16 500. He used to earn £13 200 as a civil servant. He has invested £10 000 in his business, and now asks your opinion about the profits he is achieving. Advise him, giving reasoned economic arguments.

7 An American publisher is about to produce paperback books which sell well in the USA for the British market. What uncertainties are involved in this project?

8 'In boom times profit margins are good. In slump times profit margins are bad.' Explain.

9 In what circumstances does capital move from one industry to another? What effect does this have on (*a*) profit margins, (*b*) consumer satisfaction, (*c*) the mobility of labour?

10 'You could buy debentures at a steady 7 per cent, or you could buy ordinary shares. They have paid 20 per cent for the last three years, but are rather speculative in this industry' (stockbroker to client). Clarify this information, bringing out the economic implications for this client.

20 The financial institutions

20.1 Introduction

The private-enterprise system is one where specialisation flourishes, particularly if the operations to be performed are of an intricate or technical nature. It follows that many institutions have been developed to promote particular activities where enterprise can achieve economies. These institutions are like an intricate pattern filling in the fabric of our economic life, with old institutions dying away and new institutions arising as they are required.

Nowhere is this specialised collection of institutions as fully developed as in the financial field, for money is the key that opens all doors. Some of these institutions have premises which are known to everyone, like the Bank of England in Threadneedle Street, or the Stock Exchange in Throgmorton Street. Others exist in a multitude of small offices linked through the telephone and fax systems. The 'money market', for example, is a general term used to describe all the activities of central banks, commercial banks, merchant banks, discount houses and finance houses which deal in money. You cannot visit the Money Market, for there is no such meeting place.

The true study of these institutions is Commerce, and a full description of the major institutions is given in *Commerce Made Simple*. A brief description of these operators in the financial field is essential if the next field of study, **macroeconomics**, is to be understood. Macroeconomics is the study of whole economies, rather than of individual buyers, sellers and firms. The study of such small units is called **microeconomics**. As we move from the study of microeconomics to the study of macroeconomics we enter the field of public economic policy. The institutions studied in this section are some of the most important organisations through which governments can implement policies.

20.2 The Bank of England

The Bank of England was founded in 1694, to lend money to the government. It was given a monopoly of joint-stock banking and became the government's bank. It was at that time not a nationalised institution but a private bank which wielded great influence partly because of its close relationship with the Treasury. Just over a century later Sheridan, the dramatist, described the Bank as 'an elderly lady in the City, of great credit and long standing'. Possibly this description of the Bank led James Gillray, a caricaturist of the day to depict the Bank in a famous cartoon called 'The Old Lady of Threadneedle Street in Danger'. It showed Prime Minister Pitt attacking the Bank to obtain money for the Napoleonic Wars. The old lady was putting up a spirited resistance. The nickname stuck, and has been in popular use ever since.

In 1844 the Bank Charter Act reorganised the Bank of England, splitting it into two parts: the Banking Department and the Issue Department. The Banking Department dealt with banking operations as they affected the government, the commercial banks, the money market, and the few private firms who bank with the Bank of England. The Issue Department was charged with seeing that bank notes were issued as required by the public within the limits set by the gold reserves and a small fiduciary issue of 14 million (see page 172).

In 1946 Parliament brought the Bank of England within the control of the government. The Governor, Deputy Governor, and 16 directors who form the Court of Directors are appointed by the Sovereign on the recommendation of the Prime Minister. No longer can it be claimed, justifiably or otherwise, that the Bank prevents the implementation of desirable social policies. The Treasury is able to implement government policies through the use of monetary policy. This takes effect through the Bank's control of the banking system, and its influence over the whole range of financial institutions. Monetary policy is fully discussed in Chapter 28.

One further development which cannot be overlooked here is the possibility that the Bank of England might one day become the European Central Bank. There is a good prospect that this might come about – the obvious rival for the distinction is the German Bundesbank – but it would require a considerable change in its present structure. A European Central Bank by definition could not be a nationalised institution and great merit is claimed for the Bundesbank in its independent position – not unlike the Bank of England's position before it was nationalised in 1946.

20.2.1 The functions of the Bank of England

The Bank of England is a central bank, or national bank, charged with the control of the banking system in the interest of the nation. In the last 40 years the key functions of governments have been the management and control of prosperity. Most nations are preoccupied with these activities, and an indispensable requirement is a 'central bank' which can control the general activities of the ordinary banks.

The chief functions of the Bank of England are to act as the government's bank in the widest possible sense, anticipating where possible the banking problems that may arise and examining those that do arise. It then undertakes the appropriate operations in the money, capital, and foreign-exchange markets. A full list of activities includes the following:

(a) The Bank's role as banker

(i)   Banker to the government.
(ii) Banker to, and supervisor of, the banks and the money market.
(iii) Banker to foreign central banks and international organisations.
(iv) Banker to a residue of private customers.
(v)   Manager of the note issue for the British Isles.
(vi) Registrar of government stocks, and the servicer of the National Debt.

Another important function, exchange control, was abandoned in 1979 after 40 years during which British citizens had not been free to purchase and hold foreign currencies.

(b) The Bank's operations in the markets

(i)   The implementation of government policy to control the economy by controlling the money market for short-term loans.
(ii) The implementation of government policy in both the long-and short-term loan markets by influencing interest rates and, on occasions, designating a **minimum lending rate**.
(iii) To meet the government's long-term borrowing requirements by open-market operations on the Stock Exchange; this may also influence the lending policies of the commercial banks.

(iv) Managing the exchange rate to protect the pound. At the time of writing (1995) the UK is not a member of the EMS (the European Monetary System) which operates the ERM (the Exchange Rate Mechanism). It is free to manage the exchange rate of the pound. Under the ERM all the currencies of the European Union are tied to one another in a close network of parity bonds, where every currency is fixed against every other currency. This is explained in more detail later in this book (see pages 273–7). Where a currency moves away from its parity position the Central Bank must interfere to 'manage' the exchange rate, as explained later in Chapter 23. This has always been a major part of the Bank's work in the currency markets, which have been managed in the interests of the UK only. If the UK joins the EMU again the Bank has to 'manage' the exchange rate in the interests of the European Union as a whole, not a tiny part of it. Hence the call for a single European currency, the ECU, where the only need would be to manage the ECU against the currencies of the rest of the world. Unfortunately that requires a strong European Central Bank with the power to manage the European economy free of the influence of any particular state.

(c) The Bank's influence on policy

(i) Because of its influential position in the financial affairs of the country, the Bank is able to give useful financial advice to the Treasury and to assist in forecasts of the economic situation and the balance-of-payments position.

(ii) It often advises on capital structure and the finance of companies.

(iii) It participates in the international activities of such bodies as the International Monetary Fund, the International Bank for Reconstruction and Development and holds a watching brief on the European Monetary System.

20.3 The money market

The money market is a general name for a complex of firms dealing in short-term money. This implies money repayable within short periods, from one day to one year, though occasionally money up to five years may be handled. Nearly all banks play some part in this market, including:

(a) The commercial banks, which mainly handle ordinary banking affairs for the general public, and only deal on the money market indirectly.

(b) The merchant banks, sometimes called 'accepting houses', which specialise in financing foreign trade by accepting bills of exchange for less well known merchants, but also perform many other functions.

(c) The discount houses, which operate the market for short-term loans.

(d) The foreign exchange market, in which the UK and foreign bankers exchange pounds for foreign currencies.

20.4 Commercial banks

A bank is defined as an institution which collects surplus funds from the general public, safeguards them, and makes them available to the true owner when required, but also lends sums not required by their true owners to those who are in need of funds and can provide security.

The basic functions of a bank are:

(a) The collection of surplus funds from the general public.

(b) The safeguarding of such funds.

(c)   The transfer of these funds from one person to another, without their leaving the bank by the **cheque, direct debit** and **credit transfer** systems.

(d)   The lending of surplus funds not required by the present owner to other customers who are in need of funds, in return for interest and collateral security. The interest is shared between the bank (a reward for its services) and the true owner (a reward for not using his/her money).

The English banking system is a tripartite system like a three-layer cake. The three parts are:

(a)   The Bank of England, a 'State bank' or 'national bank'.

(b)   Specialised banking institutions, such as the discount houses and merchant banks, which deal only with special customers providing funds for special purposes.

(c)   The commercial, or joint-stock banks, which deal with the general public, but are also active in most financial fields.

A full account of the part played by the commercial banks in monetary policy is given in Chapter 28.

20.5 Merchant banks

The term 'merchant banker' is very widely used today, but is properly applied to the sixteen members of the Accepting Houses Committee. These sixteen City houses include such famous names as N. M. Rothschild & Sons, Samuel Montague & Co. Ltd, and Hambros Bank Ltd. The name 'merchant banker' refers to their origin as mercantile houses specialising in the export of British goods, particularly cotton cloth, and the import of products of the countries where they were established. This involved remitting money from one country to another, and the bill of exchange on London became the means of financing the import and export trades. The merchants concerned became well known as absolutely reliable firms whose signature on a bill would make it readily discountable on the money market.

Some of the sixteen merchant bankers are still active as merchants: one owns subsidiary companies in the timber trade; one has interests in the coffee trade; one has business houses in Australia, America and Africa. The change to banking developed as the number of firms trading with overseas territories increased. Many of these new firms found that they lacked the respect and trust enjoyed by the well established houses, so that their bills of exchange were less readily discounted. The solution was found to be the 'accepting' of these traders' bills by one of the old-established firms, for a consideration in the form of commission. The term 'accepting' means that the merchant bank accepts full responsibility to the extent of the order made in the bill. Thus if the bill says '90 days after date pay the sum of £20 000 to XYZ or to order' the merchant bank will ensure that XYZ, or anyone who holds the bill because XYZ has passed it on to them, gets paid on the due date. The merchant bank adds its name to any other names appearing on the back of the bill (endorsements). All endorsers are required to accept full responsibility on the bill as far as any holder in due course is concerned. Thus a bill with a merchant banker's name upon it will be taken by any trader as being as good as money, for if there is any difficulty later the merchant banker will always honour it in full. The banker will then look to the other parties on the bill – but particularly to the original trader who wrote the bill out – for the return of the money. Gradually the merchant became a banker specialising in the accepting of bills for other merchants.

A second interest of these firms became the issue of foreign bonds for overseas governments who lacked capital. The issue of these bonds was only possible if the names of famous houses appeared in association with the issue. The merchant bankers arranged for a quotation on the London Stock Exchange, and handled the issues which were subscribed for by British and overseas investors. The London Foreign Bond Market was an international market and a source of 'invisible earnings' of foreign exchange. Today a rather similar activity goes on in the Eurobond Market, and some huge loans are floated. The Eurobond Market is largely based in London.

The accepting houses are still the specialist financiers of foreign trade, and the acceptance of bills of exchange drawn on London is still one of their primary functions. Alongside the use of foreign bills has grown up a wide-spread use of inland bills. This growth in inland business has occurred because of the more competitive rates of interest charged on bills of exchange, which are essentially short-term money and therefore provide a ready, and reasonably priced, source of funds to businessmen. The essential feature of a bill is its self-liquidating nature. That is to say, by the time the bill falls due, the trading venture it was designed to finance should have been completed and should have produced the funds for settlement of the bill. Bills are not intended to form a long-term financial alternative to bank loans or overdraft facilities. They are simply a method whereby the exporter receives his payment and the importer enjoys a period of credit, while the goods are in transit, being unloaded, going through customs formalities, etc.

The merchant banks carry out many other functions of which the issuing of new securities, activities as a confirming house for overseas orders, and the handling of bullion are the most important.

20.6 Discount houses

The 'discount market' consists of eight firms who are members of the London Discount Market Association. They specialise in **bill broking**, i.e. the provision of short-term money by way of discounting bills to borrowers who require funds which they expect to be able to repay within three months (in fact many borrowers will repay within 24 hours). This is a specialised form of banking. The discount houses provide a market-place where those who have surplus money, the use of which they are prepared to sell, can be put in touch with those prepared to buy the use of this money. The smallest unit for money on the market is £10 000, but occasionally lower amounts are used.

Today the savings of the nation are increasingly concentrated in the hands of institutional investors, such as banks, insurance companies and building societies, who assume the responsibility of caring for and earning interest on the savings of the ordinary public. As this is a competitive world the institutional investors are becoming more and more sophisticated in their outlook. Money is not allowed to lie idle, but is loaned out to earn interest when it is not required for the main activities of the institution which has collected it. Even 'overnight' interest can be earned from banks anxious to meet their daily minimum cash reserve requirements. Every institutional investor has a 'balanced portfolio' of investments of different types. Some of the short-term investments in the portfolio will have been purchased from the bill brokers of the London Discount Market Association. The commonest short-term investments are Treasury bills, bank bills, trade bills of exchange, short gilt-edged securities, corporation stocks and, more recently, sterling certificates of deposit. Some houses also deal in dollar certificates of deposit and foreign currency bills.

20.6.1
Bill-broking

Bill-broking may be defined as dealing in money: taking it from those who have a surplus and distributing it to those who have need of it. When we take money from people we must pay interest on it in due course, so that if we lend it out to people who have need of it we must clearly lend at a higher rate of interest than we are to pay to the person from whom it was obtained. The difference between the borrowing rate and the lending rate is the source of the profits of the discount house.

If this profit margin is to be kept competitive there is no room for expensive paper records of transactions. Almost all the deals are by word of mouth only, but, once given, the discount banker's word is his bond. In a single day as much as £1500 million may be handled by the market, with very little fuss or formality.

Flexible behaviour is absolutely essential to the bill broker. Changes in prices on the commodity markets or rates of interest anywhere in the world may lead to a strong demand for money, or cause a glut of money to be available. These trends must be reflected in changed interest rates or a lot of money will be lost. Since August 5, 1981, the Bank of England has sought to influence interest rates covertly rather than overtly, although it reserves the right to announce a minimum lending rate if it feels market forces are uncertain what the rate should be. If rates are being decided most of the time by market forces there are obviously fluctuations in the market rate, reflecting the demand for, and supply of, short-term funds. The discount houses must remain ever alert to possible changes.

20.6.2
Services of the bill brokers to the lending sector

Bill brokers are prepared to borrow money from anyone who has a surplus and they agree to repay it as required. Money that is to be repayable on demand is known as 'call' money because it is on call at any time. 'Short-notice' money is usually repayable in a few days.

To the banks, bill brokers offer a secure outlet for liquid funds, which can still be regarded by the banks as part of their reserve ratio. The basic rate of interest is about $1\frac{5}{8}$ per cent below the commercial banks' base rate, but the actual rate depends on supply and demand and the Treasury Bill tender. The Treasury Bill tender is a device which a central bank can use to keep other banks short of money. Since the discount houses voluntarily agree to take up all the treasury bill tender, the central bank can keep everyone short of money by raising the amount it requires the discount houses to tender for. Apart from the Bank of England's manipulation of the market in this way, it is quite profitable for the banks to lend money like this to the discount houses at negligible risk. The brokers also buy from the commercial banks those bills of exchange which the banks have discounted for customers and do not wish to keep to maturity. Such bills are promises to pay made by commercial firms, and are re-discounted by the banks to the money market.

To commercial firms wishing to lend money the discount houses offer the clearing-bank deposit rate, usually 2 per cent less than the bank base rate. This is very useful to firms which have money to spare, but do not wish to put it on deposit because they will have to give seven days' notice of withdrawal. If firms are prepared to leave it at seven days' notice they can earn $\frac{1}{4}$ per cent above the clearing-bank deposit rate.

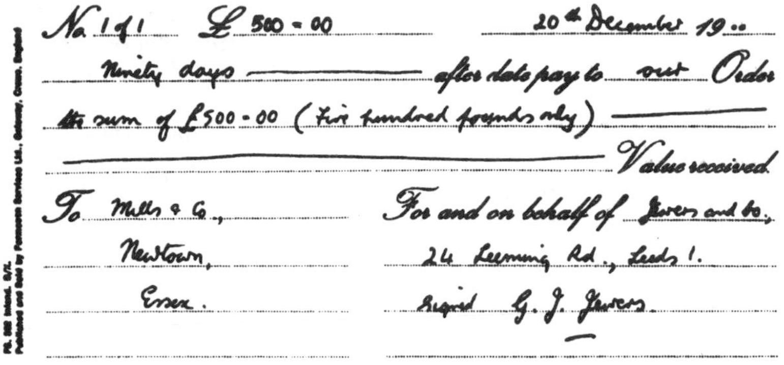
No. 1 of 1 £500 = 00 20th December 19..
Ninety days ——— after date pay to our Order
the sum of £500.00 (Five hundred pounds only) ———
——— Value received
To Mills & Co., For and on behalf of Jewers and Co.,
Newtown, 24 Leeming Rd., Leeds 1.
Essex. Signed G. J. Jewers.

Figure 20.1 An inland bill of exchange

20.6.3 Services of the bill brokers to the borrowing sector

To the government, the discount houses offer the loan of the short-term money it needs, assuming an informal responsibility for underwriting the whole of the Treasury Bill issue every Friday. It is this conventional understanding which enables the Bank of England to control to some extent the economy of the country (see page 231).

To commercial firms, the discount houses offer direct loans by discounting trade bills. These are bills given to the commercial firm by a customer who promises to pay later. By discounting these bills the commercial firm is able to obtain the money at once, less a certain rate of interest. If a discount broker does not wish to offer this facility himself he may introduce the commercial firm to a merchant banker or accepting house who will do so. The discount houses also supply banks with bank bills and trade bills for portfolio purposes.

Bank bills are bills that have been accepted or endorsed by a reputable bank. As such they are very reliable, and are discounted at a competitive rate called the 'Fine Rate'. This is an agreed minimum rate below which the eight discount houses will not buy bills. There is no maximum rate, so a bill broker who could get more than the fine rate would take it. Since the market is very competitive it is unlikely he would be able to do so often; his customer would go elsewhere.

Trade bills are bills not signed by a bank. They are usually drawn to cover a particular transaction and are more risky than a bank bill. On the other hand they are also more profitable. If these bills are passed on by the discount houses to banks building a balanced portfolio, the discount house accepts full liability on the bill. If the bill is dishonoured, the discount house immediately puts the customer in funds and looks to the parties to the bill to give satisfaction. It may therefore be said that the discount houses lend respectability to many commercial transactions and thus oil the wheels of commerce. One point about these trade bills is that they are usually for small amounts, mere hundreds or thousands of pounds. Usually the smallest unit in the discount market is £10 000, but the discount houses do handle trade bills for quite small sums. There is no limit on the size of a bill, whose reliability is judged by the names on the bill and their credit-worthiness.

20.6.4 How the discount market operates

The portfolio of investments that a firm in the discount market owns is earning interest at various rates. Gilts earn more than bank base rates, bank bills just below and the trade bills somewhere between ⅛ and 2 per cent above this rate. At the same time the discount market itself has had to borrow the money from the banks at rates varying between bank base rate and $1\frac{5}{8}$ per cent below, or from commercial firms at 2 per cent below this rate, i.e. the commercial-bank deposit rate. Naturally, like any other borrower from the bank, the discount house has to provide collateral security, hence large parts of its portfolio of investments are actually lodged as security with the banks to whom they are in debt.

If this situation continued for a few months or longer the profits earned by the money-market firm would be the difference between the interest they earn and the interest they have to pay out. In fact the situation never stays static for even one day. First, the discount houses have promised to lend the government money every day, by buying Treasury Bills for which they tendered the previous Friday. Next, the banks always 'call' money in the mornings to pay out the sums they have agreed to lend to the public, the commercial firms and the government, and also to pay tax moneys paid to them which they now have to hand on to the Treasury. If the banks do this it makes the discount houses very short of cash in the morning. Later in the day the banks will probably have cash to spare because depositors have paid in money during the day. The discount houses have to telephone round desperately to get the cash they need before 2.30 p.m., which is the closing time for borrowing from the Bank of England. Great excitement develops as they try to obtain the funds they need, calling on their screen-based electronic switchboards to raise the money. Seconds of delay may mean that someone else might get half a million pounds first.

At 2.30 those bankers whose attempts to raise cash have been unsuccessful must present themselves at the Bank of England to borrow what they need. They have been 'forced into the Bank', and if the Bank is anxious to raise interest rates all round it will charge them either a rate close to the commercial banks' base rates or even more: a penal rate. This is sad for the discount houses since they have already loaned the money to someone at less than this rate, and are therefore going to make a loss. Suppose a discount house had borrowed cash from a commercial bank at $7\frac{1}{2}$ per cent and agreed to loan it at $8\frac{1}{2}$ per cent to a metal broker. On being forced into the Bank it is up to the Bank whether it will charge the discount house a penal rate. If the Bank is satisfied with the present level of the economy it might not penalise the discount house, but if it wishes to discourage credit it may charge base rate, say $10\frac{1}{2}$ per cent or even more. A discount house forced to pay a penal rate, loses perhaps 2 per cent on the sum borrowed. On £100 000 this amounts to a £500 loss on a '3 months' bill. The bill brokers will be charging more for loans next day, and credit will be discouraged.

20.6.5 Recent developments in the discount market

The history of bill-broking is a history of adaptability to changing conditions in the money market. In the early days of the Industrial Revolution inland bills were a major source of currency, and bill brokers earned a steady living by helping to sort out uneven situations in the money market. As branch banking developed these uneven situations were adjusted by the head offices of the big banks, and the bill brokers turned to foreign bills, i.e. bills drawn on London to settle international indebtedness. During this period the saying grew up that 'a good bill should smell of the sea'.

In recent years there has been a considerable increase in the use of inland bills to finance internal trade and provide working capital, particularly in the more profitable, but more speculative, hire-purchase field. This has increased the part played by the bill broker in developing the economy of the nation. A succession of credit squeezes has made loans and overdrafts from the ordinary banks more difficult to obtain. Businessmen have had to turn elsewhere to secure funds, and the inland bill of exchange has been one way to obtain them.

Another recent development is the issue by local authorities of short-term bills and bonds with a life of one to four years. These enable the local authorities to fund some of their short-term debts, against the security of the rates. The time chosen, one to four years, lies conveniently between the three-month Treasury and trade bills and the five-year period usually chosen for short-term government bonds.

20.6.6
The economic significance of the discount market

If the discount houses had an entirely free hand in borrowing funds from savers and lending them to spenders the economy might at times get too active. Control over the economy is partly established by controlling the discount houses. This is achieved by an informal undertaking by the discount houses to subscribe for the full amount of Treasury Bills offered each Friday by the Bank of England. By setting the size of this tender sufficiently large to keep the discount houses rather short of money, the Bank of England keeps control of them. They are sure to get into difficulties (and be 'forced into the Bank') if their rates are too low, so that firms are encouraged to borrow. If they are in difficulties the Bank of England can lend to them, as 'lender of last resort' (direct assistance) or lend to banks and other borrowers to ease the pressure on them (indirect assistance). If the Bank of England is satisfied with the economy it will lend cheaply and the discount houses will be able to balance their books, and make a profit on their deals. If the Bank is worried about the economy and thinks that the discount houses are causing the economy to inflate, it will charge them a 'penal rate' and they will make losses. They will have to recoup these losses by raising interest rates next day.

20.7
The foreign-exchange market

This is another market which has no central market-place, but operates through the general offices of the banks concerned with overseas trade. The main preoccupation of the foreign-exchange dealers is to secure supplies of foreign currency as required to finance international trade. The price of foreign currencies, like all prices, is determined by the demand for that currency and the supply of it. The demand for the currency depends on the demand for that country's goods and services by foreigners, and the supply of the currency depends on how many overseas goods and services its home nationals wish to buy. Capital movements can also affect the exchange rate by making supplies of a currency available on long-term loans or investments.

20.8
The capital market

The capital market is another general name, like the name money market, which refers to a field of general activity rather than a particular place where buyers and sellers meet. Capital is required for many purposes, and specialised institutions have developed to provide it. The influence of these institutional investors has grown in the last 30 years, since a more equal distribution of wealth has been achieved. The high levels of taxation prevent rich people from accumulating large supplies of capital as in former times. Capital now has to be collected in relatively trifling sums from vast numbers of people, by special institutions.

A full list of these institutions includes, apart from the banks, the following:

(a) Issuing houses, which take on the work of issuing new shares or debentures for firms wishing to expand their activities.

(b) Building societies, collecting funds for those who wish to buy their own houses with loans financed through mortgages. Since the Building Societies Act 1986 there has been a considerable extension in their activities with the building societies providing many services previously supplied only by banks. One building society, the Abbey National, has changed its status and become a fully-fledged bank. Others may follow.

(c) Finance houses, dealing in the more risky, but more profitable, hire-purchase fields for financing the purchase of consumer durables and cars. The finance houses too have extended their activities, moving particularly into the leasing field, where durable goods such as computers, office equipment, vehicles and plant are purchased not by the company that requires the item but by the finance house. The finance house then leases the equipment to the company for a monthly payment. The purchase of capital equipment is thus taken over by a specialist provider of capital.

(d) Investment trusts and unit trusts, which specialise in collecting small sums from a great number of investors for the purchase of a balanced portfolio of shares. In this way they provide the fixed capital required by industry.

(e) Insurance companies are very active in the capital market. They have large sums to invest every week as premiums are received from the insuring public.

(f) Finally the Stock Exchange has an important part to play in the raising of long-term capital. Besides its chief function of providing a market-place for existing stocks and shares, it now plays some part in the raising of capital by granting a quotation to a new issue of shares. These shares are then 'placed' by the issuing house with one or two large purchasers of shares, insurance companies or investment trusts.

20.9 The stock exchange

A stock exchange is a highly organised financial market where bonds, stocks and shares can be bought or sold. The London Stock Exchange is situated in Throgmorton Street within a few yards of the Bank of England, and at the centre of the financial affairs of the City. It is a respected and valued national institution, but it is not alone. There are independent groups of stock exchanges in other large cities, while members of the Provincial Brokers' Stock Exchange also carry on business in numerous smaller towns.

Stock-market business is world-wide, and New York, Johannesburg, Melbourne, Tokyo, Calcutta, Paris, Amsterdam and Brussels are all famous centres of stock-exchange activity.

The function of a stock exchange is to put those who wish to sell stocks or shares in touch with those who wish to buy, so that investments can change hands in the quickest, cheapest and fairest manner possible.

When members of the general public invest their savings by lending them to the managers of a company they do not intend that the company shall have the use of their money for ever, for they do not know when fate may knock on their door and present them with problems. The investment as far as the investors are concerned is a purely temporary one, depending on good luck to some extent. If the fates are kind the investment may last for years; if the fates are unkind they or their heirs, may wish to withdraw the investment in cash form, just like withdrawing money from a bank.

From the point of view of directors of the firm the matter is quite different. They regard the investment as a permanent one, for they spend the invested money on land and buildings, plant and machinery, transport and other equipment. They cannot possibly return the money, for they no longer have it. They have turned it into assets, and in the process it becomes 'fixed'. Fixed capital is capital tied up in fixed assets, which have been purchased for permanent use in the business.

It follows that shareholders cannot withdraw their money as if it was cash deposited in a bank. They must sell the shares on the Stock Exchange to someone who has cash and wishes to invest it in the firm concerned. The price at which the exchange takes place will reflect the estimates by the two parties of the value of the share in the company which it represents. It may therefore involve the seller in some **capital gain** or **capital loss**, according to whether the price is above or below the cost price of the share when it was originally purchased.

The company whose shares are being bought and sold has little interest in the matter at all, but it will register the transfer of shares in order to keep its list of shareholders up to date. The company merely pursues its lawful activities, as laid down in its Memorandum of Association, leaving the specialist dealers on the Stock Exchange to arrange matters when the public wish to buy or sell securities.

20.9.1
Buying and selling securities

As part of the Government's recent policies to increase the freedom in business life the traditional arrangements on the Stock Exchange have been reviewed and a new system of 'market makers' introduced where brokers are able to act in both capacities, as representatives of the public in the purchase and sale of stocks and shares and as dealers with stocks and shares to buy and sell. The new arrangements came into force in October 1986 and the arrangements are now as follows:

The old system of members of the Stock Exchange who acted in a single capacity either as stockbrokers (people who acted as agents for the general public in buying and selling shares) or as stock-jobbers (stallholders in the market-place, buying shares from and selling shares to the brokers who approached them) has been replaced. Now any firm may act in both capacities (a broker-dealer) if it wishes to do so, but if it only wishes to act in a single capacity (as a broker or a dealer) it may do so. A member who elects to act as a dealer will register as a **market maker** in a certain range or class of shares and will be prepared to quote prices for feeding into the Stock Exchange Automated Quotation Service (SEAQ). These prices are in the following form:

Stock: ICI Quote 102–4 Size (10 000)

This means that the firm is prepared to buy ICI stock at 102 per 100 of stock, and to sell ICI at 104 per 100 of stock. It was originally hoped that some of the market makers would be 'Floor Market makers' actually present on the floor of the Stock Exchange where dealings take place. Others would be 'Off-Floor Market Makers' feeding prices in from their offices, not only in London but all over the country (and all over the world eventually). In the event it was soon found that the floor market makers could not keep in touch adequately with changing prices and floor trading virtually ceased. The electronic SEAQ system has made the Stock Exchange a very competitive place indeed.

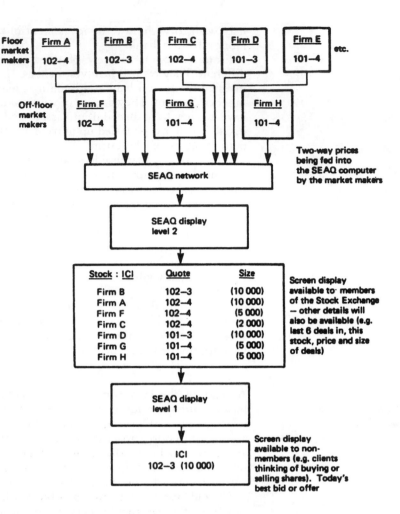

Figure 20.2 The Stock Exchange Automated Quotation System

Because of the computerised system available the prices now appear on a visual display unit like a television screen, shuffled to give the best buy or the best sale, according to whether the interested party wishes to buy or sell shares. This ability is the chief thing that protects the investor – which is made clear below. The SEAQ system is illustrated in Figure 20.2.

20.9.2
How a bargain is struck

Let us consider Mrs A, whose husband has just died and she wishes to sell £10 000 of ICI stock. She approaches a member of the Stock Exchange who has an office in her own home town. His link to the Stock Exchange only gives a SEAQ level 1 display (see Figure 20.2) but this shows the best buy on the Stock Exchange at the time Mrs A calls in. This is 102–3. It so happens that the broker/dealer needs £20 000 ICI stock himself which he believes is going to rise in price. Now this is where the Stock Exchange's new rules apply to protect the investor. It would be nice if he could buy Mrs A's £10 000 of stock at, say, £95 per £100. He knows she needs the money and will take whatever he offers her. However, this would cheat Mrs A of £7 per £100 of stock, because the fair price on the visual display is £102 per £100. Therefore the rules say a dealer may only deal privately with his client if (*a*) he tells her he is doing so and (*b*) he offers her a better price than the one on the visual display. So he might say 'Well – the best sale on the Stock Exchange as you can see is £102 for every £100 of your stock, but I can make you a slightly better offer myself of £102.50'. Mrs A will almost certainly accept this better price for her stock, and a bargain will be struck. The dealer then keys into the SEAQ system that he has purchased £10 000 of ICI stock at £102.50 and the time of the transaction. The purchase will be recorded and the Stock Exchange Council can see that he dealt honourably with Mrs A, by buying her stock under the **best-execution rule**. This rule says that the dealer must buy or sell at the best price possible according to SEAQ – or a better price if he deals privately with her on his own behalf.

Viewed from the other point of view, suppose a firm wishes to buy ICI stock as part of an investment portfolio it is building as part of a pension fund for its employees' superannuation. The best buy on the display is £103 (because the higher of the two prices is the price at which the market maker will sell to a customer wishing to purchase ICI stock). If the broker/dealer has some ICI stock he would like to dispose of – it cost him £110 a few weeks ago when he thought it would go up in price, but it didn't and he wishes to sell it. The dealer cannot charge the customer more than best-buy (£103). If he wants to deal he must – under the best execution rule – deal at a better price than the market price. So he might say 'As you can see the best price is £103 on the Exchange this afternoon, but I could sell you some that I have surplus to requirements at a better price, £102.50'. This gives the customer a better buy, and clears the dealer of the stock he wished to dispose of.

20.9.3
The economic significance of the stock market

In a free-enterprise society, capital has to be collected from individuals. In today's egalitarian society where wealth is more evenly divided than ever before, this capital is spread so thinly that special institutions are needed to collect it. These institutions are not investing capital permanently, but only incidentally as a sideline to their main occupations. Thus the bank's main occupations are safeguarding moneys and facilitating payments for their clients. The insurance companies' main occupation is to cover risks. Trade unions exist to further industrial action and the welfare of their members. For all these institutions managed liquidity is essential. Their investment policies are designed to achieve a balance between profitability and liquidity. The Stock Exchange provides the means whereby liquidity is regained, and also the means whereby a portfolio rendered unsafe by changes in the positions of governments and businessmen may be adjusted to yield greater security. Of course these services are available for individuals too, but the really significant investors today are the institutional investors.

Among the institutions of modern society central and local governments are some of the most important. In an increasingly complex society administrative control of defence, health and education extends to cover major national monopolies like fuel and power, transport, atomic energy and even certain types of land. This **public sector** of the economy requires finance too. The activities of the government broker ensure that such funds will continue to be made available through the gilt-edged market.

The gilt-edged market is an active market in government stocks. The sale of these stocks is used to finance the long-term borrowing of government departments and nationalised industries. The 'trustee status' of such stocks assists the market in maintaining an active interest in gilt-edged securities. The main object of the Bank of England's activities here is to promote the sale of long-term stock and keep the market healthy so that this type of long-term loan will always be available to the government.

All purchases and sales are made through the government broker and are largely authorised by the Bank's Issue Department. From time to time the Bank's portfolio is restored by new issues of stock. Most of these new issues cannot be sold at once to the general public but are taken up by the Issue Department. Funding is a chief aim of the Issue Department. It may be defined as persuading citizens and institutions to lend money on a long-term basis (creating a fund) instead of only for a short term.

As with all highly organised markets the activities of broker-dealers on the Stock Exchange are involved, and the general public cannot hope to understand what the specialist is doing. It follows that his activities may abuse his privileged position. The Stock Exchange Council exercises a supervisory control over members, and its Code of Dealing ensures acceptable standards of behaviour by dealers. It is also represented on a Panel, composed of representatives of banks and other institutions, whose 'Takeover Code' attempts to supervise the behaviour of bidders trying to gain control of companies. This code has been much criticised, on the ground that it does not ensure equal treatment for all shareholders. It certainly takes time for such Codes to close all the loopholes which can be devised by astute and expert specialists, but the worst abuses of speculative activities have gradually been controlled by the Panel and Council, and it seems likely that these improvements will continue.

The result of the activities of the Stock Exchange is the collection of a vast amount of capital for both private and public enterprises. This capital is not collected through the Exchange, rather it is collected *because* of the Exchange. It encourages investors to invest, because they know liquidity can be regained. This investment enables capital projects to go ahead, employment opportunities to be provided, and unit costs to be reduced as economies of scale are achieved. It even provides, by its published prices, the yardstick on which estates, inheritances and compensation (in nationalisation procedures for example) are valued.

20.10 Summary of Chapter 20

1 Financial institutions are of great importance in developing and controlling economies.
2 The Bank of England, like all central banks, is used to implement government policies by promoting expansion or contraction of the economy as required.
3 The 'Money Market' is a general name for all banks and financial institutions who are active in making liquid funds available, to promote the activities of industry and trade.
4 The commercial banks provide a wide variety of services for the ordinary public, and are also very active in making funds available to the discount houses and other specialist operators.
5 Merchant bankers promote foreign trade by accepting bills of exchange for less worthy business houses.
6 The Discount Market is the market for short-term loans. It is the medium through which the government influences rates of interest and controls the level of activity in the economy.
7 The Foreign-exchange Market is the market where the currencies of the world are compared and prices are fixed for pounds, dollars, francs, Dmarks, etc.
8 The Capital Market consists of a wide variety of institutions collecting capital from the public and making it available to various kinds of entrepreneurs. Most important are the issuing houses, insurance com-

panies, investment and unit trusts, building societies, finance houses and the ordinary banks.

9 The Stock Exchange is the market for existing securities, where those wishing to regain liquidity, by selling their shares in firms or their government stocks, may be put in touch with those wishing to surrender liquidity in favour of fixed assets.

Exercises Set 20

1 Define a bank. What are its basic functions and how does it perform them?

2 'Discount houses render great service to bankers and businessmen alike.' What services do they render and what reward do they get for these services?

3 'A financial market is just like any other market-place.' Explain, referring in your answer to (*a*) the Discount Market and (*b*) the Foreign-exchange Market.

4 The Bank of England is Great Britain's Central Bank. What are its chief functions?

5 What is a Stock Exchange, and how does it serve (*a*) the general public and (*b*) the business community?

6 Mrs A. has decided to sell 1000 shares in General Electric to buy her son a car as a graduation present. The Motorists' Insurance Co. had decided to buy 1000 shares in General Electric as part of its portfolio. How will the two parties be dealt with so that the needs of both are satisfied?

7 In what ways does a sophisticated network of financial institutions serve a nation? What is their impact upon (*a*) savings, (*b*) the factor 'capital' and (*c*) the house buyer?

Section 5: The Theory of International Trade

Section 5: The Theory of International Trade

21 International trade

21.1
Why trade with foreign countries?

Nations trade with one another for several reasons. First, Nature has been haphazard in the way she has distributed resources around the world, so that some nations possess natural ores and chemical deposits in excess of their own national requirements, while other nations have no supplies. Britain has large coal reserves but lacks copper, South Africa has gold but lacks oil (although she is still prospecting). Kuwait has vast oil deposits but little else. The exchange between nations of such resources is an obvious solution to the shortages.

Secondly, climate plays a large part in the production of many natural products. Jungle hardwoods will only grow in tropical climates while softwoods grow in the band of cooler countries in the northern hemisphere. Citrus fruits require a Mediterranean climate. Tobacco will grow in the UK, but cannot be properly cured in the British climate. Only very large countries like the USA and Russia embrace within their borders a variety of climatic regions of the world. Such nations may achieve some degree of success in practising self sufficiency. Other nations must trade.

Thirdly, it sometimes happens that a nation, despite efficient production, has such vast demands that she must supplement home production with imports. For example, Britain grows wheat very efficiently, but not on a scale large enough to support her entire needs. India grows rice, but Burma has been for centuries the 'rice-bowl of India'.

Even when a nation is able to produce all the goods it needs there may be reasons for not doing so. For years the USA husbanded its own oil resources for strategic reasons and used instead cheap supplies from Venezuela and the Middle East. Similarly, Great Britain has allowed her own cotton industry to run down in the face of competition from the newly industrialised countries of the Far East, whose cheap labour and skilful exploitation of new technologies has made them more economic than Lancashire.

Trade also takes place when it is to the economic advantage of the nations concerned to specialise in particular activities. For example both Britain and Sweden can make steel, but much Swedish steel is used in British industry because of its high quality and unique properties. Sweden buys many British cars even though Swedish cars are world famous. The explanation is to be found in the **law of comparative costs**, which is the main feature of this chapter on the theory of international trade. Before we examine this law let us consider two basic economic ideas: the principle of comparative advantage and the idea of alternative costs.

21.2
The principle of comparative advantage

Consider two men, Prof. Splitit, an atomic physicist, and Bill Greenfingers, a gardener. The professor is a highly educated scientist, earning in his normal employment £24.00 per hour. He is also a keen gardener, and because of his scientific training is actually a better gardener than Bill Greenfingers; twice as good in fact. Bill Greenfingers is a good gardener, and earns £3.00 per hour at his employment. So we have:

	Professor S.	Gardener B.G.
Normal hourly earnings	£24.00	£3.00
Earnings as a gardener	£ 6.00	£3.00

Notice that the professor has an absolute advantage in earning power over Bill Greenfingers both as an atomic scientist and as a gardener. But at which job has he a comparative advantage? Clearly, the ratios of £24.00 to £3.00 and £6.00 to £3.00 show that he has a 4:1 advantage in his specialist occupation. (24:3 = 8:1 and 6:3 = 2:1.)

Suppose the professor gives up an hour of his earning time to weed the garden. The garden will receive in this one hour the equivalent of two hours' gardening by Bill Greenfingers, for the professor is twice as good a gardener as Bill. If Prof. S. specialises in his own employment and earns £24.00, he will then be able to pay Bill Greenfingers to do eight hours' gardening. The garden will therefore look four times as tidy as if the professor had tended it personally.

Economists say that it will, generally speaking, be advantageous for mankind if people specialise in those occupations at which they have the greatest comparative advantage, or the least comparative disadvantage, leaving others to produce the goods and services for which they have little aptitude. This principle of comparative advantage is the basis of specialisation into trades and occupations, and it is of great importance in the theory of international trade.

21.3 The idea of alternative costs

'Alternative costs', also called 'opportunity costs', have been discussed earlier on page 7. Any nation has certain factors (land, labour and capital). These factors of production are available to produce goods and services. It can move its factors into or out of production at will. Suppose we say that a basic group of factors comprising an entrepreneur and 20 workers, £10 000.00 capital, and 500 acres of land, are to be devoted to the production of wheat. The result will be an output of a given quantity of wheat, say 1000 tonnes.

Had these same factors been employed in other ways, different goods or services could have been produced. They might have raised beef instead, or intensively fed poultry, or they might have made saucepans, or built roads. To move factors over to other forms of production is quite easy, but it usually involves some retraining of labour and modifications to building etc. Such little difficulties are called 'economic friction'. If there is a good deal of friction, changes will not be made easily; if there is only a little friction, changes will take place more readily.

If these factors are put to work in different ways they may turn out 1000 tonnes of wheat, or, say 100 tonnes of aluminium. The 'cost' of the wheat we actually produce is the aluminium we do not produce; or the 'cost' of the aluminium we actually manufacture is the wheat we do not grow. The factors cannot be employed on both at once, so we have to make a choice.

The alternative costs may be displayed as follows:

	1000 tonnes wheat : 100 tonnes aluminium
or	1000 : 100
or	10 : 1

The alternative-cost ratio is therefore 10:1. We can have 10 tonnes of wheat, or one tonne of aluminium, but not both. The cost of 10 tonnes of wheat is one tonne of aluminium, while the cost of one tonne of aluminium is 10 tonnes of wheat.

It is different alternative-cost ratios that give individuals a comparative advantage in one trade or another. If the factors of production (land, labour or capital) are employed where they have the greatest comparative advantage, or the least comparative disadvantage, output will be at a maximum. Let us now consider how these basic economic ideas arise also in international trade.

21.4
The law of comparative costs

The Law of Comparative Costs states that *nations will find it profitable to trade with other nations when (a) they have different alternative-cost ratios, and (b) the international terms of trade lie within the limits set by their domestic alternative-cost ratios.*

This is not an easy law to understand and the reader is urged to study the next page or two very carefully.

21.5
An example of specialisation in international trade

Imagine two countries: one is a South American republic which we shall call Garibaldia, the other is a western advanced nation (like Great Britain) which we shall call Occidentalia. Each has land, labour and capital available for employment. These factors are employed in many different activities, but we shall consider only a small set of factors comprising some land, some capital and some labour, including an entrepreneur. This set can be employed in either beef production or aluminium production. The figures given in Table 21.1 show the alternative costs of these two products.

Notice that, as stated in the law of comparative costs, these two countries *do have different alternative-cost ratios.* The cost of a unit of aluminium in Garibaldia is 2.5 units of beef. The cost of a unit of aluminium in Occidentalia is 1.2 units of beef. For every unit of aluminium production she gives up, Garibaldia can have 2.5 units of beef, whereas Occidentalia can have only 1.2 units of beef. It is clear that if one country is going to specialise in beef production it ought to be Garibaldia, because she has the comparative advantage.

Table 21.1 Comparative advantage in beef production

Country	Garibaldia		Occidentalia	
Products (in units of 1000 tonnes)	Aluminium (1000 tonnes)	Beef (1000 tonnes)	Aluminium (1000 tonnes)	Beef (1000 tonnes)
Output of a given set of factors	4:10		9:11	
Alternative cost ratios	1:2.5		1:1.2	
Effect of changing factors over from one product to another	Giving up 1 unit of aluminium	Enables this country to produce 2.5 units of beef	Giving up 1 unit of aluminium	Enables this country to produce 1.2 units of beef
Country with a comparative advantage in beef production	Garibaldia has the advantage		–	

Table 21.2 Comparative advantage in aluminium production

Country	Garibaldia		Occidentalia	
Products (in units of 1000 tonnes)	Beef (1000 tonnes)	Aluminium (1000 tonnes)	Beef (1000 tonnes)	Aluminium (1000 tonnes)
Output of a given set of factors	10:4		11:9	
Alternative cost ratios	1:0.4		1:0.82	
Effect of changing factors over from one product to another	Giving up 1 unit of beef	Enables this country to produce 0.4 units of aluminium	Giving up 1 unit of beef	Enables this country to produce 0.82 units of aluminium
Country with a comparative advantage in aluminium production	–		Occidentalia has the advantage	

In Table 21.2 this information has been rearranged to show the same figures the other way round. We now see that if one country is proposing to specialise in aluminium it ought to be Occidentalia, because she has the comparative advantage in producing this product. For every unit of beef Occidentalia gives up, she will produce 0.82 units of aluminium. For ever unit of beef Garibaldia gives up she will produce only 0.4 units of aluminium. Clearly then, Occidentalia ought to be the one that produces aluminium as its special product.

Now let us examine what happens to the total wealth of the world if these two countries specialise. For the sake of simplicity we shall pretend that the world consists of these two countries only.

Table 21.3 shows the situation before either country specialises. Since these countries have different factor endowments to start with, there is no connection between their outputs before specialisation commences. Let us assume that at this time Occidentalia produces 120 units of beef and 100 units of aluminium, whereas Garibaldia produces 110 units of beef and 60 units of aluminium.

Each country is producing for its own use, and world output is 230 units of beef and 160 units of aluminium.

Before proceeding further let us be quite clear about the fact that Occidentalia has an **absolute advantage** in both beef and aluminium production. 'Absolute advantage' is defined as a situation where a country, with a given input of factor resources, produces more of a commodity than

Table 21.3 'World' output before specialisation

World output before specialisation		
Country	Beef	Aluminium
Occidentalia	120 units	100 units
Garibaldia	110 units	60 units
'World' output	230 units	160 units

Table 21.4 Moving factors over into specialised production

Production possibility schedule - Garibaldia

(Present output shown by arrow)

Units of beef	260	250	240	230	220	210	200	190	180	170	160	150	140	130	120	110	100	90	80	70	60	50	40	30	20	10	0
Units of aluminium	0	4	8	12	16	20	24	28	32	36	40	44	48	52	56	60	64	68	72	76	80	84	88	92	96	100	104

Moving into specialised beef production (4 units of aluminium = 10 units of beef)

Production possibility schedule - Occidentalia

(Present output shown by arrow)

Units of beef	240	230	220	210	200	190	180	170	160	150	140	130	120	110	100	90	80	70	60	50	40	30	20	10	0
Units of aluminium	1.6	9.8	18.0	26.2	34.4	42.6	50.8	59	67.2	75.4	83.6	91.8	100	108.2	116.4	124.6	132.8	141	149.2	157.4	165.6	173.8	182	190.2	198.4

Moving into specialised aluminium production (10 units of beef = 8.2 units of aluminium)

another country using a similar set of factors. Thus in Table 21.1 equal sets of factors in the two countries produce 4 units of aluminium in Garibaldia (against 9 units in Occidentalia), and 10 units of beef in Garibaldia (against 11 units in Occidentalia). Occidentalia has an absolute advantage in both commodities, but her comparative advantage is in aluminium production.

In order to see what happens when these countries decide to specialise in the things they do best, we need to consider the 'production possibility schedules' shown in Table 21.4. In each case present production is shown by an arrow and a heavy 'box' round the figures.

Note carefully what happens as successive sets of factors are moved out of one industry and into the other. As Garibaldia changes over to specialised beef production her output of aluminium declines 60, 56, 52, 48, etc., while her beef output rises 110, 120, 130, etc.

In the same way, as Occidentalia moves factors into specialised aluminium production her output of beef declines 120, 110, 100, 90, etc., but her output of aluminium rises 100, 108.2, 116.4, 124.6. etc. The final result, supposing each country specialised completely, would be 'world' outputs of 260 units of beef (by Garibaldia) and 198.4 units of aluminium (by Occidentalia). These outputs are made clear in Table 21.5.

As a result of each country specialising in the industry at which it has a comparative advantage, the world is richer by 30 000 tonnes of beef and 38 400 tonnes of aluminium. How is this extra wealth to be shared between Occidentalia and Garibaldia?

One country is now producing all the beef, and the other all the aluminium. They are now about to engage in international trade, but on what *terms* will they trade? The **terms of trade** will be decided by the international demand for and supply of the products concerned. If the demand for beef is strong while the demand for aluminium is weak, the terms of trade will be favourable to Garibaldia. If the demand for beef is weak, and the demand for aluminium is strong the terms of trade will be favourable to Occidentalia.

Returning to the Law of Comparative Costs for a moment, we recall that 'nations will find it profitable to trade with other nations when (*a*) they have different alternative cost ratios'.

We have seen that these two countries do have different alternative cost ratios. These are

Garibaldia
Beef : Aluminium
  2.5 : 1

Occidentalia
Beef : Aluminium
  1.2 : 1

Table 21.5 Increased 'world' output as a result of international specialisation

	World output after specialisation	
Country	Beef	Aluminium
Occidentalia	–	198.4
Garibaldia	260	–
'World' output	260	198.4
Rise in 'World' output	30	38.4

The law continues: '(*b*) the international terms of trade lie within the limits set by their domestic alternative cost ratios'. What exactly does this part of the law mean?

Supposing the terms of trade are favourable to Garibaldia. There is a strong demand for beef, and her farmers are in a good bargaining position. Suppose her trade representatives offer to buy one unit of Occidentalian aluminium for 1.85 units of Garibaldian beef. This would be a very kind offer on their part, since they are taking up a position exactly half way between the two alternative costs 2.5 and 1.2. Since they are in a strong bargaining position they are much more likely to say 'one unit of your aluminium for 1.5 units of beef, or 1.4, or even 1.3 units of beef'. Occidentalia will have to give in to the hard bargaining because the terms of trade are against her. But if the Garibaldian traders get really greedy and demand one unit of aluminium for one unit of beef they will find that Occidentalia loses interest. She can produce her own beef by moving factors out of aluminium production and get 1.2 units of beef, so there is no point in buying from Garibaldia at a lower price than 1.2. The limit is set by her domestic alternative-cost ratio.

As the law of comparative costs says, it ceases to be profitable to trade if the international terms of trade move outside the limits set by the domestic alternative-cost ratios.

Conversely, if the terms of trade favour Occidentalia she will be able to demand more beef for her aluminium. If she demands 1.85 units, or 2.0 units, trade will still continue; but if she greedily tries to demand 2.5 units or more, the Garibaldian negotiators will refuse to trade. It would be cheaper to move factors over to aluminium production and make the metal at home.

Table 21.6 Sharing the extra output: terms of trade favourable to Garibaldia (i.e. beef is dear, and aluminium is cheap – say 1.5:1)

Country	Garibaldia		Occidentalia	
Commodity	Wealth before specialisation	Wealth after specialisation	Wealth before specialisation	Wealth after specialisation
Beef	110 units	Say 128 units	120 units	Bought from Garibaldia 132 units
Aluminium	60 units	This leaves 132 units of beef to sell. With terms of trade 1.5:1 Garibaldia buys 88 units of aluminium	100 units	For these 132 units of beef Occidentalia pays Garibaldia 88 units of aluminium. This leaves her 110.4 units
Total units enjoyed	170 units	216 units	220 units	242.4 units
Share of extra output (68 units)	46 = 18 beef + 28 aluminium		22.4 = 12 beef + 10.4 aluminium	
Conclusion:	Garibaldia is getting the lion's share			

Table 21.7 Sharing the extra output: terms of trade favourable to Occidentalia (i.e. beef is cheap, and aluminium is dear – say 2:1)

Country	Garibaldia		Occidentalia	
Commodity	Wealth before specialisation	Wealth after trading	Wealth before specialisation	Wealth after trading
Beef	110 units	Say 128 units	120 units	Bought from Garibaldia 132 units
Aluminium	60 units	Selling 132 units of beef at 2.0:1 Garibaldia buys 66 units of aluminium	100 units	For these 132 units of beef Occidentalia pays 66 units of aluminium This leaves her 132.4 units
Total units enjoyed	170	194	220	264.4
Share of extra wealth (68 units)	24 = 18 beef + 6 aluminium		44.4 = 12 beef 32.4 aluminium	
Conclusion:	Occidentalia is getting the lion's share			

Tables 21.6 and 21.7 make these matters clear, and show how the extra wealth is shared up between the two countries. Study these figures now, remembering as you do so that the international terms of trade for wheat and aluminium decide who gets the lion's share of the extra wealth created.

21.6 Reasons why nations never specialise completely

To keep the explanation simple in the above examples certain assumptions were made which were not necessarily true-to-life. Let us examine each of these assumptions in turn.

(a) The 'world' has only two countries

This does not require us to modify the original argument very much. Instead of specialisation taking place just between two countries, all the countries of the world are involved. Of course many countries grow wheat and make aluminium, but many countries that could make aluminium prefer to buy it from the nations with comparative advantages in aluminium production. At the same time it is very true that complete specialisation may never occur even when it is economically advantageous. For strategic reasons Britain continues to support home farming, although in some respects it is uneconomic. For psychological reasons many developing countries have airlines although they can't afford them, don't need them, and could get better service from foreign airlines. Specialisation will never be complete even when it makes economic sense if it makes national, strategic or social nonsense.

(b) The existence of perfect competition between nations

We have assumed that if cheap aluminium from Occidentalia floods into Garibaldia the Garibaldian aluminium industry will not attempt to stop it, because it has made up its mind to go out of business anyway. Similarly, the farmers of Occidentalia will not object to cheap Garibaldian beef flooding the country, for they have all decided to become aluminium workers and exchange their saucepans for foreign beef. In fact this is an unlikely situation, and the chief difficulty about international trade is how to overcome the opposition of 'vested interests', i.e. entrepreneurs who have sunk capital and effort into relatively unproductive home-based industries. This is a second reason why complete specialisation between nations rarely occurs.

(c) The assumption that all units of factors are equally efficient

As Garibaldia moved successive units of factors out of aluminium production and into beef production we assumed in our 'production possibility schedules' that aluminium production fell by 4 units and beef production rose by 10 units. We imagined that all the sets of factors were equally efficient. In fact of course this would not be the case. The first set of factors to be taken out of production would be those that were of least use to the aluminium industry. Probably they would also be particularly keen to change over to beef production. As the process continues, with more and more factors moving out of the aluminium industry, the factors changing over will be better and better factors for aluminium production and worse and worse factors for beef production. There will thus be twin forces at work to stop complete specialisation. The very best aluminium workers will resist strongly any suggestion to move them out of aluminium production, while the economic arguments in favour of doing so will be reduced because of their manifest unsuitability for beef production.

The same forces will be at work in Occidentalia. The very best beef farmers will resist any attempts to move them into saucepan factories, while their manifest unfitness for the work will be a strong argument against doing so on economic grounds.

The crucial point in the process is where native production is more efficient than the foreign competitor. There must come a stage where the very best Garibaldian aluminium smelters are better than the least efficient Occidentalian aluminium plants; or where the very best Occidentalian farmers are more efficient than the laziest and most incompetent Garibaldian cowboys. At this point specialisation between nations will cease. Increasing returns on one side and decreasing returns on the other bring the process to an end.

(d) Transport costs

Transport costs also interfere with the simple picture discussed, because of course such costs are inseparable from specialisation. If nations are to specialise they must transport goods and raw materials around the world. The effect of transport costs is to narrow the limits between which it will prove profitable to trade. Instead of it being profitable to trade when the international terms of trade lie within the limits set by their domestic alternative-cost ratios, it will only be profitable to trade in a rather narrower band with the transport charges being added to the domestic-cost calculations of both countries.

(e) Demand must be strong enough to justify complete specialisation

Suppose in the example chosen total 'world' demand for beef had only been 245 units. With this production everyone who wants beef can obtain it. Clearly there would be no point in specialising to the point of producing 260 units of beef. Specialisation is limited by the extent of the market, just as it is in home trade. Thus the Pitcairn Islanders, descendants of the mutineers from HMS *Bounty* make excellent souvenirs, but they do not concentrate exclusively upon production of these, since world demand is relatively limited.

(f) Absence of tariffs or quotas

The last assumption was that no artificial barriers to trade have been erected, such as tariffs or quotas. Where such barriers exist, the full competitive effect of specialisation cannot come into play, and world output will rise by a smaller amount than it should.

For all these reasons nations may not specialise completely in the real world.

**21.7
The terms of trade**

We saw in the section on comparative costs that the rate at which goods are exchanged between nations must lie *within the limits set by the domestic alternative-cost ratios*, otherwise it will pay a nation to move its factors out of specialised occupations and produce the goods itself.

What determines the exchange rate for goods is the international demand for and supply of any particular commodity. The usual market forces operate internationally and the resultant rate of exchange represents the **terms of trade** between any two countries. At any given time they may favour one country or the other, but if they become too unfavourable to one nation that nation will move factors over to new employments and trade will cease. We must now consider some of the influences on the international demand for, and supply of, goods.

**21.7.1
The demand for goods in international trade**

Demand for goods is affected by the following:

(a) *Wars, and rumours of wars*. Any signs of political disturbance make entrepreneurs and nations nervous about the possible interruption of supplies; or that demand for their products will increase at times when raw materials are not available. They therefore begin to stockpile raw materials, and this alters the terms of trade in favour of the primary producing nations. Stockpiling raises prices, and moves the exchange rate for goods farther away from the domestic cost level of the primary producer and closer to the cost level of the advanced secondary nations.

(b) *Population and income changes*. Growth in population increases the demand for primary commodities and benefits the primary producing nations. This is particularly true where increased population is accompanied by high income levels, as happened with the bulges in the birth-rates of advanced nations after World War II. Growth of population in the developing nations is less influential, since they practise self sufficiency to a great extent, but it may alter the pattern of trade by reducing the quantities of primary products they can supply for world markets. Thus increased population and incomes in South America reduced the quantity of Argentine and Uruguayan beef reaching world markets after 1945.

(c) *Depressions and booms*. Managed prosperity in the advanced nations tends to keep demand strong, to the benefit of primary producing nations. Depressions in economies which are less well managed cause serious cuts in world prices, particularly where the supply of products is inelastic. Thus rubber plantations cannot cut back production when prices fall as easily as, for example, factories. Therefore the price of rubber fluctuates more than the prices of products (e.g. secondary manufactured goods) which are in elastic supply.

(d) *Actions by influential buyers.* Some users of commodities are so influential that they can affect the prices of goods on the world markets. The chief of these are the stockpiling agencies of the US government. American stockpiles are so vast that a temporary rise in world prices can be prevented by the release of reserves which have been accumulated when prices were lower. This type of activity is like speculation on a vast scale: it smooths out fluctuations in world production and keeps prices and profit margins steadier for the benefit of both producers and consumers.

21.7.2
The supply of goods
in international trade

Supply of goods is affected by the following:

(a) *Wars, civil disturbances and strikes.* Any sort of military or civil disturbance affects the supply of goods. First, the actual production regions may be over-run, like the Nigerian oilfields in the Eastern Region during the Nigerian Civil War. Secondly, the means of transport may be interrupted, ships commandeered, bridges blown up, railway networks dislocated, or air routes closed. An example of the intricate transport network is afforded by the present-day airfreight system. Every night planes arrive at London Airport from Helsinki, Oslo, Stockholm, Berlin, Frankfurt and the other major Continental airports. Their cargoes are transferred to America-bound flights for New York, Florida, Chicago, Denver, Las Vegas and California-bound aircraft. Because of the speed of modern planes and the rotation of the earth, goods freighted from Helsinki at 5.00 p.m. one day can be on sale in the streets of Los Angeles by 9.00 a.m. next morning. Such long-haul networks are easily interrupted by any sort of civil or military disturbance.

(b) *Changes in technology.* The supply of goods in international trade is greatly affected by technological advances, and by the spread of technology to more and more countries. Synthetic rubber has affected the terms of trade to the disadvantage of the natural-rubber producers, and the invention of artificial fibres has drastically affected the wool-producing, cotton-producing and silk-producing countries. New manufacturing nations, which enter production with the most modern plants and without the encumbrances of established labour organisations, can reduce prices to the detriment of established nations whose terms of trade become more unfavourable.

(c) *Transport developments.* Changes in transport can have a dramatic effect on trade. 'Transport creates the utility of space,' says one transport economist. It opens up regions previously underdeveloped and makes them competitors of more well-established producers. The European farmers were practically driven out of business when the railways opened up the great plains of America and the Argentine. Refrigerated ships brought New Zealand lamb and Australian beef to undercut home-produced meat in the UK. Bulk carriers and containerised transport altered the economics of many industries in the 1960s and 1970s and changed the terms of trade. An example from the 1990s is provided by the humble parsnip (a root vegetable used in soups and as a roast vegetable). A supermarket chain found a parsnip grower in Australia who was prepared to grow 15 000 acres of parsnips for them and supply them washed free of all dirt for containerised delivery. On arrival in the UK the price was highly competitive with home grown parsnips stored since harvest time, out of season and of poor quality.

21.7.3
Measuring changes in the terms of trade

Favourable changes in the terms of trade benefit the citizens of a nation, because they can purchase with their produce a larger share of the world's goods. This means that of the extra wealth resulting from the international specialisation of labour a larger share is now going to them.

These changes can be measured by comparing the average price of exports with the average price of imports. The easiest way to do this is by index numbers. The UK index of export values and index of import values were originally compiled using 1961 as the base year. The fraction

$$\frac{Index\ of\ Average\ Export\ Prices}{Index\ of\ Average\ Import\ Prices} \times 100$$

gives an index for the terms of trade. Thus in 1961 when both the export and import indices were defined as 100, the terms-of-trade index was 100. A year later, in 1962, the export index stood at 101 and the import index at 99. The terms-of-trade index was then

$$\frac{101}{99} \times 100 = 102$$

indicating an improvement in the terms of trade in favour of the UK. A list over the years 1980–93 is given in Table 21.8. Note that in this new series of figures the year 1985 has been chosen as the base year and the figures for the value of imports and exports have been expressed relative to prices in that base year. Hence the figures for years before 1985 are less than 100, because prices were generally lower, in an inflationary world.

Table 21.8 UK Terms of Trade Index 1980–93

Year	Index of exports (1)	Index of imports (2)	Terms of trade (1) ÷ (2) × 100
1980	70.0	68.5	102.2
1981	76.2	74.2	102.7
1982	81.4	80.3	101.4
1983	88.0	87.8	100.2
1984	95.0	95.5	99.5
1985	100.0	100.0	100.0
1986	90.2	95.3	94.6
1987	93.8	97.8	95.9
1988	93.9	96.7	97.1
1989	101.2	103.4	97.9
1990	105.6	108.6	97.2
1991	101.4	101.2	100.2
1992	103.5	102.1	101.4
1993	114.8	110.5	103.9

Source: The Pink Book (*1994 edition*)

The higher the index the more favourable the terms for the UK. Significant changes occurred in the value of UK exports in the mid-1980s which gave unfavourable figures for the terms of trade in the last half of the decade.

**21.8
The volume of
world trade**

If world trade is not restricted in any way, countries will specialise in those industries where they have a comparative advantage and as a result of this specialisation output will increase. The world will be richer, and production will take place in the most economic location. The volume of world trade will rise and the whole world will be wealthier; but this will not necessarily mean that all the peoples of the world will benefit equally. The terms of trade will decide who gets the lion's share of the increased wealth.

Just as individuals tend to do what is best for them, nations tend to advocate free trade when they are in a strongly competitive position and are likely to profit by an expansion of world trade. When their situation is an uncompetitive high-cost situation, they tend to be 'protectionist'. This means they set up tariff walls to shut out foreign products, unless they are prepared to pay a duty on entry. For example, in the eighteenth century the infant cotton industry of Lancashire and Glasgow was a relatively high-cost industry and objected strongly to the importation of cheap Indian cotton goods. Technological advance raised productivity in the cotton mills, and by 1811 the cry of the cotton masters was for free trade: let India sell her wares freely in this country, and let Lancashire export to India in return. The resulting penetration of the Indian market by cheap Lancashire cottons brought prosperity to Lancashire. Eventually the erection of cotton mills in India and Hong Kong enabled these countries to compete again with Lancashire. Then the cotton manufacturers raised a cry for protection. Thus America, which was until a few years ago the strongest advocate of free trade, has recently been hesitating, and cries are being heard from many of its industries for protection from cheap foreign imports.

**21.8.1
How home industries
are protected**

Home industries may be protected by (*a*) embargoes, (*b*) quotas, (*c*) tariffs, (*d*) currency restrictions, (*e*) 'prior to import' deposits, and (*f*) technical specifications.

(a) Embargoes

Embargoes prohibit the import of particular commodities, or the goods of particular countries.

(b) Quotas

Quotas limit the import of particular goods, or the import from particular areas, to a permitted quota. Thus a system of quota licences has to be organised and imports must not exceed the quota. This may be a quota by volume, say 100 000 articles, or a quota by value, say to a limit of £10 million.

(c) Tariffs

Tariffs impose a duty on goods entering the country, which raises the price at which they can be sold on the home market. This means that they will be less competitive than they otherwise would be. It is generally agreed, even among advanced nations, that a developing industry may be protected. Zambia, for example, gives protection to her industries in the metal, plastic piping, refrigeration, clothing and printing industries. Ghana imposes tariffs on television sets, electrodes, bolts, nuts, screws, containers, motor vehicles and textiles. Kenya imposes protective duties on pulp and paper to protect the Broderick Falls pulp and paper mill. In general, protection of an established industry is undesirable, and international institutions like UNCTAD (the United Nations Conference on Trade and Development) try to encourage developed nations to trade with developing countries and not protect their home industries from competition from newly industrialised countries.

(d) Currency restrictions

Currency restrictions work through the foreign-exchange market, limiting the import of goods from areas whose currency is difficult to obtain for some reason.

(e) 'Prior-to-import' deposits

'Prior-to-import' deposits require the importer to deposit a percentage of the purchase price of proposed imports into a special account. By varying the percentage rate it is possible to limit imports very effectively (e.g. a small deposit for imports deemed to be necessary, but larger deposits for non-essentials). At one time in the 1960s Great Britain introduced an import deposit scheme, but it proved distinctly unpopular with countries looking to trade with the United Kingdom and with UK importers. Foreign countries, particularly third world countries whose financial position was linked to trade with advanced nations, were indignant, while other advanced nations organised retaliatory tariffs to exclude UK goods. UK importers were upset because the deposits they had to make amounted to an interest-free loan to the Government for a six-month period, which obviously reduced their cash flow and the interest they could earn on their funds.

(f) Technical specifications

Sometimes governments get round free-trade agreements by imposing technical specifications which deliberately exclude foreign goods, or delay them with time consuming modifications and adjustments. This increases the foreign competitors' costs and delays the impact of the competition on the home-produced market.

The effect of all such methods is to reduce the international specialisation of labour and decrease total world wealth. They perpetuate the continuance of production in uneconomic areas and prevent the maximum achievements of the economies of scale in the efficient areas. They result in a lower standard of living for the people of the protected country: the general body of the citizens has to bear as a social cost the expense of subsidising the inefficient home industry. Economically this type of restriction in free trade is unjustifiable, and many attempts have been made to remove such barriers. The most successful have been relatively local free-trade areas, of which the European Union (EU), now enlarged to 15 countries, is the best known.

21.8.2 Economic arguments in favour of protection

(a) Protection of infant industries

Most nations seem to accept that where a country is attempting to establish a new industry she will inevitably erect tariff barriers to protect it. This amounts to forcing her own citizens to buy an inferior and more expensive product made at home instead of better imported products. The justification for this is that, without such protection, her people cannot acquire the skill and knowledge which alone will result eventually in well made goods of improved design. There are many examples of efficient industries established in this way, but almost as many examples could be quoted of industries which started behind a tariff wall and have continued behind it, never reaching really viable status in world markets. *The same resources, devoted to other ends, might have proved more beneficial to the country.* Nowhere is this more obvious than in the Soviet Union, where for 70 years the same old industries were turning out the same old-fashioned goods irrespective of whether they were wanted by a population totally deprived of any chance to see what other nations were producing.

(b) Prevention of 'dumping'

Dumping is the export of goods to countries where they are sold at a lower price than they fetch on the home market. This discrimination in favour of foreigners may be practised in order to earn foreign exchange, or it may be made possible by increased economies of scale which would be lost if only the home market was supplied. The price to the foreign importer is deliberately kept low to ensure that the extra volume available is disposed of. Either way it represents serious competition to the importing country, whose own industry may be ruined by it. Where the competition is the result of efficiency it is legitimate; but where it is the result of a discriminatory policy, possibly even designed to ruin the industry of the importing country so as to remove it as a competitor in world markets, the importing country is justified in imposing tariffs to prevent this unfair competition.

(c) Temporary protective measures

These may be imposed for short periods. For example, the United States has from time to time introduced short-term embargoes, tariffs, etc. to meet pressure on the dollar and criticism from home-producers about the severity of competition from cheap imports. The United States also uses such methods to bring a little sense into the negotiations they hold about world trade with the international community. If negotiating states make unreasonable demands and will not yield to fair American arguments, it uses the threat of protectionist remedies to bring them to a more sensible bargaining position.

21.8.3 Non-economic arguments in favour of protection

(a) Strategic reasons

Many countries continue to produce goods, even though they could buy them more cheaply from abroad: to give up production of the goods would be unwise for reasons of national security. Great Britain continues to grow agricultural produce despite the comparative disadvantages of her small-scale agriculture. Experience in two world wars has convinced her it would be dangerous to give up farming completely.

A less well-known example is the situation that Britain found herself in during the early years of World War II. There was at this time a period called the 'phoney-war', when no battles were fought – except in Finland – and when some people doubted whether Britain was really serious about fighting Hitler. In fact she was having very great difficulty because some important industries, particularly the ceramics industries, had been allowed to decline to vanishing point. Many essential components, like electrical insulators, had previously been imported from Europe. The sudden removal of this source of supply led to desperate shortages of components for military equipment. A whole ceramics industry had to be build up from nothing before the war could be pursued.

Most nations protect their aircraft, shipbuilding and other crucial industries.

(b) Social reasons

Industries deemed to be desirable on social grounds may be continued after they become non-competitive. For example, declining industries like cotton have been protected to a limited extent to prevent undue hardship in the cotton towns of Lancashire, while compensation for mill owners prepared to shut mills has gradually reduced the industry and improved its efficiency.

The British coal industry has finally ceased to be a nationalised industry and the vast majority of pits are now closed, except where a consortium of private persons (usually the miners and managers of a previously state-owned mine) have bought the pit. Despite considerable support over more than a decade and repeated attempts to nationalise the industry, inescapable forces have finally allowed competition from natural gas, oil and nuclear power to displace coal as a fuel. The resulting changes in the life of former miners and their families can be imagined. Mining is a tough and dangerous job, which breeds men of courage and character. You cannot suddenly expect such men to become assemblers in light electrical trades, or similar work. Their physique is unutilised and they feel and become demoralised. Mineworkers are an excellent example of specific labour, difficult to resettle in other work. Some measure of protection had to be given, especially to older men, through a variety of redundancy arrangements. One aspect of the situation which was not given much attention was the strategic need for the mines. In the last war the mines produced 240 million tons of coal a year – a considerable factor in the successful prosecution of the war.

21.9 Summary of Chapter 21

1 Trade takes place between nations because resources are unevenly distributed, climate varies and the people of some areas have natural advantages over the people of other areas.

2 When discussing advantages, comparative advantage is more important than absolute advantage. Men, and nations, should specialise in those occupations at which they have the greatest comparative advantage or the least comparative disadvantage.

3 When factors can be put to work doing either one thing or another the two alternative occupations are said to be alternative costs. Thus the cost of the wheat we decide to produce is the aluminium we decide *not* to produce.

4 The student should memorise the Law of Comparative Costs (see page 242).

5 The 'terms of trade' are the relative prices of exports and imports. A country whose exports are dear relative to her imports has favourable terms of trade. A country whose imports are dear relative to her exports has unfavourable terms of trade.

6 Changes in the terms of trade may be indicated by an index number found by the formula

$$\frac{Index\ of\ Average\ Export\ Prices}{Index\ of\ Average\ Import\ Prices} \times 100$$

7 If world trade is free, nations will only carry on those occupations at which they have a comparative advantage and will obtain other goods by trade.

8 Protection of home industries may be justified in certain cases for strategic or social reasons. Its economic cost is a lower standard of living for the nation's citizens. Frequently tariff barriers shielding an unproductive home industry only perpetuate the industry's uneconomic activities, and the industry becomes a vested interest acting as a pressure group to ensure its continued shelter from competition.

Exercises Set 21

1 What do economists understand by the term 'comparative advantage'?

2 'The cost of the steel we decided to make is the cast iron we decided not to make.' Explain.

3 Outline the gains to be expected from free international trade. How are these gains shared between the trading countries?

4 What are the 'terms of trade'? How may these terms of trade be measured?

5 What is a production possibility schedule? Draw one up for a country considering specialising in beef production, instead of beef and wheat. Take diminishing and increasing returns of production from factors into account.

6 'We could make whisky, but we buy it from Scotland. Why?' Explain.

7 'The theory of comparative costs proves that free trade is the best policy.' Criticise this statement.

8 'Generally speaking it will be profitable for Britain to grow her beef in electronics factories and sow her wheat in automobile plants.' What did the speaker mean by these remarks to a gathering of farmers? Why was the farmers' reply 'Until a war comes along!' a valid retort?

9 Australia and Britain can produce both wheat and cars. A given set of factors would produce the following outputs per day:

	Units of wheat (100 bushels)	Cars
Australia	1000	200
Britain	1400	700

(a) Who has the absolute advantage in each of these products?
(b) Who has the comparative advantage in wheat production?
(c) Who has the comparative advantage in producing cars?
(d) Will trade take place when 1½ units of wheat exchange for one unit of cars?
(e) Will exchange take place when 3½ units of wheat exchange for one unit of cars?

10 Switzerland and Britain can both make watches and electrical transformers. A given set of factors would produce in one day the following outputs:

	Watches	Transformers
Britain	500	250
Switzerland	750	250

(a) Has either country an absolute advantage in either of these products?
(b) Who has the comparative advantage in watches?
(c) Who has the comparative advantage in transformers?
(d) What specialisation will take place?
(e) What will be the rise in 'world' wealth assuming five such sets of factors are at present engaged in each country on each product?
(f) How will this wealth be shared assuming one transformer cost 2.6 watches, and each nation requires the same number of transformers as before specialisation?

22   The balance of payments

**22.1
Introduction**

When nations engage in international trade they must pay one another for the goods and services being exchanged. International trade is a complex business, like all trading, and payment presents special problems. First of all there is the question of whether the currency is acceptable. Gold is at present being demonetarised, though it is still widely acceptable. Many currencies are only acceptable in their own territories. In this chapter we shall examine the problems of international indebtedness.

**22.2
Payment for
imports**

Every country has its own currency, and its merchants wish to be paid in that currency or in some currency which is freely convertible into it. For example, a German industrialist selling goods to a Portuguese importer might not be prepared to accept Portuguese escudos; but he would accept Deutschmarks, and he would be prepared to accept American dollars as his bank would freely convert them into Deutschmarks for him. Gold is generally acceptable, but the price fluctuates daily. Certain 'great' currencies are nearly always acceptable. The chief ones are the American dollar, the Swiss franc, the German Deutschmark, the £ sterling and the Japanese yen.

While the actual details of obtaining the particular currency required are arranged by the banks who deal on the foreign-exchange market, their activities do depend on a rough balance being achieved between imports and exports. If the pound is valued at 1.60 dollars and a consignment of Scotch whisky is being sold to a total value of $240 000, the American buyer will need £150 000 to make the purchase. Suppose a British manufacturer is buying 10 American machine tools at $24 000 dollars each, he will need $240 000 to complete the purchase. This will mean him/her finding £150 000 to buy the dollars. Clearly the dealers on the foreign-exchange market will be happy to arrange both transactions, for each will make the other possible. The UK purchaser will provide £150 000 to buy American goods and the American buyer will provide 240 000 dollars to buy British goods. Exports pay for imports and the result is a balance of trade.

Sometimes the goods exported are insufficient to pay for the goods imported, and an adverse balance of trade results. This adverse balance may be corrected by items which are called 'invisible' items, because they are for services rendered, not for actual goods. The chief invisible items are shipping, air transport, insurance, banking and tourist services; a full list is given on page 260.

Finally, if there is any further imbalance, and invisible items are insufficient to cover it, a nation will either have to pay out of its reserves for the goods and services imported or it may be involved in borrowing capital from overseas. Somehow or other it will have to balance its 'balance of payments'.

**22.3
UK balance of
payments**

The balance of payments of the UK is published in a special form each year, but the interest in the figures is so great that monthly reports about the progress of the accounts are given as well. These results are featured in the Press and on television, and the general public are kept constantly in touch with developments.

The annual accounts are divided into the 'Current Account' and a 'Capital Transfers' section. Readers familiar with book-keeping will appreciate that the phrase 'current-account item' refers to an item which has to be settled within the current year, whereas 'capital expenditure' refers to expenditure over a period of years. Therefore in these accounts the current account items are all matters of current trading, part of the **balance of visible trade** or the **balance of invisible trade**. The capital transfers are long-term items which will be repayable over several years, and possibly over many years. The figures are made available in a book called the *Pink Book* entitled *The United Kingdom Balance of Payments*. Each annual edition is published about the end of July, with the figures complete to the end of the previous year. Thus the 1994 *Pink Book* has the figures up to the end of 1993. One criticism of the tables as published at present is that in the interests of clarity for those who understand the tables, the figures are reduced to a 'bare bones' basis, for example in Table 1.1, the chief table in the book giving figures for the previous 20 years, the first line is the balance on visible trade. The details of visible exports and visible imports from which the balance was calculated have to be chased up in another table later in the book. This is all a bit inconvenient for the newcomer who does not really understand the tables yet. For this reason Table 22.1 (see page 260) has been expanded somewhat from the *Pink Book* tables to give the reader a clearer idea. Study this table now, before reading the detailed description of the sections in Sections 22.4, 22.5 and 22.6.

**22.4
The balance of
visible trade**

Visible items, as their name implies, are items which have a physical existence and can actually be seen. Raw materials, food and manufactured goods of all kinds are items of visible trade.

The figures are given for goods valued 'free on board'. This is the value of the goods and transit charges as far as the deck of the ship. It does not include the insurance or the freight charges made by the shipowner, since these are regarded as 'invisible' items.

A typical year's import and export trade for the UK (see Figure 22.1) shows the major headings of goods being bought and sold. Imports used to consist largely of primary products or semi-manufacturers. Today more than one half are finished manufactures, a measure of the penetration of the market by EU manufacturers and manufacturers from the NICS (newly industrialised countries). Exports, apart from oil, are nearly all manufactured or semi-manufactured goods. The 1993 figures show a serious deficit on visible trade of £13209 million. This is a very large deficit which has to be covered by a surplus on invisible trade, but as we shall see the balance on invisibles was insufficient in 1993, leaving an overall deficit on current account of £10311 million.

**22.5
The balance of
invisible trade**

'Invisible' exports make a very large positive contribution to the UK's balance of overseas payments. In the years since World War II the balance of visible trade has only been favourable in six years: 1956, 1958, 1971 and 1980–82. The balance of invisible trade has only been

Table 22.1 UK Balance of Payments, 1993 (£ million)

CURRENT ACCOUNT

				£m
Visible trade				
Exports and re-exports (earning foreign exchange) (valued fob = free on board)				121 414
Less Imports (costing foreign exchange) (valued fob)				134 623
Adverse balance on visible trade				−13 209

	Exports £m	Imports £m	Balance £m	
Invisible trade (services)				
General government	434	2 332	−1 898	
Sea transport	3 843	4 301	−458	
Civil aviation	5 075	5 526	−451	
Travel and tourism	8 951	12 257	−3 306	
Financial services	18 282	7 227	11 055	
	36 585	31 643	4 942	
Interest, profits and dividends				
General government	1 413	3 281	−1 868	
Private sector	72 531	67 667	4 864	
Public corporations	96	30	66	
	74 040	70 978	3 062	
Transfers (non-trade movements)				
General government	3 325	8 161	−4 836	
Private sector	2 050	2 320	−270	
	5 375	10 481	−5 106	
Final balance of invisibles				2 898
Final deficit on Current Account				−10 311

unfavourable in two years, 1946 and 1990. It follows that the prosperity of Great Britain since the war has to a great extent been made possible by the earnings of invisible services. What are these services? The list reads:

- Sea transport
- Civil aviation
- Travel and tourism
- Interest, profits and dividends
- Government services
- Financial and other services
- Interests, profits and dividends
- Private transfers

22.5.1
Sea transport

At one time almost the entire world trade was carried by British merchant ships. Today the protection granted by many nations to their

Table 22.1 continued

CAPITAL MOVEMENTS

	£m	£m
Deficit on Current Account (see opposite)		−10311
Overseas investments by UK firms and individuals (Outward movements of capital mean an adverse effect on the balance of payments)		
	£m	
Direct investments by UK residents	−17292	
Portfolio investments	−85603	
	−102895	
Foreign investment in the UK		
Direct	9502	
Portfolio	40009	
	49511	
Banking activities		
Loans to foreigners by UK banks (actually repayments exceeded loans)	4428	
Loans by foreigners to UK banks	24415	
	28843	
Other non-bank activities		
Deposits with and lending to foreign firms	−58671	
Borrowing from foreign firms	95882	
	37211	
General government: increasing funds available − decreasing funds available	−4357	
	−4357	
Net result of identified capital movements		8313
Final unfavourable balance overall (according to the data)		−1998
This difference is a balance item (movements not yet identified by documentation, but due to appear in due course)		+1998

Note: In effect £1998 has come in extra to expectations but the explanations for it will come in sooner or later. Such items are sometimes referred to as 'leads and lags'.
Source: The Pink Book, 1994.

own merchant fleets and the growth of 'flags of convenience' have reduced the share of trade carried by British vessels. Each year very large sums are earned as foreign exchange but unfortunately nearly as much has to be paid by our merchants to foreign carriers. Table 22.1 shows the situation as far as sea transport is concerned.

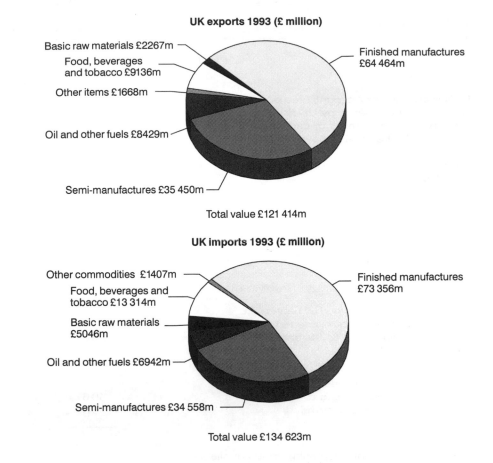

UK exports 1993 (£ million)

Basic raw materials £2267m

Food, beverages and tobacco £9136m

Other items £1668m

Oil and other fuels £8429m

Semi-manufactures £35 450m

Finished manufactures £64 464m

Total value £121 414m

UK imports 1993 (£ million)

Other commodities £1407m

Food, beverages and tobacco £13 314m

Basic raw materials £5046m

Oil and other fuels £6942m

Semi-manufactures £34 558m

Finished manufactures £73 356m

Total value £134 623m

Figure 22.1 Visible trade of the United Kingdom 1993

22.5.2
Civil aviation

Civil aviation is increasingly valuable as an earner of invisible balances, contributing favourable balances every year between 1963 and 1985 to the nation's 'Balance of Payments' accounts. With even larger versions of planes like the Boeing 757 and the Airbus, it could well be that this contribution will increase in the years ahead. This is particularly so since a wider understanding of freight economics is evident among the business community. In particular the idea of taking *total* costs into account when deciding the relative merits of air and sea freighting is leading to increased use of air transport. The high cost of the actual transport is offset by reduced insurance charges, faster transit, and other advantages. Fast and regular services by British planes are therefore attractive to overseas businessmen. At the same time the 1993 figures show adverse balances on most of these services, offset by favourable balances on other headings, for example, interest, profits and dividends. Some of these deficits probably reflect the tendency of multi-national companies to let profits be earned in foreign countries where tax levels are low, and import the earnings as profits and dividends rather than earnings in the actual industry concerned.

22.5.3
Travel and tourism

The UK usually suffers adverse balances on travel and tourism, because a large part of her population is affluent enough to holiday abroad. For many countries tourism earns net invisible balances which are a great help to the economy. Again, larger and faster aircraft are expanding the tourist market considerably. Holidays in the developing countries of Africa, the Indian sub-continent, the Pacific-fringe countries and China are proving very attractive to Europeans. This makes valuable foreign exchange available to countries which can make good use of the funds earned. In Table 22.1 the balance of payments for this particular item is adverse, but the earnings from tourism do fluctuate.

22.5.4
Interest, profits and dividends

The effect of these items on invisible earnings is very great, but it is important to have a clear picture of the difference between capital and current-account items. Suppose Britain lends Ghana £10 million for a hydroelectric power project. This sum would be a capital payment and would represent an adverse item on the balance of payments. Contrasting with this, a decision by an American company to take over a British firm at a purchase price of £50 million would be a capital receipt by Britain and a favourable item on the balance of payments. In due course each of these transactions would result in a succession of repayments in the opposite direction. The interest part of Ghana's repayments would appear as favourable current-account movements in years to come, and the repayment of the capital borrowed will be a favourable capital-account movement. The former British firm, now an American-owned subsidiary, will pay dividends to its American owners which will represent unfavourable invisible payments. In the year under discussion the figures in Table 22.1 show what the balance of payments was on this particular item, and how important overseas investment is in this respect to an overall balance of payments.

22.5.5
Government services

These include military and civil expenditure in foreign currencies, and represent a considerable loss each year on the balance of payments. Table 22.1 shows what the actual position was in the year under discussion, most of the expenditure being for military and diplomatic purposes. The EU has caused these figures to increase in recent years, not always adversely. The full figures are given in the annual *Pink Book*.

22.5.6
Financial and other services

These services are very valuable, earning substantial balances for Britain. They include banking, insurance, advertising and consultancy charges, and the licensing of foreign firms to use British discoveries and patents. This last item is increasingly important as the less developed nations become secondary producers. They must become protective towards their new industries and exclude foreign competition. Thus, if India establishes an electronics industry, it may well protect it from UK and other competition, but it may be happy to license the use of devices invented in the United Kingdom for manufacture in India. A former visible trade item, electronic components, may decline in export value, to be replaced by an 'invisible' item which is just as lucrative, royalties receivable.

22.5.7
Interests, profits and dividends

While capital movements overseas were controlled (for about 40 years after World War II) investments abroad could not be expanded and consequently interest, profits and dividends was a relatively small item in the Balance of Payments. In the 1980s this situation was reversed and the increased export of capital now brings in favourable balances of interest, profits and dividends. Some of this is profits made from actual firms set up in foreign countries – often on a 'joint venture' basis with foreign nationals. Some of it is just 'portfolio investment' (the buying of shares and debentures in foreign firms) and earning the dividends or interest receivable.

22.5.8
Private transfers

Lastly invisible items include certain movements of funds for private reasons. Thus immigrants bring funds with them which benefit the balance of payments. Emigrants take funds out, to the detriment of the balance of payments. The estates of deceased persons whose relatives live in a different country similarly move in or out as the will is executed.

22.6
Capital items

Capital items are long-term payments either outwards or inwards. The UK has for many years invested capital abroad. At one time enormous investments overseas brought in each year a flood of interest and dividend payments on current account, but these huge reserves has to be sold to pay for the two world wars and only small residual sums were left. However, when controls on capital movements were lifted in the early 1980s huge movements of capital began, with UK investors not only investing directly in foreign establishments but also in 'portfolio investments' i.e. the purchase of foreign shares and debentures through the international capital markets. Thus an investor who buys shares in Japanese electronics firms is investing capital in Japanese industry just as surely as if a joint British-Japanese company had been set up. A good deal of foreign investment is also done by British Government Agencies making loans to foreign governments.

Note that such capital movements represent an adverse movement on the Balance of Payments Accounts as the capital moves out of the UK. Fortunately much of it is offset by foreign firms and individuals investing in the United Kingdom. It does make the movements of capital rather difficult to follow, as a careful study of Table 22.1 will reveal. Those who collect the statistics for the *Pink Book* find it very difficult to follow the capital movements for all sorts of reasons. Some payments move early and are said to lead the transaction while others are delayed and are called 'lags'. Trying to detect which movements have been made in advance and which are overdue is not easy – especially since some transactions are in the names of 'nominees' and not the real names of the parties concerned. Thus, if a big multinational company is buying shares in a foreign company it may not do it in its own name – the foreign seller might put the price up or even refuse to sell.

A good deal of debate goes on as to the desirability of investing abroad. The protagonists point to the enormous need for capital in the developing nations. The antagonists are quick to retort that it is precisely these nations who do not get the investments; that private overseas investment more often goes to secure and developed nations. One can hardly blame a private investor who does not invest in insecure, unstable areas. Such regions should be helped by official government agencies who have a greater chance of securing the return

Table 22.2 Balance of payments figures 1982–1992

				£ million		
	1982	1984	1986	1988	1990	1992
Current account: visible balance	1 908	−5 336	−9 486	−21 078	−18 675	−13 104
Invisibles:						
Services balance	3 022	4 519	6 692	4 502	5 201	4 089
Interest, profits and dividends balance	1 460	4 379	4 927	4 971	4 029	4 293
Transfers balance	−1 741	−1 730	−2 157	−3 546	−4 935	−5 109
Invisible balance	2 741	7 168	9 462	5 927	4 295	3 273
Current balance (visibles & invisibles)	4 649	1 832	−24	−15 151	−14 380	−9 831
Capital transfers:						
Transactions in UK assets and liabilities						
UK exports of capital	−31 409	−32 042	−92 887	−56 243	−72 301	−82 219
UK imports of capital	28 820	24 119	84 375	63 258	+84 382	85 588
Net effect of capital items	−2 589	−7 923	−8 512	7 015	12 081	3 369
Balancing item (leads and lags in system)	−2 060	−6 091	−8 536	−8 136	−2 299	−6 462

Source: The Pink Book 1994

of their capital. While private investors can easily be expropriated, governments have long memories and can usually bring up a failure to repay at some time in the future.

Investments entering the country refer to British firms taken over by foreign investors, or shares and securities purchased by foreign nationals. Much of this foreign investment is excess capital from countries whose interest rates are relatively low. Such money is called 'hot money', because it is very liquid and can flow out just as easily as it flows in. It is a source of speculative pressure at times when the exchange rate of a currency is about to be altered.

22.7
A disequilibrium in the balance of payments

We have seen that the balance of visible trade rarely balances, and that the current account balance (which is made up of visible and invisible items) is sometimes favourable and sometimes unfavourable. The balance of payments must always balance, because even if the known capital movements when added to the current account movements show a favourable balance overall or an unfavourable balance overall the balance either way is accommodated by temporary loans. If the UK has an unfavourable balance with the rest of the world, the rest of the world will simply allow the balance to remain on its books as a sort of overdraft. Conversely, if the United Kingdom has a favourable balance with the rest of the world, we shall simply carry these debtors over into the next financial year. Since at any given moment in time there are always a great many accounts payable in both directions (i.e. UK exports will have some earnings due to them and UK importers will have some payments they are due to make) it is a little difficult to know the true position anyway, because it never gets finally sorted out. Therefore, the last line of the balance of payments accounts is an item called the **balancing item**. This 'balancing item' consists of many things. These include:

(*a*) All items, in either direction, where the movement of goods occurs in one trading period (say the present year) but the actual payment will follow a month or two later and be part of the next year's accounts. In the meantime the balance is kept on the books of the traders concerned as a part of general trade credit, as creditors (UK importers in debt to a foreign supplier), or debtors (foreign customers in debt to a UK exporter).

(*b*) There may be small foreign exchange losses or profits due to changes in the foreign exchange market which means that goods charged to customers at one rate of exchange are actually paid for later on at another rate of exchange.

(*c*) A whole host of other items may be on the move at any particular moment, such things as short-term money moving from one country to another, purchases and sales of foreign and UK stocks and shares, insurance payments, etc, etc.

Note

As may be seen, the balancing item in each case reconciles the figures to make the balance of payments balance. Thus, in 1992 the current balance was an adverse balance of £9831 million (imports exceeded exports by this amount). However some of this balance was met by a favourable balance on capital items, with £3369 million more capital coming into the UK than went out in foreign investments by UK firms. The difference of £6462 million is the balancing item (the extra balances left in the books of foreign firms to whom UK importers owed money).

What happens if the UK continues heavily in debt year after year to foreign firms is discussed in Chapter 23.

22.8 Summary of Chapter 22

1 Imports must be paid for by exports.
2 The balance of trade is the balance achieved between the import and export of goods, called 'visible trade'.
3 The balance of invisible trade is the balance achieved between the payments for services received and the payments earned by rendering services to others. The chief 'invisible' items are shipping, banking, insurance, travel and tourism, civil aviation, government services, interest, profits and dividends and private transfers.
4 The balance of trade and the balance of invisible trade together make up the balance on current account.
5 Capital movements are private or official investments abroad, set against the investments by overseas nationals in this country.
6 The balance of payments is the final result of all these influences. It is bound to balance, because any imbalance is met by temporary loans (trade credit) either by UK firms carrying balances over to the next year for foreign debtors, or foreign suppliers carrying balances over to the next year for UK customers.

Exercises Set 22

1 Would the following result in a gain or loss of foreign currency in Great Britain?

   (a) The purchase of 20 000 Swiss watches by a London businessman.
   (b) The purchase by a British merchant bank of Swiss Government securities on the Geneva Stock Exchange.
   (c) A visit to England by a party of Swiss schoolchildren.
   (d) A winter sports holiday by a London youth club.
   (e) A Lloyd's underwriter agrees to insure a Swiss cable-car company against accidents to passengers.
   (f) Claims by the relatives of victims killed in the collapse of a Swiss cable-car insured with Lloyd's.

2 During World War II all foreign investments owned by British citizens had to be sold to the Treasury for disposal abroad. Why do you think this was done, and how did it help the war effort?

3 The government has agreed to the purchase of a British motor-car manufacturing firm by an American combine. Not only has the American firm agreed to pay $67 million but they have promised to invest a further $25 million over the next three years. What are the implications of this, (a) in the short term, and (b) in the long term, for Britain's balance of payments?

4 Would the following result in a gain or loss of dollars to Great Britain?

   (a) A decision by America to transfer some military bases from continental Europe to East Anglia.
   (b) A decision by British Airways to purchase Boeing 747 planes for long-haul routes to Australia.
   (c) The purchase by the USA of a British-built mammoth tanker.
   (d) The refuelling of a British cruise ship in San Francisco.
   (e) A British investor in US stock is paid a dividend of 4 per cent.
   (f) A successful tour of the US by British pop-artists.

5 Compile a balance of payments for the country Atlantis from the data given below:

   Visibles: exports £A 2794m; imports £A 2540m.
   Invisibles: exports £A 1455m; imports £A 1600m.
   Loans from overseas: £A 230m.

6 'The balance of trade rarely balances. The balance of payments always balances.' Explain

7 How can a nation earn foreign currency to buy from countries abroad those goods that it requires?

8 What are 'invisible items' in foreign trade? List the chief types of invisible items, and consider their relative usefulness in meeting the UK's overseas needs.

9 Exports of goods helps the balance of payments. Export of capital adversely affects the balance of payments. Do you agree? Explain fully.

10 How can a surplus on current account be balanced on capital account?

23 The balance of payments and the Exchange Rate Mechanism

23.1 Introduction

When nations trade internationally they must at some time come up against a 'Balance of Payments' problem. In any given year it would be matter of the utmost good fortune if what a nation wished to buy from overseas exactly matched what it was able to sell overseas, so that a balance of payments would exactly be achieved. More likely, one year a nation will have a favourable balance of payments, and another year it will have an adverse balance of payments. Take a year when the balance of payments is favourable; we are selling more to foreigners than we are buying from them. The result will be that foreign exchange will come into our country. If a tight 'exchange control' was being exercised by central government (probably through a 'national bank' such as the Bank of England) this foreign exchange could be compulsorily impounded by the central bank and used to build up reserves of foreign exchange. As this type of central control does not exist in the United Kingdom at the present time, (1996) the foreign exchange would not necessarily add to the 'official reserves' but could be taken into the bank accounts of ordinary firms (if they maintained foreign currency accounts) or be accumulated at banks which do handle that particular type of foreign currency if they were prepared to buy it from the firms that had earned it and give them sterling instead. In a year when the Balance of Payments is unfavourable (i.e. our country is buying more from foreigners than it is selling to them) UK firms will be paying for these imports and sterling will be flowing out of the UK to obtain the foreign currencies needed. Any accumulated foreign exchange will be used up and further supplies of pounds sterling will enter the foreign exchange markets to obtain the necessary foreign currency.

Whatever the results of any particular year may be, the position of the Balance of Payments will not become unduly worrying unless a succession of bad years leads to international concern about a particular currency. In this chapter for convenience we are referring to the position of sterling and the United Kingdom, but readers who are concerned about their own country and its currency will appreciate that the same general rules apply but need to be considered in the light of their particular nation's economic position. If a nation has an unfavourable balance of payments year after year the result must eventually be that other nations are unwilling to take its currency, for to do so is simply to add more useless foreign exchange to its reserves, or more debts to the books of its business firms who have no prospect of ever being paid. No nation wants another nation's currency unless there is some prospect of being able to use it to buy something. What can be done about a nation with a permanently adverse balance of payments?

23.2
Curing a disequilibrium on the balance of payments

The fundamental problem is this. If the United Kingdom (for example) has a permanently adverse balance of payments it must be because the things that the United Kingdom is buying from other nations are worth more than the things the United Kingdom is able to sell to foreigners. Why don't foreigners buy our goods? It must be because they are less worth having than the goods they make themselves, or can get from other suppliers. If UK goods are of poor quality, or of poor design, then other nations will not buy them – but what is even worse is that the United Kingdom citizens don't want to buy them either. If the UK citizens prefer German, American or Japanese goods, then they will demand imports and a flood of sterling will be offered to buy foreign goods.

Of course, you cannot separate price from a discussion like this. If the price of UK goods is lowered some foreigners might decide they were worth having now (so that they will offer to buy them and the balance of payments will improve). Again, some citizens of the UK will also be persuaded that the UK goods are now better value for money and will buy the home-based goods instead of the foreign imports. This will again be helpful to the balance of payments. It is called 'import substitution' as the home citizen buys the home-produced good instead of the foreign good. Clearly, if we can lower the price sufficiently we shall reach a point where enough foreigners decide to buy our goods, and enough UK citizens decide to substitute the home-produced article for their imports so that overseas trade is brought into balance and confidence in our currency returns.

Although we shall return to this question of price in the next paragraph we must just say that anything we can do to improve the quality and design of our goods will help enormously to cure a balance of payments problem, because if UK goods are of excellent quality demand from overseas buyers and from UK citizens will be strong and there will be no balance of payments problem.

Returning to the question of the price of UK goods, what elements are there in the prices we charge? The 'price' of anything is the amount of money we pay to all the factors that created it and made it possible. This is, of course, what we pay in incomes to the landlords (rents), the workers (wages), the capital (interest) and the entrepreneurs (profits). If we are to cut the price of UK goods we have to cut the rewards to factors, and this means cutting rents, cutting wages, cutting interest payments to savers and cutting profit margins. However, when we are dealing with foreigners there is one other way we can lower the prices of UK goods. We can let the exchange rate fall in value, so that a foreigner seeking to buy UK goods is given more pounds for each dollar, franc or Dmark that he/she offers. If they get more pounds for their dollar the price of UK goods will really be lower. The pound is said to 'float' downwards, so that, for example:

$$\$1 = \pounds0.70$$
$$\$1 = \pounds0.80$$
$$\$1 = \pounds0.90$$

Imagine a British car costing £10 000. At $1 = £0.70 the cost to an American is $14285.71. At $1 = £0.80 it costs $12 500.00, and at $1 = £0.90 it only costs $11 111.11. As the value of sterling falls the goods become cheaper to the foreign buyer. Note that when the pound falls, the more we have to give for each dollar; 70 pence, 80 pence, 90 pence, etc.

The trouble with fluctuating (sometimes called floating) exchange rates, is that they hide the true problem to the inhabitants of the country that is using this method of achieving a balance of payments. What is really wrong when we have an adverse balance of payments is that the goods and services we are offering to the world are poor and we are paying ourselves too much for providing them. We really need to cut wages and the other rewards to factors, or to raise our productivity so that every unit of output we make is cheaper and can be sold at an acceptable price. How shall we bring home to our people the fundamental weakness of our economic position? For politicians, anxious to be re-elected, the need to tell people that they have to take cuts in wages is not a popular idea; they would perhaps prefer to let the pound float downwards on the foreign exchange market. They might prefer to erect tariff barriers at our ports and airports to impose a tax on foreign goods entering the country – thus raising the prices of imports and encouraging home citizens to buy home-produced goods. All such measures have trade-diverting effects which interfere with the working of other people's economies, and are unfair, because the real problem is that our home nationals won't work hard enough and demand too much reward for the factors they supply to industry.

The history of balance of payments problems is long, and a full discussion of the various solutions to the problem cannot be given here but we can at least list the methods and give a brief explanation before considering our present day solution to the problem – the ERM or Exchange Rate Mechanism. The list is as follows:

(a)   The 'Gold Standard' method.
(b)   The 'flexible exchange rate' method.
(c)   The 'fixed exchange rate' method or 'Bretton Woods System'.
(d)   The ERM (exchange rate mechanism), but before this method was introduced there was a return to (b) – the flexible exchange rate method for about 20 years.

Very briefly, these systems worked in the following ways:

(a)   *The 'Gold Standard' method (up to* 1914, *and from* 1925–31) When a country is on the gold standard its currency is linked to its gold reserves, except for a very small note issue called the 'fiduciary issue'. This is an issue of notes 'in good faith' because we know that some notes are always out of circulation, in children's piggy banks, and last year's cricket flannels where forgotten five pound notes languish. If the note issue is tied to the gold in the vaults of the central bank, and if everyone who wants it can have gold instead of notes, the amount of money in circulation is limited. When imports exceed exports the value of the currency will decline, but only by a tiny amount – because we soon reach the 'gold point'. This is the point where you stop paying foreigners with notes because it is cheaper to go to the Bank of England and get gold, and ship gold to your foreign supplier. This immediately affects the central bank. It is losing gold and has to cut the note issue and raise interest rates to encourage investors to leave their funds in the bank. No loans, no overdrafts and strict control of money mean no wage increases, no new equipment for industry; the dismissal of workers, etc.

However, foreign countries are receiving our gold. If they are on the gold standard too they will expand their note issues, encourage a boom in their economies, raise wages and lower interest rates to encourage investment, and their citizens will be encouraged to spend – and will hopefully spend some of their money on our goods. This will gradually restore the balance of payments. It is a self-regulating process. It works by deflating the economy in the country that is losing gold (encouraging its people to work harder because hard times are on them) and inflating the economy in the countries receiving gold (encouraging its people to take advantage of the good times by enjoying a higher standard of living and incidentally increasing their imports).

Why was the Gold Standard method discontinued then? The answer is that if it is to succeed all nations must stick to the rules, holding back their economies as gold moves out and expanding their economies as gold comes in. If the nations receiving gold do not use it to expand their note issues and let their economies expand, the whole system fails. In the years between the wars (1918–39) the Americans simply collected all the gold coming in and put it in Fort Knox. They did not expand their economy and consequently other nations – trying to achieve a balance of payments – forced their citizens to accept a lower and lower standard of living to no real purpose. Untold misery in Europe could not achieve a balance of payments and the system was abandoned in favour of 'flexible exchange rates'.

(b) *Flexible (floating) exchange rates* (1931–44) We have already seen that a disequilibrium is caused by the high price of exports which makes them a poor proposition for the overseas buyer. The price of UK exports is made up of (a) the home price in sterling, and (b) the rate of exchange between sterling and other currencies. The gold standard worked by attacking the home price in sterling, causing deflation at home and inflation abroad. The flexible exchange rate method worked by attacking the export price from the other direction: the rate of exchange between sterling and other currencies. Between the years 1931 and 1944 countries tried to alter their export prices without deflating the home economy, by letting the exchange rate look after the balance of payments. If you allow your currency to depreciate compared with other currencies, your exports will get cheaper and your imports dearer. **Depreciation** is the name given to this drop in exchange value when it occurs in a free market. **Appreciation** is the name given to a rise in exchange value as a currency becomes more valuable in a free market.

The way this method works is simpler than the Gold Standard method. Exchange rates are determined by the demand for, and the supply of, a particular currency. Suppose the United Kingdom has an adverse balance of payments. Few people want UK goods, so the demand for pounds sterling is weak. Many UK citizens wish to buy foreign goods, so the demand for dollars, francs, Dmarks and other currencies is strong. The pound weakens against these currencies, making UK goods effectively cheaper. As they get cheaper UK goods become better value for money and are more strongly demanded. Foreign goods are also becoming more expensive to the UK buyer, and therefore less desirable. Exports increase and imports decline and we return to a balance of payments. To some extent the exchange rate reflects the relative efficiencies of the industries of the two countries concerned.

Of course, this is very much over-simplified because many other aspects enter into the foreign exchange situation. Some of them we could mention are:

(i) Long-term capital movements, as banks and other lenders lend money to foreigners, or accept deposits from them.

(ii) Hot money flows. These are short-term money flows, as British and foreign investors deposit money in countries where they can earn a better rate of interest. 'Hot' money flows in and out easily and consequently affects exchange rates as it affects the demand for various currencies.

(iii) Government expenditures for all sorts of purposes (foreign bases for strategic reasons; aid to other countries; international obligations, etc).

One particularly unpleasant aspect of 'hot money' flows, which is explained more fully later (see page 277) was speculation against the currency. Speculation simply means a movement on the foreign exchange market to make a quick profit, and not for the purposes of overseas trade. Thus, if a currency is expected to fall, a person who sells the currency now can buy it back later more cheaply (thus earning a profit). To control speculative activities operating against sterling, a reserve fund of gold and foreign currencies (called the Exchange Equalisation Fund) was set up by borrowing against the security of gilt-edged stock and Treasury Bills. When the pound was under speculative pressure (e.g. because short-term money was leaving London and investors wished to sell pounds) the fund would be used to buy up the pounds on offer, releasing dollars or gold instead. The fund has increased its holdings of pounds and reduced its holdings of other currencies, but it had kept the pound stable on the foreign exchange markets, and prevented the speculators making a profit. Later, when funds were flowing into London and foreign investors wanted pounds, the Exchange Equalisation Fund was ready to supply pounds and take in the dollars and other currencies that were being exchanged, ready for the next bout of speculative pressure.

This system of managing the rate of exchange was very adaptable, because the managers of the Fund did not need to use it if the depreciation that was taking place was not a speculative one, but was the result of a genuine imbalance of payments. By refusing to buy pounds in these circumstances they could let the exchange rate depreciate to what they judged to be its true level.

Although the floating exchange rate system worked to some extent, it had serious disadvantages which included the fact that world trade declined seriously. The uncertainties of export trade increased and made it more risky. The war years interrupted trade, of course, to a considerable extent and, as the war drew to a close, the chief nations of the free world came together at Bretton Woods (outside Washington in the USA) to discuss what should be done. They decided that international trade should be encouraged by adopting a system of fixed exchange rates. This became known as the 'Bretton Woods System.'

(c) *The Bretton Woods System of fixed exchange rates* (1945–70) The problems with floating exchange rates was that if a currency was likely to float downwards and lose its value nobody wanted to hold it. Even exporters hesitated to trade if the profit they were going to make on their deals was likely to be eaten into by a fall in the exchange rate. What was needed was a system where currencies had a fixed rate against a major currency, and hence a fixed rate against one another. If all currencies were tied to the US dollar and had a fixed value against it, then any two currencies would also have a fixed value against one another. The maximum fluctuation that was allowed from this fixed exchange rate was 1 per cent of its value.

The pound started at £1 = $4.03 and was allowed to fluctuate by 4 cents (1 per cent of its value). So an exporter selling goods to the United

Kingdom at this rate knew that the most the currency could fall was 1 per cent, and as the profit margin on most deals is much higher than that (say 20 per cent), the possible loss was not enough to worry the exporter. If a currency did begin to depreciate, the central bank (the Bank of England in our case) had to step in and buy pounds on the foreign exchange market to keep the price up. To do this it had to use the official reserves of foreign currency it held. To help a country which was under pressure and likely to use up all its reserves, the Bretton Woods System set up a huge fund, the International Monetary Fund (IMF). This fund would provide extra currency as required, to help a central bank in difficulty, but only on very special terms. These were that the central bank concerned should tighten credit at home, make it very difficult for its citizens to spend money on imports, and gradually recover its 'balance of payments' position.

In effect, the fixed exchange rate system meant that the home country could allow its currency to float down 1 per cent, but after that it had to take measures to cut the standard of living, tighten credit, raise taxes and force the people either to go without or to work harder to make their goods better value for money.

Without going into the matter too deeply the system did work fairly well as the world recovered from the difficulties of the war years. The United Kingdom perhaps did, less well than most, partly because, as the country which won the war, it had to honour the debts it had incurred to win the war. Those who lose wars (and get smashed up in the process) never have to pay. The United Kingdom had to devalue to a lower level against the dollar twice in the years 1945–67, and eventually finished up at a rate of £1 = $2.40.

Unfortunately there was one real difficulty with the Bretton Woods System. If a country was coming under real pressure because its economy was less effective than most other economies, or it had good reason for being in difficulties (for example the United Kingdom in a few years around the early 1960s gave up its entire Empire and ceased to be a colonial power) it became necessary to re-align the currency against the dollar (and, of course, all other currencies). This meant a **devaluation** to a lower parity. If there was a fear that this might happen, financiers could take advantage of the impending change, by selling, (for example) the sterling they had (which lowered the price of sterling on the exchanges) and buying it back when it was cheaper. This was bad enough, but it was even worse when speculators who did not have any currency sold it anyway (as if they did have some) hoping to buy it back cheaper before they had to provide it to honour their first transaction. This just makes a profit for the speculator, without any justification at all. Although the International Monetary Fund did its best to prevent such speculation it could not entirely prevent it, and this and other defects led eventually to the abandonment of the system and a return to floating exchange rates. More is said about the role of the IMF and the World Bank later in this chapter, and Chapter 24.

(d) *The Exchange Rate Mechanism (ERM) of the European Monetary System (EMS)* As far as the European Union is concerned the present system for controlling the exchange rates is the ERM, which is part of the EMS. The EMS is based upon an artificial currency, the ECU (European Currency Unit). The ECU grew out of another artificial currency, the EUA (the European Unit of Account) used to keep the accounts of the European Economic Community in the early days when there were only six members. Small quantities of ECUs have already been minted, and a debate is taking place at the time of writing (1995) about whether this artificial coinage should be given real force by making it the single European currency, doing away with pounds sterling, French francs, German Deutschmarks, etc. This is the only sensible thing if a real Union is to be established, but there are groups opposed to it in every country. However you deride the 'little Englanders' and other groups there is some force in their argument that the time has not yet come when national currencies should be abandoned. However we are getting ahead of our story about the problem of curing a disequilibrium in the balance of payments. The EMS is a more sophisticated version of the Bretton Woods System in that it depends on the use of fixed exchange rates based on the new international unit of account, the ECU. This is explained later, but first let us be clear that if the currencies of all member states are tied to the ECU, and are worth a certain value in ECUs, then they are equally tied to one another, each currency having a parity value with every other currency in the group.

The European Currency Unit (ECU) The European Currency Unit, or ECU, is a 'currency basket', an imaginary currency which acts as a unit of account for all official transactions in the European Union. It will, undoubtedly, one day become an actual coin, and a denomination for notes of various values – 10 ECUs, 50 ECUs, etc. However, that lies in the future. For the moment its chief use is to designate a measure of value and unit of account which will be relatively stable in value because it is not tied to any particular nation's currency, but is tied to the economies of a whole group of nations, the European Union. Its actual composition is 'trade weighted', so that each unit reflects the value of international trade carried on by the different nations. The ECU composition is at present frozen at the 1 January 1994 level, and is now expressed in percentage terms using the 12 currencies in use at that time. The list is shown in Table 23.1 The value of an ECU is recalculated every day, but on 1 January 1994 it was worth US$1.16704. The effect of a currency basket, as distinct from an ordinary currency is as follows. Suppose a manufacturer offers to sell a piece of equipment for 100 000 ECU ... and the value of the Dmark rises, it is almost

Table 23.1 The European Currency Unit (ECU)

Currency	Percentage of ECU
German Mark	30.1
Pound Sterling	13.0
French Franc	19.0
Italian Lira	10.15
Dutch Gilder	9.4
Belgian Franc	7.6
Luxembourg Franc (linked to Belgian Franc)	0.3
Danish Krone	2.45
Irish Punt	1.1
Spanish Peseta	5.3
Portuguese Escudo	0.8
Greek Drachma	0.8
	=100.0

certain that the value of sterling will fall, so that the value of the ECU will not fluctuate very much at all. The value of the units is recalculated every day, and officially announced, but fluctuations will be much smaller than the fluctuations of a single currency like the guilder, the pound sterling or the French franc. Actual settlement of the debt is made in an agreed settlement currency, which will be exchanged at the rate prevailing on the settlement date. To see how this works consider the situation when 1 ECU = £0.60. The price of the machine is therefore £60 000. In three months' time, when payment is to be made, the pound sterling has fallen considerably in value but the ECU is almost the same: 1 ECU now equals £0.68. The businessman will therefore receive 100 000 ECU converted to sterling (at 1 ECU = £0.68), i.e. £68 000 – the true 'real' value of the machine in sterling.

When we say that the ECU is trade-weighted we mean that the proportion of value allotted to it from any particular currency is in relation to the size of each Member State's economy. This is re-assessed every five years and the value of the ECU adjusted accordingly. The most recent re-assessment was 1994, when the percentage amounts of the ECU were to be those shown in Table 23.1.

If the currency basket is much more stable than any of the currencies from which it is derived, we can see that an exporter or importer who wishes to be sure that the bargain he/she is making is sound will designate the price in ECUs rather than in the native currency. If a UK exporter sells goods designated in £ sterling and the value of sterling falls on the foreign exchange markets, the payment he/she eventually gets will be less than expected and will eat into the profits on the transaction. Of course, if sterling rises the exporter will make windfall profits. If the price is designated in ECUs the exporter will not gain or lose, but get the fair contract price that was originally agreed but converted to the agreed settlement currency (sterling) at the rate for the ECU and sterling on the day of settlement. Clearly there is much to be said for such an arrangement.

The actual working of the EMS is somewhat interrupted at the time of writing because of the withdrawal of the United Kingdom and some other nations from the system. It is helpful for the moment if we ignore this temporary (?) suspension of the system and consider how it was intended to work, with all member states as members.

The arrangements about parities work as follows:

(a) Each member currency is tied to every other currency by a fixed parity. This gives a complex grid of currency parities. Variations are allowed either side of any given parity up to 2¼ per cent (but the United Kingdom and Spain are allowed a wider variation of up to 6 per cent either side of the agreed parity). If two currencies appear to be drifting apart so that the limit of 2¼ per cent is being approached the problem is to decide which currency is at fault. Trouble has been caused under the old IMF system because action was required by both parties, to the indignation of the country whose finances were believed to be sound. Under the ERM this problem is solved by method (b) below.

(b) There is also a separate parity with the ECU. Since the ECU parities are very carefully calculated, a currency that is diverging will ring an alarm bell by reaching its limit against the ECU before it reaches its limit against other currencies. This is called the '**divergence indicator**' and calls for action to control the domestic economy of the country concerned. This divergence indicator only operates for the country whose rate of exchange is moving to danger point – the other party to any given exchange rate will not vary against the ECU, which, being a currency basket, cannot vary very much itself. To make this clear, suppose the lira is weakening. It will start to move away from its agreed parities with all the other currencies in the parity grid. If we take the rate of exchange between the German mark and the lira the rate of exchange will change, but how much is this due to the weakening of the lira, and how much is it due to a strengthening of the mark? We are just about beginning to think some action will be necessary by one of these parties when the divergence of the lira from the ECU rings the alarm bell. It is therefore Italy that must take corrective action.

Just what this corrective action is we shall see in a moment, but first let us ask what it could be that will set the currency concerned moving away from its agreed parities and ringing the alarm bells in the foreign exchange markets. It is, of course, the weakening of demand for a particular currency (or, of course, it could happen the other way as demand for a currency strengthened). Really, this comes down *to an individual country following policies which conflict with the general policies of other member states*. If the British, for example, pursue slack economic policies and pay our people too much for doing too little, and if we make inferior, shoddy products that no-one wants (including ourselves) then the pound will drift down on the exchanges and will reach the 'divergence indicator' against the ECU. Corrective action will have to be taken, not only to raise the value of the £ sterling on the markets, but to stop the malaise which is affecting the British economy.

The first step is to stabilise the currency on the exchange markets by supporting it. This means that the Central Bank of the currency that is in trouble uses its official reserves to buy the currency on the open market (though it can be done fairly discreetly). If we consider sterling as the currency in difficulty the Bank of England must step in and buy pounds the moment the alarm bells start to ring. In practice it is usual to start supporting the currency a little before the alarm bells ring. This is called intra-marginal intervention. When we say 'the alarm bells ring' there is of course no actual bell. We simply mean that the authorities notice that one country is nearing its divergence limit. The Bank of England, for example (called at such a time the 'intervening bank'), will use its own reserves of foreign currencies (usually Dmarks – the strongest currency at the time of writing), but asks permission of the German central bank because, of course, offering massive amounts of Dmarks to buy sterling will weaken the Dmark on the markets. If there is no serious defect in the British economy, really the action of the Bank of England may be sufficient to keep the pound within its parity levels with all the other currencies. If, however, the reverse is true, and despite the Bank of England's efforts the pound depreciates to the point where it reaches its limit against the ECU (and therefore will very shortly reach its limits against one or more of the main currencies), the **Very Short Term Financing (VSTF)** facility comes into effect. Each Central Bank makes available to other member states automatic unlimited credit facilities to finance intervention once a currency reaches its permitted margin, although in fact they may make credit available shortly before that. The idea is to buy enough of the weak currency on the market to make it stronger and raise the rate at which it is being traded on the market and keep it within the required limits (the 2¼ per cent or 6 per cent band, whichever applies). The hope is that this will stabilise the market while steps are being taken in the country under pressure to solve the balance of payments problem from which the nation is suffering. When this has been done the debts which the nation now owes to other Central Banks as a result of VSTF borrowing can be repaid, though in certain circumstances this repayment may be deferred.

To ensure that there are always funds available for intervention on the markets the Community has set up a European Monetary Cooperation Fund (EMCF). This fund is contributed to by all member states, to the extent of 20 per cent of their gold and dollar reserves. Theoretically the gold and dollars are transferred to the Fund and the country takes ECU in exchange (virtually a form of paper money which can be used in settling debts created by top-level inter-governmental dealings). Actually, the gold and dollar reserves never move anywhere; they are much safer in the vaults of the Central Banks that used to own them but have now agreed to donate them to the fund. All that happens is that the labels on certain stacks of gold bars will be changed to read 'EMCF'. Eventually, if a European Central Bank is set up, the funds might be move to that location, whenever it might be.

Before leaving this aspect of the Exchange Rate Mechanism, and turning to the more important aspect of solving a country's balance of payments problems it is necessary to say a word about speculation on the foreign exchange markets.

Speculators and the foreign exchange markets. The foreign exchange market is a market place conducted by telephone and computerised communication networks, where those who need to buy foreign currencies to pay for goods and services from foreign countries can obtain the currencies they need. Equally, where a person has received foreign currency in settlement of a debt for goods and services and wishes to turn this foreign currency into home currency the foreign exchange market is the place where this can be arranged. Since most of us do not have access to this highly organised and specialised market, and would not know how to trade even if we did have access, we ask our banks or 'bureau de change' to do it for us. These specialists are operating on the market for thousands of customers and consequently deal in bulk, rather than handling each request individually. They are prepared to quote prices – we can see them in any bank any day of the week. American dollars – 'we buy at 1.69 – we sell at 1.72'. They are able to quote these prices because they have reserves of all the major currencies, which they have purchased in the market at times when the prices seemed favourable. In other words, they speculated. No market can manage without speculators – people who buy when other people are selling and sell when other people are buying. They don't want the currencies they hold for themselves, to actually buy and sell goods and services; they only want to earn a profit on the transactions they carry out.

One type of transaction they do indulge in is a perfectly normal transaction for them, but a very undesirable transaction for a country that is in financial difficulties. Suppose the £ is depreciating (falling) on the market (and getting pretty close to its intervention level). The speculator sells pounds, because if he/she does so there is a chance that they can be bought back again ten minutes later at a cheaper price. Suppose £1 million is sold at 11.25a.m. at 2.93 Dmarks to the pound. The very act of selling pounds lowers the price of pounds on the market and, unless other people are buying pounds, the value of the £1 will fall to say 2.91 Dmarks. If the speculator now buys back at 2.91 Dmarks to the £1 he/she will receive £1 006 872.80 – a profit of £6 872.80. Such a transaction would be quite a commonplace activity for a foreign exchange dealer and there are no doubt times when the dealer loses just as easily as he/she gains. However, for a country whose currency is under pressure the fall in the exchange rate can be alarming, especially if all the dealers join in and try to sell, sell, sell. How shall we defeat such a speculative bout. The answer is to use the foreign exchange reserves of the Central Bank, and the VSTF facility to buy pounds. This will keep the price of pounds up, stop the speculator making a profit and possibly 'burn his/her fingers'. Burning the speculator's fingers occurs when instead of the price falling the price actually rises. The speculator who has sold £1 million which he/she probably doesn't even have, expects to buy back quickly at a lower price. If the price rises, since he/she must buy back in order to have the pounds necessary to cancel out the earlier sale, the speculator will lose money. For example, if the pound rose to 2.94 Dmarks the speculator would only get £996 598.63 and would have lost £3 401.37.

23.3 Solving the weakness of a currency

We now turn to the whole point of the 'Exchange Rate Mechanism' and why it is designed in the way that it is. It rings the alarm bells as a currency depreciates, and because of the divergence indicator it pinpoints which economy is at fault. The government of that country must then take steps to correct the malaise in the economy. There are several measures that can be taken, but they all have the effect of bringing home to the citizens of that country that they cannot enjoy a standard of living that is in excess of the wealth that they are creating. They must either take a cut in living standards or raise productivity by working harder and earning the standard of living they deem so desirable. The measures most commonly taken are as follows:

23.3.1 Raising interest rates

Raising interest rates makes it more expensive to borrow money, for whatever purpose. It affects the demand for goods and services from private individuals, who find the repayments less easy to afford. It affects the demand from businesses for new equipment to expand the business activity which is partly responsible for the imports which are causing the currency to depreciate. The effect of raising interest rates is to choke off the marginal project – the one that is only just profitable. For a project of this sort the extra interest is the last straw that breaks the camel's back and makes the project unprofitable. This takes the boom out of the economy.

23.3.2 Bank directives

After a decade of relatively free availability of credit in the United Kingdom, with every bank and building society pressing a credit card and 'instant availability of money' on us, many of us have forgotten that bank managers who 'like to say Yes' – as one television advertisement assures us – may in fact be forced to say 'No'. If the economy is out of control the Central Bank can issue a directive to banks telling them to restrict lending to certain levels, or to restrict it to particular needs or purposes – such as industries active in the export field. Of course, this is a great restraint on the personal choice to which citizens have become accustomed, but it has a salutary effect on the plans of everyone in the land and introduces a short, sharp shock to the whole economy.

We shall see later (see page 342) that such directives take effect through the need for banks to 'keep in step' in their credit policies. The bank that ignores the directive and continues to lend money freely will lose liquidity to other banks and get into financial difficulties.

<table>
<tr><td>

23.3.3
Physical controls

</td><td>

It is possible to bring in physical checks on the use of credit to take the boom out of the economy – for example, hire purchase restrictions are a method of reducing demand from the very poorest sector of the population which is forced to buy its durable consumer goods (cookers, television sets, washing machines, etc.) by instalments. The usual method used (which was widely adopted when the Bretton Woods System was in use) is to raise the hire purchase deposit rate and reduce the period over which repayment may be made. Thus, to make a 33⅓ per cent deposit compulsory for hire purchase means that a family seeking to pay £1 500 for a second-hand car on hire purchase must first save up £500 to put down as a deposit. If the maximum repayment allowed is two years this will raise the monthly repayment which must be met if the car is not to be repossessed. Such measures reduce demand in the economy, and also make people save harder and work harder to obtain the things they want. These are precisely the results which are needed to restore the value of the currency.

</td></tr>
<tr><td>

23.3.4
Fiscal measures

</td><td>

Fiscal measures are measures which involve taxation (the word fiscal is derived from *fiscus*, the Roman Emperor's privy purse from which he paid for the administration of the Roman Empire). If we raise taxation less money will be left in the pockets and purses of the general population, and they will be forced to reduce consumption, which will take the boom out of the economy, and reduce the number of pounds coming onto the foreign exchange market. Taxation may be raised by increasing income tax, or corporation tax, or value added tax (which affects consumers at the point of purchase) or by excise taxes such as tobacco tax, taxes on petrol, alcoholic liquors, etc.

As yet the United Kingdom has not been in the ERM system long enough for a bout of this type of restriction to have occurred, but we must remember that at present the UK is a member at the privileged 6 per cent band either side of its parity. It is intended that eventually we shall move to the 2¼ band and then such a strict system may mean that we do meet difficulties. Under the earlier Bretton Woods System (which was less sophisticated than the ERM system), the effect of these measures on the economy was described as a 'Stop-Go' system. It would in fact have been better to call it a 'Go-Stop' system; the economy was allowed to go ahead at its own pace, expanding into a boom, until balance-of-payments problems began to appear and the currency depreciated. Then the combination of fiscal, monetary and physical controls brought the economy to a 'slow', and if necessary, a 'stop' situation. This meant a serious decline in business activity, a rise in unemployment, severe restrictions on credit and a decrease in personal choice for all but the most wealthy. People started to work harder, they saved because of bad times; they travelled less abroad and they imported fewer goods, and they reduced consumption of home-produced goods leaving more goods available for export. Gradually, the balance of payments recovered, the

</td></tr>
</table>

inflation that had occurred in the boom times was reduced, wage demands were reduced and United Kingdom goods became better value for money. This improvement meant that more foreigners bought UK goods; the controls could be relaxed, and the economy entered a new 'Go' cycle. We may yet see all this as the ERM takes full effect.

Two final points about the exchange rate mechanism. Suppose a currency is so strong that it moves against other currencies and against the ECU to the point where it has *appreciated* enough to move outside its parity. The proper path to take would be to allow its citizens to enjoy a higher standard of living; to encourage them to travel more, buy more foreign goods, etc. This is all very well, but it may not be easy. For example, if they are buying home-produced goods because their home-produced goods are better than any foreign imports, it will be difficult to persuade them that they should change. If interest rates are reduced this may discourage them from saving so much, and lead them to increase consumption.

The final point is this. Suppose a country is constantly bedevilled by a depreciating currency and nothing seems to bring the balance of payments into balance. Such a country becomes a debtor nation to most other countries. Conversely, suppose a country's currency is so strong and its citizens so determined not to buy inferior foreign goods, that there is no prospect of it keeping inside its upper parity limit. Such a nation becomes a creditor nation to all other member states. What has to happen is that the exchange rate has to be either 'devalued' (in the case of the debtor nation) or 'revalued' in the case of a creditor nation. This means that such nations move to a new set of parity levels. Since 1979 this has happened 12 times with various currencies, so it is not a rare event, but it is still unusual, and prima facie undesirable.

We have now discussed the four elements in the present European Monetary System. They are:

(a)   The ECU (European Currency Unit)
(b)   The ERM (Exchange Rate Mechanism)
(c)   The EMCF (European Monetary Cooperation Fund)
(d)   The VSTF (Very Short Term Financing) facility.

In the last few pages we have been describing how the Exchange Rate Mechanism is supposed to work if all 15 members of the EU have joined the EMS. In fact the system has broken down – some say temporarily, others say irretrievably. What caused the break-down? The answer is 'the speculators'. The fact of the matter is that the total volume of money washing around the world is so enormous that even the greatest banks in the world are unable to withstand the financial pressure. We have seen how the 15 central banks are supposed to stand firm and support a weak currency, restore it to strength on the market and keep it there while the Government of the country that is in difficulties gets to work to cure the problem.

But suppose they can't withstand the pressure. Suppose, if the pound is under pressure, that they buy up all the pounds, only to be deluged with a further flood of pounds as everyone tries to sell pounds. Remember, all the speculator has to do is to sell pounds. It doesn't matter if he/she hasn't got any pounds to sell, and doesn't really mean to sell them at all, only to buy them back a bit later and take the profit on the deal. In one single day on the LIFFE Exchange (Black Wednesday 16 September 1992) the Exchange handled 886 110 futures and options contracts worth

£254 000 million. The United Kingdom in 1992 only created wealth of £407 000 million, so that the speculators on this one exchange spent a sum equivalent to more than half the total United Kingdom income for the year in one single day. No-one can stand up to that sort of pressure, and the United Kingdom left the EMS. Several other nations followed within a few days.

One final point is this. The banks, who are supposed to stand firm and resist the speculators' pressure, are putting themselves at serious risk. If they look cheerful, and keep buying the currency that is under pressure, and give out instead currency that is strong and reliable they are honouring the agreement. But if their best efforts are defeated, and they are powerless to stop the depreciation of the currency, what are they left with in the end? A lot of low value currency. As the pressure mounts they face a deteriorating situation, and to go on honouring the agreement means enormous losses for them and the people they represent. Before long they realise the battle is lost, and they must salvage their own positions. The flaw in the EMS system is the huge volume of money on the international money markets today – much of it computer controlled – where the computer detects a weakness in a currency before mere humans have noticed. The computer generates a 'sell sterling' order, and within seconds other computers pick it up and the mad scramble is on.

23.4 Elasticities and the devaluation of a currency

We have seen that under the Exchange Rate Mechanism a currency can only be allowed to depreciate to the limit of the 'band' it is allocated to – either 2¼ per cent or 6 per cent. If it then proves to have a permanent imbalance of payments which it seems impossible to correct it may need to move to a new parity altogether. This would, of course, be a lower parity, with the currency in trouble being worth less of each of the other currencies. Whether this solves the country's balance of payments difficulties depends on the elasticities on the foreign exchange market. Suppose the £ sterling was the currency that had been forced to devalue. What elasticities would affect the success of the devaluation? The three elasticities to be considered here are (*a*) the elasticity of demand for exports, (*b*) the elasticity of demand for imports, and (*c*) the elasticity of supply of exports. Each of these will vitally affect the success of a devaluation.

(a) The elasticity of demand for exports

If we are reducing the prices of our exports in order to increase earnings of foreign exchange, it is vital that the demand for our exports is elastic. Suppose export prices are devalued by 10 per cent, and the rise in export sales is exactly proportional – in other words, there is unitary elasticity of demand. The result will be that the earnings of foreign exchange have not altered. The greater volume of sales earning foreign exchange will be offset by the smaller amounts earned on each consignment. We will even be worse off in other ways, for we will have had all the extra trouble of shipping larger volumes of goods for the same result.

It will be even worse if the demand for our goods is inelastic. Then our extra effort in selling a slightly larger volume of goods will have been worse than useless, for the smaller earnings in foreign exchange on each consignment mean we will actually earn less total foreign exchange. The balance of payments may even deteriorate. Only if the demand for our exports is elastic, so that sufficiently increased volumes of sales occur, will

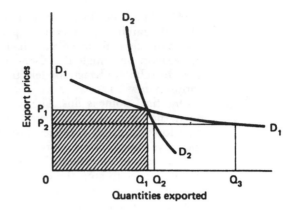

Figure 23.1 Effect of the elasticity of demand for exports on the earnings of foreign exchange after devaluation of a currency

Notes

1 If the demand for exports is elastic the curve may be as in D_1D_1.
2 If the demand for exports is inelastic the curve may be as in D_2D_2.
3 Total earnings (before devaluation) of foreign exchange are shown by the shaded area.
4 In the case of exports where the demand is inelastic, quantities sold rise only to OQ_2, less than proportionately, and total earnings of foreign exchange decline.
5 In the case of exports where demand is elastic, quantities sold increase more than proportionately to OQ_3, and total earnings of foreign exchange increase.

the devaluation bring larger earnings of foreign exchange. The situation is illustrated in Figure 23.1.

(b) The elasticity of demand for imports

Here the situation is very similar, but works in the opposite way. A country which is allowing its currency to depreciate wishes to correct its balance of payments by increasing exports and decreasing imports. How successful it will be in decreasing imports depends on the elasticity of demand for imports by its citizens. The depreciation will raise the price of imports to them. Will their demand reduce proportionately, more than proportionately, or less than proportionately to the change in price? If the imports are basic raw materials which are essential to production, it may be impossible for the demand for them to decrease at all. Indeed, higher export sales could even require larger imports of basic raw materials. If the imports are non-essentials, or if similar products are produced at home so that home products can be substituted for them, then the decrease in demand may be more than proportional. This situation is necessary if the devaluation is to be successful from the import point of view, but the situation is not quite so crucial as with exports. Since the price of imports has not changed in their own currencies we are not having to pay out more foreign exchange per unit imported, even though the home consumer is paying more for it. Therefore, any reduction is welcome, even the small reduction in the demand for goods which are in inelastic demand. Despite this, a reduction of imports is vital to the success of any depreciation of the currency, since we must now export more goods than previously to pay for each unit of imports.

(c) The elasticity of supply of exports

If exports are to be sold in increasing quantities they must be available to sell. This means it may be necessary to reduce home demand for them if the supply of exports is inelastic. Anything we do to reduce home demand will increase the supply of exports. A devaluation is usually accompanied by a serious credit squeeze, or perhaps even a total credit freeze, to reduce home demand and thus free home-produced goods for export.

**23.5
The International
Monetary Fund
(IMF)**

Although the International Monetary Fund was set up at Bretton Woods to help countries that were getting into difficulties under the Bretton Woods System, it still has many residual functions which are important even though the Bretton Woods System has largely been abandoned. It is also helpful for students to know the background to this institution because its activities have been to some extent copied by EMCF, the European Monetary Cooperation Fund. The agreements made at Bretton Woods for the establishment of an International Monetary Fund were as follows:

(*a*) By an agreed date all members should declare the par values of their currencies. Great Britain declared that the £1 should be equal to 4.03 American dollars, for example. This agreed rate of exchange would be permitted to fluctuate by up to 1 per cent on either side of the agreed parity figure. Because of two devaluations, in 1949 and 1967, the pound last stood at £1 = $2.40. Until August, 1971 it was allowed to fluctuate between $2.42 and $2.38 or 1 per cent of its agreed parity. It follows then that except for very abnormal times, like the devaluations mentioned, a foreign trader making a contract knew that he/she was unlikely to lose more than 1 per cent of the contract price by exchange fluctuations. As profit margins are much greater than 1 per cent, the proportion of his/her ultimate profit at risk was very small. World trade continued to expand under this system in a thoroughly satisfactory way.

(*b*) All currencies should be freely convertible on current transactions within five years. In fact this proved impossible, but by 1958 it had been achieved as far as non-residents were concerned. This right to exchange currencies freely has been available to British residents only since 1979, when exchange control regulations were abandoned.

(*c*) Changes of exchange rate should not normally be permitted; but if the change was of less than 10 per cent and deemed absolutely essential, a country could depreciate its currency without prior consultation with the Fund authorities. If the devaluation was to be greater than 10 per cent, the Fund authorities must sanction the arrangement.

(*d*) The International Monetary Fund (IMF), is a huge reserve of currency and gold collected on a quota basis from all the members of the Fund. Great Britain's original contribution was $1 300 million. This was raised in 1959, and again in 1965. Finally, in February 1970 a further revision raised Britain's contributions to $2 800 million. One quarter of the quota had to be contributed in gold, the other three quarters was contributed in a country's own currency. Since 1976, when the International Monetary Fund decided to phase out the use of gold in its system, the gold contributions are being disposed of – partly by returning one sixth of them to members and by selling another sixth on the open market (at a large profit). This profit is being used to help developing nations with balance of payments problems. The rest of the gold may be used to finance a fund to enable countries with excessive amounts of dollars to exchange them for other currencies. Originally there were 39 members of the Fund. By the end of 1980 there were 140 members, comprising almost the whole non-Communist world. Switzerland is a notable exception. The break-up of the Soviet bloc has led to a number of new applications to join the IMF and the majority of Eastern bloc countries will no doubt become members in due course. In 1993 the membership stood at 178 nations.

23.5.1
Use of the fund when
a disequilibrium
occurs

Today most currencies are floating, and the IMF is not being required to act in quite the same way as under the Bretton Woods agreement, but a description of the use of the Fund at that time is still largely relevant to a country with an adverse balance of payments. The original system was that when a country suffered an adverse balance of payments and its own reserves appeared inadequate to withstand the speculative pressure, the members exercised Drawing Rights against the Fund, in a series of 'tranches' (*tranche* is the French word for 'slice'). The first slice, or gold tranche, was its own contribution of gold plus any shortage of the member's contribution to the Fund. For example, the UK quota was 25 per cent gold and 75 per cent sterling; suppose some other member, wishing to buy British goods, had borrowed sterling from the Fund. The UK would be entitled to put in enough pounds to take out not only its gold share, but any extra currency it wanted up to the limit of its full quota. The fund would now hold 100 per cent of the UK quota in sterling, and the UK would go back to its battle to support the pound armed with these extra reserves. If they proved insufficient it could return for more 'tranches' – four more slices of 25 per cent each of its quota. By this time the Fund would be holding 200 per cent of its quota of sterling. However, while the gold tranche was available as of right, the successive further tranches would mean more and more stringent guarantees from the borrowing nation that it was really doing something to cure its balance of payments problems. A speculation that persisted as long as this must mean some fundamental weakness in the nation's economic affairs, and the Fund authorities might refuse help unless corrective measures were taken.

Until about 1970, this system worked extremely well and world trade grew by almost 10 per cent per annum, without inflation rearing its ugly head.

There were two problems though. The first was that a decline in world liquidity became apparent as international trade expanded. It had already been noticed that a nation whose reserves fell to about 20 per cent of its international trade was extremely vulnerable to speculative pressure, and might need to borrow to finance its ordinary deficits. A General Agreement to Borrow was arranged in 1961, with the group of ten leading banking nations extending credit facilities to one another (chiefly the UK) through the IMF. Later it was decided to create **Special Drawing Rights (SDRs)** to provide a further source of liquidity.

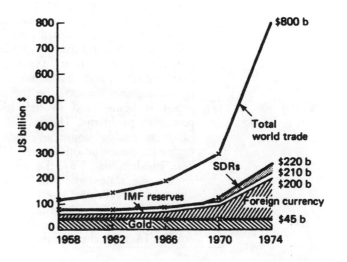

Figure 23.2 World trade and world reserves under the Bretton Woods System to 1974

Special Drawing Rights (SDRs) are a new kind of reserve asset. Keynes had suggested at the Bretton Woods Conference that if gold continued to be inadequate as a reserve currency for world trade, a new kind of international currency, for which he suggested the word 'Bancor', should be invented by the world's monetary authorities. Since the whole money system depends on acceptability, the general acceptability of 'Bancors' (bank-gold) would enable them to finance trade. The world was sceptical, and the idea was not adopted.

In the late 1960s the world situation as far as reserves were concerned worsened. World trade rose far beyond the ability of gold to back it, and although we could have revalued gold there were several good reasons why we did not do so. One reason was that the chief nations to benefit would be South Africa and Russia, and justifiably or not there was a good deal of feeling in the world that neither of these countries deserved a bonus. The other beneficiaries would be those who had hoarded gold in the past – precisely the people who had helped keep it in short supply. They had been the least cooperative in helping to make the Bretton Woods System work.

Other reasons for not revaluing gold include its inflationary effects on certain countries, and also that it represents a very primitive basis for trade. To continue to use gold to finance international trade, when all that is needed is an internationally accepted medium for payment, is a reactionary solution. Sooner or later the international system has to grow up just as domestic banking systems have had to grow up. From experience we know that a nation with reserves as low as 20 per cent is invariably in difficulties. As Figure 23.2 shows, world reserves fell relative to the volume of trade they had to finance, from 57 per cent in 1958 to 40 per cent in 1966 and 32 per cent in 1970.

A crisis was approaching. It is this situation which led to the development of Special Drawing Rights. They are not quite the same as 'Bancors'; they were designed to extend the IMF arrangements by giving all members who agree to accept them an allocation. Great Britain's share of the 3500 million created on 1 January 1970, was 402 million, each one equivalent to a US dollar. A further 3000 million were created in 1971 and 1972. A further 4000 million were created in each year from 1979 to 1981, and the situation is under constant review. The dollar basis of the SDR was later changed to a 'currency basket' (see Table 23.2).

A country wishing to use Special Drawing Rights will notify the Fund that it wishes to exchange some for usable foreign currency. The authorities will then designate which countries are to make currency available, and take SDRs instead. Clearly they will choose the countries whose balance of payments positions are strong. While this has proved to supply some

Table 23.2 The composition of the Special Drawing Rights unit

Currency	Weight (Total 100)	Amount (in units of each designated currency)
US dollar	42	0.54
D mark	19	0.46
£ sterling	13	0.071
F franc	13	0.74
Japanese yen	13	34.0

strengthening of reserves, the pace of events overtook the introduction of SDRs. The serious deficits in the British balance of payments led the UK to 'float' sterling in 1972 and by 1973 all currencies were floating.

Floating exchange rates were to reduce very considerably the calls made upon the IMF by the advanced nations. The Bretton Woods System had broken down due to the second problem that followed from Bretton Woods. This was the imperfect arrangements made at Bretton Woods about the solution of fundamental disequilibrium problems. The ability of debtor nations to devalue their currencies when faced with a fundamental disequilibrium on their balances of payments was of little help to them if creditor nations would not take steps to revalue their currencies and expand their economies to give the creditor nations a chance to earn more foreign exchange. The problem required international action – not just national corrections of the economy of the debtor nation.

These problems were suddenly made infinitely worse by the oil crisis which followed the Middle East War of 1973. The OPEC countries raised oil prices three or four times, and plunged the whole non-OPEC world into massive deficit. To finance these deficits a huge recycling programme was undertaken, largely by the commercial banks and the merchant banks. The IMF's role was not a major one, but it has gradually extended the credit facilities available. Some of these facilities have been little used, because of the conditions the IMF had to impose on borrowers under its (largely outdated) constitution. It is in the process of adjusting to criticisms of these conditions. The credit facilities available to members now are as follows:

(a) *Ordinary credit tranches*. These have already been described above.
(b) The *Compensatory Financing Facility*. Available to countries whose export earnings fall for temporary reasons only (crop failures, natural disasters, etc.).
(c) *The Extended Fund Facility*. Available to countries who require longer than usual to repay – they have up to eight years to repay the funds borrowed.
(d) *The Gold Sales Trust Fund*. This fund was set up from the sale of gold when the IMF's constitution was changed in 1976 so that gold was no longer required. One sixth of the gold was returned to members and another sixth was sold on the open market, the profits being used to establish a trust fund for the use of less developed countries (LDCs) facing balance of payments difficulties due to the oil price increases. The fund stands at about $4500 million, and to date almost 1 000 million SDRs have been paid out to less developed nations to assist them with balance of payments difficulties.
(e) *The Supplementary Financing Facility*. This was raised from the oil-producing countries to assist countries placed in difficulties by the oil price rises.
(f) *The Bufferstock Facility*. This facility exists to help nations prepared to stockpile commodities, at times when they are cheap because of a lack of demand in the recession currently prevailing.

This wider range of facilities has been helpful in bridging balance of payments deficits for many nations, but the Fund has come under criticism for its harsh borrowing conditions – i.e. the requirement it makes for countries to control their domestic economies so as to be able to repay the sums borrowed and avoid adverse balances of payments in the future. Often the money can be borrowed just as easily from the ordinary banking system without any conditions. It seems likely that the IMF will experiment with different kinds of conditions, which might make a positive rather than a negative approach to the economy. Thus if instead of the usual credit squeeze conditions it could insist on borrowers developing export industries or import-substitution industries it might help them to achieve a balance of payments in a more positive way. For example, if we have a nation with a good clay soil importing bricks for construction projects the Fund might insist they develop a brick-making industry. One agency helping a developing country found this to be the case, and earned the enduring gratitude of the government concerned by showing them how easy it was to make bricks.

23.6 Summary of Chapter 23

1   All trading nations must at the end of a given year be left with either a favourable balance of payments or an adverse balance of payments. An adverse balance of payments will usually be met by borrowing from those who have the required currency, or by trade credit (in which the debt is merely held over until the following year).

2   A balance of payments problem only becomes serious when a nation has an adverse balance of payments year after year, and some method of achieving a balance has to be found.

3   The essential solution to the problem is to convince the citizens of the nation with an adverse balance that they are enjoying too high a standard of living for the wealth they are creating, and must either reduce their demand for goods and services or create more wealth by higher productivity and harder, or more effective, work.

4   The chief methods by which an equilibrium has been established in the past have been (a) the 'gold standard' method; (b) the 'flexible exchange rate' method; (c) the Bretton Woods System; (d) a return to method (b) temporarily after 1970 and then the adoption of the present 'exchange rate mechanism' (ERM) in the European Union.

5   The Gold Standard achieved equilibrium by deflating the economy of the country losing gold because of its adverse balance, and inflating the economy of the country gaining gold reserves.

6   The Gold-Standard rules were: deflate when you lose gold, inflate when you gain gold.

7   The flexible exchange rate achieved equilibrium by letting the currency depreciate when a balance was adverse, and letting it appreciate when the balance of payments was favourable.

8   Exchange rates are determined by the demand for, and the supply of, a particular currency. To some extent this reflects the relative efficiency of the industries of the two countries, but it also reflects capital movements.

9   In order to prevent fluctuations in the exchange rate caused by short-term capital flows and speculative pressures, the Exchange Equalisation Account method of managing the exchange rate was devised. This involved buying pounds on the open market when 'a run on the pound' developed, and selling pounds when the demand for pounds was strong.

10 The Bretton Woods Agreement of 1944 introduced a system of 'managed flexibility'. This involved keeping exchange rates at a fixed parity with other currencies to encourage business confidence in trade. To help manage currencies the International Monetary Fund (IMF) was set up.

11 In a disequilibrium situation where a member's own reserves are insufficient, the member may borrow until the Fund has twice its quota of contributions. In addition, reserves have been increased by the creation of Special Drawing Rights (SDRs).

12 Managed flexibility was modified in 1971, and virtually abandoned in 1973, when all currencies floated against the dollar. Floating permits the currency to find its own level in the market.

13 In 1979 a return to a system of fixed parities began in Europe with the establishment of the European Monetary System with its Exchange Rate Mechanism (ERM). This has fixed exchange rates between each pair of currencies in the European Union, and also fixed exchange rates of these currencies with a new unit of account, the European Currency Unit (ECU). It also set up two systems to help a member state whose currency is depreciating. A member state that is in temporary difficulties may borrow reserves from other central banks using a VSTF (very short term financing) facility. This is an agreement between all the central banks to make funds available to a member whose currency has depreciated to the limit of its parity band with the ECU.

The other system is the European Monetary Cooperation Fund, which acts as a huge reserve of funds to which a member state in difficulties may turn to fight speculation against its currency. The United Kingdom joined the ERM on 5 October 1990 but left again on 'Black Wednesday', 16 September 1992 after massive pressure from speculators forced a depreciation of its currency outside the limits permitted by the European Monetary System. Before Black Wednesday the pound was worth 2.97 Dm under the ERM arrangements. After being driven out of the EMS by the speculators the pound is currently trading (1995) at about 2.40 Dm = £1.

Exercises Set 23

1 What is meant by 'a permanent disequilibrium on the balance of payments'? How may such a disequilibrium be overcome?

2 What was 'the gold standard'? Why is the Gold Standard not used today as a means of controlling the world's economies?

3 What is a speculator? How may a speculator operating on the foreign exchange market make profits even though he/she does not want any foreign currency for trading purposes?

4 What is an ECU? What is meant by saying that an ECU is a currency basket?

5 Explain how the Exchange Rate Mechanism operates to exercise control over an economy that is offering its citizens a higher standard of living than they really deserve?

6 What is the link between the Exchange Equalisation Account, the International Monetary Fund and the European Monetary Cooperation Fund? Explain how these systems work.

7 What measures can be taken to slow down an economy which is suffering from balance of payments problems? What is the alternative to slowing down the economy?

8 Explain the terms:

(a) Divergence indicator
(b) 'Very Short Term Financing' facility
(c) Depreciation of a currency
(d) Appreciation of a currency
(e) Stop-Go policies
(f) EMCF

9 What is a Special Drawing Right Unit? Why are they less important than they once were?

24   The free-trade areas

**24.1
Limited free trade**

From an economic viewpoint free trade is highly desirable, because it brings the advantages of specialisation and large-scale production. From national, social and psychological viewpoints it may have less appeal, because it is likely that the terms of trade will favour one party more than the other, and may lead the less well-placed nation to take measures to avoid the foreign competition. The most acceptable free-trade areas therefore tend to be between nations of roughly comparable economic strength, whose citizens have roughly similar standards of living and similar technologies. In these circumstances genuine comparative advantages may still lie with particular areas because of native temperament or accumulated knowledge and experience. Thus the Italian gift for style in clothes, shoes and cars is likely to prove advantageous, while Germany's engineering skill will make her heavy-industrial equipment competitive within the European Union. Britain's manufactures will be readily acceptable to Denmark, whose dairy products will compete favourably with British agricultural goods.

Where a limited free-trade area is established the degree of reciprocity in trade is high, and this reduces national, social and psychological objections.

**24.2
Bilateral and
multilateral trade**

Bilateral trade means two-sided trade, i.e. trade between two countries only. As will be seen from Figure 24.1, the volume of world trade that can be achieved when nations trade bilaterally is smaller than with multilateral, many-nation, trade. During the years 1930–40 a major depression developed in the USA and spread rapidly to the rest of the world. To protect home industries nearly all nations put up tariff barriers to keep foreign goods out, and where they traded at all it was on a bilateral basis. The result was a serious decline in world trade with loss of economic advantage to mankind in general. By encouraging international specialisation of labour, multilateral trade encourages the best use of resources. This advantage was partially lost in the years under discussion, and the experience led to an international conference at Geneva in 1947 where a General Agreement on Tariffs and Trade (GATT) was signed. Before discussing this agreement we must consider Figure 24.1, and the notes below it.

**24.3
The General
Agreement on
Tariffs and Trade
(GATT)**

This agreement was signed in 1947, by 23 nations; the number has now reached 108. The convention's aims had been as follows:

(*a*)   To reduce existing trade barrier between nations.
(*b*)   To reduce discrimination against particular nations.
(*c*)   To promote international confidence in tariff policies by promoting consultation rather than unilateral action as a means of deciding tariffs.

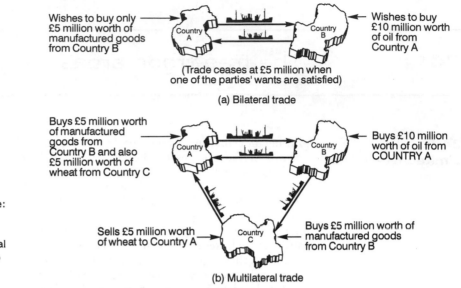

Figure 24.1 Bilateral and multilateral trade: (a) Bilateral trade – trade ceases at £5 million; (b) Multilateral trade – trade rises to £10 million

Notes

1 With bilateral-trading agreements trade can only continue to the point where one country's requirements have been satisfied. In part (i) of the above diagram, Country B would like to import a further £5 million of oil from Country A but cannot do so because Country A does not want any more of Country B's manufactures.

2 With multilateral trade the desire of Country C to buy goods from Country B enables world trade to rise in volume. Since Country A is willing to buy wheat from C, she will sell further oil to B, who will pay for it with manufactured goods delivered to C, who will pay for them by shipping wheat to A.

3 Clearly the more nations involved in world trade the better, and hence a general agreement on tariffs and trade will promote international specialisation.

The US made very generous reductions in tariffs as a result of the 1947 negotiations, and these enabled European nations in particular to penetrate the North American market. This policy of the 'good creditor' enabled Europe to recover from many of its post-war difficulties.

In 1963 President Kennedy persuaded the American Congress to cut American tariffs if other nations would agree to do so by June 1967. This initiated a new round of discussions called the Kennedy Round, which ended in 1967 with massive tariff reductions by the industrialised nations. Some 70 per cent of their dutiable import tariffs were cut, and in two thirds of the cases the cuts were of 50 per cent. A 'product-by-product' basis was the most successful method of agreeing these tariff cuts; chemicals, pulp and paper, transport equipment, machinery, base metals, and many more commodities had extensive cuts made. The one major flaw in the agreements was the extent to which primary producing countries were unable to gain concessions about agricultural products. Almost all nations have strategic or social reasons for not reducing agriculture. Developing nations tend to be agricultural, but the Kennedy Round did not prove helpful in allowing them to specialise in the activities at which they have a comparative advantage. Instead the refusal of advanced nations to cut back their agricultural programmes has given developing nations an added incentive to diversify and industrialise their economies.

One principle of GATT is that the member countries agree to give 'most-favoured-nation' treatment to all members. This means that if Britain cuts her tariff on American-manufactured electrical goods by 10 per cent she will do the same for all GATT members. With 70 nations in the Agreement it means that practically the whole world shares in the tariff cut. Such tariff cuts are made much less likely as a result.

Altogether there have been seven 'rounds' of negotiations since 1947. Since the end of the Kennedy Round we have had a Tokyo Round 1973–9 and a Uruguay Round that began in 1986 and only ended in 1994. None of these negotiations has gone easily, and the *Economist* at one stage described GATT as the General Agreement to Talk and Talk. The trouble is that it gets more and more difficult to promote free trade at a time when few nations are prepared to cut back on their farm sectors to allow third world farmers to penetrate their domestic markets. At the same time protectionism is growing, as an increasingly sophisticated set of NICs (newly industrialised countries) seeks to leapfrog over more established advanced nations. The tendency for such nations, which have rising populations that keep labour costs low, is to 'dump' goods on the advanced nations for whatever they will fetch in hard currency. The response of the advanced nations is to impose anti-dumping tariffs to raise the imported goods to price levels comparable with domestic goods. Another response is to devise unfair non-tariff barriers, such as 'construction and use' regulations on motor vehicles or slow-moving test procedures for pharmaceutical products to prevent the issue of licences for the marketing of new products. These attitudes are considered unfair by the 160 members of the United Nations who belong to UNCTAD, the United Nations Conference on Trade and Development. They are dedicated to obtaining a fairer share of world trade for the developing nations.

Another serious feature of trade developments to rebut the free competition which is encouraged by GATT are the so-called 'voluntary' restraints. A 'voluntary' restraint is one where a NIC agrees to limit its penetration of an advanced nation's market to some agreed quota, by volume or value. It is therefore really a market-sharing, anti-competitive device to prevent cut-throat competition from a NIC destroying the home industry of a developed nation to the point where it would force political retaliation by the developed nation. The USA and the EU are the two areas most keen to develop this kind of 'voluntary' restraint. There are nearly 300 such agreements.

The one area which is outside the GATT rules is the multi-fibre agreement, which limits the third world export of textiles and clothing to the developed nations. However, agriculture is an area where agreement is very difficult, and even the USA and the EU have fallen out over this area of trade. While US farmers are subject to severe market forces, EU farmers have a high level of protection, and the whole future of GATT is at present in some difficulty over the inability of EU agriculture ministers to find some way of reducing farm support payments, currently running at about $275 billion.

Another area of growing importance is the services area, banking, shipping, aviation, consultancy services, telecommunications and insurance. Here there are practically no rules; competition is difficult to introduce because many operators in these markets are multi-national monopolies or oligopolies. If developing countries seek to develop their own facilities they are inevitably high-cost, low-turnover bureaucracies with controls imposed which hinder rather than help the development of the nation. Despite this, calls for a free market in services are not listened to very sympathetically by third world nations protecting their struggling domestic operators.

Some idea of the range of topics studied in the Uruguay round of 1986–94 is given by the following list:

(a) *Trade aims* Tariffs to be cut by one third; non-tariff barriers to be reduced and where possible eliminated; natural resources (fishing, forestry, non-ferrous metals and other mineral products) to be more freely traded; phasing out of the multi-fibre agreement (MFA) to bring textiles and clothing under the normal GATT rules; review of members' trade policies to ensure greater openness.

(b) *Agriculture* Reduction in farm subsidies and support to secondary industries using farm products; opening of domestic markets to imports; tariff cuts on third world tropical products and elimination of non-tariff barriers; reduction of unfair countervailing measures. These are tariffs to keep out goods which are allegedly being dumped, but in fact are cheap as the result of a comparative advantage (cheap labour in the third world).

(c) *Services* A new General Agreement on Services needs to be drawn up to ensure fair trading in services. This includes some arrangement on fair payment for intellectual property (royalties for patents, books, franchises, etc.).

(d) *Investments* Some sensible arrangement to liberalise movements of capital is required to achieve mutual advantages and greater confidence by investors (anti-sequestration measures for example).

(e) *Administration* There is an urgent need for revision of the GATT system and for some system which guarantees the implementation of GATT rules. As a start its name has been changed to the World Trade Organisation (WTO), and world trading activities are being kept under regular scrutiny, rather than by a periodic 'round' of talks.

24.3.1 The 'World Bank' – the International Bank for Reconstruction and Development

The other major creation of the Bretton Woods Conference in 1944 was the World Bank, the International Bank for Reconstruction and Development, or IBRD for short. The bank initially received capital contributions from members, but its loan activities are financed by floating bonds designated in dollars, against the security of its capital which currently stands at $125 000 million. Only 9 per cent of this has actually been supplied by members, the other 91 per cent may be called if necessary.

The original plan was for the Bank to evaluate projects put up to it by national governments and provide the funds at competitive rates of interest (because the Bank as a prestige borrower can borrow at very competitive rates). The project itself must be capable of repaying the interest and the capital over an agreed period. Apart from the immediate post-war years when reconstruction was important, the chief activities are in the developing world. The Bank faced a dilemma with many of its early projects, in that the prestige project tends to be sophisticated and capital-intensive, whereas the developing nations need generally less sophisticated labour-intensive industries. Frequently the fundamental educational level of the less-developed countries leaves them unqualified to operate prestige projects which the Bank has formerly tended to sponsor. A sophisticated project operated by a few expatriates does little to help a developing nation seeking to develop basic skills among a large and growing population.

The Bank has therefore turned to sponsoring more 'grass roots' projects, basic training programmes, population-control schemes, improvements in basic agriculture, etc. These projects may call for research into the general development of an economy if the full implications are to be appreciated (and the loan successfully repaid).

The IBRD itself arranges the actual loans and supervises repayments. It loaned approximately $20 000 million of new loans in the year ending June 1990, a fairly typical year. Its role is to approve projects proposed by government or government-backed institutions, and to find the funds.

Three other bodies supervise activities in less developed countries (LDCs) and play a more direct part than the IBRD, although they are part of the World Bank Group. They are:

(a) *The IFC (International Finance Corporation)*. This corporation acts in the private sector in LDCs, attempting to develop and encourage private enterprise businesses. It takes a share in the equity capital of companies, securing finance for them and acting as adviser.

(b) *The IDA (International Development Association)*. This association is active in the poorest countries, lending funds for approved projects at heavily subsidised interest rates and with repayment periods as long as 50 years. Many of its projects are for developing the infrastructure of a developing nation – roads, waterways, ports, airports, power supplies, irrigation, telecommunications, etc. Although project spotting is still the main basis of these activities the evaluation procedure tends to be too slow, and the trend is towards 'programme' lending, in which a general programme is outlined and aspects can be started upon at once, while the larger projects are evaluated and approved.

(c) *MIGA. (The Multilateral Investment Guarantee Agency)*. This agency guarantees eligible investments against losses resulting from non-commercial risks (such as expropriation of assets by the host country, or repudiation of official contracts, or armed conflict and civil unrest).

24.4 The general pattern of free-trade areas

It has already been said that free-trade proceeds best between nations of similar technological status. The major free-trade area grouping is the European Union, now expanded to 15 nations by the admission of Finland, Sweden and Austria. The EFTA group (the European Free Trade Association) is reduced to a rump of three nations, with very close ties to the EU. A recent addition to the list shown in Table 24.1 is the North American Free Trade Association (NAFTA) comprising the USA, Canada and Mexico.

Removed from the list is the former Council for Mutual Economic Cooperation (Comecon) which once included the USSR, Poland, Romania, Czechoslovakia, Hungary, Bulgaria, Mongolia, Cuba and Vietnam. With the collapse of the USSR these countries are seeking to re-establish themselves as mixed economies with a higher proportion of free enterprise activities. Most hope, eventually perhaps, to join the EU.

The advantages of free-trade areas stem from the increased market which is made available to members. It is not only actual population but purchasing power that is important, so that the strongest areas are those that have affluent populations.

24.5 The Sterling Area

The Sterling Area was a formerly important bloc of countries tied by economic interests to the pound sterling. The original bloc was formed in 1931 after the UK left the Gold Standard. Today the Sterling Area is reduced to the UK, the Channel Islands, the Isle of Man and Gibraltar, so that as a world financial force the Sterling Area has really ceased to exist.

24.6
The European Union (EU)

During World War II the idea grew up of a Federal Union of Europe. The powers of Europe should be bound together by ties so strong that any further war between them would become unthinkable. The idea of a super-European State, beginning with an economic union and developing into a political union, had been born.

Table 24.1 Free-trade areas

Full name	Short title	Total population (millions)	Countries involved	1990 income per head (£)
European Union	EU	346	Germany, France, Italy, Belgium, Netherlands, Luxemburg, Great Britain, Denmark, Eire, Greece, Spain, Portugal, Austria, Sweden, Finland	6700
European Free Trade Association	EFTA	11	Norway, Switzerland, Iceland	8290
North American Free Trade Association	NAFTA	363	Mexico, Canada, USA (formed in 1995)	–
Latin American Integration Association	LAIA		Brazil, Mexico, Argentina, Colombia, Peru, Venezuela, Chile, Ecuador, Bolivia, Uruguay, Paraguay	910
Central American Common Market	CACM		Guatemala, El Salvador, Honduras, Nicaragua, Costa Rica	540
Caribbean Community and Common Market	Caricom	10	Barbados, Trinidad, Guyana, Jamaica, Tobago, etc. (22 island states)	530
West African Economic Community	CEAO		Ivory Coast, Mali, Mauretania, Niger, Senegal, Upper Volta	Not available
Econ. Community of West African States	ECOWAS		Benin, Burkino Faso, Cape Verde, Gambia, Ghana, Guinea, Guinea-Bissau, Ivory Coast, Liberia, Mali, Mauretania, Niger, Nigeria, Senegal, Sierra Leone, Togo, Upper Volta	230

The stages of its early development were as follows:

(a) Three countries, Belgium, The Netherlands and Luxemburg formed the Benelux customs union in 1945.

(b) The rebuilding of Germany, the recovery of France, and the industrialisation of Italy all took place. A useful instrument during this period which helped solve adverse balance-of-payments problems for individual countries was the European Payments Union. Undoubtedly American generosity had a lot to do with the rapid recovery of Europe.

(c) In 1952 the six nations, Belgium, France, Germany, Italy, Luxemburg and The Netherlands joined to form the European Coal and Steel Community.

(d) In 1957 the Treaty of Rome was signed, in which the six nations agreed to form the European Economic Community, popularly known as the Common Market. It actually came into existence on 1 January 1958. Its basic ideas were:

  (i) Members would still pursue their own economic policies, seeking their own best performance, but the upward harmonisation of living standards was to be a major aspect of policy.

  (ii) A sufficient degree of coordination and cooperation was envisaged to ensure an overall balance of payments.

  (iii) In choosing their own business cycle policies (i.e. their use of Keynesian economics to manage prosperity) they should consider the effect of their policies on the other members and not do anything that would harm them.

  (iv) Associate members from less developed countries would be considered, who would be granted certain benefits in trade. Turkey, Greece, and several African countries took up associate status.

  (v) Tariffs should be reduced by 10 per cent per year, and at the same time external tariffs against non-members should be raised, or levelled, to the point where a common barrier was erected to all foreign imports.

This planned programme was fully achieved by 1968 when the tenth and final instalment of tariffs between members was removed, and a common external tariff of about 12 per cent was built up against other nations.

24.6.1
Results achieved by the EEC up to 1973

Very good levels of progress were achieved in the realisation of the original objectives of the Community, but problems arose too. The trade of the Community between 1958 and 1970 rose from £10 000 million to £29 500 million. Of this, internal trade with one another rose by 500 per cent from £3000 million to £15 000 million – a very high growth rate by any standards.

24.6.2
Developments since Britain's entry in 1973

On 1 January 1973, the UK became a full member of the EEC as did Denmark and Eire. Norway withdrew at the last moment after a referendum. After a few years in which harmonisation of tariffs was achieved, full status for the new members was finally reached on 1 July 1977. Britain's trade with the EEC has improved considerably since membership began, from 29.6 per cent of total exports in 1973 to 52.6 per cent in 1993.

Imports increased similarly to 50.4 per cent of total imports in 1993. Greece became the tenth member on 1 January 1981, Spain and Portugal became the eleventh and twelfth members on 1 January 1986, and Austria, Sweden and Finland joined on 1 January 1995.

24.6.3
The European
Institutions

Figure 24.2 displays these institutions diagrammatically. There are eight of them: the Council of Ministers, the Commission, The European Parliament, the Court of Justice (supported by a Court of First Instance), the Committee of Permanent Representatives (COREPER), the European Monetary Institute and the Court of Auditors. Their organisation and functions are as follows:

(a) The Council of
Ministers

This consists of one Minister from each of the member states. Generally the Foreign Minister is regarded as the appropriate minister, but on special occasions when particular policies are under discussion the Minister for the Department concerned – say fuel and power, or agriculture – would represent his/her country. Presidency of the Council is taken in turn for six-monthly periods. The Council takes all basic decisions on Union policy, and is empowered to pass minor matters with a simple majority. On major matters a system of weighted voting is used, and a qualified majority is necessary. The weighting gives four votes to major powers, two votes to lesser powers and one vote to very small powers like Luxemburg. In practice the Council has usually wrestled with matters until unanimity is reached, since, particularly on new and controversial policies, it is not deemed wise to force policies upon unwilling partners. However, the growing size and sophistication of the Union has now resulted in there being a general feeling that such a body should be able to accept that majority voting is really enough; the minority should be prepared to accept the majority view.

(b) The Commission

The Commission consists of two commissioners from each major member and one from smaller powers, chosen by agreement. They are pledged to independence of the governments of their countries, and act in accordance with the powers laid down in the Treaty of Rome. They coordinate activity in particular fields, considering issues from a community point of view independent of national interests or aspirations. Their function is to formulate proposals for decision by the Council of Ministers and to supply information to, and answers to questions from, the European Parliament. They have a staff of Union 'Civil Servants' in Brussels, and provide the day-to-day administration of the Union.

(c) The European
Parliament

In June 1979 the first elections were held to the European Parliament. There are 410 members of this directly elected Parliament. Their function is to debate all matters of Union policy, to question both the Commission and the Council of Ministers and to supervise the Union budget. It can compel the Commission to resign en bloc by a two-thirds majority.

By 1990 the idea had developed that the European Parliament should begin to act like a real Parliament and exercise more control over the measures proposed by the Commission and agreed to by the Council of Ministers. A number of topics (about 100) became the subject of serious debate, but at present many of them are bogged down in detailed discussion in committees and it is clear that the transition to full Parliamentary

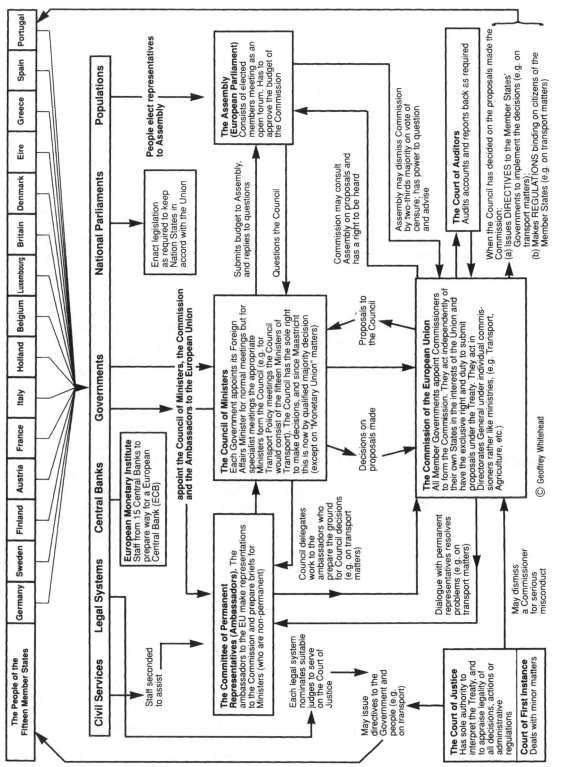

Figure 24.2 The institutions of the European Community (with special reference to transport)

The People of the Fifteen Member States

| Germany | Sweden | Finland | Austria | France | Italy | Holland | Belgium | Luxembourg | Britain | Denmark | Eire | Greece | Spain | Portugal |

Civil Services   Legal Systems   Central Banks   Governments   National Parliaments   Populations

appoint the Council of Ministers, the Commission and the Ambassadors to the European Union

People elect representatives to Assembly

European Monetary Institute Staff from 15 Central Banks to prepare way for a European Central Bank (ECB)

Enact legislation as required to keep Nation States in accord with the Union

The Assembly (European Parliament) Consists of elected members meeting as an open forum. Has to approve the budget of the Commission

Submits budget to Assembly, and replies to questions

Questions the Council

Commission may consult Assembly on proposals and has a right to be heard

Assembly may dismiss Commission by two-thirds majority on vote of censure: has power to question and advise

The Court of Auditors Audits accounts and reports back as required

The Council of Ministers Each Government appoints its Foreign Affairs Minister for normal meetings but for specialist meetings the appropriate Ministers form the Council (e.g. for Transport Policy meetings the Council would consist of the fifteen Ministers of Transport). The Council has the sole right to make decisions, and since Maastricht this is now by qualified majority decision (except on "Monetary Union" matters)

Proposals to the Council

Decisions on proposals made

When the Council has decided on the proposals made the Commission:
(a) Issues DIRECTIVES to the Member States' Governments to implement the decisions (e.g. on transport matters);
(b) Makes REGULATIONS binding on citizens of the Member States (e.g. on transport matters)

© Geoffrey Whitehead

The Commission of the European Union All Member Governments appoint Commissioners to form the Commission. They act independently of their own States in the interests of the Union and have the exclusive right and duty to submit proposals under the Treaty. They act in Directorates General under individual commissioners rather like ministries, (e.g. Transport, Agriculture, etc.)

Council delegates work to the ambassadors who prepare the ground for Council decisions (e.g. on transport matters)

Dialogue with permanent representatives resolves problems (e.g. on transport matters)

May dismiss a Commissioner for serious misconduct

Staff seconded to assist

The Committee of Permanent Representatives (Ambassadors). The ambassadors to the EU make representations to the Commission and prepare briefs for Ministers (who are non-permanent)

Each legal system nominates suitable judges to serve on the Court of Justice

May issue directives to the Government and people (e.g. on transport)

The Court of Justice Has sole authority to interpret the Treaty, and to appraise legality of all decisions, actions or administrative regulations

Court of First Instance Deals with minor matters

decision-making status has a long way to go before it becomes the normal method of making progress in Union affairs.

(d) The Court of Justice

Whenever rules and regulations are promulgated they must inevitably be the cause of disputes between parties favourably or adversely affected. It is for the Court of Justice, composed of learned judges from member nations, to interpret and declare the meaning of disputed passages. Governments, firms and individuals as well as the Community authorities have a right to appeal to the Court of Justice if they are aggrieved by the application of any Union rule.

A further court, the Court of First Instance was set up in 1988.

(e) The Court of Auditors

The Court of Auditors was set up in 1992 to establish closer control of expenditure, which was widely believed to be out of control, with corruption widespread. Its duty is to conduct random investigations where necessary, as well as systematic investigation of published reports and accounts.

(f) The European Monetary Institute

This organisation is set up to permit its members (the European central banks) to make plans for a European System of Central Banks, (ESCB) and the eventual establishment of a European Central Bank (ECB). These bodies will be needed before it is possible to move on to the 'third stage' of economic and monetary union with the creation of a single monetary policy and a single currency.

(g) The Committee of Permanent Representatives

This consists of the 15 ambassadors to the EC from the member countries. Their function is to act as permanent watchdogs on behalf of the Foreign Secretaries (or other Departmental Ministers forming the Council of Ministers). The latter are essentially part-time and rely on the permanent representatives to prepare briefs, advise on procedures, etc. This body – Coreper, the French abbreviation – has proved very effective in getting practical agreement on all sorts of detailed matters and then having them ratified by the Council of Ministers without difficulty. A proposal to make these representatives of greater importance is being aired at the moment.

24.6.4 The Union budget

The Union budget is rather like the British 'estimates' drawn up before the start of the financial year. The Union year is a calendar year, and the budget is prepared in ECUs (European Currency Units). This is a 'currency basket' whose value is related to the trade-weighted influence of the 12 countries which were members on 1 January, 1994. Its value is calculated daily. The total value of the budget when the UK joined in 1973 was 4237 million European Units of Account (EUAs), each Unit of Account being equal to one US dollar. By 1993 the budget had grown to 64 407 million ECUs, the ECU being valued at US$1.17. The details of the budget are given in Table 24.2. In 1973 the budget represented 0.43 per cent of the Community's total gross national product. In 1993, although it was 18 times as big, it only represented 1.2 per cent of the Union's total gross national product. Clearly whatever may be said about the cost per year of being in the European Union, the total budget is a very tiny part of any nation's actual wealth.

Table 24.2 Community spending 1993

Appropriations for payment	Million ECUs	%
1. Administration and staffing	2 284	3.5
2. Agricultural sector	34 943	54.3
3. Declining industries and fisheries	20 710	32.2
4. Social sector	465	0.7
5. Energy, atomic energy and environment	243	0.4
6. Consumer protection, internal market, etc.	291	0.5
7. Research and technological development	2 202	3.4
8. Aid to developing countries	2 856	4.4
9. Reimbursements to members	413	0.6
Total Commission budget	ECU 64 407 m	100.0

There is still 98.8 per cent of the gross national product to be dealt with at a national level.

The Maastricht Treaty, 1992 The Maastricht Treaty is an important document drawn up at a high-powered meeting to assess the progress of the European Community up to that time and to chart the way ahead. The fundamental difficulty was that not all nations on joining had embraced the notion that the ultimate aim of the European Community was to form a federal union of all member states – a political as well as an economic union. Maastricht was a watershed at which fundamental differences came to be aired and the weakest link in the chain was the position of the UK Government. It is significant that while several nations came away from Maastricht determined to seek a further mandate from their electorates about the ratification of the Treaty, the only government that refused to seek a further mandate was the one that really needed to – the UK Government. It hid behind an ancient figment of Britain's unwritten constitution – that once a government has been elected it is entitled to speak for the people. Yet the issue under vital discussion was not debated at all in the election, and that election was won largely by subterfuge on an election programme which proved to be undeliverable.

The Maastricht Treaty made some very important decisions, which included the following:

(a) To set up a Court of Auditors to reduce corruption and the misuse of funds.
(b) To set up the European Monetary Institute, with the 15 national central banks as members, to start the important work of establishing a European Central Bank which would eventually control monetary policy in the interests of the European Union as a whole. Its brief is 'to contribute to the realization of the conditions necessary for transition to the Third Stage of Economic and Monetary Union'. This is envisaged as strengthening the coordination of monetary policies, overseeing the development of the European Currency Unit (ECU) and ECU banknotes, promoting the efficiency of cross-border payments, etc.
(c) *Convergence criteria* Believing that any further movement to European Monetary Union could not really be effective unless the various national economies moved closer together (i.e. converged) the Maas-

tricht Treaty laid down the convergence criteria it expected to see before it would be possible to move to the third stage. They are:

(i) *Price stability* A member state that wished to proceed should have a price performance that is sustainable, with an average inflation rate over the previous year and within 1½ per cent of the three best-performance member states. Inflation to be measured by a consumer price index on a comparable basis, which takes account of differences in national definitions.

(ii) *Budgetary position* At the time of the examination of a country's affairs the Nation concerned should not be the subject of a Council decision under Article 104c(6) of the Treaty (that an excessive deficit exists which is being financed by borrowing rather than taxation).

(iii) *Exchange Rate Mechanism* At the time of entry a member state should have been maintaining its parties within the parity grid of the ERM for at least two years before, and should not, within the same two year period, have unilaterally devalued its currency against that of any other member state.

(iv) *Interest rates* For one year prior to the examination the nation should not have had an average long-term interest rate higher than 2 per cent above the three best performing member states (in terms of price stability).

The 1996 meeting of heads of state or government will decide whether sufficient convergence has occurred and if so will fix a date for proceeding to stage three of monetary union, but if this is not decided upon by 31 December 1997 stage three will go ahead on 1 January 1999.

The Maastricht Treaty goes a considerable way to achieving the aim of many of the signatories to the original Treaty of Rome, that the Treaty should lead to a full monetary union and a political union. There were to be three stages in the achievement of monetary union. They were:

(a) Stage 1. The completion of the single market, by the removal of customs barriers, the establishment of the European Monetary Institute and the European System of Central Banks. This would co-ordinate monetary policies and eventually establish the European Central Bank responsible for a single monetary policy for Europe. This will prevent the national governments manipulating their economies to manage prosperity for their own citizens alone.

(b) Stage 2 envisages a medium-term programme for economic objectives. The chief aim of such a programme would be to encourage greater convergence of economic performance of the member states. A big problem envisaged here is the question of whether the Union is to be enlarged to include all the nations that would like to join it. If this was conceded it would include such nations as Turkey, the Baltic States and possibly the Ukraine, etc., etc. The problem of building up these economies to the point where they could converge with Germany, France, the United Kingdom and Italy might prove to be insuperable. On the other hand, if the present 15 nations form a cosy club of advanced economies, the external tensions of a disunited Europe might recur at some future time. It was the possibility of future 'World Wars' that the Community was originally devised to prevent.

(c) Stage 3 envisages the irrevocable interlocking of exchange rates and the replacement of national currencies by a single European currency, the ECU.

However, this discussion moves us beyond our present discussion. The real question for that 'free trade area' known originally as the European Economic Community, and later known as the European Union, is 'Do we go on and form a United States of Europe, and does that United States of Europe include large parts of Asia (for example, Turkey and Russia east of the Urals)?' The reader is urged to watch developments closely.

24.7
The European Free Trade Area (EFTA)

The remaining EFTA states (Norway, Iceland and Switzerland) have established individual agreements with the EU to preserve the free trade they have traditionally enjoyed with states now in the Union. They have recently re-affirmed their decisions not to become members of the European Union.

24.8
'Trade-diverting' effects of free-trade areas

An important aspect of free-trade areas is their tendency to divert trade from traditional channels towards 'internal' sources of supply within the free-trade area.

24.9
Summary of Chapter 24

1 Free trade tends to be practised today within limited groupings of countries of similar living standards and levels of development.
2 Generally speaking, multilateral trade permits a larger volume of world trade than a series of bilateral trading arrangements.
3 The General Agreement on Tariffs and Trade is an international body that attempts to promote world trade by arranging for tariffs to be reduced. Its name has now changed to the World Trade Organisation.
4 The group of 160 less developed countries attempts through the United Nations Conference on Trade and Development (UNCTAD) to secure a larger share of trade for its members.
5 The main free-trade areas of the world are the European Union, the North American Free Trade Association, the European Free Trade Association, the Latin American Integration Association, the Central American Common Market, the West African Economic Community (a largely French speaking group), the Economic Community of West Africa and the Caribbean Free Trade Area.
6 The Sterling Area formerly consisted mainly of Commonwealth countries, held together in a loose association by the advantages of trading in the British market and by the facilities for finance through the City of London.
7 The European Union is a grouping of 15 major European countries pledged to secure economic and even political union. The 15 countries with their 'Associates' form a market of about 380 million people.

Exercises Set 24

1 What is a free-trade area? What advantages are likely to be achieved by joining such an organisation? Are there any disadvantages?
2 Distinguish between bilateral trade and multilateral trade. Which is more beneficial, and why
3 What is the 'Uruguay Round'? What sort of matters are discussed at such a 'round' and why has the Uruguay Round taken so long to finalise?
4 An Economic Community of West Africa has been established. Examine the economic, social and political implications for the West African nations of such a community.

5   What is the Maastricht Treaty of 1992? What new institutions has it
    founded in the European Union?
6   'Britain has abandoned the Sterling Area and assumed a leading
    European role.' What problems does this pose for (*a*) New Zealand, (*b*)
    France?
7   What was the Treaty of Rome? How successfully have the plans made
    there been achieved?
8   What are the aims of EFTA? Why has Britain left the organisation?
9   'No nation, least of all Great Britain, can remain an island unto itself.'
    What major factors require Britain to form, join and trade with free-
    trade areas?
10 The largest, and most desirable, free-trade area would be a North
    Atlantic Free Trade Area in which the USA, Canada and Europe joined.
    What (*a*) advantages and (*b*) disadvantages for Great Britain are implicit
    in the idea of NAFTA?

Section 6: Macroeconomics

Section of Macroeconomics

25   What is macroeconomics?

**25.1
Introduction**

Adam Smith thought that free enterprise and free trade would produce all the progress that was possible. The task of the economist was to display how man created wealth, but not to direct or guide the economy unnecessarily. Two centuries later there is scarcely a country in the world where the politicians and the economists are not banded together to direct and guide the economy. In most countries, in different ways perhaps, the greatest good of the greatest number is the justification for their activities. We live in an age of the consensus: 'What does everyone think should be done?' It might be claimed that it works at least as well as *laissez-faire* worked in the nineteenth century.

'Macro' is derived from the Greek word *makros* meaning 'large'. We sometimes talk of the universe as a 'macrocosm'. We say a thing is 'macroscopic' when we can see it with the naked eye, in contrast to microscopic things invisible to the naked eye. We now approach macro-economics, the economics of whole societies, after a great many chapters about microeconomics, the economics of individual consumers, individual firms and individual industries. Macroeconomics considers the whole economy from a national point of view.

In studying macroeconomics we turn our attention to the major forces acting and interacting within the economy. What forces are at work in the economy? What levels of activity are being achieved? What levels of activity are desirable? How shall we achieve them when we have decided? These are absorbing problems, made even more interesting because the whole economy stands or falls by what is achieved for the individual. If *I* am not prosperous, what use is it to me that society as a whole is prosperous? What satisfaction do I get, when I am poor, to know that others are rich? If I am unemployed, high levels of general employment do *me* no good, and what use is the general security if I am insecure?

The central problem of economics in the second half of the twentieth century is the management of prosperity to maximise individual and general welfare.

**25.2
The problems of
macroeconomics**

In the chapters which follow we have to study a number of problems which face the government of any country, for macroeconomics is concerned with what actions governments can take to achieve desired ends. In former times, and in a very few countries perhaps still today, the free play of market forces was left to decide the level of national income, and the rate of growth of the economy. As a result of this policy of *laissez-faire* ('let the thing work itself out') the economy tended to grow in spiral-like movements of business activity. Years of furious expansion, called 'booms', were followed by years of consolidation and slower progress, called 'slumps'. The economy was always growing, but it suffered from cycles of activity, spiralling upwards. The more exposed members of society, the poor, and the immigrant, suffered great misery. A cry went out for more conscious control of business activity, and eventually Keynesian economics showed the way to achieve it. More recently, after a quarter of a century of Keynesian economics and 'demand management' by politicians we have turned to 'supply-side' economics, which tries to increase production and wealth by reducing controls on enterprise, management activities, imports and exports, movements of capital, etc. Supply-side economics is to some extent a return to market forces and *laissez-faire*.

Under this final group of studies, then, we must consider:

(*a*) The national income; what it is, how it may be increased and how it may be fairly shared.

(*b*) Business cycles; their causes and cures. This involves a study of deflation, inflation and equilibrium levels of activity in the economy.

(*c*) Keynesian analysis of the economy as a problem of demand management, to ensure that there was always sufficient demand in the economy so that unemployment was largely eliminated.

(*d*) Monetarist policy which seeks to control the inflation caused by Keynesian 'demand-management'.

(*e*) Supply-side economics, which seeks to reduce the adverse effects of Keynesian economics by working in countless different ways to improve effort, productivity, efficiency, responses to changing conditions, etc.

(*f*) Public finance.

(*g*) The various policies governments follow to try to achieve these difficult – and often conflicting – aims.

Exercises Set 25 (Revision questions on microeconomics)

Before proceeding to macroeconomics a set of questions covering the general principles already discussed in microeconomics seems appropriate. The reader is urged to write answers to most of these questions. Only by written practice will the student acquire the facility he/she needs with words and ideas. The questions are deliberately *not* placed in any particular order.

1 What is the difference between private capital and social capital? Give five examples of each.

2 Consider the effects of the introduction of mammoth tankers on (*a*) the price of petrol, (*b*) the South African economy and (*c*) the Port of Glasgow.

3 What is a price index? What difficulties arise in constructing one? What use are price indices when constructed?

4 What is

(*a*) The Balance of Payments on Current Account
(*b*) The Balance of Payments on Capital Account?

What is the connection between the two? Do both balance?

5 'The International Monetary Fund is less influential under a regime of floating exchange rates than it was under the Bretton Woods System.' Explain this statement and outline the IMF's role today.

6 What factors determine the location of an industry today?

7 Why are small firms common in agriculture, building and retailing?

8 'Every additional mouth arrives in the world with a pair of hands. As a result there is no need to fear overpopulation.' Discuss.

9 For the marginal firm in perfect competition, what is the relationship between average cost, marginal cost and price?

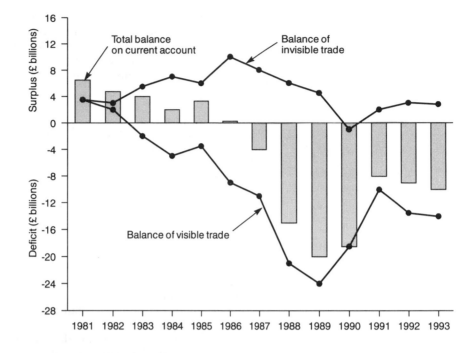

Figure 25.1

10 What is a free-trade area? How may it benefit (*a*) a developed nation, (*b*) a developing nation?

11 Analyse the economic effects of jumbo-jets, each carrying 500 passengers, on (*a*) traffic density at London Airport, (*b*) pilots, (*c*) the economy of Tunisia.

12 UK population and estimated population (thousands):

	Total	Under 15	%	15–64	%	65 & over	%
1979	55 946	12 050	21.5	35 672	63.8	8 225	14.7
1999	58 000	10 500	18.1	32 250	55.6	15 250	26.3

Comment on the economic implications of these figures.

13 What part does the Stock Exchange play in the provision of capital for industry?

14 Explain the make-up of the 'total' figures in Figure 25.1. Would a Chancellor find these results satisfactory or unsatisfactory?

15 The following changes occurred between 1958 and 1993: the index of retail prices was 1962 = 100, 1958 = 91, 1993 = 674.

	1958	1993
	£ million	£ million
Earnings from employment	13 470	118 084
Expenditure on food	4 028	23 230
Expenditure on motor cars	425	5 574
Expenditure on cinema entertainment	85	146

Comment on these figures.

16 What is the function of the rate of interest in the economic system?

17 What is the meaning of 'optimum size' in business units? On what factors does the optimum size depend?

18 Why are film stars paid more than nurses?

19 'High profits are essential for economic growth.' Discuss.

20 What gains arise from international trade? How are these gains shared between the countries concerned?

21 'If we nationalise an industry it is because it will make that industry efficient.' Do you agree?

22 Why does the price of sugar fluctuate more than the price of transistor radios?

23 'The use of container cranes will not benefit dockers.' 'The use of container cranes will enrich the nation.' Discuss these statements.

24 What is the likely effect on the price of rubber of the following?

(*a*) A war in Malaya.
(*b*) The development of a synthetic substitute for rubber.
(*c*) A 10 per cent rise in car sales.
(*d*) Legislation prohibiting the re-moulding of motor car tyres.

25 An increase in demand leads to a rise in price. An increase in price leads to a reduction in demand. Therefore prices can never change, except temporarily. Comment on this reasoning.

26 Economic forces play only a small part in wage determination these days. Do you agree?

27 What is economics? Use your definition to justify the study of economics in the further education of engineers.

28 'It is unfair to expect a nation with a favourable balance of trade to adopt policies which will lead it into balance-of-payments difficulties.' What policies might it be asked to pursue, and why are they justified?

29 What is a non-insurable risk? What is its connection with profit?

30 Why do farm labourers earn less than doctors?

**26.1
Definition**

Alfred Marshall, the English economist (see page 324), defined national income as *the aggregate net product of, and the sole source of payment for, all the agents of production*. It is an enduring definition, and the reader is strongly recommended to memorise it.

It needs, however, to be dissected carefully so that it is fully understood:

(*a*) *The agents of production.* These are the factors which create and then enjoy the national income. We are back to Chapter 1 of this book with man's 'wants' leading to production, which is destroyed by consumption. The agents of production must ceaselessly be employed to create wealth, but their reward is to share in it.

(*b*) *The aggregate net product of.* What are the agents of production producing? They are producing a total (i.e. *aggregate*) collection of goods and services. However, these goods and services cannot all be enjoyed as income, because in creating them depreciation has been suffered on the capital assets of the nation. Machines have been worn out, buildings have grown older, transport facilities have suffered wear and tear. If we do not replace this portion of the nation's capital then we shall in fact be living on our capital and consuming it. The true income created for current employment is not the aggregate product of the agents of production, but the aggregate *net* product (net of depreciation on capital).

(*c*) *The sole source of payments for.* Who will enjoy this income? Who will consume the food, wear the clothing, find shelter in the homes, enjoy peace behind the defences, laugh at the entertainment, take pleasure in the beauty that these agents have created? The answer is: those very factors of production in their human forms. Landowners will enjoy a share paid for from their rents, labourers will purchase a share with their wages, investors will spend the interest and profits that accrue to them on their investments. All these factors of production will share in the wealth. But will it be a fair share? That is a different matter, and it requires us to consider social policies, taxation to redistribute wealth etc. For the moment it is purely the income we are interested in: its distribution comes later.

Let us now repeat and memorise Marshall's splendid definition of National Income:

The national income is the aggregate net product of, and the sole source of payment for, all the agents of production.

**26.2
Why measure the
national income?**

In earlier times there was little interest in National Income statistics. The early economists believed that the economy naturally tended to produce its maximum output at all times, and therefore there was no need to measure it, or try to increase it. Income was essentially private, and if the nation had any interest at all it was in seeing that taxes (such as they were) were paid on the due date. In early Victorian times the total budget of the British Government was only about £30 million, and even by 1881 it was only about £69 million. In that year income tax raised a mere £21 million, while the tax on beer and spirits raised £31 million. This compares with the figure of about £257 390 million estimated to have been spent by various government agencies in the 1993 financial year – the most recent figures available at the time of writing.

Clearly a great change has come over the economy since Gladstone's day. This change is chiefly an increase in welfare, using that word in the widest possible sense. We have gradually come to accept that certain standards of health, education and housing are essential if society is to be kept peaceful; that income is a right to which every family are entitled even if through illness, industrial re-organisation or old age the breadwinner is temporarily or permanently unable to earn it. These principles seem to be generally accepted, although plenty of disputes are possible as to the level of services or income that should be made available.

The pressure towards equality is strong; and since resources are limited, planning becomes essential. It is quite unthinkable that we should ever return entirely to the crude *laissez-faire* of the Victorian era. It follows that a close watch must be kept on the national income, for that is the sole source of payment for all the welfare services that are to be provided. We must stimulate the aggregate net product of our people, so that they have a larger 'cake' to share out. This means we must devise optimum uses for our resources; we must train labour for a wide variety of new jobs, and we must retrain it when a change of technology results in the withering away of old industries.

The government, then, is interested in the national income. It must be measured, considered and criticised. It must be stimulated and expanded if possible, and restrained if it changes in undesirable ways. As the chosen representative of the people, the government has a mandate to pursue particular policies and exert particular influences on the nation's income.

26.3 Factors affecting the size of a nation's income

The size of a nation's income depends upon the quantity and quality of the factor endowments at its disposal. A nation will be rich if its endowments of natural resources are large, its people are skilled, and it has a useful accumulation of capital assets. The following points are of interest:

(a) *Natural Resources.* These include the minerals of the earth, the timber, shrubs and pasturage available; the agricultural potential (fertile soil, regular rainfall, temperate or tropical climate); the fauna and flora; the fish, crustacea, etc., of the rivers and seas; the energy resources, including oil, gas, hydroelectric, geothermal, wind and wave power.

(b) *Human Resources.* Here we are likely to be prosperous if we have a large population, literate and numerate, sophisticated and knowledge-able about wealth-creating processes. It should be well-educated and skilled, with a nice mixture of theory and practice. It should show enterprise, being inventive, energetic and determined in the pursuit of a better standard of living.

(c) *Capital Resources.* A nation must create and then conserve capital resources. This includes not only tools, plant and machinery, factories, mines, domestic dwellings, school, colleges, etc., but a widespread infrastructure of roads, railways, airports and ports. Transport creates the utility of space. It makes remote resources accessible and high-cost goods into low-cost goods by opening up remote areas and bringing them into production.

(d)   *Self-Sufficiency.* Although economists tend to think of the world as one inter-related group of economies, a nation cannot enjoy a large national income if its citizens are not mainly self-supporting. If the majority of the enterprises are foreign-owned there will be a withdrawal of wealth in the form of profits or goods transferred to the investing nation. It is desirable to come to arrangements which are manifestly fair to both parties when foreign development of resources is permitted.

26.4 National income statistics

Every year the Central Statistical Office (CSO) publishes a Government 'Blue Book' called *National Income and Expenditure.* It appears in the summer months and records the figures for income and expenditure up to the previous December. It also shows the figures for at least the last 20 years, so that students of trends in the nation's activity, government expenditure, etc., can compare the figures over the previous two decades.

The compilation of these statistics is clearly a very laborious task. We have to add up the total income of the nation, and there are over 58 million of us. Moreover, in order to double-check and triple-check the answers, the CSO works the figures out in three different ways, each way being based on a different aspect. The three aspects are:

(a)   *The national output* – the creation of wealth by the nation's industries. This is valued at factor cost, so it must be the same as (b) below.
(b)   *The national income* – the incomes of all the citizens.
(c)   *The national expenditure* – because whatever we receive we spend, or lend to the banks who invest it, so that the addition of all the expenditure should come to the same as the other two figures.

Put in its simplest form we can express this as an equation:

National output = National income = National expenditure

To understand the meaning of this relationship let us consider a packet of dehydrated mashed potato. What is the value of such a prepared food? The farmer rented his farm, paying rent to a landlord, and borrowed capital to buy machinery, paying interest on the loan. He employed a farmhand to help him, paying him wages, and he made a profit for himself. Suppose the price of the packet of mashed potato is 0.80. Possibly 0.08 represents the rent paid to the landlord. 0.08 represents the interest on the capital borrowed. 0.12 represents the wages of the labourer, and 0.12 represents the farmer's profit. At this point the farmer sold the potatoes to a manufacturer who also pays rent, interest and wages to his workers, and earns a profit for himself. Let us suppose that these payments are 0.04, 0.04, 0.08 and 0.08. This still leaves the wholesaler and retailer to perform their functions and there is only 0.16 left as their share. The production value of 0.80 is the same thing as the income paid to the various producers who have cooperated in the production of this commodity. Remember, to an economist a commodity is not fully produced until it reaches the final consumer, so that the income received by all these people is part of the production cost. Finally, as we all spend the income we receive, or lend it to the banks who loan it to others to spend, the total income is the same as the total expenditure (ignoring for the moment any credit creation by the banks).

Table 26.1 Calculating national income from total expenditure

UK national expenditure (in £ millions)	1993	Enter current figures here
Expenditure of consumers		
Food	46 327	
Alcoholic drink	24 395	
Tobacco	10 829	
Housing	62 316	
Fuel and light	14 618	
Clothing and footwear	23 322	
Household goods and services	26 160	
Transport and communications	69 624	
Recreation and education	40 537	
Other goods and services	78 521	
Total	396 649	
Add adjustment for tourism (see Note)	1 141	
	397 790	
Add expenditure of non-profit making bodies	7 849	
Total consumer expenditure	405 639	
Central government expenditure	88 226	
Local government expenditure	49 998	
Capital formation	94 715	
Total domestic expenditure at market prices	638 578	
Deduct:		
Decrease in stocks and work in progress	−197	
Taxes on expenditure	−91 361	
Excess of imports over exports	−8 267	
Statistical discrepancy	−91	
	99 916	
	538 662	
Add:		
Subsidies	7 458	
Net property income from abroad	3 062	
	10 520	
	549 182	
Less Estimated depreciation on capital assets	65 023	
Net national product	£484 159 m	

Note

The statistical adjustments are made in the light of experience about these estimates over the past few years.
The adjustment for tourism is made up of:

Expenditure of UK citizens abroad	11 262
Less: Expenditure of foreign visitors to UK	10 121
	1 141

26.5
Using total expenditure for calculating national income

In recent years the figures for national income published in the Blue Book have been given in a different order than that suggested above. The data required are most easily collected by adding up the nation's total expenditure and this now appears as the first method. This is followed by the figures arrived at as a result of adding up incomes, and finally the figures for national output are produced. This illogical sequence is rather unsatisfactory but since all the figures come to the same result it makes no difference really.

The first method of calculating the national income therefore is by counting up the total expenditure of citizens and of firms, government departments and local authorities. Some of this is expenditure on consumption goods, but some of it is investment in fixed assets, buildings, motor vehicles, plant and machinery, etc. This is listed as 'capital formation' in Table 26.1. To offset this, depreciation on existing assets has been deducted.

One difficulty in counting expenditure is that many items purchased have taxes added on to their sales price, while some are subsidised, i.e. sold cheaper than their cost price. Adjustments for taxes and subsidies are made in the table. The figures shown are the latest available, but a column is left vacant in which the current year figures may be entered by the reader if this is considered helpful. They will be found in the Blue Book *United Kingdom National Accounts* for the current year.

26.6
Using factor incomes for calculating national income

What has the nation received as income? The answer is that every citizen has received his/her rewards as a factor of production, i.e. he/she has received rent, wages, interest or profit. The Blue Book lists these as shown in Table 26.2. It sometimes puzzles students to know why the figures for national output should agree with the figures for national income. The explanation is that when we value output, asking ourselves what it is worth, the answer is that it is worth what the entrepreneur who arranged for its production received for it at the time it was sold. Since the sale price of the product covers all his/her costs (i.e. the rewards paid to the factor's land, labour and capital) with a profit left over which is the entrepreneur's own reward, the final sales price is really made up of the rewards to factors (i.e. their incomes). Every commodity is merely a collection of services of those who proposed its production, made its raw materials available, worked on its progress to completion, transported, warehoused, marketed and finally retailed it. The reason why the output and income figures are the same, is that they *are* the same thing. The wealth that we create is the same thing as the income we can enjoy, when viewed nationally.

In Table 26.2 the following points are of interest:

(a) The contributions made by the employer to National Health Insurance and other funds are treated as part of the incomes of the employee. Clearly these funds are accumulated for the benefit of the employees, who make use of them when their circumstances (illness, unemployment or old age) entitle them to do so. Similarly the cost of free clothing, food, etc., to members of the armed forces are classed as income of the soldier, sailor, etc.
(b) The surpluses of public corporations and public enterprises are part of the national income. Although not enjoyed by any individual they are part of the common fund administered by the government.
(c) The total income received must be reduced by the amount of depreciation suffered on the nation's capital, whether privately or socially owned.

Table 26.2 Calculating national income from factor incomes

UK national income rewards to factors (in £ millions)	1993	Enter current figures here
Incomes from employment		
Wages and salaries	301 860	
Pay in cash and kind of HM Forces	6 651	
Employers' contributions to National Health Insurance	22 707	
Employers' contributions to other funds	21 678	
	352 896	
Incomes from self-employment	61 346	
Other incomes		
Profits of companies, public corporations and public bodies (councils, etc.)	77 106	
Rent	52 872	
Imputed charge for consumption of capital	3 942	
	548 162	
Less: Stock appreciation	−2 359	
	545 803	
Add: Net property income from abroad	3 062	
Statistical discrepancy	317	
	3 379	
	549 182	
Less: Estimated depreciation on capital assets	65 023	
Total factor incomes	£484 159 m	

Note
The discrepancy is a small error (less than 0.1%) in the collection of all these figures.

26.7 Using the national output for calculating national income

The national output is the total of consumer goods and services, plus the total of the producer goods created by the various firms in the industries of the nation. The figures are collected on a 'value-added' basis to avoid double-counting. For example, suppose the forestry industry cuts timber and hauls it to a mill; the value of the timber when sold to the sawmill owner will be the value added by the primary producer, i.e. the forestry firm. When the sawmill has kiln-dried the timber, cut it to planks and finally sells them to a furniture manufacturer, we cannot value the output of the sawmill at the total price paid by the furniture manufacturer. The price he/she pays includes the forestry price, so that only the 'value added' must be counted as the output of the millowner.

The total output of all the industries gives the **gross national product**. For several reasons this is not yet a correct answer for national output. Since some of this output is for the benefit of owners abroad (i.e. foreign investors), it cannot be regarded as our output. Similarly, we have the benefit of output achieved in foreign countries by our investments abroad. The

Table 26.3 Calculating national income from national output

UK national product by industry (in £ millions)		1993	Enter current figures here
Agriculture, forestry and fishing		10373	
Mining, quarrying, oil and gas		12147	
Manufacturing		118294	
Electricity, gas and water supply		13994	
Construction		29221	
Distribution, hotels, catering, repairs		78348	
Transport and communications		46263	
Financial intermediation, real estate, etc.		133956	
Public administration, defence and social security		38199	
Public health and education services		57457	
Other services		31292	
Total domestic output		569544	
Deduct:			
Adjustment for financial services	23741		
Estimated depreciation on capital assets	65023		
		88764	
		480780	
Add:			
Statistical discrepancy	317		
Net property income from abroad	3062		
		3379	
Aggregate net national product		£484159 m	

result of these movements is a favourable balance to us, and appears in Table 26.3 as a net figure; net property income from abroad. The figures for output have been reduced in the table to take account of stock appreciation in the year. An industry which is worth more at the end of the year due to stock appreciation cannot claim this is 'output' of the current year. Another 'adjustment for financial services' was caused by high interest payments to foreigners. These reduce the output of banks, because foreigners get the benefit. The statistical discrepancy is the result of errors in the collection of figures. It is only about 0.1 per cent of the total, and is unavoidable when so many figures are collected.

Finally, the total figure for the output has to be reduced by the amount of depreciation on capital assets. The 'net' national product, which citizens can enjoy, is thus determined.

26.8 Difficulties in calculating national income

When calculating the national income there are very great difficulties to be overcome. The collection of data is never easy, but before it is even collected we must define clearly what information we require. The problems of definition, of double-counting, of collection (and compulsion if necessary), of analysis and interpretation, and finally of publication, are very great.

Definitions. A special volume of information (*National Accounts Statistics – Sources and Methods*) is published regularly by HM Stationery Office. It contains reference numbers for all the figures which appear in published tables of information. Wherever these figures are used the reference number is printed too, and the reader or student can turn up the exact definition when required. The 'Blue Book' *United Kingdom National Accounts* also has a glossary of terms which lists any changes made in definitions in the current edition. For example, the definition of 'consumers' expenditure' in Table 26.1 is:

> *Consumers' expenditure.* Personal expenditure on goods and services consisting of household expenditure on goods and services (including income in kind, imputed rent of owner-occupied dwellings and administrative costs of life assurance and superannuation schemes) and final expenditure by non-profit making bodies. Excluded are interest payments, all business expenditure and the purchase of land and buildings.

It follows that if a limited company buys headed notepaper for use in the office it will not be included; but if the Automobile Association, a voluntary association of motorists, does the same thing it will be included as expenditure by consumers.

If the reader envisages the enormous variety of purchases made of the sort just described he/she will get some idea of the work involved in obtaining these statistics.

Double-counting. We have already seen that double-counting can occur when output is considered, so that each firm must only count the 'value added' to the product by its activities. A similar type of double-accounting might occur where gifts take place. If a father earns an income of £12 500.00 and sends his son £500.00, this £500.00 must not be counted as income of both father and son. Similarly, where a husband gives his wife housekeeping money the family income is not increased. Where taxation redistributes income from rich to poor we must be careful not to count both amounts: if it is counted as income to the rich we must leave out the welfare payments to the poor.

26.8.1 Inadequate information caused by poor collection procedures

Some figures are derived from other figures collected for quite different purposes. Thus income tax payments are used to discover much information about incomes, but as many people pay no income tax there is a gap in the figures where these lower incomes are concerned. We can get some pretty broad ideas of how many there are of such persons because every employee pays National Health contributions. The difference between the number of incomes that are taxed and the number of persons paying National Health contributions must be the lower-paid workers. How much do they earn, though? We shall have to employ sampling techniques to discover this, based on statistically selected samples from a range of industries and firms.

26.8.2 Analysis, interpretation and publication

In the analysis and interpretation of these figures it is necessary to decide what will be the most useful information for the purposes of those eventually using the data. Often it is the trend that is interesting, for where public expenditure is involved the optimum use of resources requires us to avoid expenditure where possible. An education authority may force a few

Table 26.4 Consumers' expenditure at current prices and base year prices

Consumers' expenditure in £ millions	1979 Base year	1993 at current prices	1993 at 1979 prices
Food	20 998	46 327	17 118
Alcoholic drink	8 665	24 395	7 003
Tobacco	4 234	10 829	3 103

Source: National Income and Expenditure, 1993, adapted.

more children into classrooms for a few years to avoid building an extra school with a rather limited life use. The bulge in the birth-rate will soon pass, and an under-utilised building will then be left on the authority's hands.

If we wish to study trends the index-number approach may be the most useful. If we wish to know absolute figures it is desirable to publish also a table where these absolute figures have been adjusted to take account of price changes. For example, two of the tables in the *National Blue Book* are about Consumer Expenditure at Current Prices and at 'base year' prices. The extracts in Table 26.4 from a recent edition show the difference. The reader will notice what a contrast there is between the impressions conveyed about the consumption of these products by the two sets of figures. Whereas, looking at the current prices, it appears that consumption of food, alcoholic drink and tobacco more than doubled in the 14 years, it in fact fell in every case, and the nation ate more carefully, drank less alcohol and smoked less than it did in 1979. The apparent increase in expenditure was entirely due to rising prices and these rising prices, as any student of economics would expect, actually reduced demand over the 14 years.

In publication there is a further difficulty. Firms and industries using the published data will want them to be as useful as possible, but if definitions are repeatedly up-dated the figures of previous years become less useful for showing trends since the basis on which they were calculated has been changed. One has to accept a compromise between keeping a series of figures unbroken and keeping the series meaningful in a society that is changing. The reader who is interested in such statistical problems is recommended to read *Statistics for Business Made Simple*.

26.9 Uses and limitations of national income statistics

There are many uses of national income statistics, but the economist must be careful in the conclusions he/she draws. Sweeping assertions made from statistical material have so often been proved wrong, that the popular view has become that there are 'lies, damned lies and statistics'. This is often unfair to the statisticians; it is the politician or economist who uses them carelessly and without remembering their limitations, who is responsible for the trouble.

The following uses are the most important:

(a) *As a basis for assessing and comparing the standards of living.* When considering the standard of living of people at any given time we must remember the difference between money incomes and real incomes, and must remember the distribution of income. A wealthy nation may have its wealth distributed evenly or unevenly. In comparing changes in the standard of living over the years the total population affects the average income, so that average income per head will be a more valuable indication of living standards than total National Income.

Comparisons between countries must take into account such matters as the climate of each country concerned. African incomes compare more favourably with British incomes if you leave out of the British income the portion necessarily expended on shelter, heating and warm clothing. Economic welfare is not the same as social welfare, for the economist does not exclude antisocial production from production. Thus it may be argued that the creation of 'disservices' reduces national income rather than enhances it. Examples of disservices might be the creation of methods of destruction, gambling dens and 'useless' advertising. A.C. Pigou, in his great work, *The Economics of Welfare*, saw any national income as the source of the welfare of its people; but the figure of private net product must be reduced by the extent to which it embodies disservices, to give the social net product. Thus the pollution of rivers by industries is a reduction in the social welfare that can be enjoyed by the people.

The division between consumption and investment is also important when comparing the national incomes of different countries, or of the same country between one period and another. Thus if a country's wealth is being mainly used to create capital goods the standard of living will be reduced. Politicians in Britain were often accused in earlier times of promising 'Jam tomorrow, but never jam today'. This is currently true of many developing countries; the accumulation of capital is a bitter process.

(b) *As an aid to government in planning the economy.* The national income figures are a useful base from which to start the control of the economy. By measuring what that income is we can see what is needed, and what it is possible to achieve in the future. The government becomes aware of the growth areas in the economy, and the areas where growth is less than average. This helps it to plan the location of industry before serious structural unemployment starts to occur, and to keep the whole nation making progress. It can correct tendencies which appear to be undesirable because they do not conform with the expressed national aspirations of the people, and it can see which industries need developing and which should be contracted.

26.10 Summary of Chapter 26

1 Alfred Marshall defined the national income as 'the aggregate net product of, and the sole source of payment for, all the agents of production'.

2 We measure the national income because we wish to control the economy to obtain the maximum economic welfare from it.

3 There are three methods of counting up the national income. They are the aggregate-net-production method, the total-factor-incomes method and the total-national-expenditure method.

4 In all these methods care is needed to avoid double-counting.

5 Clear definitions of the measurements to be made are essential, and must be borne in mind when using or interpreting the data.

Exercises Set 26

1 What is the national income? How is it measured?
2 In what three ways can the national income be measured? Why are the three methods sure to give the same answer apart from residual errors?
3 What are the main factors affecting the standard of living?
4 The national income of Great Britain has changed as follows:

£ *million*
1948	10 517
1958	20 408
1968	36 686
1978	140 740
1988	351 710

Does this mean that the average Briton is better off? What other information would be helpful in giving a clear picture of the changes in the standard of living over these years?
5 Distinguish between 'real' national income and 'money' national income, using the following figures to illustrate your answer.

	1958	1963	1968	1978	1988
National income (£ million)	20 000	27 000	37 000	141 000	387 000
Index of final-output prices	90	100.0	120	374	790

6 What factors affect the size of a country's national income? Illustrate your answer by reference to the economy of your own country.
7 Distinguish between national income and national capital. Under what circumstances could a nation be said to be living on its capital?
8 Why is it difficult to compare the national income of one country with that of another?
9 Which of the following would you include in the national income:

(a) Wages paid to farm labourers.
(b) Compensation paid by an insurance company to a motorist.
(c) Family allowances.
(d) A win on the football pools.
(e) A husband's birthday gift to his wife of £50.
(f) The royalty earned by an author.

10 'Wages' in national incomes statistics are defined as 'the cash earnings of wage earners before deduction of personal tax and National Insurance contributions, plus income in kind less expenses of employment'. Why is such a definition necessary, and what are the implications behind each part of it?

27 The development of economic theory

27.1 Theory and practice

The early economists were essentially observers of the practical affairs of men. They wished to know how the economy worked, and began their study with careful observations of actual workshops, mines and distribution systems – the microeconomic approach which examines small units within the economic system, in order to draw general conclusions about the economy. The earliest economic theories were explanations of how the economy worked, not models for developing it along lines conceived to be desirable. There are analogies with the early development of the natural sciences here. Chemistry had to develop a body of knowledge about elements and compounds before it could recognise a pattern in their formation. Once the early theories had been developed it became possible to formulate hypotheses, predict the qualities of elements not yet discovered and eventually manufacture elements not found in nature. In the same way economic theory developed from a practical understanding of the affairs of men, to proposals for influencing economic affairs.

It is therefore helpful at this point to see how economic theory developed over the years and came to be so widely discussed in everyday life. It is unfortunate that in developing their theories economists were differently placed from their colleagues in the natural sciences, in that they were 'social' scientists. They could not conduct controlled experiments to test the truths of their theories. Having embarked upon a particular economic policy, governments and their economic advisers must see it through, at least until the point where it is manifestly unsatisfactory. Sometimes Armageddon itself is required before policies are changed. It has been truly stated that we need both theory and practice in the modern world. 'Theory without practice is barren; practice without theory is blind,' says one philosopher. How did economic theory develop over the centuries?

The modern world may be regarded as having started in the seventeenth century, when the establishment of the nation state in England was fully complete, and the struggle for the domination of the world's resources among the developing colonial powers began. Historically four main schools of economic thought developed in the UK and the USA. They were mercantilism, classical economics, Keynesian economics and, very recently, monetarism. We shall deal briefly with three of these in this chapter; a discussion of monetarism is given later (see Section 28.5).

27.2 Mercantilism

Mercantilism was the product of nationalism, and the desire to develop national power. The mercantilist philosophers sought to know how nations became wealthy in order that their nations might achieve wealth. They found the cause of wealth to be the trade carried on by merchants, and sought to increase the strength of the State so that it could support commercial interests around the world. Throughout the two centuries when mercantilism was most influential commercial wars were frequent, and sea power became all-important.

The mercantilists were preoccupied with the importance of precious metals, which alone permitted an expanding economy and the support of armed forces. The essential thing was to achieve a 'balance of payments', or rather an imbalance of payments (exports exceeding imports), the balance of which could be taken in specie or precious metal. In order to achieve this, exports must be cheap (labour cost must be kept low) and imports must be excluded by protectionist laws – such as the 'Corn Laws' which kept out foreign corn and the Navigation Acts which ensured that goods to and from the colonies were carried in British ships.

The weakness of the mercantilist system was that it believed trade, not industrial production, was the source of wealth. It was for the developing industrial revolution to burst the restrictive bonds of a protectionist mercantile society, and quicken the pace of economic growth.

27.3
Classical economics

Classical economics began with the work of Adam Smith, the author of *The Nature and Causes of the Wealth of Nations*. His life and work have been described earlier (see Section 2.4). He and those who followed him, particularly Ricardo and Mill, believed that the power-house behind the quickening pace of the economy was capital investment. The tight controls of a nation state were not, they believed, the best way to ensure efficient capital accumulation, and the doctrine of *laissez-faire* already described was developed to permit greater freedom for the individual entrepreneur. The contributions of Ricardo and Mill have already been described (see Sections 15.2 and 15.3).

In seeking to impose order upon economic theory, classical economists were most concerned to explain the enduring problems of unemployment and poverty amid plenty. The French economist, Jean B. Say, had developed a so-called 'Law of Markets' which held that every extra supply placed upon the market by an expanding production system creates its own demand. Because the factors which created the supply are rewarded with extra income, there is always just enough demand to clear the market of supplies. The economy has its own natural tendency to operate at the full employment level, with the rate of interest acting to ensure that savings and investment were always equal. That part of the national income that was not spent (savings) was available as loanable funds. If the demand for funds was strong and interest rates were high, savings would be encouraged and the supply of loanable funds would rise to meet the demand. If the demand for funds was weak and the rate of interest was low, savings would be discouraged and expenditure would rise as consumers increased consumption. Either way the market would be cleared. There might be a temporary oversupply of one product or another, but incomes would be switched to other commodities and alternative employment would become available in developing industries.

Although we now know this theory to be an oversimplification, since it takes no account of fluctuations in the flow of funds around the economy, it was accepted in its day as a sound explanation of an automatic mechanism working in the economy. The fact that hoarding and saving sometimes exceed investments, that a balance between imports and exports is not always achieved and that taxes collected and government expenditure are rarely identical weakens the theory for a real world.

In fact, Say's theory in any case took no account of the possible oversupply of factors, especially labour. Even if there was no oversupply of goods, and the money available to buy them was always of the same value, this did not mean that there would not be a surplus of labour. Later classical economists closed this loophole by using two further theories with which we are familiar: the law of diminishing returns and the marginal productivity theory.

The **law of diminishing returns** states that if successive increments of one factor (say labour) are applied to a fixed quantity of another factor (say land) eventually each extra increment will produce less – in other words, the productivity of labour will fall. The average output of labour will fall, but the marginal product will fall even faster.

The **theory of marginal productivity** holds that each unit of a factor of production will be paid the value of its marginal physical product, i.e. the marginal revenue produced by the sale of the marginal output. The more units of labour employed the less would be the wages. Any unemployed units of labour could always secure work if they were prepared to work for less. Therefore, using all these theories, there could be no *general* oversupply and no *general* unemployment.

Naturally those who believed in the free-enterprise economy found these explanations attractive, despite the evidence of widespread unemployment and poverty around them. They were well aware of the trade cycle of alternate booms and slumps. This was well documented after 1792.

**27.3.1
Business cycles**

There were 15 cycles of business activity between 1792 and 1913, with an average of eight years to each cycle. Each cycle of activity consisted of an upward movement of business activity lasting about 3½ years before reaching a peak from which it fell away rapidly into a depression, which endured rather more stubbornly, taking about 4½ years on average to recover.

No two cycles of business activity were alike, and all were to some extent related to their own peculiar economic level of development, or to some external event like war. For example, the boom years of 1791–94 were connected with a mania for building canals, and the boom years of 1825, 1836 and 1845 were all connected with surges of speculative activity connected with railway construction. The severity of the depressions following these booms were deepened by the loss of capital from private savings which had occurred during the speculations. Excessive saving is certainly connected with depressions.

Some of the chief causes of trade cycles are outlined below.

(a) Fluctuations caused by the durable nature of producer goods

When a machine-tool industry is set up, it seems inescapable that fluctuations in business activity must occur. Suppose, for example, an industry is established to make a new type of machine for which there is a demand of 1000. The life of these machines is 10 years on average. At first the industry will be looking everywhere for engineers to make the first 1000 machines, poaching labour from similar industries with offers of higher wages, and thus helping to create boom conditions. Once the first factories are equipped the boom will ease off, and eventually the industry will settle down to producing the annual requirement of, say, 100 machines. Engineers attracted to the industry in boom times will now be unemployed.

Not only this, but there is a multiplying effect in the economy of the boom enjoyed by the engineers, because they spend their wages instead of saving them. The boom wages of the engineers provided prosperity for grocers, publicans, landlords, bookmakers and many other trades. The extent to which this multiplying effect ramifies through the economy depends on the propensity to consume of the original recipients of the income. (This is explained more fully later. The point here is that there is also a multiplying effect when the depression comes along. The unemployed engineer buys less food, less clothing, less alcohol and bets less frequently.)

Pursuing the example further, this industry is now supplying 100 machines per year as a regular undertaking. Suppose there is a 10 per cent increase in demand for the product made by the machines. This requires 100 extra machines, because the industry consists of 1000 machines. The 100 extra machines mean that the size of the machine-tool industry is doubled. Once again a mad scramble starts for men to meet this increased demand; but when the order has been met there will again be a need for only 100 machines a year for nine years, when 200 will again be required.

The name 'accelerator' has been given to a movement of this sort which injects spending power into the economy and causes a surge of activity.

Clearly all sorts of variations are possible in such a cyclical activity. For instance, the 10 per cent rise in demand might fall away in the following year leaving excess capacity in the industry. This would be corrected by not ordering any machines at all, thus leaving the industry in a very depressed state indeed.

(b) Fluctuations caused by changing expectations

Some primary industries are particularly susceptible to fluctuations because of climatic conditions. Thus sugar-cane harvests can be decimated by hurricanes, wheat crops fail through diseases, frozen rivers interrupt supplies from particular regions. The initial effect is a sharp rise in prices which encourages producers in other areas to think that it will pay to turn factors over to that type of production. Once established, such new regions form severe competition to the established suppliers, and in normal or good years the world price will fall to a very low level. Sometimes in such circumstances producers band together to control the price at which they will sell the product, but this only maintains the industries in existence and often encourages further suppliers to come in. Sooner or later someone cuts the price and 'the bottom falls out of the market'. Plantations are abandoned and the jungle creeps in. The whole cycle of activity starts again.

(c) Fluctuations caused by the Gold Standard mechanism

It also appears likely that the regularity of the trade cycles between 1792 and 1913 resulted from the monetary movements inseparable from the Gold Standard mechanism. This has already been fully explained (see Chapter 23). Of the 15 cycles only three were longer than nine years and only one was less than seven years. By contrast, after the Gold Standard was abandoned in 1914, a very long depression set in once the boom war-time conditions had ended after 1918.

Whatever the causes of the trade cycle might be, in the first half of the nineteenth century the supporters of *laissez-faire* stressed the inevitable nature of recovery in any slump period, and advised against any government interference which might disturb the *automatic* recovery mechanism. We have already seen that John Stuart Mill recognised that the key to poverty amid plenty lay in a fairer distribution of wealth, but there was as yet no power that could compel the redistribution of wealth through a tax system. Humanitarians like Dr Barnardo and Elizabeth Fry did something to redress the miseries of particular groups, and many poor people emigrated to seek a better life elsewhere, but the century proved to be one of slow advance for the artisan classes and little progress for the unskilled. Gradually a slightly more optimistic climate developed.

Classical economics was to develop into the mainstream of economic thought in Britain, Europe and the USA after 1870. Alfred Marshall was its most original mind, and marginal analysis was its changed approach. The economics of Smith, Malthus, Ricardo and John Stuart Mill was transformed into a more mathematical, diagrammatic demonstration of the forces at work in the economy.

27.3.2 Alfred Marshall (1842–1924)

Alfred Marshall was the son of the cashier of the Bank of England. His father intended him to enter the Church, and gave him a strictly classical education, but eventually the young man rebelled. Instead of going to Oxford, he went to Cambridge to study mathematics and physics. Here he became an agnostic, but true to his basic philosophy never spoke against religion. Marshall disliked controversy, and claimed little originality for himself. He held that the great economists who had preceded him – Smith, Malthus, Ricardo and Mill – had developed techniques which were appropriate for their times, and which held within them the new approach he and others had developed. His great work, *Principles of Economics*, did not appear until 1890, having been 20 years in preparation. His ideas were thus later in publication than those of some of his contemporaries, but it was in Marshall's nature to rewrite and refine until he had a definitive work.

Most of the mainstream ideas of modern economics are to be found in Marshall's *Principles*. The ideas of internal and external economies of scale, of marginal utility, elasticity of demand and supply, downward-sloping demand curves and discriminating monopoly are either explicitly or implicitly included.

Marshall's work was greatly appreciated in the UK. The Victorian era was always ready to give recognition to a finished great work, even if Continental critics might justly claim that most of the ideas had already been published in lesser volumes. Marshall was optimistic about Capitalism; he wanted economics to uplift the ordinary man and, after ending his poverty, lead him on to a noble life. There would be many ordinary men today who would hold that it had done so, or has at least done as well as other systems supposedly more directly concerned to advance the underprivileged. Before this could be so, however, a change had to be brought about in many fundamental aspects of the capitalist system. The end of the trade cycle after the 1914–18 war ended any belief in the automatic nature of recovery in two decades of unrelieved depression. A new economics was required, and waiting to give it expression was a new, twentieth-century voice, a Cambridge economist called John Maynard Keynes.

27.4 Introduction to Keynesian economics

The war activity of 1914–18 provided a particularly strong boom which was followed by a very severe depression which showed no signs of responding to any 'automatic' recovery mechanism. The expected boom never came, and a long period of unrelieved underemployment and unemployment bred bitter feelings among working people everywhere. The staple industries – coalmining, shipbuilding, the iron and steel trades, cotton and woollen manufacturing and chemicals – were badly hit, and a general depression not only in Europe but in North America prevailed. Agriculture was very depressed, and the American frontier, which during the nineteenth century had done much to cushion unemployment in North America – Go West Young Man! – had now been fully developed and offered reduced opportunities. One or two industries – motor vehicles, radio and cinematography – flourished but offered little compensation for the deep depression in a whole range of major industries.

27.4.1
John Maynard
Keynes (1883–1946)

John Maynard Keynes has been called the greatest economist of the twentieth century. One has to go back to Malthus and Ricardo to find economists who influenced their own times as greatly as Keynes. His ideas were not all new, but he altered those he borrowed, and constructed an economic model of the capitalist system that pinpointed age-old weaknesses. His great work was entitled *General Theory of Employment, Interest and Money* and appeared in 1936. The basic concept of the General Theory was 'effective demand'. The level of effective demand is determined by the total National Income, and how much of it is spent or saved. If there is a high propensity to consume (the consumption function) then employers will deem it profitable to employ labour and expand production. The level of employment is therefore determined by the aggregate demand in the economy, since that alone inspires confidence among entrepreneurs. The trouble with the great slump was that too few people were spending. Too many were saving for a rainy day unaware that it had already arrived.

Thrift in the early days of capitalism had been a good thing, because the postponer of current consumption was only doing so in order to invest in industry. As the capitalist system developed, the functions of saving and investment had become separated. The entrepreneur of today is not himself a saver, but an investor only, investing other people's savings. This means that the thrift of those postponing current consumption will affect the level of activity in the economy if entrepreneurs are unwilling to invest. Nervous expectations about the prospects of profitability can lead to a reduction in business activity and a depression, or slump.

With one simple idea Keynes had solved the mystery of the capitalist system: the occurrence of business cycles which cause unemployment and poverty amidst plenty. Cycles of business activity are caused by an imbalance between savings and investment. Low levels of activity, and underemployment, are caused by a lack of demand in the economy. To cure unemployment, encourage spending: down with thrift. If the business world was unwilling to spend because it saw no prospects of profitability why should not the government influence employment directly by proceeding with public works of any and every sort? *It was for the government to manage prosperity.*

27.5
Keynes and the
rate of interest

There are several features of Keynesian economics which require explanation. First of all let us consider the rate of interest. Keynes agreed with the classical economists that people held stocks of money in order to meet their everyday needs (the transactions motive) and in order to be ready for a rainy day (the precautionary motive). He did not agree with them that after these two motives were satisfied they would either spend the rest, or lend it to some entrepreneur who would use it to expand industry. He showed that there was in fact a further motive (which he called the **speculative motive**) for holding money.

Imagine that the rate of interest is low (in Keynes' day, say, 4 per cent). A person having money to spare might invest £100 in 4 per cent stock issued by some entrepreneur, or a 4 per cent gilt-edged stock issued by the Treasury. Now, suppose interest rates rise to 8 per cent. Our stockholder, trying to recover the money invested to meet some domestic need or other, finds that the value of the stock has fallen to £50. No one is going to pay £100 for 4 per cent stock when new stock is offering 8 per cent. The only way to equate old stocks with new stocks is for the price of the old stock to fall to half its original value. Therefore, when interest rates are low, or expected to rise, there is a logical reason for holding money and not investing it. The person who invests will almost certainly suffer capital losses. Of course the reverse is true in times when interest rates are expected to fall. If interest rates fall (say to 2 per cent) the stock will increase in value (to £200). But in slump times, when interest rates are at rock bottom, a fall is unlikely. Therefore in slump times there is no automatic method of recovery. In the Great Depression the investment needed to get the economy on the move could not be obtained because the 'liquidity trap' was operating. All those who had funds available, including the banks, would not invest for fear of capital losses should a recovery raise interest rates in the economy. Unless people surrendered their liquidity entrepreneurs could not get the economy going, but people would not surrender their liquid assets while the economy was so depressed.

This destruction of the old belief that an economy would automatically aim at full employment turned Keynes' attention to the question 'What does control the level of employment?'

27.6
The national income equilibrium diagram

Keynes showed that there was a close link between the amount of income a person received and the amount of it that was spent, or consumed. Only the very poorest people spend every penny they receive as income. More wealthy people save some proportion of their income, and as incomes rise the proportion saved tends to increase. Thus the 'propensity to save' increases as income rises, and the 'propensity to consume' declines. It follows that for the nation as a whole, the national income received in any one period will be spent in the following period to the extent that it is not saved. When the national income is low there will be a tendency for most of it to be spent, because citizens will be buying essential items, but as national income rises the marginal propensity to save (i.e. the propensity to save some part of the increase in income) will rise, and the whole of the income received will not be spent. However, some of the savings will be used by entrepreneurs to build new capital assets, etc. (i.e. investment) but some portion may not be invested. We can follow the argument more easily if we consider a diagram, as in Figure 27.1.

27.7
Flows of money around the economy

If governments are to inject purchasing power into an economy where exactly should they do it? We have said several times that there is a circular flow of money round the economy, from the firms to the individual members of the public and back again. We must now build up a detailed picture of this circular flow of income, and in particular look for suitable injection points. We can do this best by considering a set of diagrams of which Figure 27.3 is the first. Study this diagram now (see page 329).

27.8
Managing prosperity – the nature of the problem

We must start our consideration of the control of the economy in the 1930s when the capitalist world was staggering through the worst slump it had ever experienced. The persistent general unemployment which had been such a feature of the troughs of the trade cycles over the previous century was more persistent and more general than ever before. A good deal of criticism of the capitalist system prevailed as a result, and since previous booms had been

(*Continued on page 331*)

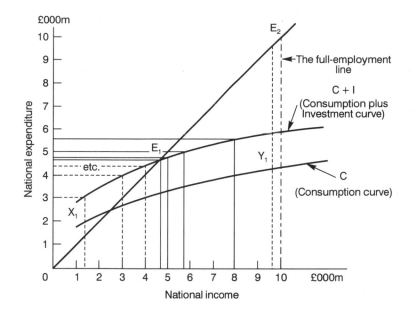

Figure 27.1 The national income equilibrium diagram

Notes

1 In this diagram the income of the nation has been plotted against the expenditure of the nation, on the same scale. The line OE_2 is at 45° to the axes and must represent the situation where income equals expenditure. In mathematical terms it is the locus of points where income equals expenditure. We shall see that whenever the nation is spending all the income it receives the economy is said to be in equilibrium. This means that the economy is not tending to expand at all, nor tending to contract, but is maintaining the same size all the time.

2 The consumption curve shown on the diagram represents the propensity of citizens to consume. At high incomes they are tending to consume a much smaller proportion of their incomes than previously – whereas at very low incomes consumption is greater than the income received. This must mean dis-saving of some sort: some citizens are living on their savings; others are – by burglary or other criminal activities – living off the savings of others.

3 Because some of the savings are borrowed by entrepreneurs for investment the actual income spent is greater than consumption, and the curve we need to look at is the C + I (consumption plus investment) curve.

4 Consider the situation where national income is £8000 million. The C + I curve shows that expenditure is nowhere near the 45° line, but much less, about £5700 million. This means that only £5700 million is going back to the entrepreneurs in the present period out of the £8000 million they paid out in the previous period. Clearly they have stocks left unsold, and cannot pay out £8000 million this time. They have only £5700 million to pay out. National income falls to this figure. Some people lose their jobs, and some assets cease to be used.

5 Do we spend all this £5700 million? No – only about £5000 million. In the next period entrepreneurs have only about £5000 million to pay out, and we spend only about £46000 million. Therefore in the next period only about £4600 million can be paid out in incomes. More people are laid off, and more factories close.

6 Fortunately, at this level we have reached the 45° line on the diagram, where income equals expenditure. This time we do spend all our income and the entrepreneurs can pay out the same income in the next period. We have an economy in equilibrium!

7 Before proceeding with the argument, note that when income is very low, as at point X_1, the economy will expand up to equilibrium at E_1. The X_1 income is only about £1300 million but we are spending on the C + I curve £3000 million. Dis-saving is taking place. In the next period the entrepreneurs can pay out £3000 million, but we shall spend about £4000 million. The process continues until we reach E_1.

8 We see therefore that for every level of national income there is a level of consumption, and a level of investment, but if this level of consumption and investment is not as large as total income then income in the next period must fall and unemployment must result.

9 What is needed to cure a slump and achieve full employment (shown by the full employment line on the diagram) is some way of increasing national expenditure so that national incomes can rise towards the necessary figure of £10 000 million on the diagram. In fact, the best income to aim for is just below the full employment level, at the figure shown by Y_1. Here nearly everyone is employed, but a few people are changing jobs, or are between jobs.

10 We can develop this line of enquiry a little further by considering Figure 27.2. Study this figure now. (*See page 328.*)

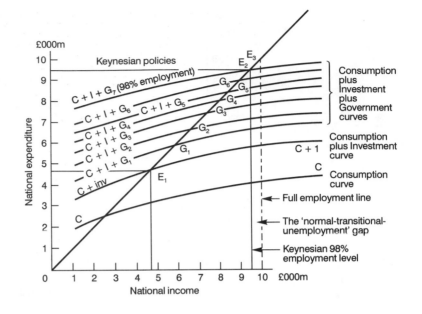

Figure 27.2 The National Income equilibrium diagram (Part II) (controlling the economy with 'Keynesian' policies)

Notes

1 In Figure 27.2 we have the same National Income equilibrium diagram as in Figure 27.1 but the influence of government policies is now shown, using Keynesian policies.

2 The starting point is the equilibrium point E_1, where incomes and expenditure are at £4800 million. The trouble is many factors are out of work. Let us call this the 'great slump' situation, with several million unemployed, factories idle, etc.

3 How did Keynesian policies cure this? They cured it by successive governmental injections of extra purchasing power. These pushed the consumption and investment curve up to higher and higher levels, shown in the diagram as $C + I + G_1$, $C + I + G_2$, etc. The purchasing power might be of many sorts. It could be payments to the unemployed, or governmental contracts for new roads, schools, aircraft, armaments, etc. As the curves rose, unemployed factors were taken on, Business began to gain confidence, the slump began to recede.

4 It is important to note that inflation does not set in at this stage. The extra income is matched by extra production, because previously unemployed factors are being taken on. The new employees are so happy to be back in work they work hard. Prices need not rise because they are making extra goods.

5 The danger begins to creep in at about 95 per cent of full employment. Now we are beginning to offer jobs to the really hard cases. The halt and the blind can't help it, but the ignorant and the lazy are a different matter. Whatever the reason the output of these hard cases does not match their wages, and inflation begins to creep in. Governments did not try to go up to the full-employment level. They stopped at about 98 per cent of full employment. At that level, apart from a very small number of hard cases, no one was really out of work. The 2 per cent unemployed were just people changing jobs. This came to be called *normal transitional unemployment*.

6 Note that this diagram appears to give the impression that once the C curve and the C + I curve are established everything is left to the government. It is for the government to manage prosperity. This is not the case. Any move by any of the forces lower down in the diagram to raise consumption or increase investment raises all the curves above it. That is why the problem of over-full employment is likely to creep in. Careful estimates of the impact of each injection of purchasing power are necessary, because each injection reacts upon the economic and psychological influences at work to affect consumption and investment. Let us list the influences at work to push government interference too far. They are:

(a) Now that the government is organising full employment there is little need to save for a rainy day. Bad times will never come, so consumption can be pushed up – our propensity to consume increases, raising the consumption curve.

(b) Part of the new policies is a more egalitarian system of income distribution (J. S. Mill's proposal at last adopted). Since the poor have a higher propensity to consume, this extra income raises consumption levels again.

(c) Consumer buoyancy raises the entrepreneurs' prospects of profitability. This raises the investment curve and makes it less necessary for the government to interfere.

(d) The increasingly expansive conditions raise interest rates and unlock the liquidity trap. Savers are encouraged to speculate, bringing funds into the market in exchange for income-yielding bonds, which they hope may make capital gains should interest rates fall again. This increased availability of funds raises the investment curve. (*These notes continue opposite.*)

7 The danger of all this is that the government injections of income into the economy may push the national income above the full employment level. If they do so shortages of labour and other factors will start to bid up prices. Inflation will develop.

8 Another danger is that since the public sector is under the direct control of the government it is frequently the public sector that the government may try to cut when the economy is too buoyant. Since many of the things governments do are essential, they can only be cut back to a limited extent. Too buoyant a private sector is therefore a disservice to the community if it cuts back the public sector too drastically. However, in Keynesian economics we are not seeking to cure inflation – that is discussed in Chapter 28. Keynes showed us how to cure a great depression. Let us return to the main text and consider some further points. (*Return to main text at 27.7 page 326.*)

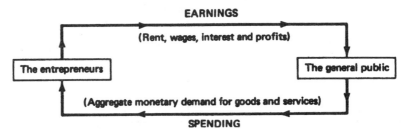

EARNINGS

(Rent, wages, interest and profits)

The entrepreneurs   The general public

(Aggregate monetary demand for goods and services)

SPENDING

Figure 27.3 Circular flow of income in a static economy (earnings = spending)

Notes

1 The entrepreneurs running the firms are paying out in rent, wages, interest and profit the entire proceeds of their activities. For the moment we can ignore corporation tax.

2 Imagine that the public spend all that they receive, so that the total monetary demand for goods and services (which are of course supplied by the firms) is the same as the earnings. The entrepreneurs are therefore receiving back all they paid out. Keynes called this total demand for the entrepreneurs' goods the aggregate monetary demand.

3 The economy is in equilibrium, i.e. in the next period of activity the level of earnings paid will be the same as in the previous period, and all the earnings received will be returned to the entrepreneurs in the form of spending.

4 The economy is static, neither expanding nor contracting. However, this is a little unrealistic, since some people will be hoarding part of their income, some will be saving with institutions and entrepreneurs will be borrowing funds either collected or created by the institutions. Consider Figure 27.4 at this point.

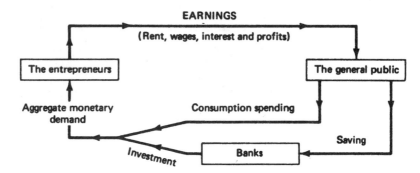

EARNINGS

(Rent, wages, interest and profits)

The entrepreneurs   The general public

Aggregate monetary demand   Consumption spending

Saving

Investment   Banks

Figure 27.4 Circular flow of income in an economy with dynamic potential (savings turned into investment)

Notes

1 People are not consuming their entire incomes; saving is now taking place.

2 If the savings are hoarded, i.e. hidden away like a miser's gold, they will be lost to the circular flow of income.

3 Fortunately most people save through one of the institutional investors, the diagram shows 'banks' collecting the savings of the general public and passing them on to the entrepreneurs. Savings become investment.

4 As both 'spending' and 'investment' return to the entrepreneurs they form together the aggregate monetary demand. If the investment exactly equals the saving, the level of activity in the economy will be the same as before, i.e. the economy is static. But now we have a possible point where a static economy could become a dynamic, or changing, economy. The banks may 'create credit' if the entrepreneurs wish to invest more than the people have saved. This will increase the level of activity in the economy, and move it up into a boom. If the banks are nervous about prospects, or entrepreneurs are not optimistic, some of the savings will lie idle and the economy will turn down into a slump. Now consider Figure 27.5.

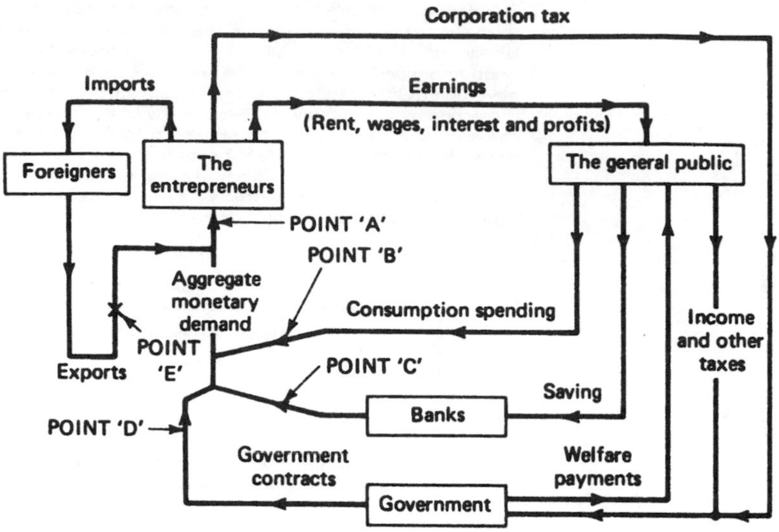

Figure 27.5 Circular flow of income in an economy with four possible agents of change (the consumers, the banks, foreigners and the government)

Notes

1 Firms have to reduce the profits they distribute to their shareholders because corporation tax is payable to the government.

2 The general public also pay taxes to the government, but in return receive, where necessary, welfare payments.

3 An additional feature in this diagram is the inclusion of foreign trade. To the extent that citizens and entrepreneurs buy foreign goods (imports) the income spent is lost to the economic system. This is compensated by foreigners' buying goods from us (exports). If imports and exports are equal in value (a balance of payments) all is well. If imports exceed exports we have an import-led slump. If exports exceed imports, we have an export-led boom.

4 The crucial point in the diagram is point A, the point where aggregate monetary demand returns to the entrepreneurs, ready to be paid out in the next period as incomes. If we have slump conditions we need to increase the flow at point A. How can we do this?

5 The flow at point B can be increased if the general public can be persuaded to increase their consumption. To do this they must stop saving and start spending. It is all this thrift that is causing the trouble. The rainy day has arrived for which the public have been saving so long; the time has come to go out and spend, spend, spend. Unfortunately they can't do it. The ones who are poorest have spent up long ago; those who have remained in employment are nervous about the future, fearing to become unemployed themselves. The rich fear to spend any more for their present prosperous circumstances are already inviting social unrest: extra expenditure now might appear ostentatious. Charitable works might help, but charity is notoriously chilly, and therefore unfavourably received. Flowpoint 'B' is therefore difficult to open. However, it may be opened if people are left with more money in their pockets – by reducing taxation and budgeting for a deficit. It may also be opened if we increase welfare payments, especially as the poor have a high propensity to consume, and will therefore spend any extra income they receive. Reduced corporation tax may also encourage firms to use retained profits for expansion.

6 The flow at point C may be made to increase if entrepreneurs are encouraged to invest – for example, by low interest rates from the banks or generous granting of planning permission. Unfortunately, the entrepreneurs are feeling particularly gloomy because the prospects of profitability are so poor. It is a vicious circle really; the prospects cannot improve unless the firms invest in new capital goods, but the firms will not invest in new capital goods until the prospects improve. The following reasons are also important why the banks are of little help in curing slumps:

(a) If the extra income to be injected is to be fully used it ought to be given to the poor. As the banks never lend to the poor they are not likely to be much help. Any extra loans they make to the well-to-do will promptly be saved by the first recipient taking the income from the borrower of it.

(b) Banks only lend against collateral, and the unemployed have no collateral. It is therefore of little use expecting banks to cure slumps, for bankers are by definition cautious, and we are looking for a spendthrift – to spend someone else's thrift.

7 The flow at point D is the easiest flow to increase. The government is the best agent to promote prosperity during slumps. Most readers would agree that there is no one like the government for spending other people's savings, and this is exactly what is required. It also has two weapons at its command in defeating general persistent unemployment. It can increase aggregate monetary demand in two ways: (i) by increasing welfare payments and (ii) by proceeding with government contracts for socially desirable projects.

(i) *Welfare payments.* As the name implies, welfare payments are payments to members of the general public whose present welfare is for some reason unsatisfactory. This means the unemployed. If we make generous payments to them they will immediately spend the money, having an infinite capacity to consume after their recent deprivations. The multiplying effect will be great, and increased demand will reach the firms through point B. The firms will cheer up and take a more optimistic view of affairs, and before long they will be worrying the banks for loans. Recovery will be on the way.

(ii) *Government contracts.* Every government has projects in reserve which it can put into operation. It may be a road, or a school, or a hospital extension, some slum clearance or an 'alternative energy' project. These will employ factors on socially useful work and the economy will receive the injection of income it requires. To replace the de-pigeonholed projects, a new set must be brought to the design stage. This will offer employment to draughtsmen, architects, etc., and will again raise the level of demand through point D.

8 Finally, the flow through A can be influenced by the flow through point E. If we import goods or services the incomes spent are not returned to the entrepreneurs for the following period, but are paid to foreign entrepreneurs instead. If we export goods and services the foreigners buying from us inject spending power into the economy. Therefore a favourable balance of payments increases aggregate monetary demand, and unfavourable balances result in reduced monetary demand through point E.

We must now return to Section 27.8 and see how Keynes explained the impact of these injections of demand on the economy (*see page 326*).

---

solved by the Boer War and World War I, one of these criticisms was that capitalism was inseparable from wars. It even proved to be true that recovery from the slump of the 1930s was largely achieved by rearmament. But just before World War II, Keynes and others showed how to cure the depression: the solution was to inject purchasing power (i.e. increased aggregate monetary demand) into the economy. The reason why wars cured slumps was that they did just that; the demand for guns, ships and uniforms raised the aggregate monetary demand. It didn't have to be wartime demand: any sort of demand would do. The more massive the unemployment, the more massive the injections of extra monetary demand that would be necessary to cure it; but however much extra spending power was injected there would be a multiplying effect, because the money injected would be spent several times, not once. Let us now consider the 'multiplier'.

**27.8.1
The multiplier**

To begin, let us consider Mr Average, who earns a low wage and has a high propensity to consume, while Mr Well-To-Do earns a very high wage and has a low propensity to consume.

Suppose Mr Average receives an increase in wages of 1.00 monetary unit per week. He will promptly spend it, and aggregate monetary demand (AMD) rises by 1.00. Suppose the person he gives it to is also rather poor, and promptly spends it. AMD has now risen by 2.00. If the third person also spends it, AMD will have risen by 3.00. If this went on fast enough and often enough, that single 1.00 would multiply around the economy an infinite number of times. This is rather unrealistic because Mr Average does not spend his money with other poor people, but spends it at shops, etc., where some of it filters off into the pockets of people like Mr Well-To-Do. When he receives the 1.00 he can't think of anything to spend it on at the moment, having all he requires. He therefore saves the 1.00; whether it gets used again or not depends on the enterpreneurs' demand for capital from the banks.

To take a simple example where on average the public saves 50 per cent, i.e. half of any extra income it receives, Mr Average's 1.00 will be spent as follows:

	Mr A	First person	Second person	Third person	Fourth person	Fifth person	Sixth person
Expenditure	1.00	0.50	0.25	0.12½	0.06¼	0.03⅛	0.01⁹⁄₁₆

The sum of these expenditures, if carried far enough, is 2.00; the seven people shown have already spent 1.98. AMD therefore rises 2.00 for every 1.00

injected when there is a 50 per cent marginal propensity to save, and the multiplier is said to be 2.

The reader should now work out for himself what will be the effect of spending Mr Average's 1.00 when the marginal propensity to save is one third, one quarter and one tenth of the income received. The multiplier in these cases are 3, 4 and 10, respectively. In fact the multiplier is always the inverse of the fraction saved, i.e. the fraction turned upside down.

It follows that in managing prosperity we must inject sufficient spending power into the economy to raise AMD and expand the economy towards the full-employment level. If we make the money available in the first place to the poorer section of the community the multiplying effect will be large. Unemployment will be cured more quickly, and we shall escape from the slump.

The marginal propensity to save is the inclination of the individual to save any extra income he happens to receive. The multiplier is found by the formula:

$$\text{Multiplier} = \frac{1}{\text{Marginal propensity to save}}$$

Thus if the nation on average saves half of any increment in its income the multiplier is 2, if the nation saves one third the multiplier is 3, if the nation saves one tenth the multiplier is 10 and if the nation only saves one twentieth of its extra income the multiplier is 20. The multiplier is that amount by which any injection of spending power into the economy will be multiplied round the economy by people passing the extra income on to others, who pass it on to third persons, etc.

Although Keynes' ideas did not receive immediate acceptance, another powerful force was at work to stimulate the economy. Hitler was on the march and the massive expenditure required to build a military machine to oppose him was to provide all the Government expenditure needed to solve the unemployment problem. It was not until 1946 that Keynesian economics was to be applied to manage prosperity, and by that time the 'establishment' had come to recognise the validity of his ideas. From 1946 to 1970 the major preoccupation of governments – not only in the UK, but worldwide – was the management of prosperity. For many people it was to seem a golden age. Keynes went on to play a leading part in the establishment of the Bretton Woods Agreement in 1944, which was to produce the World Bank, the International Monetary Fund and other influential institutions of the modern world. He died in 1946, at the start of the quarter of a century which was to put his policies into effect. Twenty-five years later international agreement on the development of a managed 'world' economy faltered in the face of exchange rate problems. A new philosophy, monetarism, rose to challenge Keynesian ideas.

27.9 Summary of Chapter 27

1 The early economists sought to study the practical affairs of men in order to discover how the economy worked. They had no intention of influencing economic affairs except to the extent of showing how extra wealth might be created.

2 The mercantilists believed wealth sprang from foreign trade. They believed exports should exceed imports and that the balance should be taken in precious metals which could be used to support strong national forces, particularly the navy. Protection for home trade was important, so as to exclude imports and develop the carrying trade.

3 The growth of manufacturing reduced the influence of mercantilism and led to the development of classical economics. Wealth was the result of specialisation in agriculture and industry, and was promoted by capital investment. *Laissez-faire* was the best policy, for in promoting their own self-interest entrepreneurs would also enrich the nation and their fellow men.

4 Classical economists believed that there was a natural tendency for the economy to operate at the full employment level. There could be no general unemployment or general over-supply if market forces were allowed to operate freely, though there might be temporary unemployment because of over-supply of a particular commodity.

5 The work of Adam Smith, Malthus, Ricardo, John Stuart Mill and Alfred Marshall is important in following the development of classical economics.

6 Between the wars (1918–39) the business cycles of booms and slumps characteristic of the nineteenth century changed to a period of unrelieved depression. John Maynard Keynes showed that this depression could not be relieved by any natural tendency in the economy. The existence of a 'liquidity trap', in which savings were held without any prospect of their use for investment, meant that businessmen were unable to reflate the economy.

7 Keynes showed that it was for the government to manage prosperity. Only direct expenditure on socially valuable projects could restore the prospects of profitability on which business confidence depended. There was insufficient aggregate monetary demand in the economy.

8 Before his ideas could be tried out the rearmament associated with the Hitler regime provided all the government expenditure required. Keynesian economics could not be put into practice until the war was over, and those whose greatest fear was a return to the depression years could experiment with the management of prosperity.

9 The reader is strongly advised to revise Keynesian economics by considering Figures 27.1–27.5, and the notes below them.

Exercises Set 27

1 Define mercantilism, classical economics and Keynesian economics.
2 What is meant by the term 'cyclical activity'? What forces are at work in the economy to create a cycle of business activity?
3 Describe the flows of money around the economy, and the alternative policies which could increase these flows to stimulate demand in slump periods.
4 What is the National Income equilibrium diagram? Explain how it illustrates policies for the management of prosperity.
5 What is persistent general unemployment? How may it be cured?
6 What elements enter into the concept 'aggregate monetary demand'? Explain why aggregate monetary demand changes and how it can be controlled.
7 'Hoarding is the worst kind of saving.' In what circumstances can saving be 'bad', and why is hoarding 'worse' than ordinary saving?
8 What do we mean by the 'propensity to save'? Illustrate your answer by considering the savings of individuals, firms and government-controlled enterprises.
9 Why is a more equal distribution of income likely to increase consumption?
10 What do economists mean by (*a*) the multiplier, (*b*) the accelerator? Explain the part each plays in controlling the economy of a country.

11 What measures are available to a government to influence the level of activity in the economy? How far would a government seek to use them?

12 When should the government (*a*) encourage personal saving, (*b*) discourage personal saving?

13 'The government should reduce taxation if it wishes to cure the unemployment in the country.' 'The government should increase taxation and welfare assistance if it wishes to cure the unemployment in the country.' Compare these two policies critically.

28 Money, monetary policy and monetarism

28.1 Changing concepts of the importance of money

Until the 1930s no real attempt was made to manage the economy, which was felt to be under the influence of inexorable forces tending towards a cycle of economic activity. One of these forces was believed to be the quantity of money in circulation. It was felt that economic fluctuation reflected changes in the quantity of money, and what little intervention there was in the economic life of the nation took the form of central bank activities aimed at encouraging, or restricting, the supply of money.

When Keynes proposed that more direct measures should be taken to relieve the depression of the 1930s, monetary policy became less important, or was seen as only one in a barrage of weapons that could be used to expand the economy out of a slump. The resulting economic prosperity – which was to seem almost a 'golden era' to many of those who had lived through the depression of the 1930s – bore within it the seeds of its own destruction. We shall trace these developments for the UK in due course, but the sign of the disease was a spiral of rising prices, to which the general name 'inflation' has been applied.

28.1.1 Inflation

Inflation is a situation where too much money is chasing too few goods and services, so that they rise in price. Long before attempts were made to manage economies, businessmen and bankers had experienced inflationary times. For example, when Spain discovered the New World and gold flooded in from Mexico and Peru, increases of prices occurred all over Europe. There was more money about, but only the same quantity of real goods, so that money was worth less and goods were worth more. Similar inflations occurred during the 'Gold Rush' days in California and the Klondyke. Mark Twain tells an amusing story of the falling value of money as he journeyed by stagecoach from the Mississippi to Nevada. At the start of the journey he gave the porter a quarter of a dollar. The man expressed his sincere gratitude at such a generous tip. Further on the same coin at subsequent staging posts aroused less and less enthusiasm. When he finally reached Nevada the porter held it in the palm of his hand, squinted at it, said he had heard of one but had never seen one, and vowed he'd remember its 'generous' donor.

These experiences led economists to see a mathematical relationship between the quantity of money in circulation, the price of goods and the quantity of goods being produced. This relationship was called the 'equation of exchange', because it sought to explain how goods were exchanged in a free economy.

Later this equation was refined by Prof. Irving Fisher to take account of another feature which may cause changes at times when no sudden increase has occurred in the quantity of money in circulation. This is the velocity of circulation of money – in other words, the speed at which it is passed on. Velocity changes with the propensity to consume of the recipient, but even more with expectations of future events. The maddest inflations occur among well-to-do rather than poor populations, for the well-to-do have so much more wealth to get rid of when the value of money is falling. Quite frequently we are treated to scenes on our television screens of wild panics on the money markets and bourses around the world as some vital currency comes under financial pressure.

Irving Fisher's equation of exchange reads

$$MV = PT$$

where M is the quantity of money in circulation, V is its velocity, P is the price of goods and T is the number of transactions that take place. What the equation says is that the quantity of money in circulation, multiplied by its velocity always equals the transactions we engage in for goods and services, multiplied by the price. Suppose that M increases, but there are no extra goods and services produced. Since T cannot alter, P (prices) must rise, and this is therefore an explanation of inflation. To control inflation, control M (the money supply).

This equation has been much criticised, chiefly on the grounds that it is so obvious that it is hardly worth saying. Clearly the quantity of money (M) multiplied by the number of times you spend it (V) must be the same thing as the number of goods you buy (T) multiplied by the price you pay (P). However, even the obvious is sometimes well worth saying, and the equation does give a useful clue in shorthand form to what happens in the economy. The following examples will illustrate the implications of Fisher's equations:

(a) Who controls M? Chiefly the monetary authorities, i.e. the government. If they reduce the quantity of money in circulation it ought to stop prices rising – in other words, stop inflation. But while the government proposes the people dispose. If the people change V by spending more rapidly, the government's activities may be undone. The classic example was during the Labour administration of 1964–69, when a massive devaluation of sterling was forced on the British Government by the refusal of the people to be 'squeezed' out of their prosperity. The more the government squeezed the more the velocity of money increased. Entrepreneurs who could not get money from the banks borrowed from the finance houses and even the moneylenders (at 48 per cent interest) to overcome their difficulties.

Similarly, in times of depression the government's activities aimed at encouraging the economy by pumping in more money can be upset by the people, who have such a low V. If the spending power the government pumps in is immediately removed as savings, the economy cannot advance. 'All we need is confidence,' said President Roosevelt in the 'Great Slump'; the confidence to spend, not save and keep V going.

(b) On the other side of the equation, the significant point is that if prices are rising they can be checked by more T. More goods, more transactions, will keep the price of each transaction down. To produce more T the productivity of our fields and factories must be raised. This is particularly noticed when a severe slump exists. If we take measures to ensure recovery by pumping more spending power into the economy this does not produce inflation because the unemployed factors which are brought into production turn out more T to compensate for the greater M available.

Before we can take our analysis of monetary policy and inflation any further we must first consider money in rather more detail.

**28.2
The money supply**

When money simply meant coins in circulation the Royal Mint was the key to the money supply. The word 'Royal' is not without significance here, for the supply of money was vital to the nation's affairs and the ruling powers reserved the right to issue and control the quantity and quality of money in circulation. Later, when banks developed to care for the surplus funds deposited with them, bank deposits became a form of money and 'bank notes' appeared as a means of transferring these deposits from one depositor to another. Later the note circulation became a matter for national control as well, and in the UK the right of other banks to issue notes was gradually extinguished and the Bank of England was made responsible for the note issue. Funds deposited in banks were now transferred by means of the cheque system, through accounts called **current accounts**. The word 'current' comes from the French *courant* (running) and implies that money is being received and paid out as frequently as the customer requires, with a running balance of funds available for the customer's use from day to day. Less mobile funds were lodged in **deposit accounts**, for which seven days' notice of withdrawals was required.

What we are leading into here is a discussion of the various definitions of 'money' which are in use for calculating the money supply. Before reaching this point it is helpful to examine basic banking procedures, and what is known as the **creation of credit**.

**28.2.1
The development of
commercial banks**

In the eighteenth century the banking system developed as a means of providing the capital for the agricultural and industrial revolutions. Not only goldsmiths, but merchants, landowners and other well-to-do people practised banking as a sideline and gradually developed the necessary expert knowledge.

Since a single banker was limited by his personal capital, the idea of partnerships in banking was adopted from an early date; limited liability came much later. It soon became clear that a bank that was too small and localised in its connections was likely to go bankrupt if hard times hit that particular area. For instance, banks in a farming area might be bankrupted if all the depositors withdrew their funds at the same time to replace cattle, machinery and fencing lost in a severe flood. This led to the amalgamation of banks in different localities to give a broader base to the bank.

The advantages of amalgamations, both with regard to the stability of the banking system and economical operation in other ways has reduced the number of banks over the years, so that by the 1920s England had only the 'Big Five' and six smaller banks. In the 1960s a further round of amalgamations began. An amalgamation of National Provincial and West-minster to form the National Westminster Group reduced the Big Five to a 'Big Four': National Westminster, Barclays, Lloyds and Midland. Similarly, the six smaller banks have tended to move more within the sphere of the large banks; Coutts & Co., for example, have joined the National Westminster Group but have not completely lost their individual identity.

The place of the commercial banks in the British economy is a particularly important one. They stand at the very centre of business activity and can greatly influence the level of activity in the economy. For this reason the banks are closely controlled in their credit policies by the Bank of England, which is itself influenced and controlled by the Treasury.

When a customer phones a bank manager and asks whether it is possible to have an overdraft, or a loan, the bank manager is able to permit the customer (if the person concerned is credit-worthy) to spend money that he/she does not really have. Thus a bank manager might agree to put £1000 in the customer's account on the credit side (which implies that the bank owes the customer £1000, which the customer is entitled to spend). Of course really this is just not true, but is corrected by opening up an equal and opposite Loan Account in the customer's name which is a debit account, the customer is a debtor for the £1000 borrowed. These two entries cancel one another out in the bank's books, but as far as the money supply is concerned the bank manager has increased the supply of money by £1000 – in other words, has 'created' money. This is called 'creating credit', because it is the credit entry in the current account which the customer actually spends. Let us see how this creation of credit actually works. A simple illustration will make it clear.

28.2.2
An example of credit creation

Figure 28.1 concerns a deposit of £100 made by Mr A to the credit of his account. The banks know from experience that on average a depositor will not, these days, withdraw more than about 5 per cent of deposits in cash. Therefore the banks keep a **prudential reserve ratio** of rather more than 5 per cent in case the customer needs cash urgently. At one time the Bank of

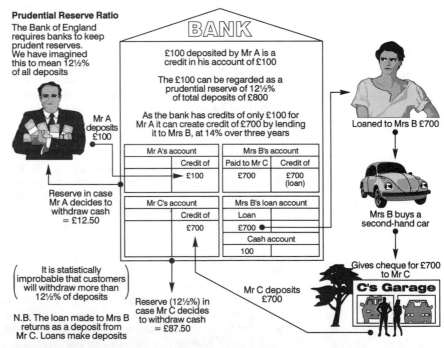

Figure 28.1 The creation of bank credit

Notes

1 The bank has made a loan to Mrs B which became a deposit from Mr C. *Loans make deposits*.

2 The statistical probability is that Mr C will ask for 5 per cent of his deposit back. That is alright, for the bank has a prudential reserve of up to 12½ per cent (£87.50) available.

3 The amount of money in the economy has been expanded by the banks from £100 to £800. With such a very large increase in spending power it is perhaps not surprising that the central bank sometimes finds it necessary to apply a credit squeeze.

4 On the bank's books it now has debits of £800 (£100 cash and £700 loan to Mrs B) and credits of £800 (£100 deposited by Mr A and £700 deposited by Mr C). Mrs B's current account is now clear.

5 This illustration does give a slightly biased viewpoint, since in fact banks do not expand credit uniformly over all loans in the way suggested. They have to preserve a reasonable measure of liquidity, and they would keep rather more than 12½ per cent as easily accessible reserves. For a long while in the decade of the 1960s they were obliged to keep a liquidity ratio of 28 per cent. Let us consider for a moment a bank's liquidity problems. (See Section 28.2.3, page 339.)

England required all banks to keep a **minimum reserve ratio** of 12½ per cent. This is no longer a requirement, but banks do have to satisfy the central bank that they are behaving prudently and keeping adequate reserves – hence the term 'prudential reserve ratio'. In our diagram we imagine the bank keeps a prudential reserve ratio of 12½ per cent and therefore needs to keep £12.50 available in case Mr A wants cash back again out of the £100 deposited. It might therefore appear that the banks have £87.50 of Mr A's money which he will not require, and which consequently is available to lend out to any entrepreneur or private individual who needs to borrow.

In fact, the bank does something much more sophisticated with the £100 deposited by Mr A. It says: 'We have cash deposits of £100, which may be looked upon as a prudential reserve of cash available for depositors. Our prudential reserve ratio is 12½ per cent. Of what is £100 12½ per cent? £100 is 12½ per cent of £800. Therefore we can have deposits (credits) of £800. But we only have cash deposits of £100 therefore we can create credits for a further £700.'

So, of the original £100, the bank keeps £12.50 in case Mr A asks for some of his money back, and lends out '£700' to Mrs B. Of course the bank can't really lend £700 out of £87.50 – it is totally imaginary money created by the bank. This loan to Mrs B is used to buy some useful asset, say a second-hand car, and returns to the bank when Mr C, the garage proprietor, banks Mrs B's cheque. He has no idea it is imaginary money, created by the bank. He puts it into his bank account, but as the statistical chances of his asking for more than 12½ per cent are very unlikely, the bank has exactly the right amount (12½ per cent of £700 = £87.50) available out of Mr A's original £100. Notice that loans to one customer become deposits from another customer – loans makes deposits. Also, the loan to Mrs B is a credit in her current account of £700. Interest on the outstanding balance of this account would be added from time to time, but need not concern us here. Figure 28.1 illustrates the process.

<table>
<tr><td>28.2.3
Liquidity versus
profitability</td><td>

Bankers earn a living by lending money at interest, and also by charging for certain services that they perform for their customers. In lending money the banks have to balance their natural desire to make a good profit with the necessity to play safe and maintain a good prudential reserve ratio. Liquidity and profitability are opposites; one cannot have both at once. A banker who lends money for long periods will earn a lot of interest, but if he/she lends so much that it becomes necessary to stop depositors getting their money out when they want it, our banker will be very unpopular.

</td></tr>
</table>

Figure 28.2 shows diagrammatically the important divisions of bank assets. The whole structure is an inverted pyramid poised on the till money. If the general public eat into this cash base by withdrawing funds unexpectedly from the bank, even for the most worthy reasons, the whole unstable edifice of banking could come crashing down, and with it the economy of the nation.

At the beginning of both World Wars the British Government's first act was to close the banks. They feared that while people were worried and agitated about their own and the country's situation, they might withdraw funds which would ruin the banking system. In a few days, when the public had grown accustomed to the idea of being at war, the banks reopened without any serious effects on their cash ratios. Successful banking depends on confidence – confidence in the political and economic stability of the whole country.

The structure of bank assets reflects the anxiety of the banks to achieve a balance between profitability and liquidity. About one fifth of all funds are

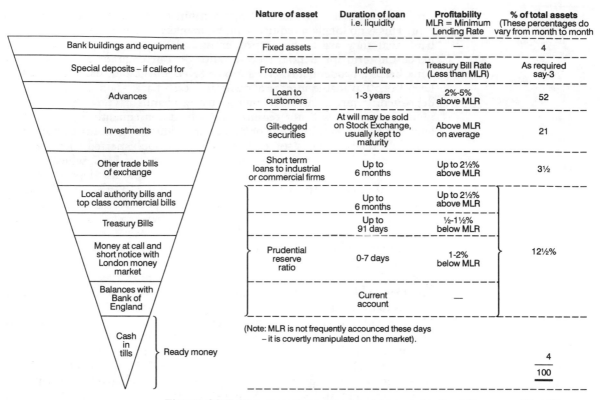

	Nature of asset	Duration of loan i.e. liquidity	Profitability MLR = Minimum Lending Rate	% of total assets (These percentages do vary from month to month
Bank buildings and equipment	Fixed assets	—	—	4
Special deposits – if called for	Frozen assets	Indefinite	Treasury Bill Rate (Less than MLR)	As required say-3
Advances	Loan to customers	1-3 years	2%-5% above MLR	52
Investments	Gilt-edged securities	At will may be sold on Stock Exchange, usually kept to maturity	Above MLR on average	21
Other trade bills of exchange	Short term loans to industrial or commercial firms	Up to 6 months	Up to 2½% above MLR	3½
Local authority bills and top class commercial bills		Up to 6 months	Up to 2½% above MLR	
Treasury Bills		Up to 91 days	½-1½% below MLR	
Money at call and short notice with London money market	Prudential reserve ratio	0-7 days	1-2% below MLR	12½%
Balances with Bank of England		Current account	—	
Cash in tills	Ready money			4
				100

(Note: MLR is not frequently accounced these days – it is covertly manipulated on the market).

Figure 28.2 The structure of a bank's assets; liquidity v. profitability.

kept in cash or near-cash form, so that only the most extreme conditions could possibly affect the bank's ability to repay depositors. A further fifth of bank assets is kept in relatively liquid gilt-edged securities which could be sold fairly easily (though this might involve some capital loss). The other half of the bank's assets are loaned to customers, repayable over relatively short periods of about two years on average. These loans are repayable at regular intervals with interest, so that even with these relatively illiquid loans some funds will be returning to the banks for redeployment every week of the year.

28.2.4
Limitations of bank
credit policy

Although it might appear that the creation of bank credit places unlimited resources at the disposal of the banks, in fact there are some severe limitations on their creation of credit. These are:

(a) The need to maintain liquidity in a system based almost entirely on confidence.

(b) The need to ensure security for the loans. A high proportion of bad debts would cut into the profitability of loans as a whole, since absolute safety must be given to depositors who have entrusted funds to the bank. Very often banks will not give loans unless adequate security called collateral (literally 'side by side') security is available. The deeds of property are usually good security, for land and buildings nearly always have some value. A life-assurance policy is often offered as security, but it is less acceptable because, apart from its surrender value, if any, the policy will not be paid unless the borrower dies. Gilt-edged securities are acceptable collateral, as are shares in reputable firms, but the best guarantee for any bank is the known integrity of the customer. Where risks are taken they are calculated risks; good reliable loans are balanced against less worthy ones, and the principles of a 'balanced portfolio' of assets are followed.

(c)   The third limitation on credit policy is the climate of economic affairs at the time. The new Bank of England controls include regular reviews of a bank's liquidity, as well as overall surveillance of the economy. These controls, introduced in August 1981, are explained more fully later.

Returning to the subject of 'credit creation' there is one difficulty about lending money that has been 'invented' to customers who may spend it wherever they like. What would have happened in the illustration (Figure 28.1) if Mr C had not banked in the same bank as Mr A and Mrs B? This is explained in the next section.

28.2.5 **Keeping in step**	As there are in fact several commercial banks, it is quite likely that Mr C will deposit his cheque in some bank other than the one which made the loan to Mrs B. If this happens, at the end of the day Mrs B's bank will have to pay Mr C's bank a large sum of money which it has only invented. It follows that the system can only work satisfactorily if some sort of reciprocal activity is taking place at the same time. Thus if some customers of Mr C's bank are borrowing funds and spending them with firms that bank at Mrs B's bank, the funds due from each bank to the other may come out equal.

This will happen only if all the banks in the banking system follow a policy of 'keeping in step'. This means that the banks must create deposits only in proportion to the amount of business they do. In this situation we speak of deposits resulting from the creation of credit as 'active' deposits and other deposits as 'passive' deposits. In Figure 28.3 we are imagining a two-bank system, in which Bank A is four times as large as Bank B – in other words, it has, over the years, collected four times as many deposits as Bank B. Suppose now that Bank A makes loans to a total value of £10 000 – in other words, it actively creates deposits of £10 000 by writing credit entries into the accounts of some customers to that value. These are 'active' deposits, but when the favoured customers spend this money the shop-keepers, etc., who receive it will deposit it in their ordinary accounts as 'passive' deposits. The probability is that the borrowers who have received loans from Bank A will spend their money with shopkeepers and others, four fifths of whom bank with Bank A; the rest will be banking with the other bank in the system, Bank B. This means that £8000 will return to Bank A, but £2000 will be 'lost' to Bank B. Bank A would therefore be liable to pay to Bank B £2000 it has 'created', and does not really have. In order to prevent any undue stress in the banking system Bank B must keep in step by lending its customers enough money to ensure that £2000 returns to Bank A. Since the ratio is 4:1 the amount must be in the ratio

$$4:1 = £2000:?$$

The missing figure is clearly £500.

Therefore if Bank B lends its customers £2500 and they spend this money, the probability is that four fifths of this will be banked with Bank A (£2000)

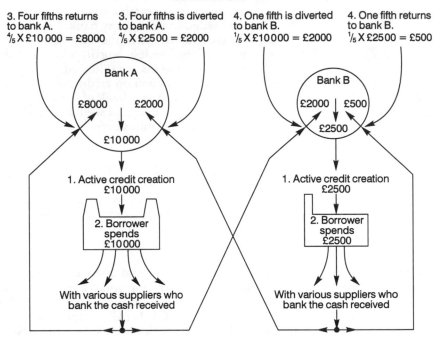

Bank A:Bank B: – 4:1

3. Four fifths returns to bank A.
⁴/₅ X £10 000 = £8000

3. Four fifths is diverted to bank A.
⁴/₅ X £2500 = £2000

4. One fifth is diverted to bank B.
¹/₅ X £10 000 = £2000

4. One fifth returns to bank B.
¹/₅ X £2500 = £500

Bank A

£8000   £2000

£10 000

Bank B

£2000 │ £500

£2500

1. Active credit creation £10 000

2. Borrower spends £10 000

1. Active credit creation £2500

2. Borrower spends £2500

With various suppliers who bank the cash received

With various suppliers who bank the cash received

Figure 28.3 'Keeping in step' in credit creation

Notes
1 Bank A is four times as large as Bank B and their creations of credit must therefore keep in step in the ratio 4:1.
2 The probability is that any loans will be spent with retailers, etc., four fifths of whom bank with Bank A and one fifth bank with Bank B. If the loans are 'in step' each bank will receive back 'passive deposits' equal to the 'active deposits' it has created, and no real money will need to pass between the banks.
3 Now work out what would happen if Bank A's loans were £10 000 but Bank B's loans were £8000. Which bank would owe money to the other and how much? (See 4 below.)
4 Bank A will receive deposits of cheques for £6400 drawn on Bank B but Bank B will receive deposits of cheques for only £2000 drawn on Bank A. Bank B must therefore settle at the daily clearing by paying Bank A £4400 (the difference). As it has only invented this money it has no funds with which to settle.
5 We should also note that the need to keep a certain 'prudential ratio' imposed by a controlling authority like a central bank helps banks to keep in step. A bank that gets out of step will lose money to other banks; its prudential reserves will be depleted and it will have to refuse customers further loans until its reserves build up again as repayments come in from loans already issued.

and one fifth with Bank B (£500). Each bank will therefore receive back the amount of its active creations of credit. Figure 28.3 illustrates the process.

Measures of money supply

In order to keep control of the money supply it is necessary to know exactly how much money is in circulation. The various measures that have been proposed over the years have invariably been found to leave out some important element of money which had previously gone unrecognised, or been thought too trivial to include, but which then turned out to be significant after all.

The measures that have been used over the years total eight. They are called M0, NIBM1 (non-interest-bearing M1), M1, M2, M3 (formerly called Sterling M3), M3c (formerly called M3; the 'c' stands for currency, i.e. foreign currency), M4 and M5 (formerly called PSL2). These new definitions were introduced in 1987 and consequently earlier figures for some of them are not available. The distinguishing feature of the various types of money is their liquidity (how easily they can be made available to purchase goods and services). Table 28.1 shows the various measures and their constituent components. While a great deal of effort goes into defining measures of money supply and building up the collections of data which tell the Treasury what is going on, actually controlling the money supply is not easy. Economic life goes on best in situations where entrepreneurs are free to buy and sell, to borrow or lend, to pay higher wages or dismiss staff as they think fit. Any attempt to control such basic activities requires an army of administrators to police the incomes or other monetary policy, and their role is largely unproductive. (Study Table 28.1 now.)

The difficulty with all measures of money supply is that the general public, or perhaps we should say the sophisticated money market operators who handle the savings of the general public, can take practical steps to move funds out of areas where they are controlled, and into areas where they are insusceptible to government measures. As with all political measures, control of the money supply is conducted in open market, in the full glare of the media floodlights. The *Economist* magazine quotes a law called 'Goodhart's Law', coined by Mr Charles Goodhart of the Bank of England, which states 'any measure of the money supply that is officially controlled promptly loses its meaning'. This is a sobering thought for anyone advocating close control of the money supply. It is easier said, apparently, than done. The Bank of England now only calculates M0 and M4, as shown in the last few years in Table 28.1. Let us return to look at developments of monetary policy since 1945.

28.3 Monetary policy 1945–70

The failure of such attempts as there were to cure the great depression by monetary policy led in 1945 to the adoption of Keynesian economics. The 'cheap money' policy of pre-war years, which kept interest rates down to 2 per cent in the belief that cheap money would encourage what entrepreneurial ability was about, had failed miserably. There were no prospects of profitability because there was insufficient aggregate monetary demand. It was the actual expenditure on rearmament which started the recovery, and the direct involvement of the Government in every aspect of industrial and commercial activity to win the war which kept the economy busy. By the end of the war, which Keynes spent at the Treasury, the importance of Government responsibility for the management of prosperity had been realised. The chosen method was fiscal policy: taxation would place funds at the disposal of the Government which would spend them in such a way as to rebuild the nation after its wartime losses, and manage prosperity in the general interest of the greatest number of its citizens.

In this situation monetary policy had its part to play but it was not an active role. The 'cheap money' policy was continued. Now that there were prospects of profitability, entrepreneurs were about and low interest rates would encourage them. Cheap interest rates would not encourage thrift, and the whole emphasis of government policy was to encourage spending. In the 10 years after the war even the National Savings officers, who had encouraged savings to pay for the war, turned to discouraging savings. Cheap interest rates also helped with servicing the massive debt built up during the war. This debt was now to be painfully repaid, as 'blocked sterling credits' accumulated during the war years were gradually released to the benefit of overseas creditors.

Slowly the economy recovered, and with it the confidence of business management. The strong demand in the economy began to bid up interest rates as more and more capital was required, but even more important it

Table 28.1 Measures of money supply

Name of measure	M0	NIBMI	M1	M2
Purpose of measure	A very narrow definition of money supply (somewhat anomalously called 'the wide monetary base')	Non-interest bearing component of M1 (see next column)	Measures of stock of money on a narrow definition	A slightly broader definition covering the funds available to the private sector for transactions of all types
Items included:				
(a) Notes and coins in public circulation	Yes	Yes	Yes	Yes
(b) Banks' till money	Yes	No	No	No
(c) Banks' operational deposits at the Bank of England	Yes	No	No	No
(d) Bank current accounts of private sector (adjusted for items in transit)	No	Yes, but only the non-interest-bearing current accounts	Yes (both interest-bearing and non-interest-bearing)	Yes (both types)
(e) Bank deposit accounts in sterling, of the private sector	No	No	No	Yes
(f) Private sector holdings of sterling certificates of deposit	No	No	No	No
(g) Bank deposit accounts as in both (e) and (f) but designated in foreign currencies	No	No	No	No
(h) Private sector's holding of money market instruments (bank bills, Treasury bills and local authority deposits)	No	No	No	No
(i) Certificates of tax deposits	No	No	No	No
(j) Private savings in National Savings Bank	No	No	No	No
(k) Private savings in building societies	No	No	No	Yes
Some seasonally adjusted figures for each measure:				
End 1987 (£m)	15 661	45 069	91 916	187 375
End 1988 (£m)	14 447	50 270	108 475	215 247
End 1989 (£m)	15 358	47 730	150 448	236 615
End 1990 (£m)	15 198	45 563	152 363	255 412
End 1991 (£m)	15 734	45 932	160 469	278 288
End 1992 (£m)	20 586	–	–	–
End 1993 (£m)	21 729	–	–	–

Where gaps are shown in the figures it means that the figures for this measure of money supply have not been published recently (in some cases because of industrial action). Now return to page 343, paragraph two.

M3 (old £M3)	M3c (old M3)	M4	M5 (formerly PSL2)
Measures stock of money on a broader definition but relates only to funds available in sterling held by the private sector	As for M3 but it also includes foreign money held by UK nationals (the 'c' stands for currency)	The private sector's money M3 (old sterling M3), plus the private sector's holdings of building society shares and deposits and sterling certificates of deposit, less the building societies holdings of bank deposits and bank certificates of deposit, notes and coin	The same as M4 but including also private sector holdings of money market instruments, certificates of tax deposits and short-term national savings (but leaving out the building societies' holdings of these instruments)
Yes	Yes	Yes	Yes
No	No	No	No
No	No	No	No
Yes	Yes	Yes	Yes
Yes	Yes	Yes	Yes
Yes	Yes	Yes	Yes
No	Yes	No	No
No	No	Yes } But not building society holdings of these	Yes (but not building societies' holdings of these
No	No	Yes	Yes (but not building societies' tax deposits)
No	No	No	Yes (but not savings certificates, SAYE and other long-term deposits)
No	No	No	Yes (but not term shares or SAYE)
185 760	216 534	303 999	319 443
315 237	–	357 302	372 661
381 120	–	425 600	439 857
421 578	–	477 004	495 276
–	–	501 688	–
–	–	520 334	–
–	–	544 569	–

began to suck in imports, at a time when many exports were being 'given away' to repay wartime debt. The balance of payments became an overriding concern of governments. True the imports were largely foodstuffs and raw materials, not manufactured goods as they tend to be in the 1990s, but they still represented a considerable burden on the balance of payments. The era of 'stop-go' had arrived.

It is a pity that 'stop-go' was chosen as the phrase to describe economic policies in the years from 1952 to 1970; the phrase 'go-stop' is so much better. The government was seeking to manage prosperity and to get the economy to 'go' – and it was so successful that many entrepreneurs concluded that bad times would never come again. If the government was committed to prosperity there could never be a slump again, and therefore there could not be much risk in showing enterprise. As part of the process of managing prosperity that large sector of the economy now under the government's direct influence, the nationalised industries, was encouraged to keep costs down to the private sector by charging less than the true cost for services – the bill for the difference was met by the taxpayer. This encouraged the private sector to expand, and resulted in balance of payments problems at a time when the fixed exchange rate mechanism devised at Bretton Woods did not permit the value of a currency to depreciate to correct such difficulties. The result was that the 'go' had to be replaced by a 'stop', with a massive check to the economy, largely implemented by fiscal changes – heavier taxation and discouragement of consumption in a variety of ways. Interest rates also rose, chiefly to encourage the funding of long-term debt, which was rising due to the deficit policies being pursued in periods of 'go'. Monetary policy was, however, much less important than fiscal policy, and was to remain so for a decade following the Radcliffe Report of 1959.

28.3.1 The Radcliffe Report of 1959	This report followed a searching enquiry into the working of the monetary system. It found that even to define the money supply was no easy task. The wider liquidity – which means the many other sources that people needing funds could turn to besides the banks – was almost insusceptible of definition. More direct controls on bank lending and on hire purchase were expected to have a greater effect than any attempt to control the money supply. Thus hire purchase controls, with their immediate impact upon the poorest class of purchaser, were found to be very effective in 'stopping' the economy. The imposition of a minimum deposit and a maximum period for repayment caused both private citizens and businesses to cut back demand. Similarly, quantitative and qualitative controls on bank lending had more salutary effects on the credit policies of the commercial banks than manipulation of interest rates, bearing in mind the levels of interest rates prevailing at the time. Industry at this time was still earning reasonable profits, of about 15–20 per cent. Interest rates in the 6–7 per cent region were unlikely to stop a firm proceeding with a desirable project. Suppose rates were raised by 1 per cent: this was only a marginal reduction of profits. No one at that time envisaged interest rates of 20 per cent (or even 30 per cent) as they have been at times in the 1980s. By contrast, quantitative limits on the amount of bank lending, and qualitative controls (for example, restriction of loans to exporters only) had an immediate impact on credit creation.

Unfortunately, as the years passed, it became clear that disruption of bank lending in this direct way had side effects that were undesirable. Imperfect control of other financial bodies – particularly finance houses and less scrupulous money lenders – meant that the banking system was distorted. Control was exercised on the strange basis that the more reputable and honourable you were, the tighter you were controlled; while the 'fringe' financial institutions were not controlled at all. Some changes were clearly necessary, but governments hesitated for fear of adverse effects on the foreign exchange markets in view of persistent balance of payments deficits. The one device introduced in the 1960s was the **'Special Deposits' scheme**. Under this scheme a portion of the liquid assets of each of the commercial banks was frozen in the Central Bank in a 'special deposit' account. Interest was paid initially on these deposits at the Treasury Bill rate, but not of course at the much higher rates which could have been earned had the funds been left free for loans to the private sector. Remembering that any cash available can be multiplied up by the 'credit creation' mechanism to much higher levels of loan than the actual cash itself, it can be seen that if the Bank of England imposed special deposits of, say, 3 per cent of the bank's total assets this represented a very large slice of cash, and an even bigger slice of bank lending which the banks must forgo. As a result severe restrictions on overdrafts and loans had to be implemented.

By 1971 the injustice of the prevailing system – close control of the banks with no control over other organisations – was so apparent that the Bank of England introduced changes, outlined in a paper called *Competition and Credit Control*.

Before looking closely at competition and credit control let us first consider the 'failure' of Keynesian economics.

28.3.2
The 'failure' of Keynesian economics

The fact is that Keynesian economics did not fail: it is just that it was too successful. Keynesian economics was designed to cure a slump, and this it did most effectively. For 25 years the UK enjoyed an era of egalitarian prosperity. The standard of living increased out of all recognition compared with the inter-war years; the condition of the very poor was transformed; a general welfare programme eliminated dire poverty; the rich were squeezed to a very considerable extent out of their excessively privileged position and a juster, fairer society was realised. A 'wind of change' swept away imperial power and conceded self-government to all but the merest vestiges of empire and the sterling area shrank until it only included the Channel Islands, Gibraltar and the Isle of Man. Unemployment hovered around the 2 per cent level, known as normal transitional unemployment (about 500 000 unemployed out of a workforce of 25 million). No one was really out of work, but people were 'between jobs' now and again.

The trouble was that, as economics teaches us, appetite grows with feeding, and those who have at last been enabled to raise their heads only succeed in focusing their eyes upon wider horizons. Gradually a host of minor changes, each perhaps only seeming in itself to be a minor adjustment, produced major changes. Inflation gathered speed, broke into a canter and was barely restrained from a gallop. We may list:

(*a*) Total wealth created, which had in any case suffered a major setback by the loss of imperial privilege, could not now expand further without going through the full employment barrier. The situation was eased to some extent by the arrival of immigrant labour from the Commonwealth, but this was to produce its own range of distortions eventually. In general this immigrant labour was not highly skilled, and consequently as far as skilled trades were concerned the supply of labour was too small compared with demand; employers began to

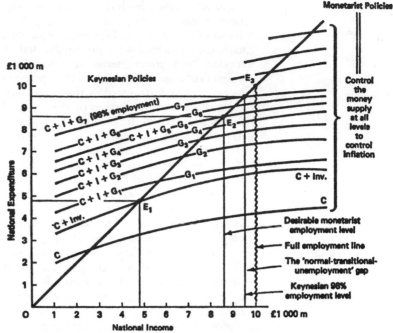

Figure 28.4 The National Income equilibrium diagram (Part III) (controlling the economy with 'monetarist' policies)

Notes

1 In Figure 28.4 we have the same National Income equilibrium diagram as in Figure 27.2, but the influence of monetarist policies is now shown.

2 The starting point now is the full-employment line, where equilibrium is at E_3 and everyone is fully employed. Keynesian prosperity abounds. People come to expect that their standard of living should double every 25 years. They resent 'stop-go' policies; a little 'stop' to check inflation, a little 'go' to get back to 98 per cent of full employment. We are all more sophisticated; we know how the 'other half' of the world is living. Setbacks in the economy are necessary, but not if they affect me. Like an uncontrollable rabble we burst through the full-employment barrier.

3 The trouble with full employment is that once you have it it is difficult to increase output any more. You cannot produce more goods, unless you use new technology. You cannot use new technology if trade unions demand the full fruits of its output, for there is nothing left for the inventor, or the tertiary services which are also trying to grow. Most of these services are run by the government as non-profit-making services. If the public sector policies for which the government was elected cannot be implemented because of over-full employment the government must hold down the rest of the economy. Keynes is abandoned, for of course his policies are no longer necessary; we have too much aggregate demand. The problem now is to hold down the money supply to control inflation.

4 National income has now gone up well above the full employment level (E_3 on the diagram). What has pushed it there? Clearly it is not deliberate injections of government spending because Keynesian policies have now been abandoned. There is a strong mixture of forces at work to raise all the curves in the diagram. Briefly we may list:

   (a) High incomes paid to strongly organised work forces;

   (b) Easily available credit – not just hire purchase but sophisticated help-yourself schemes like Barclaycard and Access, and large-scale loans from fringe banks and finance companies;

   (c) Sophisticated behaviour by the mass of the people – especially the tendency to increase the velocity of money, i.e. to spend money as soon as we get it;

   (d) Low productivity, work-sharing and other devices which make it necessary to employ three men to do one job;

   (e) Wage drift under the influence of bogus productivity deals;

   (f) Generous welfare arrangements, redundancy payments, golden handshakes and silver-lined retirement benefits;

   (g) The rescue of lame duck industries of notional (rather than national) importance.

5 To control the money supply government policies can act at every level. Since each layer in the diagram is built upon the layers lower down it will help to reduce incomes anywhere in the scale. Monetarist policies try to reduce incomes wherever possible by putting a tight framework on wage-bargaining, credit, public expenditure (including local government expenditure), taxation, bogus productivity deals, the rescue of lame ducklings (some ducks just have to be saved), welfare dodging, etc.

6 The aim of all these policies ultimately is to bring income down to about the 90 per cent level of full employment. This is because, with more generous welfare, etc., the band of 'normal transitional unemployment' is widened – people take a holiday between jobs, even if this lowers their consumption level. The actual measures taken, and the effect of monetarist policies on unemployment, are described in the main text.

poach labour by offering it higher rewards, and too much money began to chase too few goods.

(b) The increased sophistication of all classes led them to seek to preserve their own standard of living. For the rich this meant a more strenuous resistance than formerly to the expansion of the share of the national income going to labour. Interest rates were pushed up, and prices were increased to keep profit levels not only steady, but increasing at the same pace as inflation. Rents rose. For labour the problem was to keep wages ahead of inflation, even if the only way of compelling attention to their 'just' claims was by strike action. In a sophisticated economy it is easy to bring industry to a standstill, and the eventual results may be difficult to foresee compared with the temporary successes of the achieved wage claim, soon to be eaten away by further inflation. The almost complete collapse of the major British ports may have had many causes, but the last straws that broke the camels' backs were the strikes of the 1960s and early 1970s. Similar developments in all major industries occurred, and only the high unemployment of the 1980s stopped the 'English disease' (industrial unrest).

(c) The original concept of welfare in the years between the wars had been that no nation should be content to allow citizens to be degraded by abject poverty, or suffer ill-health. It was never envisaged that this should extend further than the relief of dire need. However, this attitude gradually changed over the 20 years of increasing affluence between 1945 and 1965. The idea grew up, and was fostered by a growing body of political activists as well as by many well-meaning individuals in all walks of life, that everyone had a *right* to unlimited prosperity. For example, those forced out of employment (presumably because of the weakness of the capitalist system) were held to be entitled to the same wage as 'unemployed' that they had received as employed people. Earnings-related benefits, however rational they might be, still had to be paid by someone, and the only source of national income is wealth-creating industry. Burdens were heaped upon industries that were already facing severe competition from other advanced nations and newly industrialised countries as well. The welfare burden, exaggerated by a certain amount of free-loading, began to approach the insupportable.

Keynesian economics was no longer required, for the problem was not one of curing a depression. The problem now was excessive demand, and a firm control of the money supply was seen as one way to grasp the nettle. We can consider the situation by looking again at the national income equilibrium diagram. Study Figure 28.4 now. The implementation of monetary policy began in the 1970s as inflation developed. It was to lead eventually to a fully monetarist policy. Before looking at monetarism, we must first look at an alternative model of the economy, the aggregate demand – aggregate supply model.

28.4
The aggregate demand– aggregate supply (AD–AS) model

An alternative way of looking at the economy, and monetarists think it is a better way than the national income equilibrium diagram, is the AD–AS model. They maintain that it gives a clearer picture of what is happening in the economy, because it deals with aggregate demand (i.e. the demand of the whole nation) and aggregate supply (i.e. the total wealth that the nation will create in any given set of circumstances). The model is sometimes called the neo-classical model, because it is a return to the virtues of 'classical economics' – the economics that prevailed before Keynes introduced his ideas for the management of prosperity in times of slump.

The 'virtues' of classical economics may be listed as follows:

(a) The idea of *laissez-faire* (let things work themselves out). Do not interfere with entrepreneurs seeking to get rich, because they will, if left alone, enrich us all.
(b) The market contains all the forces necessary to maintain prosperity. Supply and demand will interact to arrive at prices which will clear the market every day and call forth a further round of production tomorrow.
(c) The economy has its own natural tendency to operate at the full employment level (or at least fairly close to the full employment level – because some people are quite unemployable and must be cared for in other ways).

Of course we know that these 'virtues' have, at times in the past, failed miserably to provide a satisfactory level of life for many people. However, that was long ago, and in more prosperous times, where inflation is a major problem because demand has been allowed to grow larger than the ability of the nation to supply, the neo-classicals maintain that an AD–AS model gives a better picture of the economy.

28.4.1 What the AD–AS model offers us

The aggregate demand–aggregate supply model views the whole economy as a massive demand and supply diagram, with an AD curve looking very much like a simple demand curve, and an AS curve looking very much like a simple supply curve. However, these two curves are not the same as demand and supply curves in microeconomics, which are used to analyse changes in prices and outputs. In macroeconomics, AD and AS curves are used to analyse fluctuations in the aggregate price level (i.e. inflation and deflation) and aggregate output (booms and slumps).

28.4.2 The aggregate demand curve

To start, we will look at the aggregate demand curve. Study this diagram (Figure 28.5) and the notes below it.

The aggregate demand curve represents the aggregate demand for domestic goods and services by households, firms, the Government and foreigners (the net effect of exports – imports). This demand may be expressed as:

$$AD = C + I + G + (X - M)$$
$$= \text{Consumption} + \text{investment} + \text{government expenditure} + \text{(the net effect of exports – imports)}$$

The AD curve is a downward sloping demand curve for three main reasons.

(a) Interest rate effects

When there is a rise in general prices, interest rates rise because the lenders of money know they are going to be repaid in money the purchasing power of which will have fallen in the time between granting the loan and receiving the repayment. The higher interest rate is to compensate for the loss of purchasing power. This makes borrowers of money hesitate to go ahead with the purchase of interest-sensitive goods, such as cars, consumer durables, computers, etc.

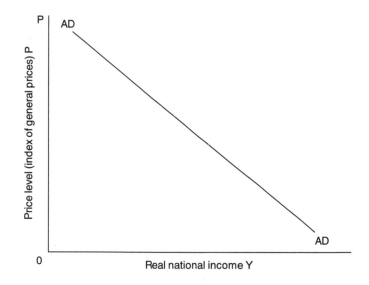

Figure 28.5 The aggregate demand curve

Notes
1 The vertical axis measures the aggregate price level (the index of general prices, also known as the GDP deflator because it is used to reduce the GDP (Gross Domestic Product at current prices) to GDP at base year prices when we are trying to see the changes in GDP in real terms, not money terms).
2 The horizontal axis measures real national income, which as usual is designated Y.
3 Increases in the price-level means that the prices of goods in general (not any particular good) have risen. Demand will be low when the price level is high, and will increase when the price level is low. So the AD curve is a downward sloping demand curve.
4 The AD curve is downward sloping for three reasons (a) interest rate rises reduce the demand for interest sensitive goods; (b) general price rises mean a reduction in wealth for almost all people; (c) imports become more attractive (cheaper) and home goods less attractive (dearer). A description of this is given in the main text.

(b) Wealth perceptions

A rise in general prices decreases real wealth for all those who hold their assets in money form. Since almost all people have at least some of their wealth in cash or near-cash form (such as balances in current accounts at their local bank) the purchasing power of this money falls. The perception that they are less wealthy leads individuals to spend less, and this perception is confirmed by their discovery that they can no longer really afford the project they were considering. Consequently the marginal project is postponed to a better day.

(c) Increased imports (M) and decreased exports (X)

As prices rise, home-produced goods become less attractive and foreign goods, which have not increased in price, seem better value for money than formerly. This leads to increased imports. At the same time exports decline, since foreigners find the prices of the goods they wish to buy have risen. They turn to home-produced goods, or the goods of competitors which have not risen in price.

The net result of all these changes is that AD falls. Consider the formula:

$$AD = C + I + G + (X - M)$$

In this formula C, I and G have all declined because all the elements of home demand, whether private consumers, business firms or official government bodies have reduced demand, while (X) exports have declined and (M) imports have risen, to make the combined effect (X − M) less than it was, and possibly adverse.

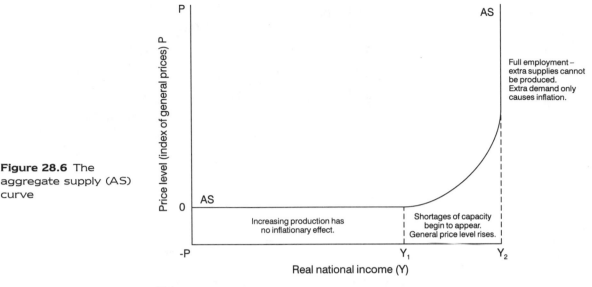

Figure 28.6 The aggregate supply (AS) curve

Notes

1 Where there is practically no demand at all, the AS called forth will be mere 'subsistence supply'. This happens in wars and other calamities. It is a situation of unused capacity and under-employment of factors.

2 As recovery begins, the previously unused factors are combined to increase production (real national income) but prices do not rise because higher prices are not needed to coax factors into production. The supply curve is a horizontal line at the current price level and inflation (a general increase in prices) does not occur. Supply is infinitely elastic, and P in our diagram is equal to 0.

3 As higher levels of output are reached, shortages in particular areas begin to develop and prices begin to rise. Wages of some types of labour begin to rise to attract the scarce labour away from its present employer. 'Golden hallo's' (a lump sum payment to induce an employee to leave one firm and join another) begin to appear; head-hunters are busy finding key personnel and costs begin to rise. The supply curve begins to slope upwards, and rises more and more steeply as full employment is approached.

4 By definition, at full employment no increase in supply is possible and the AS curve is vertical.

28.4.3 The aggregate supply (AS) curve

The AS curve represents the aggregate supply of goods and services produced by all firms in the economy. Since we need to see what happens when prices are not rising (P = 0) the vertical axis has been shown starting at a point lower than 0 (i.e. a point showing deflationary times). The AS curve has limits; zero production (no real national income) and full capacity production (the real national income is at its 'full employment' level, when the factors of production are producing maximum output given the state of technology and enterprise available at the time). The aggregate supply cannot be increased in this situation, however much prices rise to give suppliers' added incentive. Consider Figure 28.6 and the notes below it.

28.4.4 The AD–AS diagram as a model of the economy

When we put the aggregate demand curve and the aggregate supply curve on the same diagram, we can see how the economy varies. The AS curve represents the aggregate supply that will be called into the market place as the response of entrepreneurs to the demand prevailing at any particular time. AD and AS are in equilibrium where the AD curve intersects the AS curve. The various levels of demand shown in Figure 28.7 decide what the real national income (aggregate supply) will be, and what price level they will be at. Study this figure now and the notes below it.

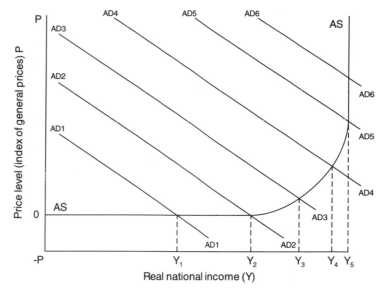

Figure 28.7 The AD–AS model of the economy

Notes

1. The AS curve shows the range of responses of entrepreneurs to varying levels of demand in the economy. Outputs (real national income) can vary from 0 to Y_5, which is the total aggregate possible output of wealth in this economy given its level of technology and skill.

2. Demand is low at AD_1 and AD_2 and calls forth outputs (national incomes) of Y_1 and Y_2. The price level is P_0 (zero inflation), since inflation does not occur when there are under-utilised factors waiting to be employed.

3. After Y_2 shortages of labour, components, raw materials, etc., begin to creep in, and prices begin to rise.

4. At demand AD_5, national income rises to Y_5, the maximum possible. Any further increase in demand only results in higher prices (inflation). Thus AD_6 cuts the AS axis at a price well above that prevailing at AD_5 but no further output can be induced to appear.

28.4.5 How can a higher national income be achieved when full employment prevails?

If increases in demand cannot achieve higher output, what can we do to achieve it. The answer can only be that we must try to increase supply-side measures. Supply-side measures are measures that make the markets for factors operate more efficiently. If we can get our factors more cheaply, use them more economically and raise productivity so that we create more wealth from the same input of resources, we shall effectively postpone the time when the AS curve becomes vertical. The final part of the AS curve will be moved to the right; inflation will creep into the system more slowly and growth in the economy will take place. This should make a higher standard of living possible (but of course how this increase is shared out among citizens is open to debate). This is illustrated in Figure 28.8

28.4.6 The cycle of economic activity around Y_n (the 'natural level')

Monetarists believe that the economy has a 'natural level' at which it operates best, and to which it will return eventually no matter what influences are brought to bear upon it. Where this 'natural level' is it is almost impossible to know, but if we accept the idea for the present it will enable us to see what happens when the economy is disturbed from this natural level. Figure 28.9 shows the cycle of activity around an economy whose 'natural national income' is Y_n.

28.4.7 Conclusions about the AD–AS model

The AD–AS model is an improvement over the national income equilibrium diagram in this respect, that it looks at the management of prosperity from both sides – the demand side (in which prosperity is to be achieved by

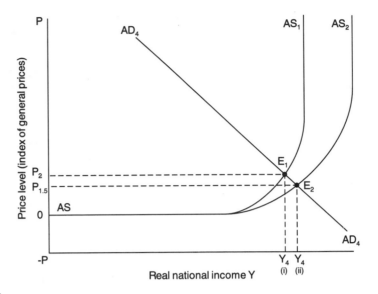

Figure 28.8 Supply-side measures to increase national income (Y)

Notes
1 A series of supply-side measures (reducing the power of trade unions, ending monopoly controls of raw materials, freeing-up of road transport operation, etc.) enables productivity to rise and the AS curve moves to the right.
2 AD and AS are in equilibrium at E2 instead of E1. At this point real national income has increased and the inflation experienced in the economy is at a lower level, $P_{1.5}$ (not P_2).

ensuring that demand is strong and full employment encouraged) and the supply side (in which prosperity is to be achieved by higher productivity and supply-side measures to make the factor markets work better). The weakness of the model is that it assumes that the economy has some natural state, to which it will always return whatever attempts are made to expand it towards full employment or rein it in when it gallops too fast. Just where that natural level is, and whether it is anywhere near the place where we would like it to be, is not exactly clear. Presumably it is some way below full employment but somewhere above the point where excessive unemployment causes social unrest. Market forces appear to be playing their true part in keeping the economy vibrant and competitive, but underneath it all the Government is attempting to manage prosperity by adroit manipulation of … well, probably the social security budget (but any public sector activity will do). Whatever part market forces may play, it is against common sense to say that the Government does not, and should not, play any part in keeping the economy prosperous. That is what governments are for!

28.5 Monetarism and monetarist policy to cure inflation

Persistent inflation has been the distinguishing feature of most economies since 1972 when the Bretton Woods System was finally abandoned. Imperceptible rises in the post-war years had given way to serious single-figure inflation in the late 1960s, and in the seventies double-figure inflation began to appear. When more than 10 per cent of income is eaten away by inflation in a single year people do begin to get alarmed. Those who take no steps to keep incomes in line with inflation will soon find their real incomes seriously reduced. The business community and organised labour can usually keep abreast of inflation. The one pushes up prices to keep profit margins adequate; the other pushes up wages to keep them ahead of inflation. The unrepresented, the retired and the unsophisticated are left to

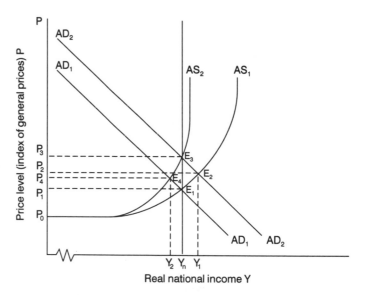

Figure 28.9 The cycle of economic activity around a 'natural level' of income of Y_n

Notes

1 *Starting position* The economy is in equilibrium at its natural level, with the AD curve intersecting the AS curve at E1, a national output (income) of Y_n and a slight degree of inflation with the general price level at P_1.

2 *Expansionary phase* Aggregate demand begins to rise, and gathers power as all the forces at work $(C + I + G + (X - M)$ gain in confidence. Y increases to Y_1 as the economy slides up AS_1 to E_2, where the ultimate demand curve AD_2 intersects the AS_1 curve. This is the top of the boom. There is increased wealth, but inflation is beginning to build.

3 *Uncertainty phase – the boom busts* In this phase trade unions attempt to preserve real incomes by seeking wage increases; firms attempt to preserve profits by raising prices and the government attempts to control inflation while at the same time protecting the vulnerable (who all have votes). These activities cause a decline in confidence. Aggregate supply begins to fall, the AS curve shifts to the left, demand is still strong and the price level rises to P_3 as the national income falls back to Y_n.

4 *Disillusion and recession* Demand weakens too as the prospects of profitability fall, trade union pressures decline, consumers save for the 'rainy day' which is approaching, the $(X - M)$ balance worsens and the Government postpones marginal projects. Demand falls back to AD_1 again, inflationary pressures ease, the national income declines to Y_2 and the recession equilibrium position is at E_4.

5 *Recovery* At the low point in the recession, productivity is higher from those in work. Possibly, too, the exchange rate is weak making goods better value for money to foreigners. The $(X - M)$ factor in the economy turns favourable and a slow export-led recovery begins. The AS curve begins to move to the right and demand extends to the original point of equilibrium E_1. The cycle is complete; the economy is back to its natural level of Y_n national income, and the price level declines to its former rate of P_1. (*Now return to Section 28.4.7, page 353.*)

face falling standards of living. The only group that can 'hold the ring' for these groups is the government, and hence the various attempts to organise an 'incomes policy'. Whether such policies can be achieved by voluntary methods – the government persuading the strong to limit their claims in the interests of the weaker groups in society – or whether a 'statutory' policy is better, is debatable.

Monetarists believe that an alternative to incomes policy is close control of the money supply. Their chief spokesman, Professor Milton Friedman from the Hoover Institute, California, popularised the idea that the cause of inflation was simply the excessive supply of money. With inflation becoming a major problem all over the world (and in some countries inflation is in three figures and almost a way of life) the monetarist remedy is to restrict the growth of the money supply.

The basic idea behind monetarism is that money is unique: it represents all the other things that can be bought with it. The demand for money represents a demand for purchasing power. The holding of money brings a reward in the form of convenience, which is often higher than the reward (interest) which is gained from a loss of liquidity. Thus many people leave balances in current accounts at the bank simply because the convenience of meeting daily payments with absolute certainty is worth more to them than the interest they could get by transferring the money to a deposit account. As soon as the current account is in danger of becoming overdrawn they transfer funds out of their deposit accounts to top it up. In order to prevent this happening interest rates have to be very much higher than, for example, in the Victorian era, when 2½ per cent was deemed to be a worthwhile rate of interest. Money is therefore seen as one asset in a portfolio of assets, possession of each of which yields a certain rate of satisfaction. If the money supply grows money loses its attractiveness relative to other assets, which will be purchased with the increased money available. This will build up their price. To control inflation, control the money supply.

This was the policy followed by the Conservative administration led by Mrs Margaret Thatcher from 1979 onwards. To be fair, the policy had already started as early as 1976, when the Labour administration, following a world-wide trend, set monetary targets in the form of a range of permissible growth in the money supply, based upon Sterling M3. The IMF has insisted on the use of this definition (now called M3) as being the one least likely to distort the inflation in the UK's domestic economy. The target is expressed for the year ahead, but is reviewed every six months and consequently 'rolls over' in a continuous series of forecasts. The government might appear to be well-placed to control the money supply, since it spends roughly half the national income in public sector activities of various sorts. Unfortunately, even the closest controls over departmental expenditure are inadequate in a dynamic situation. Thus if unemployment rises welfare payments must increase, and it is impossible to impose rigid controls over the expenditure. Many workers in government employment are poorly paid – even Members of Parliament get considerably less than most of them could earn in industry. It is not possible to cut wages in the public sector at the same time as a free-for-all is being encouraged in the private sector. If the free-for-all results in bankruptcies for some firms in the private sector we cannot allow the same thing to happen to hospitals, schools or the armed services.

Some further mention will be made of monetarist policies later in this chapter, but the second thread in Conservative policies in the 1980s was in fact more important than the monetarist idea. It came to be known as 'supply-side economics'.

28.6 Supply-side economics

Ever since the days of John Maynard Keynes economics has been dominated by the idea that the amount of *demand* in the economy was the vital thing. In the big slumps of the 1930s there was no confidence in the triumph of prosperity anywhere; and the least of all in that power house of capitalism, the USA. It was the 'New Deal' programme of Franklin Delano Roosevelt (and Keynes was one of his advisers) which taught that if no-one else could pump demand into the economy the Government must do it. Government projects started the recovery – only to be overtaken by the rise of militarism and re-armament before World War II.

All the same, the seed that had been planted grew during the war years, and the quarter of a century after the war proved to be a period of growing and unparalleled prosperity. The secret of the management of prosperity was to keep the demand steady, or better still, growing. A touch on the accelerator to speed things up; a touch on the brakes when inflation threatened. Lots of 'go' and a little 'stop'. That was the secret. Demand was all, and government management of demand was crucial.

However, it bore within it the seeds of its own destruction. If prosperity is everything, and the government has supreme control, we can safely leave it to the government. Our capacities for consumer goods and services were infinite, and they included more leisure and less work. Greater equality of income raised demand to enormous heights; consumption rose at the expense of investment, and the supply-side of the equation faltered. Highly organised labour demanded an excessive share in the fruits of production, imports were sucked in and balance of payments problems developed. One economist lamented in the popular press:

> John Maynard Keynes
> Took incredible pains
> To teach us to manage prosperity,
> And for twenty-five years
> We aimed, amid cheers,
> For an egalitarian prosperity,
> But some of our brothers
> More equal than others
> Demanded an excessive ra-tion,
> And the English disease
> Brought us down to our knees
> Where we're up to our necks in inflation.

The English disease was a tendency to go on strike at the drop of a hat. The supply of goods and services was being strangled by anti-competitive forces.

What is supply-side economics? It is economics that holds that the emphasis given in Keynesian economics to the management of the amount of demand in the economy has gone too far, and has led to a disregard of the supply-side of the economy. The supply-side of the economy is that part which is the result of free-enterprise activity. Keynesian economics has adversely affected this side of the economy by imposing many impediments to free activity, so that firms and individuals cannot respond to changing conditions and changing market demands. In practical terms supply-side measures are measures which restore the influence of market forces, and make markets (such as the market for labour) operate more freely.

There is a popular misconception that 'market forces' has got something to do with the distribution of goods, and buying and selling in shops and supermarkets. This is completely wrong. When supply-side advocates call for the free play of market forces the markets they are talking about are the markets for the factors of production, for land, labour (especially labour) and capital, and of course the entrepreneurial skills which alone make capitalism work. What the supply-side advocates say is that the forces of production have been weakened by excessive attention to consumption activities and the infinite demands of the consumer. We all know that man's wants are infinite, for each level of consumption to which we rise only reveals a wider horizon to which we instantly aspire. The means to satisfy those wants are limited, and take land, labour and capital to produce.

Although supply-side measures are government inspired they are not macroeconomic for they operate at the level of the firm and the individual. They are therefore microeconomic. They are intended to achieve growth in the economy not by increasing demand (which monetarists believe will only result in inflation) but by increasing productivity and therefore the supply of goods and services available. The measures are designed to remove any hindrances which prevent people working harder, or showing new enterprise. What we have to do is undo the adverse developments of fifty years of Keynesianism and return to some traditional *laissez-faire*, or market forces. The adverse developments of Keynesianism are the impediments to free activity – a persistent protectionism of those in entrenched positions – which prevents individuals and firms responding quickly to changing conditions and changing market demands. *Supply-side economics may be characterised as policies designed to make the markets work better.* The markets referred to are the factor markets for land, labour, capital and enterprise.

In every sector of the economy there are built-in frictions which prevent the markets operating freely. There are many nationalised industries which are overmanned, overcapitalised, oversupplied with land, etc. Throughout industry there are restrictions on the movement of labour, and on free competition in the wages field. There are restrictions on land use, and on enterprise and on the freedom of capital. The argument is that if all these artificial brakes on production were removed the UK could compete more effectively in the world and unemployment could be solved. This would be the creation of real jobs, not artificial job-creation. It is not so much that the UK wants to export its goods all over the world, as to substitute home produced goods for the imports at present flooding in. We have to make goods not only better, but better value for money because the price has come down. This is certainly a new attitude to unemployment, and perhaps one that is long overdue.

The measures taken in supply-side economics include the following:

(a) The labour market

Here one of the problems is the mobility of labour. Workers in dying industries have to be turned out of them and into productive work elsewhere. A year-long coal strike in 1984–5 had been fought precisely on this principle – can a dying community be forever maintained on social grounds. A National Mobility Office has been set up to encourage the mobility of labour; council houses have been sold to tenants – since owner-occupiers move more easily. Conveyancing of housing has been made cheaper and the solicitor's monopoly of the process has been ended. Pensions have been made transferable to encourage people to change jobs. Another problem is the need to retrain if skills are to be developed in the areas where they are required. A wide variety of courses has been developed and archaic apprenticeship practices are under sustained attack, while strike action (the English disease) has been curtailed by a requirement to ballot members before a strike can be held.

The poverty-trap (a better name is the low-income trap) which prevents people taking work while unemployed because the jobs available pay (after tax) less than social security, has been a problem. Tax thresholds have been adjusted upwards (and social security payments adjusted downwards).

The disinclination of employers to employ has been met by reduction in national insurance charges and the phasing out of wages councils – which forced employers to pay high wages to poor-quality labour, public sector pay has been reviewed and is now fixed by market forces (supply and demand) not by national comparisons with other work elsewhere in private sector employment. The official view is that 'government regulations should not impose such a burden on employers that they prefer not to employ'.

(b) The capital market

The first measure taken on the capital market was the ending of foreign exchange control. The result has been a massive export of capital – which has not done a great deal for jobs at home – but it was felt that freedom to move capital to the place where it offered the best economic situation had to be fully appreciated by everyone.

Dividend controls, hire purchase controls on the size of deposits and the periods for repayment and control of bank lending were all abolished and building societies have been allowed to compete more with the banks and other financial institutions. Stock exchange arrangements have been changed to make the market more competitive and changes in capital gains tax and taxation on pensions have made it easier to compare investment opportunities.

Tax changes have made borrowing by companies less attractive and equity finance (finance by the issue of shares) more attractive. Corporation tax has been reduced to make profitability more important and tax avoidance less of a growth industry.

The net effect of many of these measures is to help the rich rather than the poor, but perhaps that is what is needed. The incentive to work hard for personal advancement has been greatly reduced in recent years where welfare (and playing the welfare system) has been too great a preoccupation of too many people.

(c) The market for land

The major improvement here is a massive move into privatisation of excess land held by nationalised industries, local authorities and central government. Not only have sales of land made much of it available for development but a lot of it has been used to set up small business premises which are in real demand as measures to expand the small business sector have pressed ahead.

(d) The encouragement of enterprise

A great many measures to encourage enterprise have been undertaken at a grass-roots level. Almost every local authority has its enterprise agency; small firms services have been developed in most regions, a 'start-up' allowance of £40 per week for one year is available to unemployed people who elect to become self-employed and 1 250 people every week are taking advantage of this offer. Loan guarantee schemes and a business expansion scheme encourage investors to help small businesses get established.

These and other supply-side measures are certainly having an impact in many areas at many levels, and doing at least something to change the climate of business towards greater enterprise and more enthusiastic wealth creation.

There was one other aspect of supply-side economics which gathered pace as the success of microeconomic measures to free industry began to prove successful. The idea grew that nationalised control of many industries was no real benefit to the economy. Central planning and supervision was counter productive, and it would be better to privatise the public sector as far as possible.

28.6.1 Privatisation and supply-side economics

Privatisation (the sale of nationalised industries back to the private sector of the economy) became one of the major gangplanks of supply-side economics. The official Treasury viewpoint on the need for a privatisation programme is given below, by courtesy of the Treasury. It has been abbreviated to some extent, and students are advised to read current literature – *The Economist* etc. – for developments in privatisation.

28.6.2 Privatisation in the United Kingdom

(a) Introduction

The UK Conservative Government's privatisation programme, begun in 1979, ranks among the most radical economic changes in the UK since 1945. Privatisation is a key element in the Government's economic strategy, one of a range of policies to reduce the size of the state-controlled sector of the economy and to increase the proportion of assets owned privately. Other elements of this strategy include giving state sector tenants the right to buy their own homes, inviting tenders for the performance of a wide range of services at present within the public sector and (where cost-effective) contracting these services out to private firms.

The privatisation programme has two main aims: to promote efficiency, whether through competition or other means and to widen share ownership (see below). Competition is the best way to ensure that goods and services desired by the customer are provided at the lowest economic cost. Giving customers freedom of choice enables market forces to provide sustained pressures on companies to increase efficiency. Privatised companies generally operate in a competitive market environment. But the Government does not wish to confine the benefits of privatisation to business in competitive areas of the economy. Privatisation is therefore being extended to the 'natural monopolies', where competition is either unworkable or very limited in scope. To the extent necessary, regulatory arrangements take the place of the market in holding down prices and ensuring good service for the customer.

(b) Background

In 1979, the nationalised industries in the UK accounted for about a tenth of the Gross Domestic Product, a seventh of total investment in the economy and around a tenth of the Retail Price Index. They employed about $1\frac{1}{2}$ million people, and dominated the transport, energy, communications, steel and ship-building sectors of the economy. But despite the high hopes of their founders, their performance has consistently been disappointing. Criticisms have been voiced about their total return on capital employed, their record on prices, productivity and manpower costs, and about the low level of customer satisfaction they have provided.

The reasons for these shortcomings are complex. In many cases, it can be seen that the fault lies not with management and workers, but with the system. The industries are constantly open to political and bureaucratic involvement. Social and commercial objectives become intertwined, to the detriment of both. Because the industries' borrowing is underwritten by the Government, it is indistinguishable in market terms from other forms of public sector borrowing, with the result that the needs of individual state industries must on occasion be subordinated to macroeconomic requirements. Financing constraints spill over to the industries' investment programmes and lead to problems of allocation. Their claims – which may be absolutely justifiable in commercial terms – always have to be viewed against the totality of public expenditure. There are also other checks and restrictions in matters of detail. All these constraints stem from the paramount need to preserve public accountability through Parliament for the use of public money.

Successive governments have attempted to grapple with the poor performance of nationalised industries through increasingly stringent control frameworks. The cumulative effect has been to create a set of external stimuli that, in the absence of real competitive forces, try to provide pressure similar to that normally provided by market mechanisms. The intention behind the Government's privatisation and competition policies is to replace the surrogate market with the real market, in the belief that this represents the logical conclusion of the control philosophy that has evolved over the years.

(c) Benefits and achievements of privatisation

Privatisation is intended to benefit customers, employees and the economy as a whole. Customers benefit when the greater efficiency that can be achieved through privatisation is passed on to them; for example, in the form of prices which are lower than they would otherwise have been, wider choice and better service. Privatised businesses are likely to be more responsive to changing customer demands, and more innovative in introducing new products to the market. They are likely to produce a better return on capital invested, and more economic operations.

For employees, privatisation means working in a company with clear objectives, the means to achieve these and rewards for success. This, in turn, reinforces the concern for the customer that is at the heart of any successful business.

The economy benefits through higher returns on capital in the privatised industries, which can no longer pre-empt resources from elsewhere in the economy but must compete for funds in the open capital markets. And as the products and services of privatised industries underpin much activity elsewhere in the economy, there are substantial benefits for other businesses.

These advantages are borne out in the success of privatised companies. Amongst companies which have been in the private sector for a number of years, the profits of Cable and Wireless, British Aerospace, Amersham International and the National Freight Consortium have increased significantly. Among more recent entrants to the private sector, British Telecom has eliminated waiting lists for installations, Jaguar has made major advances in product quality, sales and profits, and British Gas has increased profits and the number of its customers.

Sometimes the Government has needed to retain specific limited powers over the future ownership, control or conduct of a privatised company. In such cases it has retained a special share or 'golden share' in the company. This does not allow the Government to intervene in the running of the company but may secure certain aspects of national interest or guarantee the company's independence during its early years in the private sector.

To sum up the programme to December 1993, 47 major state corporations and many smaller bodies have been privatised. Receipts so far have been £55 000 million with future sales projected at about £5 billion per year. An interesting side light on these statistics though is that in 1990 it was possible to say that employment in public corporations had declined by 876 000 (to 786 000 from 1 662 000). However, by 1993 employment in public corporations had increased again to 1 203 000.

(d) Wider share ownership

The promotion of wider share ownership – both among employees and the general public – is a major objective of the privatisation programme. This is part of the Government's policy of extending the ownership of wealth more widely in the economy, giving people a direct stake in the success of British industry, and removing the old distinctions between 'owners' and 'workers'. The privatisation programme and the flotation of the Trustee Savings Bank have contributed much to the increase in the number of private investors in the UK. Together TSB and British Gas attracted some 3 million people into share ownership. This means that the number of shareholders has roughly trebled since 1979. And about 90 per cent of eligible employees became shareholders in their companies on privatisation.

The special arrangements that are made to encourage small investors and employees to participate in privatisation sales have contributed to this extension of share ownership. Employees are typically given an offer of free shares and matching shares in proportion to what they buy. They are also given priority over the allocation of a proportion of the total offer. Small investors are made aware of individual sales through extensive marketing campaigns and through the wide distribution of prospectuses and other information. And when an offer is oversubscribed, priority in the allocation of shares is given to small investors.

(e) Mechanics of privatisation

The mechanics of privatisation are complex, and each case raises its own problems. The main options are: trade sale, where a company is sold to a single firm or a consortium; a placing with a group of investors; a public flotation on the Stock Exchange, either by a fixed price or by a tender offer with a minimum price; a management/employee buyout.

Pricing a share issue is always a difficult matter of judgement, whether it is a state-owned or a privately-owned company that is being sold, especially when the company's shares have not been traded before or where there are no directly comparable companies. Moreover, it is impossible for any vendor to anticipate accurately the movements of the stock market between price fixing and the receipt of applications. The UK Government always seeks the best professional advice available, both on pricing and on other aspects of a sale. It has also shown that it is ready to experiment and innovate in the interests of achieving successful privatisations at a fair price for the taxpayer and the investors. However, the effect of privatisation on the Government's finances is incidental to the programme's main purposes, which are to increase efficiency and to widen share ownership to the benefit of the whole economy. Privatisation in the United Kingdom has been widely copied around the world.

The results of privatisation of such a wide range of activities must inevitably be patchy. Some activities are highly competitive or can quickly become so, while others are natural monopolies with heavy capital costs that do not encourage competition. We cannot pay to install four or five telephone lines to our homes in the name of competition. The telephone affairs of the nation are still in the hands of only two suppliers, British Telecom and Mercury, but a network of cable companies is beginning to establish itself.

Practically all privatisations have led to significant increases in productivity as labour forces have been reduced (sometimes whole layers of management have been removed en bloc). However, turning a natural monopoly from a state monopoly into a private one has on the whole not proved particularly beneficial and in particular has not produced significant reductions in price to the ordinary householder or business customer. There may be some evidence of a marginal improvement in services to customers but there is also evidence that after an initial shake-up the monopsonist supplier sinks back into the cosy atmosphere the industry formerly enjoyed as a nationalised corporation.

28.7
Controlling the monetary sector of the economy

To return to the attempt to control the economy by monetary measures which has been such a feature of the period from 1979–90, there can be no doubt that monetarist theories were given the most lengthy trial by the succession of Conservative Governments led by Mrs Thatcher. The experiment was allowed to proceed for so long because there was a conviction that fiscal policy, which attempted to manage prosperity by stop-go policies using high levels of taxation had been proved to be inappropriate. The idea that the money supply could be controlled fitted in well with supply-side economics and the climate of free enterprise that it generated. Part of the procedure of controlling the money supply required the control of the monetary sector – the banks and other institutions which could create credit. First a new Banking Act 1979 gave the Bank of England much closer control over the banking system than it had previously enjoyed, but there is little point in discussing this Act since it was completely repealed and replaced by the Banking Act 1987, which repealed some of the parts of the earlier Act which bankers disliked. The chief effect of the closer control over the banking system was announced on 5 August 1981, and is still effective. It took the form of a paper **Monetary Control-Provisions** which changed the system in force during 1971–81 for control of the banking system. In the first place the Banking Act, 1979, had already established much more stringent controls over the banks after the failure of the 'fringe' banks in 1973–74. The new arrangements reserved the use of the word 'bank' to those institutions which did actually offer a complete range of banking services to wide sections of the general public, and to the specialist, traditional 'merchant banks' who had always offered a rather more limited service. Other institutions were registered as 'deposit-taking institutions' and had to change their names to delete the word 'bank'. Thus the 'industrial banks' generally are reclassified as 'deposit-taking institutions'. With all these institutions now under the control of the Central Bank it was time to change the rules of Competition and Credit Control which had applied from 1971–81, and from 20 August 1981, the Monetary Control Provisions apply. All institutions have had to deposit ½ per cent of the value of their eligible liabilities as cash at the Bank of England. These deposits do not bear interest. The clearing banks must also deposit adequate sums to cover their likely requirements for clearing purposes.

In addition to this all eligible banks agree to keep further assets available as reserve assets easily convertible to cash if required. An 'eligible' bank is one of such a standing that its acceptances on bills of exchange are eligible for discount at the Bank of England. Any bank may apply to become an 'eligible' bank, and the Bank of England will then check whether it meets the necessary criteria. Such a bank must have adequate cash reserves, readily available.

The Bank's document reads as follows on this point:

11   From August 20, 1981, each eligible bank undertakes to maintain secured money with members of the London Discount Market Association and/or secured call money with money brokers and gilt-edged jobbers – all at market rates appropriate to the nature of the lending – such that:

(i)   the total funds so held normally average 4 per cent of that banks's ELs (as defined in paragraph 5);
(ii)   the amount held in the form of secured money with members of the LDMA does not normally fall below 2½ per cent of ELs (as defined in paragraph 5) on any day.

12 *In relation to the above undertaking, each eligible bank will:*

(i) *aim to meet the daily average ratio over either six- or twelve-month periods (having first notified the Bank of its choice of period), the ratio on any particular day in a banking month being calculated as a proportion of ELs at the last but one make-up day. For example, the relevant ELs figure for each day in banking September will be those as at make-up day in banking July.*

and

(ii) *to provide monthly returns of its daily figures, which the Bank will use to assess the bank's performance relative to its long-term commitment.*

A bank will go below the minimum only in exceptional circumstances and will be ready to explain such action to the Bank when the relevant monthly return is made.

(Reproduced by courtesy of the Bank of England)

The effect of these measures is to ensure reasonable liquidity for eligible banks, but the Bank of England has also had discussions with all banks to ensure that their own systems of 'prudential controls' are adequate for the overall safety of the bank concerned.

To list the measures of monetary policy we have:

(a) *Interest rate policy.* The Bank of England's policy on interest rates is explained in the new document. Previously the bank had announced changes of Minimum Lending Rate (MLR) on Thursdays. This is discontinued, but the Bank reserves the right to promulgate MLR when it feels the market needs a clear signal, so MLR is not quite dead. Instead of a weekly announcement the Bank will allow the market to decide interest rates – but covertly the Bank influences the rates in what it considers to be desirable directions. In general rates are kept high, to discourage individual spending, and encourage the sale of gilt-edged securities.

(b) *Direct controls.* The 'corset', a system calling for special deposits from banks lending too generously, has now been abandoned, but the ordinary system of 'special deposits' which are frozen to restrict bank lending has been retained, although it is not in use at present (1995). The Bank obviously feels it needs to have this right to call for special deposits should tighter credit control prove to be essential in the future.

(c) *Open-market operations.* The Bank of England's improved knowledge of the banking sector since the 1979 Act, and its struggles to control the money supply, have enabled it to know with greater accuracy than ever before what the money supply is, and how it varies from day to day. If a shortage of money is likely to develop on a particular day it buys bills on the open market to relieve the shortage, rather than forcing the discount houses into the Bank. If a surplus is likely to occur at some future date it arranges to sell Treasury Bills on that date to mop up the surplus, and to mature on a date when a shortage is likely to develop. The shortage will then be relieved by the Bank repaying the loan and redeeming the bill. The bank is thus seeking to control day-to-day events by the most careful forecasts of the flow of funds.

(d) *Foreign exchange dealings.* When foreign exchange payments flow in or out of the country the money supply fluctuates. If the Bank refuses to intervene on the foreign exchange markets the price of the pound rises and falls instead.

(e) *Fiscal policies*. These are still a major weapon in the war to control inflation, since they have a strong impact on the money available to consumers and reduce the funds available in the economy.

(f) *Public spending controls*. These are usually called 'cash limits' – a budget for spending departments is drawn up and may not be exceeded without the most severe examination of the supplementary expenditure proposed. In a famous phrase one chancellor said: 'In former times programmes have decided how much money will be spent – in future the reverse will be the case.' Keeping the expenditure within the budget allowed is a salutary control over spending departments.

Monetarism works by defining a measure of money supply (see pages 344–5) and setting a limit to its growth in the coming financial period.

A major problem for monetarists is the existence of 'lags' in the economy. This means the amount of time required for a given monetarist measure to take effect in the economy. Government policy is implemented through a variety of **instruments** aimed at achieving a given effect – in this case an impact on the money supply. To measure the effect it is necessary to designate certain variables as **indicators**. Even if the variables chosen are reliable indicators of what is happening to the target aimed at, there may be a considerable time-lag before the instrument has any impact at all. It is also difficult to be sure that something else has not caused the indicator to react. The following examples may be helpful:

(a) *Information lags*. Where policy-makers are expected to act to take preventative measures when certain information comes to light, they may not receive the information, or may distrust it, before taking corrective action. There is a strong tendency to 'wait and see'. Action is delayed and a deteriorating situation may get out of hand.

(b) *Decision lags*. Even when policies are clearly laid down and discretion within a policy has been allocated to officials responsible for executive action they may not implement the policy at once. It is even worse where the decision has to be referred up to higher authorities, and action must be delayed until approval is given. President Truman is reputed to have had a notice over his desk in the White House saying 'The buck stops here'. There is a strong tendency for those who have to take decisions to pass the responsibility to someone else.

(c) *Interest rate lags*. Monetarists believe that the supply of money responds to changes in interest rates, and therefore government (or central bank) activity to manipulate interest rates is a useful instrument for influencing the money supply. Unfortunately, the impact is not instantaneous, and a climate of opinion takes some time to develop before the general public begin to respond by buying (or selling) a particular type of investment. This type of lag may lead to excessive adjustment of interest rates because the effect appears at first sight to be too small, resulting in overshooting once the time-lag has passed.

Targets may be missed for various reasons from year to year. Generally speaking the government has only an imperfect idea of what causes changes in money supply. There is, for example, a tendency to raise interest rates in order to convince investors that a fall in interest rates must follow sooner or later. As Keynes showed, when gilt-edged interest rates are high investors will buy gilts because they will rise in price if interest rates fall. In buying gilt-edged securities investors will take the funds from their accounts in the banks and thus decrease the money supply.

The conviction during the 1980s that only interest rates would have any real impact on the money supply, and the many attempts to define the money supply and discover what it really was at any given moment in time, had a very serious effect on the economy. Despite the fact that even as early as 1986 some economists had decided after some six years of trying to define, and control, the money supply, that it was to some extent indefinable (and perhaps even uncontrollable) the experiment continued. Goodheart's law (see page 343) seemed to rule, but the use of interest rates as the sole measure to control the money supply continued to be used, with very serious effects on some vulnerable people, small businesses, home buyers, etc. However, the need to proceed with affairs in the European Union began to exert an impact on domestic policies. The UK joined the ERM, bringing UK interest rates closer to the rates prevailing in the rest of the European Union. As belief grew that naked monetarism in the Milton Friedman style was no more a panacea for economic problems than Keynesianism had been, and that a return to Government action was desirable to cure the depression of the early 1990s, our economist versifier wrote:

Let's ignore the old man from Chicago,
Against thrift let's bring in an embargo;
A prosperous trend
Will return if we spend
So let's order champagne and escargots.

The great experiment of monetarism was allowed to draw to a close and a greater variety of measures may now be used to secure control of the economy. Close definitions of the money supply have ceased to be a major preoccupation of Chancellors of the Exchequeur, and King Canute has been restored to his chair as the only ruler of the United Kingdom who tried to hold back the tides on the advice of his 'wise' men.

28.8 Conclusions about monetarist policies

There are four main threads in any government's policies. They are:

(a) To maintain a high and stable level of employment,
(b) To secure continuous economic growth,
(c) To keep inflation at a low level, and
(d) To avoid balance of payments difficulties.

These threads are mutually irreconcilable to some extent, and any one of them can only be fully achieved at the expense of the others. For monetarists, facing the realities of the last quarter of the twentieth century, the aim of keeping inflation at a low level seems to be dominant.

The best that can be said for the pursuit of monetarist policies in the UK is that the Conservative administrations led by Mrs Thatcher had been a real test of monetarism. Seldom has an economic idea been so whole-heartedly pursued with such single-minded determination. The prospect of going through the three million unemployed barrier and even the demise of major industries have not been allowed to interfere with the monetarist experiment.

On the credit side of the account we may claim that a greater sense of realism in employment and in industrial relations exists after ten years of industrial restructuring, de-featherbedding, privatisations, mergers and closures. Industry is now much leaner: the question is whether the patient is too emaciated to recover. The balance of payments is now once again a cause for concern despite enormous savings made possible by North Sea oil, now that the huge oil imports of previous decades are replaced by domestic supplies. Industry has moved into the microcomputer age, with a general acceptability of microprocessor techniques throughout industry.

Against this must be set the really massive decline in UK secondary manufacture as a result of free trade. There is no way to keep imports out even when they appear to be infringing international anti-dumping agreements. Many of the developed nations, the newly industrialised countries and the developing nations are able to undercut British-made goods, though possibly there is some overt or covert assistance to industries. The criterion here is whether the goods sold in the UK are being sold at prices which are lower than those charged to home nationals. In many cases they are, in some cases blatantly so. Against this may be set the success of UK goods now selling abroad from British, Japanese-run factories. It seems the traditional way UK industry was run was part of the problem.

A monetarist anti-inflation policy is essentially a low-growth policy. If your approach is one of meeting national needs, when the entire world is in need of massive expansion of economic activity, it makes it very difficult to play a full part in world recovery. We have widespread poverty in a world where there is excess capacity in almost every industry. It is illogical not to put unemployed factors to work, but it has to be a coordinated international effort. Governments with a blinkered approach – so worried about their own internal problems that they cannot be roused to support a sustained effort for growth internationally – do a disservice to their own nationals as well as all the rest. Monetarist policies, both in the UK and the USA are essentially introverted, narrow, selfish and self-defeating. It is relatively easy to manage an impoverished society – the management of prosperity and a fuller life for mankind calls for the opposite policies: wealth creation on a massive scale.

To be fair, the monetarist policy has now largely been modified. Its good side is that it is clear that the new realism in economic life is producing growth and greater competitiveness in world trade. The present position of the United Kingdom is that it is managing its own economy and not seeking to play any vital part in developing the economic structure of Europe as a whole. Re-joining the European Monetary System would be an essential pre-requisite to returning to the heart of the EU, and probably would be possible now that the UK currency has been depreciated down to a realistic position. The speculators can only win if the currency is over-valued. If it is realistically valued, return to the EMS should be possible. 'Black Wednesday' has blighted the part the UK hoped to play. We should try again!

28.9
Summary of
Chapter 28

1 Early economists noted a relationship between the amount of money in circulation and prices. Professor Irving Fisher expressed this in the equation of exchange $MV = PT$.

2 The most important element in changes in the money supply is the ability of the banks to 'create credit' by granting loans and overdrafts to their customers.

3 Any attempt to control the money supply requires us to measure it. The measures of money supply in use at present are M0, NIBM1, M1, M2, M3, M3c, M4 and M5 (see Table 28.1 in text).

4 The success of Keynesian economics in achieving reasonable prosperity for all led to increased expectations, and eventually to inflation. To

combat inflation Keynesian economics was abandoned and monetarist policies to control the money supply were instituted.

5 The chief aim of monetarism is to control inflation. A close control of the money supply is achieved by a quiver of fiscal and monetary weapons; monetary targets for growth of the money supply are set and every effort is made to meet them.

6 The measures available to implement monetarist policies are: (*a*) interest rate policies; (*b*) direct controls over bank lending; (*c*) open-market operations; (*d*) floating exchange rates; (*e*) taxation policies; and (*f*) public spending cash limits.

7 Many of the improvements in the economy have been achieved by 'supply-side' measures – measures designed to act to promote wealth creation and the supply of goods and services – as distinct from Keynesian economics designed to operate on the economy by influencing demand. Supply-side measures work by making the markets for land, labour, capital and enterprise work better. They remove restrictions built into the factor markets by vested interests such as trade unions, or by oppressive legislation of a social nature which heaps costs onto industry.

8 Privatisation of socially owned enterprises is another feature of the monetarist experiment, and it has had considerable success and been widely copied.

Exercises Set 28

1 What is an equation of exchange? Explain the elements of the equation and why it has been held to illustrate the workings of a market economy?

2 What is the 'prudential reserve' ratio of a bank? What influence does it have on the activities of bankers?

3 'Loans make deposits.' Explain this statement, and the importance of the creation of bank credit in the economy of a country.

4 The banks are preoccupied with achieving liquidity, profitability and security. Explain the importance of each of these to the banker. How does he achieve all three at the same time?

5 'Bankers can only lend what is lent to them by others.' Discuss.

6 Explain the term 'keeping in step' as applied to the activities of commercial banks when sanctioning loans and overdrafts to customers.

7 What are the main objectives of governments' economic policies? To what extent are they mutually irreconcilable?

8 What are monetarist policies? How may they be implemented?

9 'Any measure of money supply that is officially controlled promptly loses its meaning.' (Goodhart's Law.) Explain.

10 What is meant by (*a*) M3, (*b*) M0?

11 Why are 'lags' such a nuisance to monetarists seeking to control the economy? In your answer refer to (*a*) interest lags, (*b*) information lags, (*c*) executive lags.

12 'Fiscal policies are dead; monetarist policies are the only ones that will control the money supply.' Discuss.

13 What are 'supply-side' measures and how do they differ from Keynesian measures to improve the economy?

14 What is the aggregate demand – aggregate supply (AD–AS) model of the economy? In what way is it an improvement on the national income equilibrium diagram?

29.1
**The public sector
of the economy**

At one time the activities of a central government were limited to the keeping of internal and external peace. In return for the security which it provided, a portion of the national output in the form of taxation was surrendered to the sovereign power. The extent of this tax contribution varied with the rapacity of the sovereign, and the ability of the lesser nobles, merchants, and ordinary people to resist or to control him.

Today the situation is very different; the powers of the sovereign have been curbed by a code of laws and conventions, and the duties of governments extend far beyond the traditional powers of peace-keeping. Governments now control a large sector of the economy, providing not only security but welfare services of all sorts, and also providing through nationalised industries a range of goods and services which for some reason are produced more satisfactorily in this way. Thus in the UK a National Health Service provides a wide range of benefits from before birth until death. These services could be provided privately, but we have chosen to provide them socially. Similarly, but by a different process of development, atomic power stations and other matters affecting the nuclear industry are under the control of the Atomic Energy Authority.

A full picture of such activities can be gained by considering the set of figures for public expenditure given in Table 29.1.

29.1.1
The public sector and
the private sector

Public debate rages over the level of resources which should be allocated to the public sector. During the early 1960s management of the economy tended to act against the interests of the public sector and in favour of the private sector. The Keynesian idea was to expand the public sector whenever the private sector suffered a setback. When governments became adept at keeping the economy booming by injecting an appropriate amount of AMD into the economy, setbacks in the private sector did not occur, and the public sector was starved of resources. In the late 1960s this imbalance was corrected, and socially desirable policies were pushed ahead, particularly in education and higher education, but also in the social services, and welfare fields.

These advances in social aspirations could only be achieved by a reduction in the private sector or by growth in the economy. In the late 1960s and early 1970s growth proved very difficult to achieve, so that controls over the private sector increased. Not only was taxation heavy, but the social aspirations included measures to promote such aims as security of employment, equality of opportunity, equality of the sexes, etc. These measures raised cost to the private sector. It soon became clear that the private sector was being reduced more than was wise. If a public sector service is not self-financing (for example defence, education, health services, etc.) any deficit must be financed from taxation on the private sector. To reduce the private sector to less than 50 per cent of the total activity in the economy is to place too great a burden on it, and tax revenues may be inadequate.

Table 29.1 UK public sector income and expenditure 1993 (£ million)

Current Account

Payments	£m	Receipts	£m
Defence	23 621	Taxation:	
Public order	13 979	On income	73 070
Education	32 293	On expenditure	91 361
Health	35 845	National Insurance	38 503
Social security	96 023	Community charge	8 001
Housing	5 617	Trading surpluses	294
Recreational/cultural	3 186	Rents	5 736
Fuel and energy	−522	Interest and dividends	4 803
Agriculture, etc.	3 828	Imputed charge for	
Mining, etc.	1 165	consumption of non-trading	
Transport and communication	2 101	capital	3 308
General services	11 405		662
Other economic services	4 796	Other transfers	
Other expenses	5 607	Total funds available	225 738
Debt interest	18 446	Deficit on Current Account	31 652
	£m257 390		£m257 390

Capital Account

	£m		£m
Deficit on Current A/C	31 652	Taxes on capital	2 627
Gross domestic fixed capital formation	11 097	Total deficit	48 664
Physical increase in stocks	−24		
Grants and transfers to other sectors	8 566		
	£m51 291		£m51 291

Deficit financed by	£m
Increase in liabilities to overseas creditors	−45 562
Decrease in assets held overseas	−1 836
	−47 398
Balancing item (Figures becoming available but not yet clear)	−1 266
	£m−48 664

Source: Blue Book of National Income and Expenditure 1994

The privatisation of parts of the public sector has been an important feature of economic policy in the late 1980s (see pages 360–2) and as a result the public sector has fallen to almost 38 per cent of the economic activity – a much more sensible figure. This is financed by taxation. What principles govern such taxation?

**29.2
Adam Smith's
canons of taxation**

Adam Smith listed four principles of taxation policy which should, he said, be observed by governments. These were:

(*a*) Taxation should be equal, by which he meant proportional to the taxpayers' incomes.
(*b*) Taxes should be certain, and not at the whim of the tax collector.
(*c*) Taxes should be arranged so that collection is convenient.
(*d*) Taxes should be economic, that is the yield should be greater than the cost of collection.

A modern chancellor might add other principles, such as:

(*e*) Impartial treatment of all taxpayers.
(*f*) Absence of disincentive effects on hard work or enterprise.
(*g*) Consistency with government policies.
(*h*) Adjustability if necessary.
(*i*) The cost of compliance should be kept as low as possible.

*(a) Taxation should
be equal*

There are three ways of collecting tax from individuals so that it falls 'equally'. These are:

(i) The *per capita* tax, in which everyone pays the same contribution, say £250.00 per head.
(ii) The proportional tax, in which everyone pays the same proportion of their income in tax, say 10 per cent. This was Adam Smith's 'equal' tax.
(iii) The progressive tax, in which the amount of tax is adjusted to fall most heavily on the rich. The opposite is a 'regressive' tax, which falls more heavily upon the poor. Thus in Table 29.2, the line for proportional taxation shows all parties paying the same proportion of their income in tax, but the tax is regressive because the loss of 20 per cent of his income is nothing to the rich person, but a very severe burden to the poor person.

Table 29.2 shows the tax burden falling on three individuals under each of these three classes.
Which of these tax systems gives the fairest tax? We must judge them not from the weight of the burden in absolute terms, but relative to the utility to

Table 29.2 'Equal' taxation: the three methods

	Income per annum					
	Mr A £1 500		Mr B £5 000		Mr C £50 000	
Type of tax	Tax	Balance to spend	Tax	Balance to spend	Tax	Balance to spend
Per capita (£250.00 per head)	£250	£1 250	£250	£4 750	£250	£49 750
Proportional (20%)	£300	£1 200	£1 000	£4 000	£10 000	£40 000
Progressive	£–	£1 500	£ 500	£4 500	£20 000	£30 000

the taxpayer of the income surrendered. Clearly the *per capita* tax is most unfair, while even the proportional tax is unjust. The point here is that the utility of each pound given up is very much greater to Mr A earning £1500 than the utility of that same pound to Mr B or Mr C. Mr B is still left with 2⅔ times Mr A's whole income, while Mr C is left with 26⅔ times Mr A's whole income. If the total tax needed is only £11 300, the 'fairest' way is for Mr C to pay it all.

The progressive system is therefore the 'fairest' system for direct taxation, and this system has been adopted by most nations. However, it is not possible to take enough tax from the rich to finance all the nation's needs, and tax does fall upon all citizens in an indirect way.

(b) Taxes should be certain

A system of tax collection which is not certain will almost invariably cause discontent. For example, the system of tax-farming used in medieval times gave a local official the power to collect taxes from a given area. So long as the required sum was paid to the ruler no questions were asked as to how much profit the collector earned from his 'farm'. A rapacious and extortionate tax gatherer could therefore collect whatever taxes he wished, and could show favouritism or discrimination as it pleased him.

(c) Taxes should be arranged so that collection is convenient

Taxes are invariably a burden at the time of payment, even when the taxpayer agrees that they are just and equitable. To collect them at the most convenient point reduces losses by non-payment and simplifies the whole process. For example, income tax in Britain used to be a very nominal sum, twopence or threepence in the £1, and it was reasonable to collect it as a lump sum every six months. It now represents a very much larger fraction of earned income and payment every six months would require the ordinary citizens to save up several weeks' wages to pay taxes when required. A great many of them might default on such payments. The PAYE (pay-as-you-earn) system relieves them of this necessity. The tax is extracted from the pay packet before it is even received and the employer pays it over to the Inland Revenue authorities. In 1972 a new system was suggested in a Green Paper called '*Proposals for a Tax Credit System*'. Under this system not only would tax be deducted from the wages of taxpayers, but the welfare payments to families with children, or those in need of rent allowances or family income supplements would be added to the wage packet. This would be done by a system of 'Tax Credits', to those needing extra income. A person whose tax credits exceeded tax debits would find money added to the pay packet by the employer. The scheme has not yet been approved by Parliament in the form outlined above; although a scheme bearing the name 'Tax Credit' has been developed to help particular groups of disadvantaged low-income families.

(d) Taxes should be economic, i.e. productive of revenue

Any tax which costs more to collect than it raises in revenue is clearly a waste of time. Of course taxation might be introduced for reasons other than raising revenue (for example to discourage an undesirable habit like gambling), but if it is a revenue-raising tax it ought to be abandoned if it is uneconomic. During the nineteenth century dozens of taxes which were barely economic were abandoned. They included taxes on windows, shops, horses, carriages, servants, coal, salt, wine, beer, leather, calico, candles, slates, earthenware, sweets, glass, brick, soap and paper. By 1881 the entire revenue (admittedly only £69 million) came from five taxes: income tax £21 million, stamp duty £4 million, spirits £31 million, tobacco £9 million and tea £4 million.

(e) Taxes should be impartial	Complete impartiality is achieved by direct taxation, if it is designed so as to be progressive in as 'fair' a way as possible. Two citizens in the same situation as regards income, dependents etc. are taxed the same. Impartiality is much more difficult when indirect taxes are imposed. A tax on hair-dressing will not affect some people, the non-smoker avoids tobacco duty and the teetotaller avoids the alcohol tax. In many cases of tax on goods the incidence of the tax is on someone other than the person who consumes the goods, and it is usually the supplier or the manufacturer who is forced to suffer the tax. This is explained more fully on page 382.

The impartiality achieved by progressive taxation is often called 'vertical equity'. 'Horizontal equity', by contrast, seeks to ensure that two persons with the same income and the same commitments pay the same tax. While this is fairly easy to achieve with direct taxation it cannot be achieved with indirect taxation unless all taxpayers have the same scale of preferences for goods.

(f) Absence of disincentive effect on hard work or enterprise	It is very important to a nation that its people should work hard, should be industrious and busy. They will work best when personal incentives are great since personal prosperity is desired by all. Only a particularly dedicated person will keep working year after year for philanthropic or patriotic reasons. If taxation is so heavy that overtime becomes pointless, so progressive that responsibility is not worth accepting, then the tax is having a disincentive effect. People will 'vote with their feet' and leave the country; a 'brain-drain' or a 'capital-drain' develops as useful factors which cannot, in their estimation, earn a suitable reward, emigrate to other countries where their services are required.

(g) The costs of compliance should be as low as possible	It is expensive to comply with tax laws, and to employ accountants who will discover exactly what the laws say so that you need not pay more than a proper amount. If costs of compliance can be reduced, dissatisfaction will be avoided.

29.3 **Tax structure of the UK**	The first classification of taxes is into **direct taxes** and **indirect taxes**. Direct taxes are levied directly on the individual taxpayer; the burden is personal and inescapable. Indirect taxes are not levied directly on individuals, but on the activities of individuals. They can be avoided by refraining from the taxed activity, or they may be passed on to other people if the economic conditions are favourable. Thus we need to study the *incidence of taxation*, i.e. on whom does the tax fall, with indirect taxes.

29.3.1 Direct taxes	Direct taxes have in the past included income tax, surtax, corporation tax, capital gains tax and estate duty (death duty). Today income tax takes the form of a graduated personal tax. The main features of taxation now are given below.

(a) *Personal taxation*   The income of individuals, instead of paying income tax, followed by surtax for those with very high incomes, now suffers a graduated personal tax. It includes (a) certain personal allowances which all may enjoy which prevent very poor people from being caught in the tax net at all, since they do not earn enough to reach even the lowest scale of tax (currently the 20 per cent band); (b) a lower band of tax which, if it catches poor people at all only charges them a low rate of tax; (c) taxation at a basic rate on a broad band of income (this catches most of the middle income people but only takes a relatively reasonable rate of tax (currently 24 per cent); (d) higher rates of tax at the 40 per cent level – to bring in a 'fair' share of taxation from the well-to-do. A new system of self-assessment of this and all other direct taxes is described on page 284.

(b) *Corporation tax*   Corporation tax is a tax levied on companies. It is at present being revised downwards to reduce the tax payable by small companies to a level closer to the figure for ordinary citizens. It is currently (1996) at the 24 per cent level.

(c) *Capital taxes*   It sometimes happens that where wealth has been accumulated to an excessive extent by particular classes of people, the government will wish to redistribute it by taxing away the actual capital. Such a tax has been popularly designated a 'wealth tax'.

(d) *Capital-gains tax*   A 'capital gain' is an increase in the value of an asset arising from some change in demand or market situation. There is an element of luck in some capital gains, which arise as a result of events rather than any special effort on the part of the asset's owner. For many years there was no tax payable on this kind of capital appreciation, for it was held that capital gains could not be taxed as income. This was an anomaly in tax law, because it gave immunity from tax to a class of relatively affluent persons who conducted regular activities on markets like the Stock Exchange, the New Issue Market, the property market, the markets for fine art etc. Where these transactions are occasional there might be some case for holding that only a capital appreciation is involved, but where they are repeated frequently as a series of short-term activities, they are clearly in the nature of business activities. The 1962 and 1975 Finance Acts therefore brought these short-term activities within the tax net.

    If you buy certain assets and resell them, it is assumed that you are trading in them, and the profit is taxable. If you make a loss you can set this off against any profits which you have made on other things. Examples are investments, property (apart from private dwelling houses), and works of art. It follows, although the rules on any given transaction are complicated, that if your income is increased by capital gains you are caught in the tax net.

(e) *Development gains tax*   This tax was first introduced in the UK in 1974. It was payable at a flat rate of 60 per cent when the development value of land was realised. Aimed at the profits of land speculators it resulted in less land becoming available for development, and was discontinued in 1985–6.

(f) *Inheritance tax*   This tax is the new name for Capital Transfer Tax since the concept of taxation on gifts made in the lifetime of the donor was abandoned in the

1986 Budget. The tax is not payable on the first £200 000 and the rate is 40 per cent. A wide variety of small gifts, (for example gifts made to children at the time of their marriage by the parents of the married couple) are now exempt. The principle of death duties is that where a person makes a fortune, that fortune must be contributed by the mass of the citizens in the excellent profits made by the person's trading or professional activities. It has been generally agreed that such rewards, however well deserved, ought to be returned to the mass of the people at death (while still leaving reasonable provision for heirs or dependants).

29.3.2 Advantages of direct taxation

The chief advantages of direct taxes, like personal taxation, and corporation tax, are that they have a high yield relative to cost; they are reasonably certain in their application, and equitable because they fall most heavily on those who can afford to pay.

A personal tax of one penny in the £1 raises about £2500 million in the UK, and gives a Chancellor considerable control of any uncertainty in the economy. (The use of the budget as a regulator of the economy is discussed on page 379). Direct taxation is thus a very effective method of regulating the economy. By removing money from, or restoring money to, the pockets of the nation's citizens, it enables very rapid alterations in spending policy to be achieved, to change the level of aggregate monetary demand.

The progressive nature of personal taxes and death duties redistributes national income and national capital to avoid gross inequalities of income and wealth. This promotes social harmony.

29.3.3 Disadvantages of direct taxation

The chief disadvantage of these taxes is that they constitute a disincentive to hard work. Cases are on record where authors who write a single volume which sells well are forced to emigrate because taxation removes such a large proportion of the income. The author's next book will earn income for another country. The author's talents are effectively lost. Similarly a dramatist who could write several film scripts or plays per year may decide to write only a single script because any extra output would yield so little extra income. At more routine levels a high rate of tax on eventual earnings discourages individuals from working overtime, or taking extra responsibilities even if salary is raised. Leisure becomes more attractive than income.

High tax levels increase the advantages of avoiding taxation by discovering loopholes in the tax laws. Clever accountants can save their companies enormous sums, and a transference of good brains into socially unprofitable tax-avoidance activities wastes talent. High taxation repels foreign capital which would otherwise seek investment in a country, and encourages firms and individuals to invest abroad in tax havens. The development of 'flags of convenience' in the shipping field enables entrepreneurs to escape taxation.

Direct taxation on a company's profits reduces the capital available for ploughing back into the industry. This lowers productivity since the latest equipment would usually mean faster working speeds and higher output. The overall effects of corporation tax are very difficult to assess, but the tendency to regard companies as an inexhaustible source of tax revenue should be resisted. If extra taxes are imposed on business activities prices must rise, and the tax falls, not on the company, but on the mass of consumers who use the company's products.

During the 1980s tax avoidance has been less of a growth industry and tax levels on the business sector have been reduced to more reasonable

Table 29.3 Yield of UK taxes 1993

	£ millions
Taxes on wages and salaries (including National Insurance)	96 526
Taxes on companies (Corporation Tax)	11 262
Taxes on expenditure (including motor vehicle tax)	91 361
Taxes on public corporations	151
Taxes on non-residents	3 634
Community charge	8 001
Royalties and franchises	951
Taxes on capital	2 386
	£m214 272

Source: Blue Book on National Income and Expenditure 1994

proportions. Corporation tax on company profits fell from 52 per cent to 33 per cent during the decade (25 per cent for small companies). The actual figures for the yield of UK taxes in 1993 are shown in Table 29.3.

29.3.4 Indirect taxes

Indirect taxes include purchase taxes, sales taxes, value-added tax, selective employment tax, taxes on tobacco, spirits and wines, petrol and fuel oil, motor taxes, betting and gaming taxes, stamp duties and many more. All of these have been tried in the UK at one time or another.

Some of these taxes are specific taxes, i.e. a definite sum is charged per unit. For example, petrol duty stands at 46.6 per cent of pump prices and tobacco duty at 56.6 per cent of retail price. Value added tax has now been raised to a flat rate of 17½ per cent on all goods and services, except those designated as 'zero rated' or 'exempt'. The rate on fuel is 8 per cent.

Indirect taxes called **customs duties** are levied at the port on imported goods. Others called **excise duties** are levied on home-produced goods or services. Tobacco tax and the tax on wines are examples of customs duties. The alcohol taxes on whisky and beer produced within the UK, and the licences charged for betting shops and gaming houses are examples of excise duties.

Motor taxes are payable on all vehicles, and form an additional cost to the motorist of £135 per annum. On commercial vehicles they are very heavy indeed, and may be as much as £2000 per vehicle per annum.

A widespread change in indirect taxation took place during 1973, when Britain entered the EEC. It involved the abolition of purchase tax, an *ad valorem* tax imposed on wholesalers at the point where goods were passed on to retailers. The retailer then passed the tax on to the final consumers, who were therefore taxed upon the 'purchases' they made. Selective employment tax was also abolished. This tax was imposed in 1966, by the Labour administration. Its purpose was to reduce employment in service industries. These taxes were replaced by value added tax.

(a) Value added tax

Value added tax is a tax imposed at every level of economic activity, over the very widest ranges of goods and services. The tax is applied at each stage

Table 29.4 Tax collection under the VAT scheme

Tax calculation	Gravel pit owner £	Manufacturer £	Civil engineer £
1 Cost price of output (without tax)	–(gift of nature)	1 000	3 000
2 Sale price of output (without tax)	1 000	3 000	10 000
3 Value added	1 000	2 000	7 000
4 Sale price (with tax at 17½%)	1 175	3 525	11 750
5 Tax position	Input:Output 0:175	Input:Output 175:525	Imput:Output 525:1 750
6 Tax collected: Output – Input (payable to HM Customs)	175	350	1 225
7 Tax paid personally	0	0	0
	(The entire tax falls upon the final consumer – the local authority who bought the bridge, since they paid £11 750 for a £10 000 bridge.)		

where value is added. Imagine a gravel pit owner whose product is bought by a manufacturer of precast concrete bridge sections. These are purchased by a civil engineering contractor for use in a roadbuilding project. Value is added at three points: (*a*) where the natural product is removed from the pit for use; (*b*) when the raw material is manufactured into the semi-finished product; (*c*) when the pre-cast units are assembled into the civil engineering facility. At each stage value added tax is levied at – say – the 17½ per cent level. Let us imagine that £1000 of gravel is turned into £3000 of pre-cast units which are turned into a £10 000 bridge. Tax is added by the pit-owner at 17½ per cent (£175), by the manufacturer (£525), and by the civil engineering contractor (£1750). The total tax payable by the consumer (say the local authority that ordered the bridge) is £1750. This sum will be collected in the manner shown below, using a system of calculations involving input taxes and output taxes.

- *Input tax* is that part of his/her 'purchases' which the individual is paying extra as value added tax.
- *Output tax* is that part of his/her 'sales' which the individual is receiving extra as value added tax.

The difference between the two, output tax – input tax, is the net tax collected by the individual on behalf of HM Customs. This is accounted for to the Customs and Excise Department.

**29.3.5
The advantages of indirect taxation**

The chief advantages of indirect taxation are that the effects are spread more widely throughout the community, and the tax is often paid without the taxpayers being conscious of it, as it appears to be part of the purchase price of the commodity or service being supplied.

Without indirect taxation the government would find it difficult to raise the revenue it requires to finance its activities. Direct taxation would have to be raised to a level where the disincentive effects were very strong. Indirect taxation, by spreading the taxes over most citizens, promotes a sense of social responsibility. The demand for free goods is highly elastic, and without their present tax increments many goods would appear to be so cheap as to be almost 'free'. This would increase demand to points where the marginal utility of the goods was very small, so that the commodity was almost being wasted. When indirect taxes raise prices they cause citizens to take a desirable interest in the uses made of these revenues.

Indirect taxes do not have a disincentive effect on effort; they may even increase effort if they are placed on desirable goods and services. So long as the level of tax is kept reasonable, so that goods are not placed hopelessly out of reach of ordinary people, the incentive effect of indirect taxes may raise productivity and benefit the nation as a whole.

Indirect taxes may be used for a wide variety of government purposes, to promote policies deemed desirable. For instance, an infant industry may be protected by tariffs from foreign competition. Improvements in social standards may be achieved by the removal or imposition of taxes: thus the abolition of the window tax in nineteenth-century Britain produced improvements in house design to give better light to the inhabitants. The imposition of betting taxes may reduce undesirable gambling, and the tobacco tax may reduce lung cancer. Links with overseas countries may be strengthened by reciprocal trading agreements involving tariff changes, and effects on the balance of payments may be achieved by encouraging exports and restricting imports.

29.3.6
Regressive nature of indirect taxation

One criticism that is often made of indirect taxation is that it is regressive, in other words it falls more heavily on the poor than on the rich. For example, to tax household durables like vacuum cleaners, washing machines, or refrigerators with perhaps 20 per cent VAT is to tax regressively. Since no household really needs two of these articles the poor person and the rich person will pay the same tax. As the income surrendered in tax has greater utility to the poor person than it has to the more wealthy individual the burden falls more heavily. Similarly, as motor tax is the same on a small saloon car as on a Rolls-Royce it is a regressive tax. The adverse effects of regressive taxation are to some extent reduced if basic necessities are not taxed at all. Thus it is rare to tax bread or potatoes, meat, eggs and vegetables. Indirect taxation, by contrast, is often quite heavy on tobacco, alcoholic beverages and tea, which have been called the poor man's luxuries. The heavy tax on these items is partly connected with the inelastic nature of the demand for them which makes them particularly suitable for taxation purposes (see page 119).

Other criticisms of indirect taxes include their lack of impartiality, since they can be avoided by abstaining from the use of the article taxed. Thus the teetotal non-smoker who does not drive a car escapes enormous tax burdens in the UK.

Nearly all indirect taxes are inflationary. They lead to demands for higher wages to offset the higher taxes, and when these are granted the Chancellor is forced to raise taxation again. It is particularly difficult to avoid this sort of spiral in a free-enterprise society. For example, after the oil states raised their prices in 1973 heavy levels of both direct and indirect taxation were imposed with the deliberate intention of reducing the standard of living being enjoyed by the British public, which was out of step with their productivity at the time. The complex price rises that followed included three elements:

(*a*) an element caused by the increased raw-material prices due to depreciation of the currency as the pound floated downwards;
(*b*) increased indirect taxation deliberately imposed by the government;
(*c*) an element of unfair price increases caused by the desire of corporations to keep ahead of inflation.

To avert massive pressure for increases in wages the government formed a 'social contract' with the trade unions to limit wage increases to agreed levels. This, and high levels of unemployment, forced a reduction in real incomes.

29.4
The budget as an instrument of economic management

In the UK the Chancellor of the Exchequer usually presents his tax proposals to Parliament every December. The budget is not just designed to raise revenue to meet government expenditure, but is an instrument for achieving control of the economy during the coming year. The true function of governments in modern advanced societies is to preserve the general prosperity. This is done by keeping aggregate monetary demand strong enough to avoid recessions and slumps, but not so strong that inflation develops. The new budgetary measures are later set out in a Finance Bill which, upon receiving the Royal Assent, becomes legally enforceable. Powers to collect taxes have to be renewed annually as a protection to the common people, so that the budget can never be delayed without the whole administrative machine being in grave danger of illegality.

The Chancellor's main task therefore is to assess the economic situation. Does the economy need stimulating severely, or moderately, or does it need to be restrained? He brings in a budget which will have an accelerating effect, or a neutral effect or a restraining effect, according to the government's estimates of what is required.

29.4.1
Budgeting for a deficit

When the Chancellor 'budgets for a deficit', he plans to spend more in the year than he collects in tax. This can only mean that in his view the economy is in need of stimulation; the level of aggregate monetary demand needs to be raised. The signs will be obvious to all. Unemployment will be higher than the normal transitional-unemployment level. Entrepreneurs will have lost confidence a little and will be waiting to see whether the prospects of profitability are going to improve or worsen before proceeding with marginal projects. Order books will be looking rather thin in some of the major industries, and stocks will be accumulating in warehouses and retail outlets.

By budgeting for a deficit, i.e. reducing taxation, the Chancellor leaves the average citizen with more money to spend. If the average citizen does go ahead and spend, the economy will revive. If he/she does not do so, the government will proceed to increase welfare benefits to needy persons and to press ahead with capital projects already in the pipeline. This will accelerate the economy, and recovery will start.

29.4.2
Budgeting for a surplus

When the Chancellor's view is that there is inflationary pressure in the economy, he will take measures to raise taxation and reduce spending. This will leave him with a surplus. The resulting contraction of aggregate monetary demand will reduce the demands for goods and services. This will prevent prices rising and ease the inflationary pressure in the economy.

Whether the policy is successful or not depends on the reactions of the taxpayers. The extra taxation may lead to such a round of wage demands that it proves inflationary not deflationary. The people may give up extra work because the tax burden is too heavy, so that productivity falls. Again, this is inflationary. Fearful of heavier taxation in the future, they may increase the velocity of money and keep the inflation going by using their smaller incomes more rapidly.

29.4.3
A neutral budget

Where the economy is believed to be about right, with neither a stimulus nor restraint required, the Chancellor will bring in a 'neutral' budget. This means that any tax changes he makes will cancel one another out. They may still be important as far as individuals are concerned. For example, an increase in the tax on petrol and a reduction in higher rates of income tax would effectively transfer incomes from motorists to the well-to-do, but leave the aggregate monetary demand unchanged if the amounts concerned were the same (assuming the well-to-do do not save the extra income).

The effects of these alternative policies have already been studied in Chapters 27 and 28.

29.4.4
The budget accounts

There are two accounts where records are kept of Government Income and Expenditure. The **Consolidated Fund** is an Account which records current transactions, expenditure against income. The National Loans Fund records the government's lending and borrowing, The Consolidated Fund records taxation moneys received and expenditure disbursed, most of it on 'supply services'. This name is given to the major expenditures of government departments for civil and defence purposes, education, local-government activities etc. The surplus or deficit for which the Chancellor has budgeted will appear as a balance on this account at the end of the year. This surplus or deficit is transferred to the National Loans Fund and either reduces or increases the amount which the Government has to borrow to finance the loans which it makes. The government finances most of the capital expenditure of the nationalised industries and the local authorities, using the surplus, if one was achieved, or borrowed money. The borrowed money may be National Savings, or money from the sale of gilt-edged securities. The increase or decrease of the National Loans Funds during a year is thus the final measure of the government's surplus or deficit, and the change in the National Debt.

29.5
The national debt

The national debt came into existence in its modern form in 1694 with the establishment of the Bank of England. The first loan made to the government was £1.2 million. In December 1993 the national debt stood at £231 435 million, which is over 178 000 times as large as the original debt.

The national debt increases only when the money raised from taxation is insufficient to cover the government's expenditure, and hence the government has to borrow the extra money that it needs. Wars are notoriously costly – for example, in World War I it was estimated that £1 million per day was being spent on the war in the trenches. Over the years we can see that the national debt always increases in war-time. However, a considerable change has come over government expenditure in recent years, as the figures that follow will explain. In 1967 the national debt stood at £32 000 million

Table 29.4 Increases in the national debt

Year	Amount of National Debt (£m)	Increase in year (£m)
1984	172 209	15 712
1985	189 712	17 503
1986	197 589	7 877
1987	205 342	7 753
1988	213 527	8 185
1989	200 080	–13 447
1990	189 730	–10 350
1991	193 415	3 685
1992	205 528	12 113
1993	231 435	25 907

Source: Financial Statistics

and most of it could be explained by expenditure in various wars from 1694 to 1945, when World War II ended.

In 1993 the national debt stood at 231 435 million so that in the peacetime years from 1967 to 1993 the national debt had risen by £199 435 million to about seven times the 1967 figure. This is a measure of how seriously the UK has been living beyond its means, with the Government spending much more than it receives in revenue. The actual figures for the last few years are given in Table 29.4.

In the worst year, 1993, the national debt rose by £25 907 million, which is £71 million per day (71 times more than was spent per day in World War I.

It is interesting to see how this huge amount of debt is financed by borrowing from the general public. The full details are given in an official publication *Consolidated Fund and National Loans Fund Accounts*. The public are persuaded to lend money to the Government by the purchase of various types of loan stock. For example, it might be '13 per cent Treasury Stock 2000'. Such investments are called 'British Funds' and the day-to-day prices are shown in the daily press. Suppose a person buys £1000 of such stock on the day of issue, it means that the money will be repaid in the year 2000, and in the meantime interest will be paid at 13 per cent per annum. It follows that as the years go by the stock will move closer and closer to repayment date, and become what is known as short-dated. Most long-dated stock has at least 15 years to run, while medium stocks have about ten years to run.

All British funds are spoken of as 'gilt-edged stock because, when they were first issued, they were recorded in a book with gilt-edged pages at the Bank of England. For the clerks in the Gilt-edged Department at the Bank of England the issue of such stocks makes a great deal of work. Not only does interest have to be paid at regular intervals, but there is always some stock reaching its redemption date and having to be repaid. However, in order to repay it the money has to be borrowed again, so there is the problem of persuading the public to buy enough new stock to enable the bank to repay the old stock. Of course, if the Government also wants to borrow more, someone has to be persuaded to buy stocks to that extra value as well. In one recent year the Government borrowed £98 871 million and repaid £91 118 million. That is quite a lot of work.

One final interesting point which we can see if we look back to Table 29.1 is that in 1993 the interest paid on the debt was £18 446 million. That is just the interest, not repayment of any of the debt. As the entire housing budget was only £5 617 million it means we could have quadrupled the housing budget and housed every homeless person in the country if we had not had to bear this burden of debt.

29.6 The incidence of taxation

Taxation is an unpleasant experience for the person taxed, since it removes a portion of his/her income for the public use. It has been established in the courts of law that citizens are entitled to do their best by all legal means to reduce their tax burdens; it is for the tax authorities to make the tax net secure. The Chancellor proposes taxation on particular persons, goods and services, but is by no means sure that the burden will eventually fall where it was expected to fall. The 'incidence' of a tax is the place where it falls; it is of interest to the economist to be able to predict this so that the tax burden can be adjusted fairly.

(a) Direct taxation

The incidence of most direct taxation is clearly upon the individual taxed. The individual can rarely pass on his/her tax to any other person, though collectively a group may be able to negotiate a compensating rise in wages. Heavy taxation may be inflationary if it leads to a round of wage demands, and the burden of such wage increases is shared among the entire population as an increase in the price of the goods or services produced. This means that those strongly organised workers whose goods are in inelastic demand, or who occupy 'bottleneck' positions in the economy, pass on their taxation to workers in less well organised industries, or to pensioners.

Similarly, corporations may very easily pass on some of their increased taxation by raising prices to the public. Although this results in increased profits which bear tax in the normal way at 33 per cent, say, there is 67 per cent of each extra pound left to compensate the shareholders for the extra burden the Chancellor has imposed. Once again an inelastic demand for the product is essential if prices are to be raised without loss of trade.

(b) Indirect taxation

Here the incidence of the tax can be demonstrated diagrammatically, and there are useful implications for a Chancellor attempting to devise a tax system which will raise the revenue required or implement the social policy proposed. Although a full discussion is too advanced for our present purpose, the main points are illustrated in Figure 29.1.

(c) A specific tax on consumer goods

This acts like an increased cost of production to the manufacturer, who will therefore bring in a smaller quantity at each price. In other words, the supply curve moves to the left, forming a new supply curve above the previous one and displaced from it by the amount of the tax. How this will affect the price of the goods, and on whom will the tax fall, depend on the elasticity of demand for the goods. Figure 29.1 illustrates the position.

The implications here are important. If a Chancellor wishes to raise revenue, taxes must be imposed on goods which, because they have no

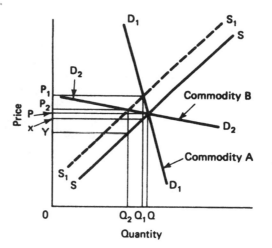

Figure 29.1 Incidence of an indirect tax

Notes

1 D_1D_1 and D_2D_2 are the demand curves of two goods. Commodity A is in inelastic demand; the demand for B is elastic. The supply curves are similar.

2 When the tax is imposed, suppliers lose the amount of the tax from whatever price they receive. As a result they are only willing to bring in a smaller supply at every price, and the supply curve moves to the left. The vertical distance between SS and S_1S_1 is the amount of the tax.

3 The effect on Commodity A is that the price rises a good deal, and the quantity supplied falls off slightly to OQ_1. Of the total price OP_1, the entrepreneur is now receiving OX, compared with OP before tax was imposed. The industry has only contracted a small amount, and the bulk of the tax is being paid by the consumer.

4 With Commodity B, which is in elastic demand, the consumers abandon their purchases to a much greater extent, turning to other substitutes. The result is that price only rises to P_2, the entrepreneurs only receive OY, and the incidence of the tax is largely upon them. Moreover the industry is seriously affected, with excess capacity forced upon it by the Chancellor's policy.

5 The reader should try to draw a similar diagram with a more elastic supply curve. The result is to place a bigger share of the tax on the consumer, and a reduced burden on the supplier. The fact is that the incidence of the tax varies with both the elasticity of demand and the elasticity of supply. As the elasticity of demand is less affected by time than the elasticity of supply, the incidence of the tax will fall more lightly at first on the consumer, but as time goes on and suppliers adjust their outputs to take account of the less profitable situation the consumer's burden grows.

close substitutes, are in inelastic demand. The consumer, being unable to change to other goods, will bear most of the tax burden, and the industry will be affected only to a small degree. Thus cigarettes, alcoholic drinks, petrol and tea will support quite heavy taxation. Similarly, a tax on goods in elastic demand will raise little revenue, but will seriously affect the industry concerned. This may be an agreeable result of the taxation if the industry is antisocial in the Chancellor's view, or if it causes social costs which amount to disservices to the community. Thus a tax on betting may reduce gambling, while raising very little tax. A tax on vehicles emitting harmful exhausts would encourage a change to other forms of transport.

(d) Taxation of economic rents

Where a factor is in inelastic supply and the factor owner is able to command economic rents, the imposition of tax will not cause any change in either supply or demand. The tax will have to be borne entirely by the supplier and will reduce the benefits the monopolist has been enjoying hitherto. Thus a monopolist earning economic rents cannot alter his/her position, which is already the most profitable one, and the tax will simply cream off these profits (see Figure 29.2).

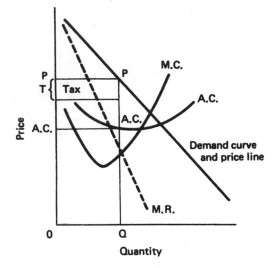

Figure 29.2 Taxation of 'economic rents'

Notes

1 The monopolist is making 'economic rents' equal to A.C., A.C., P, P.
2 The tax T will be paid by the monopolist, since at an output of OQ he is already producing at maximum profit.
3 Whatever proportion of this maximum is taxed away the monopolist will still be better off staying at the present level of output rather than changing to a different level. Sixty per cent of maximum profits is still better than 60 per cent of less-than-maximum profits.

29.7 Self-assessment of tax due

Starting on 6 April 1996 the United Kingdom is turning over to a 'self-assessment' system of taxation. This will not affect employees paying tax under the PAYE (pay as you earn) system, unless they are very high earners, but it will affect sole traders, partners and other persons who have income from several sources, including pensions and investments. Designed to reduce the work carried out in Inland Revenue offices the new requirements call for the taxpayer to calculate the tax due on all his/her various types of income (with some help provided in the early years for those feeling unsure of themselves). The arrangements are not finally decided at the time of writing (March 1996) but are along the following lines:

(a) Everyone must keep adequate records of documents, receipts, payments, etc. *which are adequate to support the statements made in the self-assessment tax return completed each year.* These records must start on 6 April 1996, and there is a fine of up to £3000 for failure to keep proper records.

(b) The tax returns (to be called SA Tax Returns) will be sent out in April each year – the first one being sent out in April 1997.

(c) On receipt, the taxpayer must check that he/she has all the Schedules needed to account for all the different types of income received, including any guide notes or Help Sheets on offer. The Inland Revenue will send out all the Schedules they expect the taxpayer to need (based on their past experience) but it is for the taxpayer to call for any others required. Failure to reveal a source of income by not requesting the appropriate Schedule may lead to more fines, and interest on unpaid tax.

(d) The likely Schedules are:

Schedule 1 Employment
Schedule 2 Share Schemes and Share Options

Schedule 3   Self-employment (sole traders)
Schedule 4   Income from Partnerships
Schedule 5   Income from Land and Property in the UK
Schedule 6   Foreign Income
Schedule 7   Income from Trusts and Settlements
Schedule 8   Capital Gains
Schedule 9   Non-residence and Non-domicile.

(e)   Having completed those Schedules that apply to him/her, the taxpayer transfers the various income figures arrived at to a Work Sheet provided in the Tax Return Guide. This Work Sheet enables the taxpayer to calculate the tax due.

(f)   It is then possible to complete the SA Tax Return, which must be sent in, with any instalments of tax due. In general, tax is payable in two instalments, by 31 January and 31 July each year. Failure to pay may lead to the Inland Revenue charging interest, penalty payments and a surcharge.

29.8 Summary of Chapter 29

1   The government today provides a wide range of goods and services: security, education, welfare, basic economic services and housing. These services have to be financed by taxation.

2   Taxation should be fair, easy to collect, of certain amount rather than at the whim of the tax collector, and impartial between different taxpayers. It should not discourage enterprise or hard work. It may be in the form of direct taxes levied on persons, or indirect taxes levied on goods and services.

3   In the UK the chief direct taxes are income tax, capital gains tax, corporation tax and inheritance tax.

4   The chief indirect taxes are customs and excise duties, motor taxes and value added tax.

5   Direct taxes are usually arranged so that they are progressive, i.e. falling most heavily on the well-to-do. Indirect taxes are nearly always regressive, falling more heavily on the lower paid.

6   The budget is an instrument of economic management, used to control the economy. The final result may be a surplus or a deficit.

7   A budget deficit increases the National Debt, while a budget surplus decreases the National Debt.

8   The incidence of taxation is the place where the tax falls. It is usually upon the individual in personal taxation, but with indirect taxation it depends on the price elasticities of demand and supply as to whether the tax can be passed on by suppliers to consumers.

9   Taxation of economic rents does not affect supply or demand, and falls on the rentier. (A rentier is someone who enjoys unearned income.)

Exercises Set 29

1   Why should a good system of taxation include both direct and indirect taxes?

2   What were Adam Smith's canons of taxation? What other criteria might a modern Chancellor add to them?

3   Explain the difference between progressive and regressive taxation. On what grounds can each be justified?

4   Outline the tax structure of the UK. How are the revenues which have been raised eventually disbursed?

5   Direct taxation falls on the person taxed; indirect taxation falls more uncertainly. Explain.

6　In what ways may the budget be described as an instrument for managing the economy? Who decides what management policies are to be followed, and what pressures are at work to influence these decisions in your own country?

7　Distinguish between 'budgeting for a surplus' and 'budgeting for a deficit'. In what circumstances is each appropriate?

8　What influence have the price elasticities of demand and supply on the incidence of an indirect tax? Illustrate your answer by the tax on tobacco, which is deemed to be a product in inelastic demand and fairly elastic supply.

9　'If the demand for a particular commodity or service is elastic, the Chancellor can reduce its consumption by taxation. If it is in inelastic demand he/she can only make those consuming it pay heavily for the privilege.' Explain.

10　For each of the following give an example of an actual tax:

(*a*)　A direct tax on a business enterprise.
(*b*)　A tax convenient to the taxpayer.
(*c*)　A tax which the taxpayer cannot possibly notice.
(*d*)　A tax that is fair to different income groups.
(*e*)　A tax that is highly regressive.

30 The future of economics

30.1 The Greeks had a word for it

The modern word 'economics' has its origin in the Greek word *oikonomos* meaning a steward. The two parts of this word *oikos*, a house, and *nomos* a manager, show what economics is all about. How do we manage our house, what account of our stewardship can we render to our families, to the nation, to our descendants?

From Socrates and Aristotle to J. M. Keynes, and Prof. J. K. Galbraith is a span of 2250 years. It takes us from a slave society, where all but the few were poor, to an affluent democracy. Great changes of taste and fashion have occurred. Socrates rose in the morning, put on his cloak and went out into the public square to engage in conversation and discussion. His needs were few, and he was unencumbered by worldly possessions. Today we are obsessed with material wants, and struggle to the beach with a car loaded with deck chairs, aqua-lungs, and assorted paraphernalia, towing a yacht or a power boat behind us.

Economics is the study of mankind in the everyday business of providing this enormous variety of goods and services. This book has attempted to describe the major aspects of production, distribution and exchange. It is clearly only a beginning to the vast study of specialised aspects of the economy. The author hopes the reader will continue into this more specialised field of applied economics. Before doing so, and to conclude this book, let us note two final points about elementary economics. First, economics is a valuable liberal study in its own right. Secondly, while economics can never cease to be important, the time is fast approaching when its relative importance should decline.

30.2 A liberal study

The current fashion is to advocate liberal education, that is education over a wide field. Specialisms are condemned in education on the ground that specialists become divorced from everyday life, immersed in their own peculiar interests. The author does not subscribe to this view, for economics is about specialisation as the key to a fuller life. Specialisation increases wealth; as a general principle the ploughing of deep furrows is as advantageous in education as it is in agriculture. There are many liberal men who are also specialists.

Certainly economics is a liberal study. Everyone needs to know some economics, for it explains the framework of prosperity and a liberal life is only possible when prosperity exists. Follow historically the flowering of art, literature, and science around the world and you will find they flourished most where prosperity was to be found. Even today only where the economy is strong can people be spared from production to think sublime thoughts, create beautiful objects, paint immortal pictures or compose imperishable melodies. The humblest workers in such societies are ennobled by their labour, for it alone makes possible the culture of their times.

30.3
No longer the
dismal science

For 30 years, from 1945–75, Thomas Carlyle's characterisation of economics as the 'Dismal Science' seemed to have been invalidated. Economists seemed at last to be able to handle the cycles of depression which gave such distress in the early years of the capitalist system. Keynesian economics could manage prosperity, with a touch on the accelerator to get the economy to go, and a touch on the brakes to steady it when it got out of hand. Since then, two things have happened.

First, socialism, or perhaps we should say communism, has been found wanting. The ideal has been proved illusory, at least as far as economics is concerned. The dictatorship of the proletariat proved too severe a regime for a delicate bloom like productivity; a million flowers withered in China and only began to revive as the peasantry were set free to seek consumerism instead. In the Eastern bloc most progress was made by those seeking to press least heavily on their populations with the dogmas of a bygone era. The middle way of controlled capitalism has proved the better solution.

Secondly, the full implications of a Welfare State have been realised, and they have been found wanting too. If you manage prosperity to the point where full employment is reached inflation must sooner or later appear. If prosperity includes increased amounts of leisure time and less onerous working conditions productivity must decline unless self-discipline replaces enforced discipline. If a world view is to be taken and other nations are to be given the chance to develop, the resulting competition must bring unemployment in some areas of the developed nations. Unemployment in times of stagflation and slumpflation seems to be as difficult a problem to solve as the 'persistent general unemployment' Keynes wrestled with in the 1930s.

Even economics has changed. The science of econometrics has raised its lovely head. Made possible by the development of computers, it has at last enabled us to test what would happen if we did this, rather than that, or the other. We can express policies in mathematical terms, envisage various events mathematically and run them through the computer to envisage every possibility – a technique called the Monte Carlo method. One economist described this as 'more or less plausible, but entirely arbitrary, assumptions leading to precisely stated, but irrelevant conclusions'. Our study of mankind in the everyday business of life has become a highly theoretical, and abstruse, but – those who can understand it maintain – an extremely practical discipline. All they need to do now is convince the politicians who have to transform theory into practice. Today we need not, like Socrates, don our cloaks and go out into the market place to discuss the state of 'the Republic'. We can do it in the comfort of our own homes, by watching television, where the finest minds of the nation make almost hourly presentations. There is a nice mixture of cheerfulness and despondency. The latter is not surprising in a world facing the prospect of supporting 20 billion inhabitants in the next century, compared with the 800 million alive in Adam Smith's day. Those studying economics can take consolation from this fact – that whatever happens in other disciplines, economics is king. Music, literature, art and even science cannot flourish without it and neither can education, welfare or any other socially desirable policies. We still have to create wealth before we can distribute it.

Index